Instructional and Cognitive Impacts of Web-Based Education

Beverly Abbey
Texas A&M University-Commerce

IDEA GROUP PUBLISHING
Hershey USA • London UK

Senior Editor: Mehdi Khosrowpour
Managing Editor: Jan Travers
Copy Editor: Maria Boyer
Typesetter: Tamara Gillis
Cover Design: Connie Peltz
Printed at: BookCrafters

Published in the United States of America by
Idea Group Publishing
1331 E. Chocolate Avenue
Hershey PA 17033-1117
Tel: 717-533-8845
Fax: 717-533-8661
E-mail: jtravers@idea-group.com
Website: http://www.idea-group.com

and in the United Kingdom by
Idea Group Publishing
3 Henrietta Street
Covent Garden
London WC2E 8LU
Tel: 171-240 0856
Fax: 171-379 0609
http://www.eurospan.co.uk

Library of Congress Cataloging-in-Publication Data

Instructional and cognitive impacts of Web-based Education / [edited by] Beverly Abbey.
p. cm.
Includes bibliographical references and index.
ISBN 1-878289-59-4 (s/c)
1. Internet (Computer network) in education --Psychological aspects. 2. World Wide Web. 3. Instructional systems--Design. I. Abbey, Beverly, 1944-

LB1044.87.I545 2000
371. 33'44678--dc21 00-025657

British Cataloguing in Publication Data
A Cataloguing in Publication record for this book is available from the British Library.

Instructional and Cognitive Impacts of Web-Based Education

Table of Contents

Preface

There is not one simple approach to using technology, especially one as unique as the World Wide Web. As innumerable people rush to "become a presence" on the Web, educators too feel the pressure to become Web-savvy. This press to make classes, and indeed, entire degrees available through the Internet, has led to a plethora of flashy, often pedagogically unsound sites.

This book represents a compendium of current international thought and issues on assessing, designing and delivering instruction via the Web. There are many books and articles providing quick fixes on the mechanics of how-to put your classes on the Web, and ignore or omit matters of instructional import. A major concern of many professional educators is the quality and efficacy of the instruction being delivered in this manner. Public schools are required to use textbooks and other instructional materials that have been stamped with a "seal of approval" regarding content and pedagogy. However, an increasing number of instructors, at all grade levels, are using Internet sites as both content sources and delivery mechanisms: sites that have not been evaluated by state organizations and commissions to assess theoretical and instructional appropriateness.

How should instructional delivery be modified for Web access? What independent cognitive responsibilities have been placed uniquely on the learner? How may we ensure that Web instruction is more than an electronic correspondence course?

The contributors to this collection offer a variety of points of view dealing with Web site instructional design issues and the cognitive impacts of learner interactions with the Web. The chapters range from theoretical analyses of student-centered learning to guidelines reflecting appropriate educational constructs. Due to the nature of the topic, there is no obvious way to organize the content. Therefore, the chapters are arranged alphabetically by first author.

Bastiaens and Martens from the Open University of the Netherlands (Conditions for Web Based Learning with Real Events) argue for the importance of real cases for independent learning. An Electronic Performance Support System (EPSS), based on the Web, provides students the opportunity to work in a professional context as opposed to the artificial environments in classrooms. They provide excellent explanations of terms and impacts of issues related to real world learning.

Berg, Collins, and Dougherty of the University of Maryland, Baltimore Campus (Design Guidelines for Web-Based Courses) discuss design elements and considerations of students and instructors for three types of courses – Web supplemented, Web enhanced and Web based. They emphasize prototyping using input from representative users, most of whom have learned their Web skills outside of academia.

Berry, University of Pittsburgh, (Cognitive Effects of Web Page Design) presents an overview and background of major theoretical and design issues. Of major importance are his suggestions for future research topics such as text presentation, windowing, visual complexity, browser mentality (instructional intent), wayfinding and cognitive load and effort.

Bonk, Cummings, Hara, Fischler, and Lee from Indiana University (A Ten Level Web Integration Continuum for Higher Education) clearly explain and analyze instructional considerations to help faculty integrate the Web in instructional situations. Their continuum offers guidelines for an instructor at any level of Web commitment.

Fisher from Marquette University (Implementation Considerations for Instructional Design for Web-based Learning Environment) using a model of staff development for middle school teachers, discusses the importance of aiding learners in transforming information into meaningful learning experiences. She provides authentic assessment rubrics that promote the use of a range of approaches enabling students to communicate and make meaning in collaborative Web learning environments.

Leflore of North Carolina A&T (Theory Supported Design Guidelines for Web-Based Instruction) discusses how to present to-be-learned material and how students are required to interact with and interpret the material from three perspectives - Gestalt, cognitive and constructivist. She presents guidelines with examples of Web instruction and activities based on these theoretical bases.

Lockee, Danielson, and Burton, Virginia Technical University, (ID and HCI: A Marriage of Necessity) address user interface considerations using the traditional instructional design linear model. They emphasize the greater importance of the interface for Web-based courses and present a number of factors for the instructional designer.

Lowther, Jones and Plants from the University of Memphis, (Preparing Tomorrow's Teachers to Use Web-Based Education) present an organizational scheme for preparing teachers using levels of Web integration and Web information literacy (browser, Boolean searches, and Web technical skills). They close with suggestions and guidelines for some instructional approaches and recommendations for integrating the Web into teacher education programs.

Maddux and Cummings of the University of Nevada, Reno, (Developing Web Pages as Supplements to Traditional Courses) present pedagogically sound guidelines for instructors who are without support services, yet desire to incorporate the Web in their classes. Their lists of example Web sites should prove very helpful to novice site designers.

Miller and Miller from Texas A&M University-Commerce (Theoretical and Practical Consideration in the Design of Web-Based Instruction) contend a correspondence between cognitive models of memory and the structure of the Web and present suggestions on how to apply this similarity in planning instruction on the Web. They emphasize the relationship between theory and practice in designing Web course structure, media and communications.

Oliver and Herrington, Edith Cowan University, Australia, (Using Situated Learning as a Design Strategy for Web-Based Learning) present an instructional design model for situated learning. Their model describes and applies the integration of the elements of situated learning (content, learning activities and learning support) to a Web-environment.

Persichitte from the University of Northern Colorado (A Case Study of Lesson Learned for the Web-Based Educator) relates first hand experiences with problems (and solutions) of conducting a Web-based class. Throughout her narrative, she emphasizes the importance of the instructional design process in preparing a Web-course.

Powers and Guan, Indiana State University, (Examining the Range of Student Needs in the Design and Development of a Web-Based Course) argue that a needs assessment must consider more than discrepancies or gaps. Learners' technology skills, interpersonal concerns and possible physical or learning disabilities are factors that must be taken into account in designing instruction for the Web.

Rogers of Bemidji State University (Layers of Navigation for Hypermedia Environments: Designing Instructional Web Sites) discusses characteristics of learners and of Web sites. She promotes the importance of considering the interactions of users and sites as a whole in order to provide appropriate structures that enable learners to learn.

Smith-Gratto, North Carolina A&T, (Strengthening Learning on the

Web: Programmed Instruction and Constructivism) addresses the role of programmed instruction in designing Web sites for building knowledge bases which learners may then manipulate in a constructivist manner. She argues that although the Web promotes open-ended explorations, exploration is not enough - learners need to be focused toward achieving outcomes.

Spector and Davidsen from the University of Bergen, Norway, (Designing Technology Enhanced Learning Environments) offer a well-constructed argument for the use of models in designing for complex learning. Using an instructional design methodology called model-facilitated learning (MFL), they present six basic principles to guide the development of designing cognitively engaging interactions and activities around the content of system dynamics.

Hopefully, this collection of ideas by international authors will prove thought provoking and engaging. Comments, contentions, confutations and complaints are welcome.

Bev Abbey, Ph.D.
Sherman, Texas
babbey@austinc.edu

Chapter I

Conditions for Web-Based Learning with Real Events

Theo J. Bastiaens and Rob L. Martens
Open University of the Netherlands

This chapter presents two converging developments. Traditionally, learning at schools or universities and working in a professional context were relatively separated. Companies often complain that students know a lot 'facts' but are not 'competent.' On the other hand at schools and universities students often complain that they can't see the relevance of a certain subject.

This chapter deals with the two converging worlds: traditional distance training (such as employed at for instance open universities all over the world) and in company training. ICT and competence-based education are bringing the two together, resulting in a combined working/learning mode, which we will describe as learning with real cases. This leads to more self-study or independent learning. Figure 1 presents an overview of the different facets of the tendency to learn with real cases.

This chapter will start with a description of distance education since many things can be learned from this. Then, developments in the business or professional context will be presented. We will stress that there is a convergence leading to 'learning with real cases'. After a description of this development, learning with real cases, as well as pitfalls and recommendations will be discussed.

DISTANCE LEARNING

This first section deals with distance learning. This will also be referred to as distance education or distance training, which are in this context largely overlapping concepts. Where we put 'student' the reader may also fill in employee.

A more or less generally accepted definition of distance education is proposed by Holmberg (1990, p. 1): 'The term distance education covers the various forms of teaching

Figure 1. Toward learning with real cases

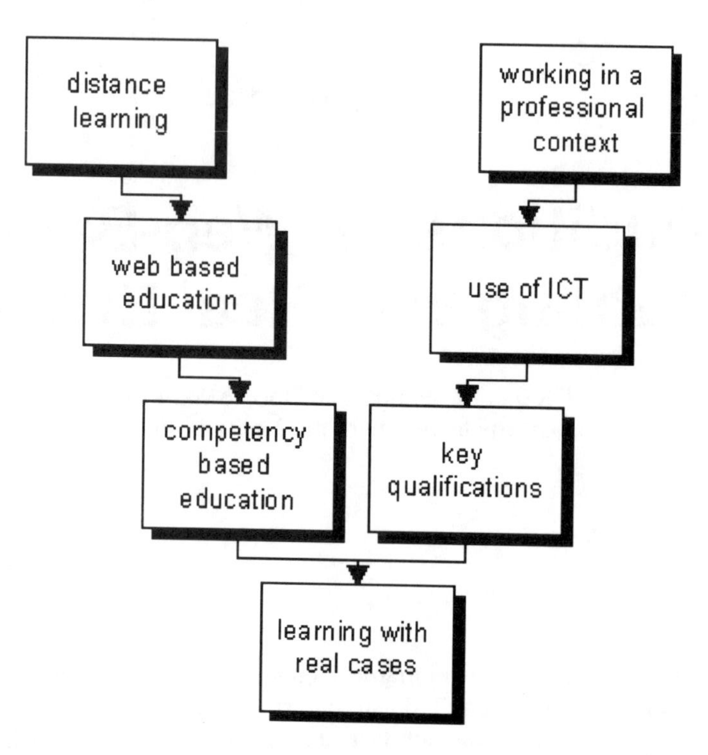

and learning at all levels which are not under the continuous, immediate supervision of tutors present with their students in lecture rooms or on the same premises, but which nevertheless benefit from the planning, guidance and tuition (i.e., tutoring, teaching) of the staff of a tutorial organisation. Its main characteristic is that it relies on non-contiguous, i.e., mediated, communication. Distance study denotes the activity of the students, distance teaching that of the tutorial organisation.' This definition indicates the relation with the concept 'self-regulated learning,' although it is not the same. If the student is able to learn in an adequate way with a low degree of external support, the learning is self-regulated.

Gradually, distance training began attracting more attention. Although a teacher who stands before a moderately sized group of students might be able to provide better support, tutoring, and encouragement, as well as determine and monitor the pace and contents of the course he is teaching, a shift towards distance training is still in evidence. Not only is it becoming more important in terms of the number of educational institutions around the world which specifically provide distance teaching, but mainstream education is also adopting more and more of the techniques of distance training. Some authors predict a 'big bang' in distance training, pointing to the explosive growth of the Internet (Hawkridge, 1995). The objections to distance education have been largely overcome for economic reasons and because 'distance learners' tend to outperform students in mainstream education (Granger & Gulliver, 1995; Martin & Rainey, 1997). Meta-analyses which compare 'conventional' educational methods to computer-assisted education emphasising independent study frequently show that the latter group performs better, for example in terms of the pace of study (Fletcher-Flinn & Gravatt, 1995; Montague & Knirk, 1993). The same holds for comparisons between conventional education and modular education, with programmed instruction using a variety of media and interim testing.

There are, incidentally, researchers who argue that open (distance) education is only an upgraded version of a common phenomenon at universities in the previous century. The enormous increase in the number of students meant that universities became bigger, unwieldy, restrictive and 'supply-led' (Bell & Tight, 1995, p. 3): 'But these trends— along with the associated jargon of assessment of prior knowledge, distance education, modularisation, student-centred learning and so on—while in many ways welcome, should not be seen as modern or radical innovations. What they really represent is a reversion to earlier and more open patterns of higher education.' In *Pittmans Journal* open learning/ distance education is described as 'one of the most interesting developments of recent years in the educational world'. The article appeared in 1924. In Germany, Isaac Pittman launched his correspondence courses in stenography as early as 1840. The idea of distance training is at least as old as the first reliable railway and postal services. Educationalists appear to have faulty memories, however, and educational researchers succumb to the tremendous pressure to present something as 'innovative'.

Quite apart from the question of whether we are dealing with an entirely new discovery or a revival of something which has been around for a while, distance training and the associated educational techniques (e.g., open learning) have clearly grown in importance. The birth of modern open distance learning at the university level is frequently dated from the founding of the British Open University in 1969. For many governments, it was a sign that higher distance education was to be taken seriously.

EDUCATIONAL ARGUMENTS FOR DISTANCE TRAINING

Demand-Driven Paradigm Replaces Supply-Led Paradigm

In considering how best to optimise education, many authors have hit upon the idea that the teacher plays a much too central role in conventional education. Students focus on what the teacher wants and reproduce her views as much as possible. The teacher is highly autonomous and determines the course of teaching and learning. She often composes the tests and examinations herself and is therefore actually testing herself. Many authors believe that it would be much better to focus more on the student, with the student working on his own, at his own initiative, and more out of his own interest and curiosity than the teacher's. The instructional material and the teaching should be tailored more to the needs and wishes of the students, in terms of form and content next to time and place.

This shift coincides to some extent (with the usual delay in educational theory) with a shift in the field of psychology from behaviourism (with its emphasis on input and output, the learner as a black box. Any former pupils who used to find their exercise books [or their foreheads!] covered with stamps or stickers are the typical products of the behaviourist tradition) to a more cognitive approach which accentuates mental processes and, accordingly, the importance of the learner's own role (constructivism). This seems to be in line with a shift in society. It is not the teacher who is central to the learning process, but the learner, who functions as an information processor and who has his own set of responsibilities. The term 'demand-driven education' is used in this connection. Valcke & Thorpe (1995, p. 113) state that distance education is 'a field of research that is of particular importance for a growing body of educational institutions, many of which have not, until now, focused on self-study, distance learning formats or independent learning. These are increasingly interested in the distance learning/distance education paradigm. The growing trend away from 'supply-driven' towards 'demand-driven' education is a key feature in causing such institutions to change their teaching-learning approach and to look for alternative ways to engage/involve their 'clients' in learning experiences.

Many authors point out that a similar trend has become apparent in the thinking about education. Advances in information technology have made a specific contribution to this trend.

Inadequate Conventional Education

Sometimes conventional teaching and learning can be an excellent form of education. In actual practice, however, it is sometimes disappointing. In this section we look at the shortcomings as they have been observed.

Most forms of conventional education are in fact modelled on pre-adult education, with the emphasis therefore being on the supporting role of the teacher. There are quite a number of educational objectives which are difficult to achieve through the offices of a teacher. While it is true that teachers can stand before the classroom and convey what they know, it is still up to the pupils or students to do the learning by working with the subject matter, for example by reading a lot, by completing exercises, or by repetition (e.g., when learning definitions). The advantages associated with conventional education are largely irrelevant when it comes to certain subjects, for example reading comprehension, arithmetic, achieving certain educational objectives at a specific level of knowledge, et cetera. Independent study is also an equally good or even better method of attaining objectives at an 'advanced' level. A study carried out by Aarnoutse and Weterings (1995) demonstrated, for example, that in the conventional approach to teaching reading comprehension, less than 1% of the pupils' time is devoted to reading skills or strategies. They spend most of their time completing exercises (answering questions) or reading on their own.

Another important drawback to conventional education is that quite a lot depends on the quality and the motivation of the individual teacher. Good teachers are few and far between. If the teacher lacks motivation and/or quality, the advantages of conventional education disappear. The same is obviously also true for distance training: if the material is unsatisfactory, distance training will also not function well. It is, however, much easier to monitor quality, since the material only has to be well written once. Once it is satisfactory, it will stay that way for a time.

The size of the class is another important factor. If a conventional university class becomes too big, the quality of the teaching often suffers. Gibbs, Lucas & Simonite (1996) demonstrated this connection in higher education in the UK. Lectures attended by more than 100 students, for example, actually offer no more than a semblance of the original advantages of conventional education, e.g., interactivity and individualisation.

ECONOMICAL AND BUSINESS ARGUMENTS FOR DISTANCE TRAINING

Distance training has always been driven by economical arguments. Much of its current popularity has to do with a still-growing tendency to use cost effectiveness measures in education. Educational institutes are more and more 'reckoned' on their effectiveness. In this section it will be exemplified what distance training has to offer.

Freedom to Choose Place and Time

Distance training has from its beginning (it started off as a commercial enterprise) been ruled by economic and business arguments. Cost effectiveness and efficiency have always been put central in arguments that plead for distance training. Many teachers have been distrustful to distance training precisely because of this emphasis on business instead of educational arguments and out of simple fear of losing their jobs. In this section we will briefly provide some underpinning for these economical and business arguments.

Holmberg (1995) shows that it is precisely the freedom to determine the time and place of study which is crucial for adult education, since adults usually have jobs as well. The demand for adult education has grown enormously since the mid-nineteenth century, leading to the founding of institutions for distance training all around the world, from Japan to Sweden. An indication of the size of the market for adult education was given by Sorenson & Walberg (1993), for example: in the USA, companies spent over $45 billion in 1990 on adult training programmes. Many of the students who enroll in distance training institutions gain access to a level of education that would have otherwise been closed to them.

Geographic Accessibility

In distance training, it is not the student but rather the curriculum which moves from one place to another. That saves the student a lot of time. The cost of moving the curriculum is considerably lower than the cost of moving the students. This advantage is important not only in wealthy Western nations but also in the Third World. Once a country's postal service becomes somewhat reliable, distance training facilities generally soon flourish (for example in Zimbabwe). If the post office is unreliable, however, attempts to set up higher distance education facilities usually fail (for example in Mozambique).

Although it can scarcely be imagined in a densely populated country such as the Netherlands, there are many countries, such as Australia, where physical distance is a major problem in education and where distance education is hence considered of paramount importance.

Costs

When labour is a major cost factor, as it generally is in a high-wage country such as the Netherlands, savings can be obtained by reducing the cost per product. There is a growing trend, not only in business but also in education, to reduce costs by means of labour extensification, although the trend is less pronounced in the latter. Distance training can be viewed as a form of labour extensification within the field of education. The labour factor (i.e., the teacher) is replaced by an intermediate agent such as a computer or a written course. This does not mean that the teacher's role becomes superfluous, however. Rather, this role is upgraded, for example to that of tutor or facilitator.

From a cost perspective, there is naturally a certain point at which the scales tip in favour of distance training. Distance education is generally accompanied by relatively higher fixed costs and lower variable costs (per student). The greater the number of students enrolled in a course, the lower the cost per student will be. That is much less the case in conventional education; the costs are largely variable, consisting of teacher-hours. It is, after all, unlikely that a teacher can teach a classroom of 50 students instead of his normal class of 15 without feeling the effects. The quality of conventional education usually declines as the classroom size grows. There is no such inverse relationship between quality and classroom size in distance education. Indeed, some distance learning courses have an enrolment of over 50,000 students.

It is impossible to describe the point at which the scales tip in terms of a general, constant relationship (Montague & Knirk, 1993). It depends on the salary of the teachers teaching the course, the amount of effort involved in making the course subject suitable for distance training, and so on. Because the variable costs, for example in conventional higher education, are attributed to teacher-hours, distance education is often a much cheaper alternative, however. Indeed, universities in all over the world are making increasing use of distance learning techniques as a cost-control measure. The use of information technology, for example computer networks, can also make distance education more cost effective than other forms of education (see for instance Sutton & Gross, 1994; Kearsley & Lynch, 1994; Athey, 1997).

ICT

When ICT is used in education, it is often accompanied by a greater emphasis on independent study, on the freedom to determine time and place, because physical barriers are removed. The concept of 'just-in-time-teaching' is often mentioned in this connection. Computers have played an increasingly greater role in education since the sixties. In about the past ten years, the availability of relatively inexpensive, powerful personal computers (Bates, 1995) has introduced a new, almost unexplored source of innovation in educational technology. The number of households in Europe with access to multimedia computers is increasing rapidly. As the Windows™ operating system is gradually elevated to industry standard, it is also becoming much easier to develop a certain uniformity. Specifically, in the past two years a rapid drop in prices and a huge leap in the processing capacity of PCs (internal memory and processor speed) have unleashed new opportunities for useful educational applications. This can, without a doubt, be described as the most important reason for the enormous increase in application software, for example computerised testing, in various forms of education. What should also not be underestimated is the fact that authors who have access to a PC are now able to produce texts quickly and efficiently, and that this task is even easier when done by a team. All these developments are grist for the mill of distance training.

The flourishing use of networks, such as the Internet, also offer tremendous educational opportunities. One example is computer conferencing.

DEVELOPMENTS: WORKING IN A PROFESSIONAL CONTEXT

Thus far we concentrated on the developments in traditional distance education institutes such as Open universities. In the next section we will look at the developments in private enterprise.

Through a far-reaching globalising effect, the world economy is no longer predictable.

This influences the supply of products and services. Flexibility becomes the key word instead of stability. On the job, flexibility demands the necessary know-how from employees.

Another development is the shift towards an information economy, in which capital, raw materials and labour are no longer the most important means of production, but more important is the application of knowledge. This knowledge combined in products and services forms an essential surplus value. In an information economy, knowledge is therefore seen as a tool for competition.

Both factors, flexibility and knowledge as a competitive tool, explain the increased demand for training. Training is an important way of distributing knowledge. The importance of knowledge is therefore directly tied to training. Because of this, training becomes more and more of strategic importance within an organisation. Through this strategic importance, more attention is paid to the end result of training. This end result is formulated less and less in terms of learning results but increasingly in terms of work performance.

If knowledge counts as the most important economic factor in the information economy, then it is important to educate effectively and efficiently. Unfortunately many organisations have had disappointing experiences with the effectiveness and efficiency of professional training. Training often does not lead to the desired improvement in performance. This is also caused by the fact that training is often given too early or too late and often does not meet the individual needs of the target group. The disintegration of working and learning also could play an important role.

Competence

Although much money was spent on technological innovation in the seventies and eighties, industrial productivity and economic growth did not skyrocket. A reason for the rather marginal grow, in spite of innovative technology, was the fact that training and education were underestimated (Danish Ministry of Education, 1994). Whenever companies have to innovate they also have to train and educate their workforce.

Nowadays the rate of change is enormous. It is more a revolution than a period of change. With all the innovations on the work floor, knowledge is treated as a product this time. Knowledge is the main industrial factor in business today. Companies are downsizing and concentrate on core business today. They have to invest in technology and in a well-trained workforce. Also in the field of training there is a movement to concentrate on core business. Only here it is called key qualifications or core competencies. The difference between key qualifications and competencies lies in the fact that 'key qualifications' originates from economics and can be regarded as a systematic link between knowledge and skills learned and professional practice. Competencies comes from the field of competence and performance theories, which have their roots in the psychology of learning and knowledge (Streumer & Bjorkquist, 1998). In this article we use the term competence. Although definitions may differ, in general the term competence is referred to as the potential capacity of an individual (or a collective) to successfully accomplish a task or deal with situations (Ellström, 1997). It is possible to distinguish four categories of competencies (Bunk, Kaizer & Zedler, 1991);

- *Vocational competence*: carry out the work in a specific field of activities, expertly and without supervision;
- *Methodical competence*: to react in a systematic and systemic manner to difficulties

that may arise during work performance, to find solutions independently and to be able to apply the experience gained in a meaningful way to other problems encountered in the work;

- *Social competence*: to communicate with others and to work with them in a cooperative manner, to display group-oriented behaviour and empathy;
- *Participative competence*: to shape one's own workplace and the working environment in a broader sense, to be able to organise and make decisions, and be prepared to take responsibility upon oneself.

Effective Training on the Job

Knowledge and skills are often taught in a classroom situation, outside the context of the actual working environment. This results in a rather low transfer of the knowledge and skills to the work situation. From the current training paradigm, characteristics can be distilled that meet the new requirements and expectations which are set for more effective forms of training. The first characteristic is the demand for flexibility in the form of training, which can be implemented quickly. Second, the information economy requires employees to constantly increase their competence. This demands a form of training that is continuously present. The third characteristic is that the transfer value of training up till now has been rather low. New alternative forms must meet these demands. Measures such as offering a training just-in-time, taking into account the individual wishes of employees, and integration of working and learning could increase this transfer. The integration of working and learning means that training returns to the actual job location.

It is expected that training on the job will have three advantages that will lead to more effective training.

1. With on-the-job training, the learning environment and the job location are one and the same. The transfer of knowledge and skills will therefore increase.
2. The learning process will be more active and concrete. An employee sees a problem and immediately sees the value of the training material in practice.
3. The cost effectiveness: there are no travel or hotel expenses, and the costs resulting from absence are avoided by training on-the-job.

Some Reservations

Taking into account the advantages due to the characteristics named before, there are also some reservations to be made.

Tied to the first characteristic, the quick implementation, on-the-job training can be implemented quickly if the knowledge and skills that are to be learned are already present and if the target group is not too big. In other words, if there is an expert within an organisation, he can train a select number of employees as a trainer/coach on the job. However if we are looking at innovative developments which require a large number of employees to be trained at the same time, the application possibilities of on-the-job training is relative.

The second characteristic is the continuous presence of the possibility to increase competence. Training on-the-job is a form of training that can be constantly present. However if one is working with a coach or a mentor, this person can also be absent or not available for the 'pupil'. Therefore, a form of on-the-job training that is constantly present is hard to realise.

Thirdly, new alternative forms lead to expectations of an increase in transfer possibilities. This specifically applies to on-the-job training due to its characteristics. Characteristics such as just-in-time training and taking into account the individual differences are only possible up to a point. If an employee is involved in some form of on-the-job training, a coach can suggest a remedy or elaborate further on a topic. Especially compared to classroom training, this action can be just-in-time. But just-in-time can also mean at the same moment. Not 10 minutes, 15 minutes, or an hour later, but immediate action. The chance that a coach will do this is rather small. A coach also has his tasks and obligations elsewhere. The same applies to the individual differences. By training on-the-job a coach offers the tuition. The employee does not know exactly what the possibilities are and cannot determine this beforehand. The coach sets the tempo and the progress for the employee. The preference of the coach for a certain method or outlook is often decisive. The individual freedom of the 'pupil' is hereby limited.

DEVELOPMENT: ICT AND COMPETENCE-BASED DISTANCE TRAINING

Where behavioural objectives, knowledge, skills and attitudes have been the key factors in curriculum design for several decades, competencies and competence standards are now becoming the main focus.

Competencies refer to the ability to operate in ill-defined and ever-changing environments, to deal with non-routine and abstract work processes, to handle decisions and responsibilities, to work in groups, to understand dynamic systems, and to operate within expanding geographical and time horizons. In other words, competencies are built upon the combination of complex cognitive skills (encompassing problem solving, qualitative reasoning, and higher-order skills such as "self-regulation" and "learning-to-learn"), highly integrated knowledge structures (e.g., mental models), interpersonal skills and social abilities, and attitudes and values (e.g., the will to believe in taken responsibilities). In addition, competencies assume the ability to flexibly coordinate these different aspects of competent behaviour. Acquired competencies enable learners to apply complex cognitive skills in a variety of— not yet learned—situations ("transfer of learning") and over an unlimited time span ("lifelong learning"). In other words: competent students are supposed to act more or less as skilled and experienced employees. This means that educationalists argue more and more that students should not learn (by heart) in order to complete their exams, but should learn to solve lifelike problems.

It is not difficult to see that there is an economical drive behind this development, besides the educational drive. Companies have been complaining a lot about graduates who know a lot but who don't do a lot. Instead of theoretical knowledge, employees who know how to acquire knowledge, who know how to cooperate, and so on, are better suited to the demands of business. As already stated above the status of knowledge is changing.

To date we see many initiatives by which educational institutes such as universities are responding to this demand. In most cases, two major changes can be distinguished:

- *Adaptation of the educational approach.* Problem-based education, competency-based education and case-based education all point in the same direction. Learners have to work on realistic cases. They have to solve problems instead of take exams. Of course the tremendous growth of possibilities that are provided by ICT stimulate this development.

- *Adaptation of the assessment.* The tail wags the dog. In other words: changing the educational system without changing the exams won't help a lot. A new and sophisticated case-based education will not lead to effects if the exams remain traditional. Students will always try in the first place to obtain high marks. This concealed influence of the assessment is often referred to as the hidden curriculum. In order to really change the educational system, the exams have to change as well. Methods such as peer and self-assessment, as well as progress tests, are used for this. Replacement of paper and pencil exams by more active assessment procedures or projects can be seen in this light as well.

Computer-Based Training On-The-Job

The paragraph above proves that on-the-job training in its current form has its restrictions. As a result of new alternative forms of training and through far-reaching computerisation of the professional environment, a new form of on-the-job training developed. This new form, computer-based training on-the-job, combines training on-the-job with training through computer software. Computer-based training on-the-job in its most simple form is educational software, which can be used by the employee at his own desk. Experiments with this form of training have taken place. The idea behind this was that employees would use the slow hours to follow a course individually at their own desk. A much more extensive and complex form of computer-based training on-the-job developed out of Performance Technology. In this form an Electronic Performance Support System (EPSS) takes care of delivering information, advice and training at the individual's desk.

What is an EPSS?

An Electronic Performance Support System (EPSS) is an electronic environment which is easily accessible for every employee and structured in such a way that the employee instantly and individually can go online to reach a wide variety of information such as electronic coaching, advice, dàta, images, tools and assessment systems. The appearance of such an environment is dependent on the task execution.

Let's look at an insurance company as an example. The tasks of employees of an insurance company consist of advice, calculation and sales. In the past insurance agents priced their products orally to their clients, they calculated the financial position of the client, the possible costs for the premium based on index lists, and used application forms. These application forms were then sent to the head office for review. At the head office a special department checked these forms and entered the data in the computer. After a couple of days the client would receive the insurance policy at home. If mistakes were made filling out the form, the insurance agent would return to the client to correct the mistake. In order to guarantee a high level of advice, insurance agents were trained on a regular basis. The traditional method of training used was mainly classroom training in groups of insurance agents. Looking ahead to the future, this innovative insurance company has switched to working with EPSS.

Every insurance agent now uses a laptop which he takes along to the client. At the start of his visit the insurance agent pulls up the main menu, which shows the products offered. Together with the client the agent can chose a product. For example a client wishes to mend a break in his pension build up through an insurance policy. The agent will click on pensions and can show the client the importance of a solid pension plan by means of a graphic presentation. Normally the next question from the client would be: 'What is that going to cost me?' The agent then switches from the graphic presentation to calculating the cost for the client. With new clients, the personal data is entered once. With a regular client the agent can pull up the personal data from the database. The personal data of the client, his income and his other insurance coverage appear on the screen. The computer will calculate the insurance premium for the agent. The agent only needs to ask a couple of questions, such as when the client wishes to retire and what the desired monthly income is. With one click, the computer calculates the monthly pension paid upon retirement and the monthly premium to be paid now. Different situations can be shown on the screen at the same time and in a table the client can see the difference instantly. After this advice the client can decide. The traditional application forms have become obsolete. The insurance agent saves the information in his computer. The insurance policy can be printed on a portable printer. The client information is later sent to the main office by modem. The control department at the main office is no longer necessary. The computer checks the data and calculates the premium. The client now knows immediately if an insurance application has been accepted and he has all the required information. The insurance agent can be satisfied.

An EPSS has additional advantages. In the electronic environment the agent can search for information which he needs for his job. He can also ask the system for advice in certain situations. In addition he can increase his knowledge of new products by calling up a computer-based training (CBT) module. The insurance company sends him a CD-rom every month with CBT lessons. Prior to a visit to a client or just after the agent can learn just-in-time. With the EPSS the insurance company has taken a step forward to more efficient and effective training. Besides advantages in quality, such as the standardisation of products and processes and an optimising of the advisory role, agents can be trained flexibly and quickly. The know-how on products and processes is located in the EPSS. Not only in the help and advisory functions (extrinsic support), but also in the interface. The agent goes through the system by a certain route (intrinsic support). Competence can be increased by a continuous presence of CBT. When a problem arises, information, advice or training can be called up instantly. This benefits the transfer value.

Another advantage of the EPSS is the control function. The EPSS checks the data entered, it warns when a mistake is made, and even gives the agent a training advice. A manual, human check is no longer necessary. The process of the advice up till the final policy arriving at the client's house takes far less time, and therefore appreciation by the client is higher.

Tele-Learning

There are many changes taking place in the field of working and learning. Even though no one can predict what the future will bring, it is expected that electronic alternatives as EPSS and tele-learning will become more and more important. Tele-learning is defined as the intentional acquisition of knowledge, skills and attitudes with the help of information and communication technology (ICT). Tele-learning is a very broad concept supported by a variety of devices and tools. An important dimension of tele-learning is the communication between the learners and (electronic) sources, and communication among learners themselves. An obvious and popular example of tele-learning is the intranet. This is a network specific and only for employees to share information and knowledge. Especially tele-learning via intranet seems to play an important role in the knowledge economy today.

Tele-Learning Applications

As stated before tele-learning can be supported by many applications. The choice for these support devices and tools must be closely linked to the goals of the training. Of course choices have to take in mind the limitations of the workplace also. In Table 1, tele-learning applications that are of main importance for tele-learning are provided. The applications are divided in three categories: low-tech, medium-tech and high-tech applications. These categories refer to the speed and capacity of the companies' network.

For low-tech applications, like e-mail and discussion groups, a network with limited capacity and speed is sufficient; almost every network today can support these applications. Medium-tech applications can contain more information, therefore these applications need more capacity and speed. High-tech applications, like videoconferencing, need networks with high speed and high capacity. At the moment only a few organisations have networks which can support high-tech applications, like videoconferencing. So, a few companies can support their tele-learning program with videoconferencing applications.

Table 1. Applications for tele-learning (Bastiaens & Krul, 1998)

Tele-learning Applications	Example	Category
E-mail	Electronic mail between employees	Low-tech, a few hundred bytes per second, delay of a few seconds
Bulletin board	Relative simple way of conferencing systems (short announcements, reactions and positions)	
Newsgroups	World wide conferencing system for discussions, etc.	
Non-interactive audio	Audio in WWW pages to support the content	Medium-tech, hundreds of kbits per second, delay less than one second
Non-interactive video	Video in WWW pages (limited length)	
Interactive audio	Audio conferencing between two or more sites	
Videoconferencing	Combination of audio and vision between two or more sites	High-tech, more than 1 mbit per seconds, almost no delay
Multimedia conferencing	Combination of audio, video, pictures, employees can work on one and the same document (application sharing)	

The Surplus Value of Tele-Learning

In the field of business and industry, it is hard to attach a certain surplus value to only the concept of tele-learning. Although most of the time more influences like the work process, colleagues and customers play an important role, we will try to describe important dimensions of the surplus value of tele-learning in this paragraph.

Supporting the performance of employees with tele-learning is meaningful whenever the learning process becomes more efficient and effective. Also the gain of positive attitudes towards learning may be an important surplus value of tele-learning. Collis (1996) describes three variables for the successful implementation and use of innovations like tele-learning. According to her, tele-learning will only be successful whenever the combination of the variables—perceived payoff, level of difficulty and subjective personal interest—are positive.

Perceived Payoff

One of the main problems of specifying the perceived payoff of tele-learning is the fact that the benefits are often interwoven with the general business process. Although it is hard to isolate the real profits from tele-learning, it is important to do so. The long-term innovation process will take advantage of it.

Supporting the performance of employees with tele-learning applications will be useful when it is clear that the employees' performance will become more efficient and effective and that the employees' attitude will be affected in a positive way. Collis (1996) has put the three variables—efficiency, effectiveness and attitude—in a model (see Figure 2) and calls them gain, comfort and enjoyment. The metaphor of her model poses that innovations will only be implemented successfully when the results of a combination of the three variables—gain, comfort and enjoyment—will be positive. The underlying paragraphs will go into detail and describe the Collis model on the implementation of tele-learning applications.

The gain vector

The gain vector in the model (see Figure 2) refers to the expected advantages of the tele- learning application that has to be implemented. The gain vector is related to the effectiveness of the application. It is expected that tele-learning, first of all, will improve the quality of the learning processes (Romizowski, 1994). For example, it is easy to work and learn in project teams and communicate and exchange point of views by telecommunication. This will enhance the processing of conceptions and principles and improve problem-solving strategies.

Tele-learning can also mean a more active and concrete learning process. People who work and learn together have to make their knowledge more explicit and they have possibly to defend their opinions in cooperation with others. This means that people become more actively involved in the learning process and the content.

Next to the advantages for the learning process, tele-learning can improve the quality and productivity of the performance of employees. Especially more complex tasks can benefit from the support of tele-learning applications. The gradual dissemination of knowledge and information, the accessibility of important sources and procedural knowledge can improve the performance of individuals and teams. Next to this it is possible to share information and experiences. Employees can learn form each other and have the opportunity to broaden their tasks. The possibilities of communication and knowledge sharing can have a positive effect on the collaboration and support knowledge management initiatives.

Tele-learning also saves time travel and accommodation expenses. At the same time employees do not have to leave the workplace at all (withdrawal expenses). With tele-learning it is a possibility to learn at the job at off-peak hours. It is also cheaper regarding the training of large numbers of employees (compared with traditional classroom training).

The comfort vector

The comfort vector refers to the efficiency of an application. Tele-learning can improve the availability of training material. The possibilities to use material are increased. For example, through the World Wide Web it is possible to access material quicker. An employee can easily consult the expertise of other people. The borders between, for example, training events and coaching become faint. This can improve the balance between different learning activities.

Tele-learning can make the learning process more flexible. Learning becomes independent of time and place. Employees can, to a certain extent, choose whenever and whatever they will learn at the workplace. Is it easy to communicate with each other, so coaches or trainers can easily provide feedback to a learner and respond to his needs. Quick feedback is very important, nowadays. In many situations it is the employees own responsibility to obtain new skills and knowledge. A training event, which keeps the employee waiting for feedback, is out of date.

With tele-learning it is easy to obtain new (training) material. Not only is it possible to buy standard computer-based training modules but also to use sources which are not training material *per se*. Examples are on-line encyclopedias and homepages of profes-

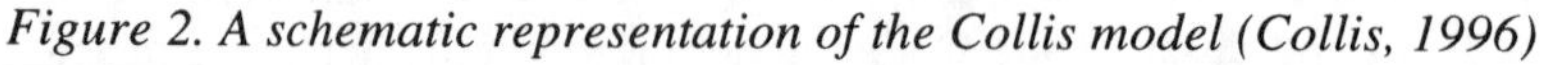

Figure 2. A schematic representation of the Collis model (Collis, 1996)

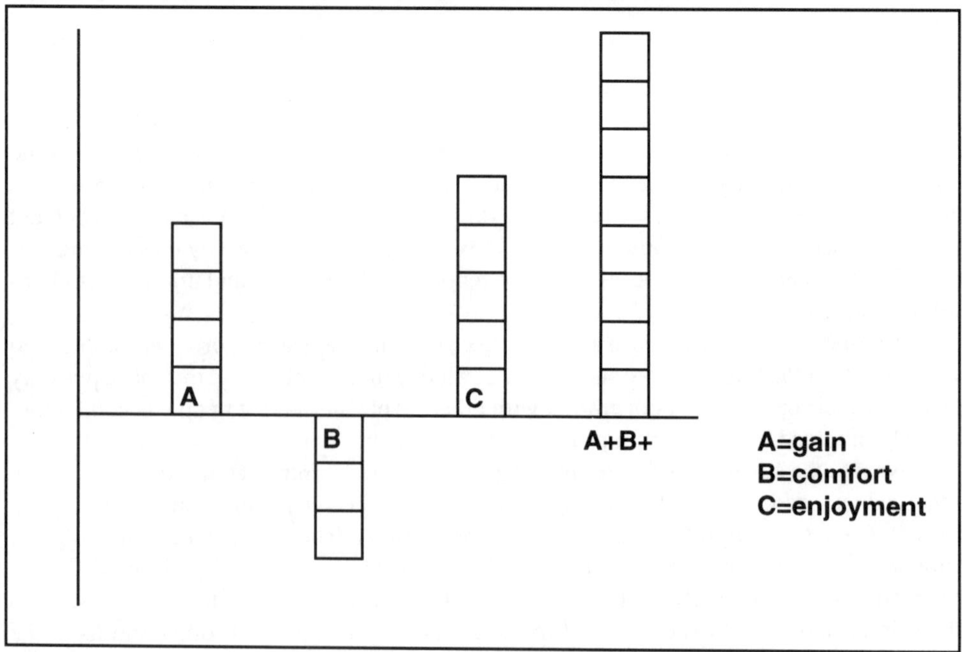

sional- and employers- organisations.

The enjoyment vector

The enjoyment vector refers to the attractiveness of an application and the joy people have whenever they are working with the application. Tele-learning can provide attractive learning material. Interactivity, video, sound and animations in applications are just a few characteristics that can simulate real-life situations, and by doing so enhance the joy and motivation of the learner.

The enjoyment vector is partly an exogenous factor, which depends heavily on personal opinions. Every individual reacts in one's own way to innovations. In general learners in distance training programs complain of a relative isolation. Tele-learning can take away these complaints by working and learning in an interactive way in cooperation with other colleagues on the job.

LEARNING WITH REAL CASES

In the above sections we signalled a trend: on the basis of economical and educational arguments, distance educational techniques have become more popular. The availability of affordable and powerful ICT has boosted this development. Distance education with ICT not only brings blessings. In the worst case, learners learn the wrong things, become demotivated, mainly start learning by heart, and so on. Therefore, another trend that we signalled, is the growth of competency-based education. This educational approach, which shows many similarities to case-based education or problem-based education, presents real problems to students. These problems are intend to stimulate active learning, instead of surface learning. Learning becomes much more similar to working.

Figure 1 depicted that in companies, working comes closer to learning. So, it seems that the differences between educational institutes and companies are becoming smaller. Learning with real cases is the key concept in this. It is expected that situated social practice in which participants' interpretations are continually being negotiated, will stimulate the creation of meaning and will have a positive impact on learning results. For that reason the learning process is contextualized with real-life cases. Important and basic issues in the design of learning environments are often derived from instructional design theories. Too often, however, these issues are not a response to a real instructional need. We suggest using real-world problems as a starting point. Learning with real cases is particularly useful in this situation, as they provide an environment in which students can explore a real problem, attempt to understand it, and then consider and generate a response. This methodology is especially effective if students are required to identify facts and issues, to de-center and view events from different perspectives, to apply current professional knowledge and research, and to predict consequences of various courses of action (McNergney, Herbert, and Ford, 1993).

In our view the concept of learning with real cases is a combination of on-the-job training and on-site learning combined with ICT. Learning-by-doing with real assignments from practice is the main focus. The ICT environment serves as a workspace for students who work together on a real case and reflects on the following four central tenets (based on Narayanan et al., 1995):

1. Learning is enhanced by problem solving. Learning is more effective when it occurs

through activities associated with solving problems (e.g., identifying and formulating the problem, generating alternatives, evaluating, decision making, reflecting, and articulating) rather than through transmission models of instruction.

2. The ICT tools have to reflect a realistic problem (for example the metaphor used for the interface has to look like a realistic 'real-world' tool) and use authentic activities that the learner will engage in during their (future) career roles. Besides that, the tools have to provide intrinsic support and structure which heavily relates to the problem-solving process.
3. Collaborative work is central to learning with real cases. Students are expected to solve problems and completes assignments in groups. As students work in collaborative groups, they are forced to articulate and reflect upon their thinking. The workspace has to support collaboration and provide procedural facilitation that enables students to use their own thinking, share knowledge and reflect on the way knowledge is used in real life.
4. Learning and the acquisition of problem-solving skills need to be scaffolded. The experiences implementing effective problem-based learning environments teach us that solving real-world problems requires help from facilitators, knowledgeable experts, and the learning environment. The goals of scaffolding are to enable students to carry out a reasoning process or achieve a goal that they would not be able to do without help. Students must have access to expert performance and modelling of the process involved.

A shared electronic learning and working space that seamlessly integrates a full variety of functionalities for the above will enhance learning. This workspace will tie together tools that students will use while solving problems.

In an idealised picture students learn in a 'virtual company' which prepares them for real life. They cooperatively learn and work on their assignments. This 'virtual company' is always on standby, and provides information and tools for learning and for keeping knowledge up-to-date. In this environment it is easy to consult colleagues or a coach whenever this is necessary.

Designers of an electronic learning and working space have to concentrate on teaching, learning and working processes. They have to consider what actions students can take when they are learning (e.g., how can they learn more about the topic business process redesign?). They have to think about the possibilities for the teaching process ('how can individual students be monitored and supported while working on an assignment?') and they have to design real-life actions for the virtual company (which operations can a counter clerk perform in a virtual bank?).

In the next sections we will provide guidelines associated to learning with real cases and try to answer the question, "how do we support people while they are working and learning with real cases?".

GUIDELINES

Use Embedded Support Devices

Alongside its advantages, distance education with ICT obviously has disadvantages as well. Learning with real cases is to some extent a type of distance education, because often a knowledge base is constructed, for instance available on an intranet. Using and understanding this often has to be done relatively independently, thus quite similar to distance training. Research over the years has shown important disadvantages of distance or independent learning. Some of the most important of these are the relative lack of support, guidance and interactivity, the fact that course material is often static and is not tailored to meet the needs of the users, and the lack of interim adjustments to take account of what students actually do. It is argued here that these are critical problems which are at least partly to blame for the difficulties students encounter in the process of self-study. Such problems may express themselves in the form of students' falling behind in their studies or dropping out. Distance training attempts to solve these problems by making use of embedded support devices (ESDS) in (written and electronic) course material (Martens, 1998). These devices consist of a whole spectrum of additions such as examples, questions with feedback, study tips (e.g., Write down the most important points raised in the summary), advance organisers (e.g., Your next task will be to explore the theory mentioned above), exercises and margin texts. All these ESDS are in fact an attempt to replace the teacher at the front of the classroom. In a distance education context, there is hardly contact between students and teachers/tutors, so the material has to be sufficiently supportive (Lowe, 1995; Dekkers & Kemp, 1995). Therefore an essential part of self-study material consists of embedded support devices. The central role of embedded support in distance education can be illustrated by the fact that learning materials in this context consist for about 40% of ESDS. ESDS represent a set of formal and content-related add-ons, extensions and elaborations of the learning materials, such as pre- and post-questions, schemes, illustrations, content pages, indexes, tasks, summaries, advance organisers, objectives, prior knowledge references, study tips, et cetera. ESDS aim at scaffolding the learning process.

A few short examples of ESDS are presented in below.

Advance Organiser

'In the previous section we treated the classical view on economics, thus emphasising the free market. Another and contrasting view is proposed by Milton Keynes, who stresses the importance of financial stimulation of the economy. This interesting view is presented in this section.'

Pre-question

'What would you take into consideration if you were to start a bookstore in the centre of town X?'

Add-on

'More information about this subject can be found in the interesting book of Mrs.... She describes the macro-economical implications of the Keynes' theory with clear examples.'

Objective

'After finishing this chapter you understand the basic principles of the labour market.'

Functions and Effects of Embedded Support

Since ESDS aim at supporting the learning process from the point of view of the student and aim at supporting the teaching process when taking the view of course developers, they can be structured following a traditional model of the teaching-learning situation:

starting conditions/situation
objectives
learning content
learning activities-didactical methods
media
evaluation

The way the ESDS are expected to support the learner are diverse. From the literature and from an analysis of current practice in developing study materials, we can derive certain functions in relation to each specific support device. These ESDS will be presented in an overview.

We distinguish more than 40 different ESDS, but some of them are to be considered as set categories rather than single, specific, supportive facilities. It has to be noted that sometimes the same text can contain several ESDS. In other words the same text can have more than one supportive function.

Most ESDS can be used in electronic learning environments/interactive learning environments (ILE) as well as in printed learning environments (PLE). Where support devices are especially designed for use in one type of learning environment, this will be indicated. Note that particularly the list of ESDS related to ILE is not treated exhaustively since to date this type of support in distance education is still in its infancy.

Of course the distinction between basic content and ESDS is not always a straight forward one. Research has shown however that in practice it is quit easy to divide text in basic content and ESDS. In distance education this distinction is often made explicit as a means to support learners. Explicit and structured embedding of ESDS is seen as one of the tools to enhance quality in distance education materials.

The next paragraph will discuss ESDS. For an overview of all ESDS, we refer to Table 2.

Starting Conditions

Starting conditions are related to the information students should have at the beginning of a case. They are often neglected which may cause problems. This section describes some ESDS that have proven to be helpful.

Indications about Required Prior Knowledge

If a course builds on necessary prerequisite knowledge or if prior knowledge about specific topics facilitates studying the study materials, information about this is needed for the student.

Indications about Study Skills Required

The way a student is to work through the study materials can imply the mastery (or learning) of specific study skills; for example, certain law courses presuppose that the student is skilled in handling multiple law sources, jurisprudence, et cetera.

References about Required Prior Knowledge

If prior knowledge is required, students can be helped by providing them with references of books, places, tools, etc., where they can acquire this prior knowledge.

Starting Level Tests

If students do not feel sure if they are 'ready' for a certain course, starting level tests are useful. Students can determine for themselves if they meet the starting conditions.

Prior Knowledge State Assessment

Starting level assessment measure starting conditions. Prior knowledge state assessments measure the extent to which students already mastered the course they intend to study. The test results can be helpful to navigate the student more selectively through the study materials by paying less attention to study contents that are sufficiently mastered.

Learning Objectives

Sometimes it is relevant to indicate learning objectives. The following support devices are recommended.

Course Introduction

Course introductions are general orientation sections for students that are helpful to answer questions about: What can I expect from this course? What are the general aims of this course? How many time will it take to study the materials (study load)? What extra support facilities are foreseen next to the study materials?

Learning Objectives

If defined at an operational level, learning objectives give clear indications about 'what' and 'how' the study content is to be mastered. The phrasing of objectives in observable terms is an important standard. In literature, many researchers have studied the potential benefits of incorporating objectives into the study materials.

Rowntree (1992) emphasises the importance of learning objectives in distance training since they are often a guideline to what is to be learned and how it is to be learned. He discusses four conceptions of learning:

- learning as memorising
- learning as understanding
- learning as application
- learning as personal development

He states that learning objectives should not be exclusively aimed at for instance the first two types of learners, since then learners from the last two categories would be frustrated.

Learning Content

In the actual learning or course content, many improvements to the readability, for instance, can be realised. Many of these ESDs will help to get an overview and to make relations in the material more explicit.

Structure Pages

Structure pages orient the student through the materials. This is especially relevant if the study materials consist of different types of materials: study book, text book, a reader, additional source materials, and/or software packages.

Glossary

Glossary is a support device that is especially designed for ILE. A student can click on a word and then get more or less extra information, definitions etc., related to this word.

Hotwords

A support device related to Glossary consists of Hotwords. These are words in a text in ILE that can be clicked on. By means of hypertext links, the reader can then easily skip from one theme to another. These ESDS are also referred to as hyperlinks.

Content Pages

The content pages present the overall structure of the learning content. They help to detect interrelations in the course content and help to embed a specific course chapter or part into the broader course content setting.

Both 'structure pages' and 'content pages' can be considered as 'pre-instructional strategies'.

Repeat-units

Repeat-units help to recapitulate the course content studied so far. Repeat units can be developed at the micro-unit level, rehearsing only the content dealt with in one specific learning unit. Other repeat units are developed at the meso-level and link together all learning contents discussed so far. The interdependence of the learning content is stressed in this way.

Registers and Indexes

Each content domain builds on special conceptual frameworks, sets of agreements, postulations, abbreviations, formulas, and so on. A handsome overview of this information enriches the course content and can present additional access devices to the course content (Hartley, 1995).

Advance Organisers

Initially conceptualised by Ausubel (1963), advance organisers are a regularly used support device in study materials. The fact advance organisers are of higher abstraction level than the course content itself helps to structure, introduce, put into context, et cetera, the learning content that follows. Advance organisers can be expositive (stressing the agreements) or comparative (stressing differences). They serve as connections between former text parts and new text parts. Research in relation to the effects of advance organisers has resulted in conflicting findings. An overview can be found in Montague & Knirk (1993).

Schemes

Schemes embrace a large set of complex information into an abstract but more translucent small set of information. Schemes reflect the major 'structure' that is to be found in the information. Some schemes are called 'processes' or a 'classification' if the structured information reflects chronological, hierarchical or comparison interrelations.

Course Additions

In certain types of courses, the course content is to be commented. This is especially true if the course if based on a text book of an author who explicitly makes choices, colours information or distorts certain facts.

Content Extensions

Next to content additions, content extensions give the student additional information where 'more' can be found since the study materials only deal with part of the existing knowledge of the domain. References, for instance, of literature, places and people can be useful in this perspective.

References to Other Learning Units

Studying the separate learning units of course materials can invoke a crumbled perception of the course content and as a consequence on the knowledge domain. References to other learning units can help to prevent this.

Text Structure

The way text is structured and divided into text parts has an impact on the perception of the basic structure of the domain knowledge. Most research and research overviews about 'text structure' focus on specific elements of this set of support devices (e.g., Bernard, 1990). Rowntree (1992) mentions 'signals' such as white spaces, headings, boxes and bullet lists as important tools. Also Hartley (1995) stresses the importance of appropriate layout in distance training textual materials. The use of colours can be added to this. Colours can play an important role in making the text structure more visible. Pett & Wilson (1996) give guidelines for this.

Summaries

Summaries can be considered as commented schemes of broader text parts. They compress information to a readable but short outline of the major topics deliberated so far (Montague & Knirk, 1993; Hartley, 1995).

Text Documentation

Text documentation is a 'set category' comprising pictures, maps, charts, graphs, tables, photos, cartoons, et cetera, that help to substantiate elements or parts of the abstract course content. Lowe (1995) and Goldman & Schwartz (1995) stress the importance of illustrations in (distance) education materials. Text documentation is especially an effective way to present multiple representations of the same course content. Illustrations can have motivational-affective and cognitive effects (Lowe, 1995). Many authors have studied this set of support devices: diagrams are for instance heavily studied. Also the representation of quantitative information has attracted attention. To date many researchers agree that pictorial information especially if it is dynamic (in an ILE) can add much to learning gains, without agreeing on exactly what cognitive processes are responsible for this.

Examples

Examples can be considered as a special case of 'text documentation'. They add to the course content an alternative representation of the same knowledge element. Rowntree (1992, p. 132) says: 'Good open learning will include plenty examples.' Examples bring principles to life.

Learning Activities

Support devices in relation to study activities can be subdivided into two categories: devices that help to structure and organise the learning process and devices that help to motivate and activate the student.

Indications about Study Load

Clear indications about the study load to be expected can help students to structure and plan their study time. The course study load is, in the Open University-context, given in study-hours.

Indications about Support Provisions

At the same level, students can also structure their work according to the support provisions, rendered by e.g., study centres, peer groups, et cetera. The indications comprise information about properties and strategies adopted under the specific circumstances.

Indications about the Expected Study Approach

The course content can be documented, at the micro-level, with information, indications, guidelines, about the way to tackle the course content, specific subparts of the course content, certain tasks, questions, et cetera.

Questions, Tasks about the Study Approach

When discussing the 'Indications about required study skills,' we already referred to the fact that studying specific content domains can imply the mastery of specific study skills. But it is also possible to teach students to acquire these skills in the course of their actual learning process (Montague & Knirk, 1993). This implies that the course developer incorporates into the study text information on a meta-level when he gives indications about how to deal with the tasks, questions, materials, et cetera. The example we gave about the skills in handling multiple law sources can be, for instance, demonstrated in a separate text section before the student is expected to do it on his own.

Prequestions

Prequestions are a special support device that presents the student with questions before actually elaborating the course content in more detail (Montague & Knirk, 1993). The questions can help the student to make the needed prior knowledge available. Questions are also helpful to relate the new learning content to information already dealt with or they induce explicit reflection from the student in relation to the new course content. Research about the potential benefits of incorporating questions into study texts is abundant. For extensive overviews we refer to Bernard & Naidu (1992); Duchastel & Whitehead (1980); Rickards & Denner (1978); and Winne (1983). Some of this research is not only related to 'pre-questions' but is also relevant for the use of questions in general.

Questions

'Questions' is a commonly used type of support device in study texts to continuously encourage the student to question himself about his knowledge, comprehension or mastery of the learning content (Lockwood, 1995 a; Montague & Knirk, 1993). Assessment can be formative (not graded) and summative (graded). Students tend to be very well aware of summative assessment and many students direct their learning process on this (Lockwood, 1995b). In practice these two forms of assessment often resemble each other. In conventional education a teacher continuously monitors the comprehension process. This important role of the teacher has to be substituted somehow in distance training. Questions with feedback are therefore crucial in self study.

The literature references mentioned in relation to pre-questions can also be repeated here. Questions with feedback are among the most important and most used support devices in distance education (Rowntree, 1992; Dochy, 1992; Naidu & Bernard, 1992). Naidu & Bernard (1992) report that sometimes questions are avoided by students. Therefore they should be well designed and placed close to the relevant text.

Tasks

'Tasks' are support devices that demand from the student further actions, especially at the application level and going beyond the information presented in the study text. In practice authors distinguish application tasks, construction tasks, action tasks, algorithm tasks, et cetera.

Concept Mapping

Concept mapping is a strategy for representing meaningful relationships between concepts in the form of propositions. It is a learning strategy which allows the reconstruction of course content into personal representations, stimulated by exercises based on graphic procedure. A concept is a perceived regularity in events which is designated by an arbitrary level. For example rain is the label used for water dropping from clouds. Propositions are the linking word(s) between concepts that form a semantic unit to illustrate a specific regularity (Naidu & Bernard, 1992). Concept mapping is a study strategy that is stimulated by means of exercise in the learning material. It takes some practice and persistence with mapping before significant positive outcomes become manifest (Naidu & Bernard, 1992; Montague & Knirk, 1993).

Simulations/Microworlds

A special form of new embedded support is formed by simulations or microworlds. These are simulations of processes that can be manipulated by the learner. They represent typically new forms of ESDs that are coming up with the emergence of ILE (e.g., Edwards, 1995; Hensgens, Van Rosmalen & Van der Barren, 1995; Montague & Knirk, 1993). Simulations/microworlds are relatively often used for mathematics and science teaching.

Feedback

The learning activity can further be intensified by giving feedback in relation to questions and tasks. Revision and reflection behaviour are incited and can help the student to look at the same study content from a different perspective. In reviewing the literature especially the study of Bernard & Naidu (1992) is of importance in this context since these researchers focused on the combined effect of post-questions, concept-mapping and feedback in a distance training context. Biemans & Simons (1992) found that embedded regulation questions must be accompanied by regulation hints to be effective in a computer-assisted instruction on word processing. A more general overview of research in relation to feedback in relation to self-regulated learning can be found in Elshout-Mohr, 1991.

In ILE, feedback can be generated automatically and can provide extra information to students taking into account students' responses to questions. Questions with feedback are one of the most important support devices in distance training.

Notetaking Tools

A tool typically used in ILE is a support device for notetaking by students. It gives students the advantages that text processors have such as copying, printing and editing. Quade (1995) found that notetaking from computer-based instruction using an on-line notepad promotes higher achievement then pencil and paper methods.

Media

Use of Additional Media, Media-mix

The printed course text can be appended with information that can only be delivered by other media. Information and references about these media are to be given.

Support for the Use of Media

Moreover, the student is also to be told what is expected from him when he is studying or working with these additional media.

Network Connections

ILE can provide network connections, allowing students to communicate more effectively with other students or tutors.

Evaluation

Sometimes systematic evaluation is required. Again important examples of useful support devices are presented.

Mastery Requirements

The expected mastery levels in order to pass examinations are guidelines to help students to estimate their readiness after studying the course content.

Information about Test Formats

Students are disoriented if they are questioned, evaluated by unexpected test formats (e.g., special types of multiple choice where they expect free format questions). The way they prepare themselves for a test is influenced by this type of information.

Table 2. Overview of ESDs

Part of the learning model	ESD
starting conditions	indications about required prior knowledge
	indications about study skills required
	references about required prior knowledge
	starting level tests
	prior knowledge state assessment
learning objectives	course introduction
	learning objectives
learning content	structure pages
	glossary
	hotwords
	content pages
	repeat-units
	registers and indexes
	advance organisers
	schemes
	course additions
	content extensions
	references to other learning units
	text structure
	summaries
	text documentation
	examples
learning activities	indications about study load
	indications about support provisions
	indications about the expected study approach
	questions, tasks about the study approach
	prequestions
	questions
	tasks
	concept mapping
	simulations/microworlds
	feedback
	notetaking tools
media	use of additional media, media-mix
	support to the use of media
	network connections
evaluation	mastery requirements
	information about test formats
	tests (formative, summative)
	feedback

Tests (formative, summative)

Examples of tests and examinations give directions about what and how to study. These examples can have a strong influence on the way students study. Students often learn with this final exam in mind (Lockwood, 1995 b), so assessment can have a strong influence on the study process (Buttler & Winne, 1995).

Prior knowledge (at the beginning of a study) and progress (during a study) assessment can be influential forms of ESDS that are often incorporated into courses. They are intended to give students feedback, hints and cues, about their study process. In printed courses the feedback (e.g., correct answers) are usually immediately available to students, with 'electronic' procedures this type of information can be delayed and/or personalised (Dochy, 1992).

Feedback

Examples of correct answers have more than an illustrative function. They shape the way students will prepare themselves to answer questions. Research has shown that delayed feedback often gives better results than immediate feedback (e.g., De Klerk & Eerland, 1977; Bangert-Drowns, Kulik, Kulik & Morgan, 1991). Delayed feedback prevents students from immediately looking up and simply memorising the right answers. ILE could in this perspective be far more effective than PLE, also because they can react to answers given by students.

PITFALLS

We have pleaded for a certain approach to learning with real cases. In that approach, working and learning have become more the same. In a learning condition (e.g. students following a course), real life is simulated. Real problems and cases will be the starting point for learning. In a professional context, where the cases are real, learning is supposed to occur as a side effect. Think of a company that provides its employees with a knowledge management system on an intranet. In that case coaching functions and ESDs have to support these employees. In this section we will briefly discuss some topics, considerations, or if you like, pitfalls. Where appropriate, we'll indicate what ESDs may be useful to employ.

Minimal Learning Versus Acquiring Overview

Minimal learning is a concept employed in professional contexts. The basic idea is that employees should not lose time in learning all kinds of irrelevant subjects or get lost in a forest of knowledge that the company has put on the intranet. In other words: you want learners to read, study or look only for that information that is relevant for them and that will actually improve performance.

But on the other hand you don't want employees to get an incomplete image, or even worse, when students use real cases, try to solve problems but miss the overview of a certain learning content. They learn for example to use a program for statistical analysis without really understanding the statistical concepts that underlie this program. Minimal learning has the risk of causing incomplete or even false or confusing knowledge.

The solution to these controversies lies in the organisation of the learning contents, by means of ESDs or coaching functions. There are many ESDs that are designed to solve this problem. So to put it with all crudeness: it is not a good idea to have learners or employees solve problems and tell them that if they need tips, guidelines, theory or whatever, they can refer to a multimedia encyclopedia. That information should be organised, by means of structuring ESDs. This can be done by setting learning goals, structure pages and overviews.

Action Mode or TV Mode?

Many ESDs in distance training have been designed to prevent or stop students from a passive learning mode. In a passive learning mode students learn by heart, don't really think about concepts and don't come up with any creativity. Using multimedia can worsen the problem. This is sometimes referred to as the 'TV mode'. Learners absorb things in a very passive manner, as if they were watching a soap television program. ESDs designed to get students out of that passive mode all have to do with activation: intriguing problems are presented, questions are asked or even tasks are required. This is often related to a monitoring function. The computer program monitors progress. Much research has shown that this can stimulate students and prevent them from switching to the passive mode. But of course there are risks in this approach. In the first place this monitoring is expensive. It costs a lot of development time. This is mainly because it has to be done in a good way. When you give the wrong advice to students, for instance because the tasks are not well designed, the effect may well be worse than without using these ESDs or monitoring function. Then there is the problem control or inspection. People often don't like the idea of being monitored by a program they work with.

Content or Procedures?

Another distinction that is important to notice is that of providing employees with content (e.g., knowledge, theory, databases) or procedures that only support or organise the work. Examples of the latter case are form fields, procedural tips (e.g. 'first do this, then do that and then do next'). Tools often support procedures and content is offered by, for instance, online information systems. In the practice of real cases this distinction is often not very clear. But it is a distinction that is important to keep in mind. In the one case you really want people to learn things, and accept that this may take some time, in the other case you try to make people act as fast as possible in an efficient way without caring much about a learning effect or transfer of knowledge.

Misconceptions

We already pointed at the danger of minimal learning or learning with real cases: people may not get a proper overview. They might act in a 'see monkey do monkey' way. Real events are very problem oriented; learners or the employees want to do things. They want to solve a problem or perform a certain action. And when that works they think it is fine. But there is the risk of inadequate, inefficient or even wrong solutions that only seem to work well. A 'classic' example of this is when people don't know how to use their text-processing program. A typical beginner's error in WordPerfect 5 was to use tabs or interspacing to make a paragraph indented. This seemed to work well, until there was a slight change in font type, printer settings, or whatever. Again, this is a risk of learning with real cases. People may become too task oriented without taking their time to look a little bit deeper into the tools they are using. And, again, we strongly recommend the use of ESDS to prevent this from happening. Suited for this are questions with feedback, tasks, tests and examples.

Social Interaction

Working with real cases behind a computer screen seems a lonely business. Although it may be effective, cheap and so on, criticisers believe that nothing compares to learning in a classroom or a university with all its social interactions. This may be true to some extent but this objection has largely been overcome in recent days. The solution to this is Computer Supported Collaborative Learning (CSCL). In many projects teams of students work together, for instance in a virtual company. There have become many tools available for this, varying form e-mail to groupware and tools to actually share applications on different computers. In a business context this cooperation via the computer is becoming the standard. enterprise storage, intranet, knowledge management, and so on have become key factors.

These entire developments make learning and working with real cases more and more into a social event instead of a soloist tour.

Wrong Starting Points

In classroom-like teaching situations it is relatively easy to check if all students know enough to begin with a course. But when working with real cases, it is easy to make wrong assumptions about prior knowledge of employees or students. Too much help, guidance and explanation is boring and too little is even worse. There are many ESDs that are designed to tackle this problem. We recommend use of indications about the expected study approach, prequestions, references about required prior knowledge, starting level tests, and prior knowledge state assessment.

Pitfalls Related to the Introduction of Tele-Learning

Regarding the organisation it must be mentioned that tele-learning requires a change of culture. Due to our knowledge-society, companies have to concentrate more than before on information retrieval skills and knowledge building. This demands for an integrated learning and working environment in which employees cooperatively build and maintain a knowledge base.

With tele-learning, organisations have to invest in hardware and software. Next to this there are implementation costs for information meetings and induction costs.

The shift towards a knowledge-society in which the utilisation and development of knowledge are the central tenets, demands flexible and fast working processes in an always changing environment. Unfortunately, the working environment is often too dynamic to learn or read information. For example, an employee has to concentrate on the production process or has to serve a waiting customer. At that moment he doesn't have the time to learn his lessons or even search for information.

Responsibility and Dependence

Whenever employees learn to trust in computers for their information, there is a possibility that they will trust the computer 100 percent and will not think for themselves. They will become dependent on computers for their knowledge. Whenever the server is down there is a shortage of knowledge and information.

Other pitfalls refer to the learning process. As mentioned before, looking for information in an effective way will become more important (information retrieval skills). But it is also important that employees take responsibility for their own learning. Some employees may not have the ability to take responsibility or will not have adequate information retrieval skills. They may make wrong choices and learn less effectively.

It is doubtful whether tele-learning applications are suitable for learning a certain attitude. Learning attitudes most of the time requires the involvement of other people. It is expected that it will not be possible to teach all the learning processes in an organisation. Tele-learning will probably be just one out of a range of training and support possibilities.

WRAPPING UP

This chapter presented two converging developments. Traditionally, learning at schools or universities and working in a professional context were relatively separated. We have argued that these two are converging. This leads to what was called 'learning with real cases'. It is expected that situated social practice in which participants' interpretations are continually being negotiated will stimulate the creation of meaning and will have a positive impact on learning results. In our view the concept of learning with real cases is a combination of on-the-job training and on-site learning combined with ICT. Learning-by-doing with real assignments from practice is the main focus. The ICT environment serves as a workspace for students who work together on a real case. We presented guidelines, examples, and pitfalls that are associated to this new approach to working and learning.

REFERENCES

Aarnoutse, C.A.J., & Weterings, A.C.E.M. (1995). Onderwijs in begrijpend lezen [Education in reading comprehension]. *Pedagogische Studiën, 72*, 82-101.

Athey, T.A.(1997). *Virtual learning and its impact on the university*. Paper presented on 'the new learning Environment'. The 18th ICDE conference, The Pennsylvania State University, June, 1997.

Ausubel, D.P. (1963). *The psychology of meaningful verbal learning*. New York: Grune & Stratton.

Bangert-Drowns, R.L., Kulik, C.C., Kulik, J., & Morgan, M. (1991). The instructional effect of feedback in test-like events. *Review of Educational Research, 61*, 213-238.

Bastiaens, Th. J., Krul, Y. (1998). Teleleren in Bedrijven: Een afweging waard?.*Gids voor de opleidingspraktijk*. Afl 27, oktober 1998.

Bates, A.W. (1995). *Technology, open learning and distance education*. London: Routledge.

Bell, R., & Tight, M. (1995). Open universities in the nineteenth century Britain. *Open Learning, 10*, 3-11.

Bernard, R.M. (1990). Effects of processing instructions on the usefulness of a graphic organizer and structural cueing in text. *Instructional Science, 19*, 207-217.

Bernard, R.M., & Naidu, S. (1992). Post-questioning, concept mapping and feedback: a distance education field experiment. *British Journal of Educational Technology, 23*, 48-60.

Biemans, H.J.A., & Simons, P.R.J. (1996). Contact-2: a computer-assisted instructional strategy for promoting conceptual change. *Instructional Science, 24,* 157-176.

Bunk, G.P., Kaizer, M., Zedler, R. (1991). Schlüsselqualificationen- Intention, Midofication, und Realisation in der beruflichen Aus- und Weiterbildung. *Mittteilungen aus der Arbeitsmarkt- und berufsforschung*, 24(2), 365-374.

Collis, B. (1996). Tele-learning as a Pedagogical Re-Engineering, Idylle. WWW document at http://www.to.utwente.nl/user/ism/collis/presents/ped-eng.htm

Danish Ministry of Education (1994). Technology-supported learning (Distance Learning). Report no. 1253. Copenhagen. Ministry of Education Publishing Office.

Dekkers, J., & Kemp, N.A. (1995). Contemporary developments in the typographical design of instructional texts for open and distance learning. In: F. Lockwood (Ed.), *Open and Distance Learning Today* (pp. 311-322). London: Routledge.

Dochy, F.J.R.C. (1992). *Assessment of prior knowledge as a determinant for future learning*. Utrecht/London: LEMMA, Jessica Kingsley.

Duchastel, P.C., & Whitehead, D. (1980). Exploring student reactions to inserted questions in text. *Programmed Learning and Educational Technology, 17*, 41-47.

Edwards, L.D. (1995). The design and analysis of a mathematical microworld. *Journal of Educational Computing Research, 12,* 77-94.

Fletcher-Flinn, C., & Gravatt, B. (1995). The efficacy of computer assisted instruction (CAI): a meta-analysis. *Journal of Educational Computing Research, 12*, 219-242.

Gibbs, G., Lucas, L., & Simonite, V. (1996). Class size and student performance: 1984-94. *Studies in higher education, 21,* 261-273.

Goldman, S.R., & Schwartz, D.L. (1995). *Viewing versus doing in the integration of text and graphics*. Paper presented at EARLI, 1995, Nijmegen, the Netherlands.

Granger, D., & Gulliver, K. (1995). Toward a new approach to quality in open learning. In: D. Sewart (Ed.), *One world many voices*, ICDE June 1995 (pp. 81-84). London: Eyre & Spottiswoode Ltd.

Hartley, J. (1995). The layout and design of textual materials for distance learning. In: F. Lockwood (Ed.), *Open and Distance Learning Today* (pp. 279-287). London: Routledge.

Hawkridge, D. (1995). The big bang theory in distance education. In: F. Lockwood (Ed.), *Open and Distance Learning Today*. London: Routledge, 3-12.

Holmberg, B. (1990). A paradigm shift in distance education? Mythology in the making. *ICDE bulletin, 22*, 51-55.

Holmberg, B. (1995). The evolution of the character and practice of distance education. *Open Learning, 10*, 44-47.

Kearsley, G., & Lynch, W. (1994). Combining television and computer networks to provide cost-effective distance education (pp. 443-452). *International distance education: a vision for higher education.* Preconference papers of International Distance Education Conference, Pennsylvania, USA: Pennsylvania State university.

Lockwood, F. (1995, a). A cost benefit model to describe the perception and use of activities in self-instructional texts. *European Journal of Psychology of Education, 10*, 145-152.

Lowe, R. (1995). Using instructional illustrations for distance education. In: F. Lockwood (Ed.), *Open and Distance Learning Today* (pp. 288-300). London: Routledge.

Martens, R.L. (1998). *The use and effects of embedded support devices in independent learning*. Ph.D. Thesis. Utrecht: Uitgeverij Lemma BV.

Martin, E.D., & Rainey, L. (1997). *The effect of distance learning on student achievement and student attitude: a longitudinal, controlled study*. Paper presented on 'the new learning Environment'. The 18th ICDE conference, The Pennsylvania State University, June, 1997.

McNergey, R.F., Herbert, J.A. & Ford, R.D. (1993). *Anatomy of a team case competition*. Paper presented at the annual meeting of the American Educational Research Association. Atlanta.

Montague, W.E., & Knirk, F.G. (1993). What works in adult instruction: the management, design and delivery of instruction. *International Journal of Educational Research, 19,* 329-331.

Naidu, S., & Bernard, R.M. (1992). Enhancing academic performance in distance education with concept mapping and inserted questions. *Distance Education, 13*, 218-233.

Narayanan, N.H., Hmelo, C., Petrushin, V., Newstetter, W., Guzdial, M., & Kolodner, JL. (1995). *Computational Support for Collaborative Learning through Generative Problem Solving*. Paper presented at the CSCL conference 1995. Indiana University Bloomington.

Pett, D., & Wilson, T. (1996). Colour research and its application to the design of instructional materials. *Educational Technology Research and Development, 44,* 19-35.

Quade, A.M. (1995). *A comparison of on-line and traditional paper and pencil notetaking methods during computer-delivered instruction.* Proceedings of the 1995 annual national convention of the association for educational communication and technology (AECT), Anaheim, USA.

Rickards, J.P., & Denner, P.R. (1978). Inserted Questions as Aids to Reading Text. *Instructional Science*, 7, 313-346.

Romizowski, A.J. (1994). Opleidingen op afstand, de toepassingen [Applying training at a distance]. *Opleiders in Organisaties, Capita Selecta,* afl 18. Deventer. Kluwer Bedrijfswetenschappen.

Rowntree, D. (1992). *Exploring open and distance learning*. London: Kogan Page Series.

Sorenson, R.C., & Walberg, H.J. (1993). Preface on: What works in adult instruction: the management, design and delivery of instruction. *International Journal of Educational Research, 19,* 329-331.

Streumer, J. N. & Bjorkquist, D.C. (1998). Moving Beyond Traditional Vocational Education and Training: Emerging Issues. In: Nijhof, W.J. & Streuer, J.N.(1998). *Key Qualifications in Work and Education*, 249-264. Dordrecht. Kluwer Academic Publishers.

Sutton, D.F., & Gross, C.D. (1994). Bridging the cultural gap with distance learning (pp. 171-179). *International distance education: a vision for higher education.* Preconference papers of International Distance Education Conference, Pennsylvania, USA: Pennsylvania State University.

Winne, P.H. (1983). Training students to process text with adjunct aids. *Instructional Science, 12*, 243-266.

Valcke, M., & Thorpe, M. (1995). Distance education: A particular context for teaching and learning. *European Journal of Psychology of Education, 10,* 111-120.

Chapter II

Design Guidelines for Web-Based Courses

Zane L. Berge
University of Maryland Baltimore County, USA

Mauri Collins
Old Dominion University, USA

Karen Dougherty
McCormick & Co., Inc., USA

Successful course creation for the Web environment means much more than the use of documents uploaded and electronically linked together. Course content should be designed specifically for use with an interactive, electronic medium that is capable of accommodating different types of audiovisual information (Porter, 1997, p. 128). This content can include video clips, animation, sound effects, music, voiceovers, photographs, drawings, and linked and unlinked pages. It means maintaining high standards of quality while promoting accessibility, motivation, and interactivity for students who are learning in this environment. Students in Web-based courses can become problem solvers involved in real-world problems as they take responsibility for their own learning.

WHY TEACH AND LEARN ONLINE

Teaching and learning online is flexible. Key features of Web-based learning environments are:

> "Interactive, multi-medial, open system, online search, device-distant-time independent, globally accessible, electronic publishing, uniformity, worldwide, online resources, distributed, cross-cultural interaction, multiple expertise, industry supported, learner-controlled, convenient, self-contained, ease of use, online support, authentic, course security, environmentally friendly, non-discriminatory, cost effective, ease of coursework development and maintenance, collaborative learning, formal and informal environments, online evaluations, virtual cultures, etc." (Khan, 1997, p.8).

Using a Web browser, all of the above are available to faculty and students at a click of the mouse. Students can take a virtual tour of another country, or a local museum, or have a virtual seminar with visiting lecturers in a way they might not be able to do without access to such technology (Dodge, 1996). Students can search libraries the world over and access journals, books, and information quickly and easily. They can access more than 50 million Web pages, with hundreds of new Web sites bearing up-to-the-minute information appearing every day. This could support a national and international student body that can share ideas and thoughts no matter where they live in the world, and renders moot the inaccessibility to educational opportunities that a particular student might face within their own geographic boundaries, finances, or work schedule.

Students Perspective

Students can be challenged with problems that require them to analyze and connect concepts and summarize those concepts for themselves and others. Because of the proliferation of Web pages containing unverified – and sometimes unverifiable—information, students can practice analysis and discernment and apply filtering criteria to the pages they are reading to estimate their reliability. To the extent lifelong learning is seen as a necessary condition for work and life's activities in the 21st century, an instructor can always have as one course goal guiding students to learn how to learn and to evaluate their own learning experiences. A continuum of methods can be delivered via Web pages from instructor-led lectures through guided learner-controlled activities to eventually independent, student-controlled.

Online, Web-based classes can often "fit around" students' lifestyles and obligations. The classes offer advantages to active, involved learners who are motivated to learn. The relatively self-paced learning style of most Web-based classes can be adapted to students who each learn differently and at different rates. The material is presented in text and graphic form, with everything from plain text pages to those holding Web-streamed images where students can actually watch live course proceedings or access them from archive at convenient times. Material can be reviewed for missed concepts as many times as the student would like, without holding up other learners who are not stalled at mastery of a specific skill or constructing this particular unit of knowledge.

Instructors' Perspective

For instructors, the initial commitment of time and energy is large as course materials and presentation need to be converted from face-to-face to Web-enhanced or Web-based delivery and the conversion of "digital instructional resources" (a fancy name for existing word-processed documents) may require the instructor to learn new technology skills. An instructor may even have to acquire a new teaching style or new methods of content delivery. One of the benefits of Web-based course delivery is that the course materials are often easier to update, often easier for learners to access and use, and the Web can be used to distribute most or all of the course content to students (Saltzberg, 1995). Feedback and evaluation can be more timely and achieved more conveniently through e-mail and on-line conferencing. Phone costs may be reduced, depending upon the amount of previous long-distance phone calls to students that had to be made. Problems can more often be handled as they arise (Dodge, 1996). In addition to instructors tracking students and seeing what each has and has not submitted, students can often see what work has been turned in and what still needs to be done. When the syllabus, readings, assignments, and testing schedules are on Web pages they are constantly available for reference by students and not easily mislaid. If the instructor wishes, tests can be given online, graded and recorded, usually in less time than if done off-line (Saltzberg, 1995). With the use of forms, assignments with "one right answer" can be submitted privately to the instructor, even in a course where class discussion spaces are open to all.

WEB-ENHANCED AND WEB-BASED COURSES

There are three delivery models for Web-based instruction discussed below, each having somewhat different emphases regarding instructional design. The models discusses are: 1) using the Web as a supplement to face-to-face instruction, 2) using the Web in a mixed mode with face-to-face instruction, and, 3) using Web-based instruction instead of face-to-face instruction.

Web-Enhanced Courses: A Supplement to Face-to-Face Meetings

Historically, the "traditional" classroom model requires students and faculty be in a particular place at the same time. In a face-to-face class, generally the whole class proceeds through the course content at the same pace, regulated by the instructor. This instructor-paced classroom occurs regardless of the interest, prior experience, or scheduling demands of students or instructor. The distributed classroom model (IDE, 1997) is similar, except students may physically attend class from several locations. For instance, there might be a group of students at another site with Web-based synchronous communication used to link the classrooms (e.g., audio or videoconferencing). The Web, used as a supplement to classroom activities here, could be used for the distribution of documents including lecture notes, test reviews etc., as a resource for information, or for asynchronous computer-conferencing to allow interaction among and between students at different sites and to do it at convenient times.

Instructional design focuses on analyzing what the course learning objectives are and how to best present them to students. So the design of a Web course would involve providing readings online, links to Web sites to visit, or providing a place for face-to-face classroom discussions to continue, or sometimes discussions about new topics to take place. Continual assessment of student learning during the course and at its completion is important to ensure that the goals and objectives are/were being met. Planning for the identification and implementation of changes necessary so that the course can be improved in future iterations, both in face-to-face meetings and on the use of the Web, is important to the design of future courses.

Web-Enhanced Courses: Mixed mode

Web-based learning plus classroom sessions (Butler, 1995; Saltzberg, 1995) necessitate students being in a particular place at a specified time occasionally, but a significant portion of the instructional goals and objectives can be met online. Ownership of learning is given more to the learners, and they are encouraged to reach new levels of understanding. The learning materials used are both in print and online (Dorbolo, 1996). From a learning materials design point of view, one challenge is to match the media used with the shelf-life of the material being distributed. When that information is expected to change relatively often or quickly, it is well to plan for those documents to be online. If documents or other information is stable and will be used for a relatively long time, then print may be the most convenient medium.

Analyzing the existing course content to see what should be done face-to-face or synchronously, and what could be done as well or better online, is an important first step in content delivery design. Designing a course that uses the advantages of each medium available to the class will maximize benefits to the learners. A program to bridge or make the transition from the classroom to online as easy for the learner as possible must be integrated into the very early stages of the course.

Web-Based Courses

In the past, traditional institutions of higher education would insist that students wanting an education must come to the university to fulfill some term of residency. Likewise, trainers often still gather students into a central location. Both professors and trainers, using this Fordian-style mass production model, pace the instruction, with little regard for student *learning* (Berge, 1999). Today, nontraditional students' lifestyles place value on part-time study, and study when and where convenient to each of them. Add to this business managers who can no longer afford to have employees gone for days or a week or two at a time for training at central location. For maximum effectiveness, training and learning opportunities must go to the students and arrive just-in-time. For these and other reasons, demographics and competition no longer allow instructors or trainers to insist on "my place at my pace." Totally online, Web-based courses offer benefits for learners and trainers/instructors alike.

A hyperlearning model (George Mason University, 1997) can work well in these situations, with the designer thinking about interactivity for the student regarding what resources are linked, what text should be archived and available, the demonstrations that would be valuable in learning, how testing can be done to match the real-world circumstances a learner would find him or herself in, and the practice the students need to reinforce their learning.

Advantages of Web-based courses include instructional work areas that are open for use at any time. Collaboration among distributed learners is possible and often more convenient than with face-to-face classrooms (Goldberg, 1996). Experiential learning models where the learner participates with control over the nature and direction of the learning process can be more easily used (Polyson et al., 1996). Many experiences can be simulated virtually in ways that interact with students to give them real-life experiences that they may never be able have otherwise.

DESIGNING WEB-BASED COURSES

Regardless of the delivery method, in all courses the following elements must be accounted for in their overall design:

- *Administrivia*— syllabi, schedules, contact information, course objectives and expectations, etc.

- *Course Content*—textbooks, readings, lectures, video/audio tapes, graphics and images etc.
- *Interaction*—between student and instructor and among students.
- *Additional Learning Resources* (which can be developed by students themselves).
- *Monitoring* of ongoing student learning.
- *Final assessment* of attainment of course learning objectives.

Structured in the above manner, course design frequently causes instructors some difficulty as they are not used to considering the chunking of course content into the above categories. Most faculty are required to develop a syllabus, the format and content of which is often spelled out in institutional accreditation documents. A syllabus document is a sound initial framework or "map" for laying out the content and learning processes to be included in the course. Thinking this through carefully can also assist in planning the navigation strategies. If information will be referred to frequently, it might be placed on a page that may be linked to/from several other pages. A document that may be referred to once or twice during the course may be linked only to the syllabus. Time spent with pencil and paper planning the number and kinds of course pages and the links among them, can save hours of later frustration. Course Web sites rarely benefit from Topsy's "just growed" style of development (so-called from the character in Harriet Beecher Stowe's novel *Uncle Tom's Cabin*).

General design considerations for the development of Web-based courses also includes analyzing the target group, the skills students will need to develop, the technology needed by both instructors and learners, the cost to get the course up and running, the course content itself, the skills needed to design and put the course online, and the time and skill needed to maintain the course (Polyson et. al., 1996). Designing might mean starting with the content and process of the face-to-face class and determining how best to restructure both the content and learning process for Web-based delivery.

Most Web-page development has taken place outside of academia and the learned behavior of persons accustomed to "surfing" the Web must be taken into account during the Web-based course design process. Most print materials appear in linear fashion, even though the content itself might be skimmed, chapter summaries or final chapters read first, and the index consulted to find particular topics of interest. Not so with hyperlinked information. Pages are skimmed and the reader rapidly gathers nuggets of information. The reader's impatience rapidly mounts as the loading time for images or whole pages increases. When information is designed for the Web, it must be in a form that is both attractive and usable, and dense information needs to be broken down into manageable pieces or *chunked* so that people can find it quickly. This partitioning of information into manageable units and linking the chunks to form a comprehensive and easily usable Web of information is the structure of the Web. The chunks must provide information in the appropriate textual or visual formats for the type of information being conveyed (Porter, 1997, p 129). Valuable message and page design principles can be derived from print-based materials. The use of color, graphics, white space and text arrangement can be used to visually represent the structure of the information.

There are many different types of computers and several varieties of Web browsers that students and instructors will use, so the final design must be thoroughly tested, using several different Web browsers and screen definitions to be sure the pages will appear close to the way that the designer intends. HTML has only recently become more than "strong suggestions" to a browser about how the designer intends that the page should appear. This can be very frustrating to designers used to working in print materials with the ability to place design elements accurately—to the hair's breath. Some flexibility in design is necessary to accommodate the endless combinations of screen size and resolution, operating system and browser versions. Browsers attempt to display pages to fit the available screen real-estate and in so doing may distort the original page design. Especially annoying is the need to scroll pages to the right when page elements have been set in a fixed design greater than 500 pixels wide.

Decisions must be made about the "extras"– beyond text and simple graphics—that might be included on pages. When considering the use of video, animation, or sound, or sophisticated scripts or browser plug-ins, it is well to remember that not all students will have machines capable of receiving and displaying them. The term "eye candy" has been coined to refer, in a derogatory manner, to visual elements of a page that, while looking "flashy," add nothing to understanding the content.

Software for developing courses must be chosen for its ease of use and flexibility, especially if faculty will be expected to build and/or maintain their own course Web sites. Deployment of course Web sites requires careful beta-testing of the entire course site to make sure all links and buttons work properly. The infamous "404 not found" error message presented by browsers when a link fails to work can quickly become a source of great irritation. Most quality Web page editing software includes site management facilities and can check all internal and external links as part of the site verification process and indicate where links are broken.

Proper planning for prototyping also includes input from a representative sample of learners and the instructor who will be using the Web pages. They must be asked to let the design team know if there are design or navigation errors that will be frustrating to both user and instructor. Loading times for images and pages should be checked again at this stage on modems of varying speeds.

ASSESSMENT

Monitoring of student learning during and after the course must be conducted to ensure that quality learning took place. Interim monitoring can be accomplished with interactive quiz sections where learners can read a question, choose an answer, and have that answer locked in. The instructor can then receive the student's completed quiz by private e-mail, comment on it personally and return the quiz to the student, or post grades with coded personal identification, to a course Web page. Immediate feedback from quizzes can also be programmed into Web pages to reinforce students' learning and to quickly correct misapprehensions. All the "time on task" in the world will not result in effective learning if the student's time is spent incorrectly completing an exercise.

The designer must also take into account the fact that the instructor and the student may never see one another face-to-face, which may have implications for the evaluation of student performance, knowledge, or attitudes (Polyson et. al., 1996). Faculty frequently ask how they can be certain that a student actually taking a Web-based quiz or examination is the same student registered for the course, or is doing so without outside assistance. Because this is so difficult to ensure without the use of proctored tests, wisdom might be served in using alternative forms of assessment of student understanding. This could be accomplished by a series of sequential exercises building upon one another throughout the semester.

GUIDELINES FOR USERS

Using new technology requires a new set of skills and a different attitude on the part of both instructor and students. Some of the competencies that should be included are:

- Take responsibility as a self-directed learner. There is no one to remind the student to sign on or to make the student stay online for two hours. The student and instructor must be open to new ideas, concepts, and ways of doing things.
- Use sound time management skills (University of Central Florida, 1997). Time becomes very important as the student cannot count on signing on during the last day of a course and expect to complete it. A student is required to find the time and have the self-discipline to sign on regularly for the time it takes to complete the course goals.
- Practice sound study skills (University of Central Florida, 1997) that include learning and exploring on the Internet and using a host of on-line resources. Often there will still be a text book that will need to be read, plus extra readings from newspapers and journals. Being a self-directed learner and having sound organizational abilities will help tremendously here.
- Show personal efficacy and a willingness to learn in a new environment. Students in on-line courses should do some preparation ahead of time. The student must take the initiative in locating back-up equipment (e.g., public libraries, college campuses and their employer in either the training or MIS department of the company) and arranging as much as possible for its use should the student's primary system go down or otherwise fail. These can be anticipated and arrangements made as contingencies.

SUPPORT CONSIDERATIONS FOR FACULTY AND STUDENTS

Faculty

- State clearly in the course description the minimum technology, software and connectivity requirements students will need to meet. Also state what other skills will be necessary (e.g., using a word processor, using a Web-browser, etc.)
- Make sure faculty are accessible either online at specific times in their offices or by fax or telephone. Office hours should be known from the start. This is especially important at the beginning of learning periods while students become accustom to learning online.
- Be prepared to teach students how to interact effectively online; it is a skill that must be acquired.
- Communicate feedback on course performance to students and suggestions related to the course or on-line environment in a timely manner.
- Listen to what the students are saying and respond to them, and encourage them to respond to and collaborate with each other.
- Establish policies, goals and clearly defined objectives so students know what is expected of them.

- Become sufficiently knowledgeable of the software you are using to answer student questions, and know who to call for help and answers beyond that. Provide a set of "frequently asked questions," and determine if there are students in the course who can serve as "peer tutors."
- Use a variety of teaching/learning styles and techniques. Recognize that lectures translate to very long text documents on-screen and that there may be other, more effective ways of covering the same materials (Paulsen, 1995).
- Encourage students to collaborate with each other and, if an on-line conferencing system is used, to read and comment on each others' contributions.
- Be proactive and attempt to solve problems before they become an issue.

Students

- Make sure prior to the beginning of the course that you can meet the minimum technology, connectivity and skill requirements for the course. Check before the course begins that you can connect with the course site.
- Know how to access on-line help and helpers.
- Make sure your Internet browser has the necessary features to receive all course materials. Know who to call if there is a problem.
- Get and maintain an e-mail account. Learn how to transfer and receive files and documents between your desktop and your Internet service provider.
- Become Internet savvy; spend time exploring on your own.
- Learn the polices, goals and objectives of the course. Ask if something seems uncertain or unclear to you.
- Understand and use the rules of "netiquette." Realize that interacting online in text is different than face-to-face interaction along several dimensions, including the lack of body language to assist in the interpretation of meaning. Communication must be clear and explicit to minimize misunderstandings.
- Be proactive in your contributions to the course, especially to course discussions. To be silent online is to be invisible.
- Contact your instructor immediately if you feel you are falling behind or not understanding the course content.
- Realize that on-line classes require the same or a greater time investment than a face-to-face course, and be prepared to make that time investment on a regular basis.

CONCLUSION

Educators should view Web-based learning as a continuum ranging from supplementing in-person instruction to programs that are completely online. In the near future, I doubt there will be a time when all students receive all their learning online. By the same token, I doubt there will be many students who do not receive some part of their formal learning through technologically-mediated delivery. As more institutions of higher education and also within the training field begin to use on-line delivery of education and training, it will become more difficult for any learner to escape using on-line teaching and learning.

Teaching and learning online may be new skills for both instructors and students. It is important that each become accustomed to the technology before learning can take place.

Many instructors and learners believe learning involving this new media is worth the struggle, since the use of Web-enhanced and Web-based courses can provide significant advantages for learners, instructors and employers.

This chapter has supplied the more significant elements of Web-based learning regarding administrivia, course content, interaction, learning resources, monitoring and final assessment. Through experience, you will learn and add to this list.

REFERENCES

Berge, Z.L. (1999). Educational technology in post-industrial society. In J.G. Webster (Ed.) *Encyclopedia of Electrical and Electronics Engineering*. New York: Wiley & Sons.

Butler, B. S. (1995). Using the World Wide Web to Support Classroom Based Education: Challenges and Opportunities for IS Educators. Presented at *Association of Information Systems* in Pittsburgh, PA. [Online.] http://www.gsia.cmu.edu/bb26/papers/education/aiswww/

Dodge, Bernie. (1996). Distance Learning on the World Wide Web. [Online.] http://edweb.sdsu.edu/People/BDodge/ctpg/ctpg.html.

Dorbolo, Jon. (1996). Web Course Study: Oregon State University Challenging Students' Paradigms. [Online.] http://www.uoregon.edu.

George Mason University. (1997). Prototypes of Hyperlearning Environments. [Online.] Available: http://www.cne.gmu.edu.

Goldberg, M.W. (1996). Student participation and progress tracking for Web-based courses using WebCT. Proceedings of the Second International NAWeb Conference, October 5-8. Fredericton, NB, Canada.

IDE. (1997). Models of distance education. [Online.] http://www.umuc.edu/ide/modlmenu.html

Kahn, B. H. (1997) *Web-based Instruction.* Englewood Cliffs, NJ: Educational Technology Publications

Paulsen, M. F. (1995). An Overview of CMC and the Online Classroom in Distance Education. In Zane L. Berge and Mauri P. Collins (Eds.) *CMC and the Online Classroom,* Vol. III. Cresskill, NJ: Hampton Press.

Polyson, Susan, Steven Saltzberg, & Robert Godwin-Jones. (September, 1996) A Practical Guide to Teaching with the World Wide Web. *Syllabus.* [Online.] http://www.umuc.edu/iuc/cmc96/papers/poly-p2.html

Porter, Annette. (1997) *Creating the Virtual Classroom: Distance Learning with the Internet.* New York: Wiley

Saltzberg, S and Polyson, S. (September, 1995). Distributed Learning on the World Wide Web. *Syllabus.* [Online.] http://www.umuc.edu/iuc/cmc96/papers/poly-p.html

University of Central Florida (1997). On-line Learning Critical Competencies. [Online.] http://www.ucf.edu.

Chapter III

Cognitive Effects of Web Page Design

Louis H. Berry
University of Pittsburgh, USA

INTRODUCTION

The advent of Web-based instruction, which relies upon hypertext models of interaction and design, reemphasizes the need for a clear understanding of how learners process and encode information presented in Web sites intended for instructional purposes. The unique nature of Web page design, mandated by constraints in the technology which limit student interactivity, and yet which support divergent exploration, necessitates a deeper consideration of how learners interact with various Web site design factors. The purpose of this chapter will be to address the cognitive implications of those factors. This chapter will not focus on specific graphic layout and design criteria or visual display specifications that have been extensively covered in the research literature on computer screen design. The intent, rather, is to review and discuss the major theoretical and design issues impacting contemporary instructional Web page design. It is essential however, to understand the basis for much of the Web page design that occurs currently, and that stems from much of the earlier work in computer screen design.

History and Research in Screen Design

The history of computer screen design has been scattered across disciplines and has addressed questions of need rather than of cognition. The vast majority of early research studies addressed the perceptual aspects of how users viewed and interacted with data on the screen (Galitz, 1989). In most cases, these studies were technology driven, that is to say, they were conducted to test out or validate new screen display technologies such as higher resolution monitors and the utility of pointing devices such as the mouse (Card, English & Burr, 1978; Lu, 1984; Buxton, 1985; Foley, Wallace, Victor & Chan, 1984). The end result of this work generally reflected an attempt to answer the question of "How can we most effectively display data on the screen given the current or newest technology?" (Heines, 1984).

Of particular significance, however, was the research conducted at the Xerox Palo Alto Research Center (PARC) which led to the innovation of the Graphical User Interface (GUI) (Smith, Irby, Kimball, Verplanck & Harslem, 1982; Herot, 1984) which has come to dominate computer interfaces.

Research in some of the parent technologies has also been applied to the field of screen design, particularly in the area of visual perception. In many of the early studies, the act of interacting with the computer screen was seen as almost solely being one of maximizing visual perception (Heines, 1984). Clarity of image and recognition of display elements were the primary variables investigated (Rubinstein & Hersh, 1984; Brown, 1988). Little consideration was given to how the viewer used the information that was presented, or to how it was encoded into memory. Some of this research was useful, particularly that which was done in the area of visual complexity (Dwyer, 1978; 1987). While these studies were focused on other types of media rather than computer screens, the findings have become important to the design of screen displays and interfaces.

In a similar way, research into the perception of printed copy has contributed significantly to our understanding of how text is perceived and interpreted on the computer screen (Gropper, 1991; Gillingham, 1988; Jonassen, 1982). This research has worked almost at cross-purposes, however, to inform us on computer text display. In one sense, a good deal of the text-based research has enabled designers to specify optimum text size, font, style, and layout, but it has also made it quite apparent that the computer screen differs substantially from hard copy in important aspects (Garner, 1990; Hartley, 1997), a fact that many Web page designers fail to recognize.

When the research in computer screen design is viewed from a historical perspective, it becomes readily apparent that little attention has been given to the cognitive effects of screen design and even less to the educational implications of such design. A review of the work done previously is a useful place to start.

The Cognitive Aspects of Screen Design

Those aspects of computer screen design which are of most interest to educators are related to the ways in which information displayed on the screen is perceived and encoded into memory. Typically the processing of information has been viewed, from the perspective of cognitive theory, as falling into two general areas. The first of these is the perception and pattern recognition of information. The second is the processing and encoding of information into long-term memory. Earlier work in screen design was strongly oriented around the former, while the more recent studies focus on the latter. Hannafin and Hooper (1989) have defined screen design as "... the purposeful organization of presentation stimuli in order to influence how students process information" which is much more related to the semantic aspects of screen design than to solely perceptual aspects.

It has been suggested by Norman, Weldon, and Schneiderman (1986) that computer information is organized in three different "modes of representation". These include the machine layout which describes the internal data representation in the computer, the surface layout which describes the physical organization of objects on the screen, and the cognitive layout which describes the mental model of the information developed by the user. Of these, the latter two are of most interest to screen or page designers because they represent the two aspects of screen design which impact on students. The surface layout is analogous to the traditional view of screen design which specifies the nature and layout of objects on the screen as well as the visual and perceptual characteristics of them. The cognitive layout is analogous to the encoding and representation of knowledge in memory.

Perceptual aspects. Screen layout and the relative salience of visual elements constitute the most relevant studies in screen design. The focus of researchers, particularly in education, is the role of such elements in gaining and maintaining the user's attention (Rieber, 1994). Other studies address the importance of directing the user's attention to the more relevant aspects of the display while de-emphasizing the less relevant attributes (Hannafin & Hooper, 1989; Grabinger, 1989). The role of color and type characteristics has also been studied in the context of attention and in terms of text readability or recognition (Galitz, 1989).

It is important to recognize that the perceptual aspects of screen design, while of concern to designers, is not the only component that Web page designers should consider. The task of organizing the perceived information into coherent and encodable units is of equal importance, as well as promoting the building of mental models of the knowledge by the user. These may be considered the semantic aspects of screen or Web page design.

Semantic aspects. Research directed specifically at the encoding and retrieval of screen information has been less frequent, but in those instances where researchers proposed theory, it was of significant impact.

The ROPES Model, introduced by Hannafin and Hooper (1989), is an approach describing the various activities associated with the learner's interaction with a computer-based instructional presentation. The model addresses both the perceptual/attentional and semantic encoding aspects of screen design and represents one of the first attempts to provide guidelines for screen design that move beyond purely graphical specifications.

Another cognitively-based orientation is the Syntactic-Semantic Model of Objects and Actions (SSOA) described by Schneiderman (1992). In this model, Schneiderman discusses the different components of processing which occur as the user interacts with the computer. Syntactic knowledge deals with the device-dependent details of the computer and represents the most basic of cognitive processing. Semantic knowledge in Schneiderman's view consists of two parts, that which he refers to as computer concepts or knowledge about the interface and how it is accessed, and the second part, task concepts which he suggests relate to the task to be completed. It is this part of the processing that we can interpret as the domain knowledge that is the object of instruction. In the Syntactic-Semantic Model, Schneiderman recognizes that different types of cognitive processing and learning activities are related to the different concepts or tasks, an important point when determining how the user should be interacting with a given screen or Web page.

THE NATURE OF WEB-BASED INSTRUCTION

The term Web-based instruction has been used to describe a number of informational uses of the World Wide Web. Among these are the use of Web sites as purely deliverers of information. In these instances the Web site is not designed with any particular educational intent other than making specific information available to the visitor. In the case of an informational site, there is no intended objective of promoting learning, but rather a "use the information if you want" reasoning. An educational Web site, on the other hand, has generalized educational goals or objectives much like public or educational television. In this case the intent is that the visitor will gain some more specific knowledge, but no attempt is made to assess whether or not learning occurred. In other, instructional sites, specific instructional objectives are developed and the act of instruction is more structured and the degree of learning is carefully assessed. Instructional sites such as these are used in many on-line courses today.

Web-based instruction can be all of the above, but in every case, the means whereby the user interacts with the Web site is very different from more traditional forms of informational, educational, or instructional media.

The differences between Web-based media and the familiar types of media fall into three distinct areas: technological differences, pedagogical differences, and variations in the way users interact with the information or instruction.

Technology

The technology of the Web site is a strong determiner of how users will interact with the site. The World Wide Web is based on a hypertext model of interaction which emphasizes a search and browse method of access. The use of clickable buttons, images or hot text reduces the user's behavior to rapid hand movements which occur only slightly behind the visual scanning of text and images. The fact that the decisions to select and click can be made quickly minimize the reliance on detailed reading of text or even interpretation of pictures. A consequence of this behavior is the reliance of the user on small bytes of information which can be scanned, read, and acted upon quickly and often without reflection. Additionally, the knowledge that the site can be revisited encourages even more cursory browsing behavior.

Pedagogy

Web-based instruction is very different from traditional instruction in that knowledge is often contextualized in an effort to make it real or, more significantly, more interesting and attention maintaining. While contextualized learning is important, it does not constitute the majority of instructional strategies that can or should be employed to promote learning.

A second pedagogical criticism leveled at Web-based instruction is that much of the content delivered to the screen is of questionable validity or depth. While the question of validity is probably best debated in other forums, the matter of depth of knowledge is significant. Knowledge representation on the Web has been described by one colleague as being "like Swiss cheese, broad, thin and full of holes."

The last pedagogical difference in Web-based instruction is inherent in the hypertext environment, particularly when encountered by novice users or learners with unsophisticated search strategies. In these cases, the visitor may form erroneous conceptualizations of the content presented and may even become disoriented, experiencing the state of "hyperchaos" described by Marchionini (1988).

Interactivity

While one might expect browsing on the World Wide Web to be a highly interactive experience, this is true only to the degree that the visitor can select and access a particular site. As the technology stands today, limited two-way interaction can be achieved between the instructor and the student. In instances of on-line courses, use is frequently made of e-mail, drop boxes, threaded discussions and occasionally chat rooms, but for the most part these are rare in most informational or educational sites.

The limited two-way interactivity results in consequent limits on instructor guidance and coaching. The ability to carry on a dialogue with the instructor while interacting with the information presented in the site is simply not possible on today's Web.

Focus of this Chapter

The characteristics of the World Wide Web described above make it a very unique instructional medium with great potential. On the other hand, however, it is essential that these characteristics are understood and factored into any design of computer screens or Web sites.

While much of the research and theory related to screen design is widely known and used, it is not always applicable to the design of Web sites, and it often does not inform us as to how Web-based information is most effectively processed by learners. This chapter will focus on selected cognitive factors which appear to be significant areas for research and application in the design and development of educational Web pages and sites.

COGNITIVE FACTORS IN WEB PAGE DESIGN

The primary intent of this chapter is to identify and discuss the major theoretical and design issues impacting contemporary instructional Web page design. These can be organized into two areas: those which relate to the physical design of the message and presentation, and those which are derived from how the learner interacts with the pages or site.

The selection of relevant factors was determined by a review of current research literature as well as other popular and professional literature related to Web page design and utilization. Of particular value is the Web site maintained by Jakob Nielson (1997) at http://www.usit.com/alertbox/. It is important to note that many of the factors have not been identified in the education literature, but rather from sources in computer and information science, graphic design, and psychology.

Message Design Factors

The first of these, message design as defined by Grabowski (1995) consists of two components: message design for instruction and message design for learning, both of which are critical to the integration of knowledge into an individual's cognitive structure. Message design for instruction is defined as "...planning for the manipulation of the physical form of the message" (Grabowski, 1995). This definition fits much of what has been termed screen design. Concern has been concentrated on how to graphically lay out the screen for maximum perceptual efficiency. The definition of message design for learning according to Grabowski (1995) "...involves the planning for the inductive composition of the message which induces the learner to meaningfully relate the target information to the old." It is precisely this view that reflects the more contemporary approach to screen and Web page design.

Three significant areas of research have become important to the design of instructional Web sites, particularly with regard to the cognitive aspects of the process. These evolved from either screen design research or the "parent" technology, visual learning research. These seem to be relevant specifically to the design of Web pages or sites because they deal with some of the physical attributes of site design, but are much more closely related to how Web visitors process the information obtained from the Web site. The three most frequently referenced areas include text presentation and text density, the implications of windowing environments, and visual complexity.

Text presentation and density. The first of these factors addresses text characteristics, text formatting and text density on the screen as well as the screen density of text. In each of these instances, the early research was drawn from typography, under the assumption that text on the computer screen was identical to text on the printed page. Research (Hartley, 1997) has refuted this assumption however. Recent research into the presentation of text in Web pages further suggests that Web page displays may differ substantially from other computer displays such as those employed in computer-based instruction (Nielson, 1997).

The earliest research on computer screen design was primarily related to typographical characteristics such as font size, type, style, and color and frequently was reflective of the sophistication of the computer display technology in existence at the time, rather than associated with a *pure* standard related to the viewer's visual perception (Grabinger, 1989). Secondly, these principles were often simply a reflection of earlier research in print typography. While useful guidelines can and have been derived from such research, it should probably be considered an evolving science, dependent on the resolution and display characteristics of the technology at any given time.

Of greater significance to educational designers are the concepts of text density and screen density. Of particular significance is the work conducted by Morrison, Ross, and O'Dell (1988) and Ross, Morrison, and O'Dell (1988). These researchers have defined two variables which relate to the organization of textual information on the screen both quantitatively and qualitatively. The first construct is termed text density and represents the richness of contextual detail presented on the screen. The second is the concept of screen density which refers to the amount of expository information presented on an individual screen.

Research in the area of text density has suggested that low density text is a viable technique for presentation of lengthy text. This is congruent with the suggestions of Nielson (1997) that text should be presented on Web pages in short chunks and should be edited to simplify content.

Conversely, research on screen density has suggested that users prefer higher density screens as opposed to those with quantitatively less information. This may, however, merely reflect the fact that most users prefer to move quickly through text, and accessing a greater number of screens is more work for the amount of text obtained.

A number of contemporary writers have suggested that the browsing experience is unique in terms of reading text (Nielson, 1997; Lynch and Horton, 1999) and that users may not even read text, but rather skim it, looking for comprehensible key words and shoulder headings. Such a process may indeed be used by the casual browser, but this may not be the case when users are attempting to gain more detailed content. The sophistication of the user and their intentions may be the most critical factor dictating how text should be displayed. The degree of domain knowledge the user brings to the site visit has been described by Dillon and Zhu (1997) as being critical to the amount of textual and contextual detail preferred. Those users with a high degree of domain knowledge will prefer higher density information screens, while those users with little domain knowledge will prefer less information and more explanations (Dillon, 1996).

Clear and concise organization is important in any instructional transaction, but the current research implies that Web-based materials could profit from particularly wel- edited textual material, supported by frequent and meaningful headings and other organizational pointers. Research is less clear with regard to the prose style most effective, although concise, newspaper styles appear to be indicated (Lynch and Horton, 1999).

Windowing environments. The second set of factors related to the design of the message is one of organization of information on the screen. The cognitive layout theory proposed by Norman, Weldon and Schneiderman (1986) was formulated to describe how information can be represented in different ways on the screen. This was not a new concept, because as early as 1984, Heines described functional areas on the screen. These areas represented the consistent dedication of specific screen areas to standard informational tasks. This concept is similar to the notion of windows and windowing environments. Windows are defined by Card, Pavel and Farrell (1984) as "areas of the screen which provide a particular view of some data object in the computer". Windowing environments therefore consist of the windows, palettes, icons, buttons and tools associated with a particular interface which enable the user to interact with and potentially reorganize the various information sources available. The use of these objects has been a standard feature of computer screen design since the advent of the Graphical User Interface and exists in Web pages in the form of frames or even individual pages themselves. Of particular importance is the concept, noted by Norman, Weldon and Schneiderman (1986), that the cognitive layout is a complex representation of the elements and the relationship between elements that appear on the screen.

All windows are used to represent or display information and may be used to expand the amount of information available to working memory. In some cases, this information is presented directly on the screen, while in others, the information is implied or understood to exist in some other, non-visible, location in the memory of the computer.

Windows can be defined by form, function, or whether they are explicit or implicit. The physical forms of windows relate to their spatial design and layout on the screen. The functions of windows refer to the information representation inherent in the window or intended by the designer. The degree to which the window is explicit or implicit is determined by the user's ability or need to physically view the contents of the window, i.e. computer clipboards are implicit whereas work areas or documents are explicit.

Windows serve a variety of functions, many of which are noted by Jonassen (1989). Among those described are: *navigational*, in which windows serve as directional or browsing aids; *organizational*, in which the windows help the user spatially relate or organize information; *explanatory*, which help the user by providing guidance or substantive coaching; and *metaphorical* which employ a metaphor to represent or symbolize an operation or informational concept. In each of these functions, the window(s) aid the user in developing a mental image or organization of the knowledge being presented. Furthermore, windows can be placed under designer control to represent or model some previously determined organization, or they may be placed under user control, in which case the window can be reorganized to conform to a specific user's own mental model of that information.

In hypertext environments such as the World Wide Web, multiple pages and frames within a single page serve the same function, implying to the user that different information exists in different locations in the site or on the Web. In this manner, the user's personal representation of the organization of available knowledge forms an idiosyncratic mental model of the information which is used by the visitor to aid in processing and encoding knowledge into long-term memory, as well as holding that knowledge in working memory for subsequent use. This interpretation of the information by the user can function as a powerful cognitive tool which may be used to facilitate deeper processing of new knowledge.

Windows can also serve a negative function if they are used in a disorganized or casual manner. Research (Gaylin, 1986) has shown that the display of too many windows may be distracting, especially for inexperienced users, and suggests an average of 3.7 open windows at any time.

Visual complexity. The popular literature on Web page and site design consistently suggests that the World Wide Web is essentially a visual medium and that designers should rely primarily on visual displays to communicate their message, at the same time de-emphasizing lengthy text passages. The classic literature in instructional message design is abundant with supporting research to the effect that visuals are equivalent and frequently superior to text in communication effectiveness. Early theoretic orientations (Dale, 1946; Morris, 1946; Gibson, 1954) have all suggested that the more complex or realistic an instructional visual is, the more effectively it will facilitate learning, presumably because it will provide more meaningful cues which assist in encoding.

Other classic research and theory originally proposed by Travers (1964) contradicted this orientation in suggesting that the human information processing system is of limited capacity and, in times of increased information transmission, some information may block the processing of other, more relevant information. This information overload position has received substantial empirical support, but the debate has largely been unresolved (Dwyer, 1978; Dwyer, 1987). The fact remains that most computer applications rely heavily upon visual-based information, which not only appeals to many users, but seems to provide a good deal of the primary information which is communicated.

The extent to which complex or realistic visuals are incorporated into Web pages and sites seems to be much more a function of the image download time for larger, more complex (bit depth wise) files. This may for the present make the decision to rely strongly on realistic visuals more of a technical rather than a design decision.

The fact remains, however, that learners appear to differ with regard to the amount of time and cognitive effort required to read a visual (Dwyer, 1978). Research has shown that visual details are processed at successive levels with more basic information related to form and location being analyzed first, and more contextual elements such as color and tonality being processed later and possibly in different ways (Berry, 1990). Without engaging in a detailed discussion of the complicated field of visual processing, it can be said with reasonable assurance that more complex, realistic and detailed visuals require a correspondingly greater processing time to be effectively analyzed (Dwyer, 1978).

Web sites and pages are no exception to this rule, and the act of browsing, which may entail more cursory examination of visual materials, may increase the discrepancy between the amount of information presented and the amount that can be effectively processed. The nature of Web-based instruction may represent an important instance of the high information transmission described by Travers in 1964.

The potential of information overload due to the combination of browsing forms of interaction and complex visualization may result in imperfect or incomplete processing by students, particularly those who have not developed an adequate mental map or structure of the knowledge being presented (Norman, 1983). Visuals which have not been related to the accompanying text may not be understood and may actually work to confuse or disorient the learner. Research has not addressed this issue as yet. One research-based guideline which may be useful is to relate visual material to textual material in a meaningful manner. This will require careful organization of the information on the page as well as the use of additional cueing devices such as arrows, highlighting and spacing to direct the user's attention. Other actions which slow down the student's interaction with the visual materials can provide more processing time and make distinctive aspects of the visual salient for more detailed encoding. The incorporation of visual materials in Web sites is essential, but requires additional planning on the part of the designer to ensure that the materials are fully processed and furthermore that they do not represent an element of confusion in interpreting the site information.

Learner Factors

There are those factors which are more related to how the Web site visitor or learner views or perceives the information presented rather than to how the site designer has organized the site. These aspects of the interaction process that occurs between the student and the site may be related to individual differences across students or they may be related to the unique ways in which the student interacts with Web-based materials. To some extent, this is a function of the materials and how they are designed, but in a larger sense, these aspects are tied to the perception by the user of how the information should be approached. Student perceptions may not be accurate however and may result in misconceived strategies for gaining and processing target information. It is these concerns that are discussed in this section.

Browser mentality. The very nature of hypertext, as it has been described over the years, is one of nonlinear, searching activity (Lynch and Horton, 1999), and the technology has encouraged this type of behavior with the familiar point-and-click graphical interface. Decisions are made based more on recognition of options or paths rather than on recalled information or choices. All of this encourages a quick decision-making type of interaction augmented by an increased anticipation of the next choice or option. Researchers have not addressed these types of behaviors in any but the most mechanical ways. Substantial research has focused on such variables as menu search times, data selection and entry, and scanning times for screen targets (Galitz, 1989; Tombaugh, Lickorish and Wright, 1987). Few if any of these have, however, been related to the intentional behavior exhibited by learners as they browse Web sites.

Only recently have researchers noted that hypertext browsing engenders a different type of instructional strategy or intent (Campbell, 1998). This phenomenon may be termed browser mentality because it reflects the intentional strategies employed by individuals in browsing or searching the Web. It is described by such characteristics as skimming rather than reading text (Nielson, 1995), rapid visual search and selection of buttons or hyperlinks, and an undefinable impatience to move on to the next page. Virtually no empirical support for these descriptions is yet available, but all one needs to do is spend an hour or two observing students interacting with the Web to recognize the effects. The technology of hypertext and the Web is based upon and obviously supports this type of interaction. This does not mean to say that interaction of this type is bad or that it is inherently counterproductive to learning, particularly when creative and divergent thinking is desirable. The difficulty arises when this form of interactivity is applied to instructional settings or content where deeper interaction with the content is desired or required. The user who simply skims over the contents of a Web page may identify terms and general concepts, but the conceptual base and elaborative aspects of the material will be lost (Nelson, 1991).

Cursory browsing may also have significant implications for the processing of information in that students cannot (or do not) take the time to reflect on the content presented. In so doing, less effort is directed at employing particular cognitive or generative strategies which have been shown to be effective in encoding new knowledge (Jonassen, 1988; Weinstein and Mayer, 1985; Rigney, 1978).

These effects will be compounded if designers adhere to the text criteria suggested by contemporary design guides (Lynch and Horton, 1999;) or include text with a low degree of text density as described earlier in this chapter (Morrison, Ross, O'Dell, Schultz and Higginbotham-Wheat, 1989).

Navigation and wayfinding. One of the earliest identified effects of hypertext navigation, user disorientation, was described by Marchionini (1988). He attributes this effect to the large amount of relatively unstructured information inherent in most hypertext environments as well as to the corresponding high level of user control provided by the system. The two of these characteristics can work together to increase the amount of cognitive load imposed on the user, resulting in what Marchionini refers to as "hyperchaos". Those Web sites that provide a rich hypermedia environment do so at the risk of overloading the novice user with navigation and informational choices that can easily overwhelm or confuse the student (Turoff, 1995).

Research has been as supportive of hypermedia environments as one might expect. Studies reported by Nelson and Joyner (1990) and Jonassen and Wang (1991) favored linear presentation of material over hypermedia formats because they provided less disorientation and provided more structure.

Wayfinding is a term that has emerged from the research on how individuals traverse a hypertext environment. As the term implies, wayfinding means the ability to move through a physical or (in terms of hypertext) information environment without becoming lost (Jones, 1988). Effective wayfinding is dependent not only on knowing where one is going, but also on knowing where one has been, which suggests that not only should designers provide consistent and intuitive navigation tools, but also clearly defined maps of the information space that constitutes any instructional Web site.

Wayfinding is strongly dependent upon the learner's cognitive skills, particularly those that relate to spatial orientation. Spatial visualization ability was studied by Alonzo and Norman (1998) to determine the degree to which one's ability to mentally manipulate spatial information is related to the ability to navigate through an information space. They found that by increasing interface apparency through graphical cues or map structures, all users could be aided, but particularly those with lower spatial abilities.

Cognitive overhead. The concept of cognitive overhead has been identified by researchers for a number of years, but was first addressed in terms of complex cognitive functioning by Sweller (1988) and Sweller and Chandler (1991). Cognitive load refers to the demands placed on the learner's working memory during instruction. In the case of computer-based instruction or Web-based instruction, the term covers both the mental processing necessary to access and interpret the screens, icons and objects, and the cognitive processing devoted to processing the actual content of the instruction. The goal is, of course, to reduce the amount of processing directed at interacting with the system and maximizing the processing of knowledge being taught.

Cognitive load is an ever-present factor in the design of computer screens and interfaces because each of the screen elements or objects must be interpreted by the user and consequently occupies some of the user's mental energy. A complex or unconventionally designed screen which uses different fonts, objects, navigation tools, and layout patterns will generally have a high procedural or functional cognitive load because each component will need to be perceived and interpreted by the learner. A screen which uses standard conventions in text, graphics, navigation, and layout will be more easily interpreted and consequently have a much lower cognitive load. One of the reasons many screen and interface designers have, for years, advocated the use of consistent screen design conventions is to reduce the cognitive load of interacting with the screen (Heines, 1984; Schneiderman, 1997).

Web sites and pages frequently (and unfortunately) are haphazard design attempts which combine a vast number of different and often incomprehensible screen elements in a format which is awkward and difficult to follow. In those instances where the design is planned, the intent is usually to make the site bright and flashy in an effort to gain and hold the attention of the learner. In most of these sites the design elements are difficult to interpret easily and consequently make high demands on the learner's cognitive resources (Tauscher and Greenberg, 1997).

It is difficult to train learners to devote less cognitive effort toward processing system related activities, but it is relatively simple to design Web sites that display information in a consistent and transparent manner. Transparency describes Web sites or computer pages that require minimal cognitive resources to perform system-level tasks. The term transparency means that the functions of relating to the system requirements are only peripherally obvious to the user and consequently involve minimal cognitive effort (Berry & Olson, 1992). This can be achieved through the use of accepted symbolic standards for screen elements and through explicit labels or icons which describe choices or tasks. The key aspect of transparency is that the user should not have to think about his or her actions, but simply respond in an intuitive manner.

FUTURE DIRECTIONS IN WEB PAGE DESIGN

Based upon this review of the most frequently noted cognitive factors in screen and Web page design, a number of speculative recommendations can be made regarding the future directions for research and theory building. Of course, many of these factors may change in relative importance or interest depending upon changes and innovations in the technology.

Further research is called for in regard to the development of mental models of knowledge that can be generated via Web site or page structure. Some researchers have even suggested that training in creating such models may increase the limits of memory and processing (Mayhew, 1992).

Other researchers have described complex symbol systems (such as windowing environments) that are learned, over time, by users and may indeed be useful in modeling cognitive processes (Salomon and Gardner, 1986). Research attention should focus on the cognitive effects of these more complex page design features.

The phenomenon of browser mentality needs to be studied more deeply, not only to understand how users interact with and extract information from hypertext/hypermedia systems such as instructional Web sites, but also to assess any transfer of the same effects to other study and learning situations. If, indeed, this type of browsing behavior is learned and pervades other instructional activities, then it will have significant implications for the design of many different instructional materials and experiences.

Researchers are only beginning to look at how screen design criteria affect deeper processing of knowledge, although some fairly comprehensive guides have been published to aid designers. The question of greatest interest here, however, is whether this knowledge can transfer to the medium of Web page and site design given the unique nature of the medium. In the highly user-controlled environment of Web-based instruction students may not be interacting with the same screen elements or in the same manner as they have traditionally done in CBI applications. In a similar way, the newer technologies of Web-based instruction may exert different priorities or capabilities on users which could influence the usability of the instruction.

As the technologies evolve, newer and different interfaces emerge. The means of navigating through information spaces which employ these interfaces tend to change also and this will necessitate an alteration in how we view the act of navigation. To reduce the cognitive load imposed by navigating and interacting with Web-based instruction, we need to understand how to maximize the degree of intuitiveness that is inherent in the materials.

Additionally, research must address the need for effective wayfinding strategies that orient any user at any time, even in complex information environments. We also need to explore, in much greater depth, the role of user cognitive variables such as spatial ability and cognitive style in terms of how they relate to wayfinding.

CONCLUSION

This chapter has addressed only some, although perhaps some of the most significant cognitive aspects or problems related to the design of pages and sites for Web-based instruction. The list of topics is certainly not exhaustive, nor will it remain exclusive for long, because as the technology changes, there will be a corresponding change in design capabilities and instructional needs. Web-based instruction is only beginning to show its potential and researchers are just becoming aware of the problems or benefits of the new medium. It has been said that designers tend to view new technologies in terms of older, yet similar technologies, particularly with regard to design methods (Rieber and Welliver, 1989). A substantial block of knowledge exists with respect to computer screen design, but it is yet unclear just how valid much of this will be in the design of Web-based materials and particularly those intended for instruction. The World Wide Web is an exciting and powerful tool for learning, but only if we know how to make it effective.

REFERENCES

Alonzo, D. L. & Norman, K.L. (1998). Apparency of contingencies in single panel and pull-down menus. *International Journal of Human Computer Studies*, 49, 59-78.

Berry, L. H. & Olson, J. S. (1992). *Hypermedia: Cognitive factors in screen design*. Paper presented at the annual convention of the Association for Educational Communications and Technology, Washington, DC: February, 1992.

Berry, L. H. (1990). Effects of hemispheric laterality on color information processing, *Perceptual and Motor Skills*, 71.

Brown, C. M. (1988). *Human-computer interface design guidelines*. Norwood, NJ: Ablex.

Buxton, W. (1985). There's more to interaction than meets the eye: Some issues in manual input. In Norman, D. A., & Draper, S. W. (Eds.). *User centered system design: New perspectives on human-computer interaction*. Hillsdale, NJ: Lawrence Erlbaum Associates.

Campbell, R. (1998). HyperMinds for hypertimes: The demise of rational, logical thought? *Educational Technology*, January-February, 24-31.

Card, S. K., English, W. K., & Burr, B. J. (1978). Evaluation of mouse, rate-controlled isometric joystick, step keys, and task keys for text selection on a CRT. *Ergonomics*, 21(8), 601-613.

Card, S. K., Pavel, M. & Farrell, J. E. (1984). Window-based computer dialogues. In B. Shakel (Ed.), *Human-computer interaction - INTERACT R84*, Amsterdam, NL: Elsevier.

Dillon A. (1996). Myths, misconceptions and an alternative perspective on information usage and the electronic medium. In J. Rouet et al. (Eds.), *Hypertext and cognition* (pp. 25-42). Mahwah, NJ: Lawrence Erlbaum Publishers.

Dillon, A & Zhu, E. (1997). Designing Web-based instruction: A human-computer interaction perspective. In B. H. Khan (Ed.)*Web-based instruction*. (pp. 221-224) Englewood Cliffs, NJ: Educational Technology Publications.

Dwyer, F. M. (1978). *Strategies for improving visual learning*. State College, PA: Learning Services.

Dwyer, F. M. (1987). *Enhancing visualized instruction; Recommendations for practitioners*. State College, PA: Learning Services.

Foley, J. D., Wallace, V. L., & Chan, P. (1984). The human factors of computer graphics interaction techniques. *IEEE Computer Graphics and Applications*, 4(11), 13-48.

Galitz, W. O. (1989). *Handbook of screen format design* (Third Edition). Wellesley, MA: Q.E.D. Information Sciences

Garner, K. H. (1990). 20 rules for arranging text on a screen. *CBT Directions*, 3(5), 13-17.

Gaylin, K. B. (1986). How are windows used? Some notes on creating an empirically-based windowing benchmark task. *Proceedings CHI T86 Human Factors in Computing Systems*, (pp. 96-100).

Gillingham, M. G. (1988). Text in computer-based instruction: What the research says. *Journal of Computer Based Instruction*, 15(1), 1-6.

Grabinger, R. S. (1989). Screen layout design: Research into the overall appearance of the screen. *Computers in Human Behavior*, 5, 175-183.

Grabowski, B. L. (1995). Message design: Issues and trends. In G. J. Anglin (Ed.) *Instructional technology: Past, present, and future* (pp. 222-232). Englewood, CO: Libraries Unlimited.

Gropper, G. L. (1991). *Text displays: Analysis and systematic design*. Englewood Cliffs, NJ: Educational Technology.

Hannafin, M. J., & Hooper, S. (1989). An integrated framework for CBI screen design and layout. *Computers in Human Behavior*, 5, 155-165.

Hartley, J. (1987). Designing electronic text: The role of print-based research. *Educational*

Communication and Technology Journal, 35(1), 3-17

Heines, J. M. (1984). *Screen design strategies for computer-assisted instruction*. Bedford, MA: Digital Press.

Herot, C. F. (1984). Graphical user interfaces. In Y. Vassiliou (Ed.), Human factors and interactive computer systems (chap. 4). *Proceedings of the NYU Symposium on User Interfaces*, New York, May 1982. Norwood, NJ: Ablex.

Jonassen, D. H. & Wang, S. (1991, February). *Conveying structural knowledge in hypertext knowledge bases*. Paper presented at the annual meeting of the Association for Educational Communications and Technology, Orlando, FL.

Jonassen, D. H. (1988). Integrating learning strategies into courseware to facilitate deeper processing. In D. H. Jonassen (Ed.) *Instructional designs for microcomputer courseware*. Hillsdale, NJ: Lawrence Erlbaum Associates, Publishers.

Jonassen, D. H. (1989). Functions, applications, and design guidelines for multiple window environments. *Computers in Human Behavior*, 5, 183-194.

Jones, M. K. (1989). *Human-computer interaction: A design guide*. Englewood Cliffs, NJ: Educational Technology Publications.

Lynch, P. J. & Horton, S. (1999). *Web style guide*. New Haven, CT: Yale University Press.

Marchionini, G. (1988). Hypermedia and learning: Freedom and chaos. *Educational Technology*, November, 8-12.

Mayhew, D. (1992). *Principles and guidelines in software user interface design*. Englewood Cliffs, NJ: Prentice-Hall.

Morrison, G. R., Ross, S. M., & O'Dell, J. K. (1988). Text density level as a design variable in instructional displays. *Educational Communications and Technology Journal*, 36, 103-115.

Morrison, G. R., Ross, S. M., O'Dell, J. K., Schultz, C. W. & Higginbotham-wheat, N. (1989). *Computers in Human Behavior*, 5, 167-173.

Nelson, W. A. & Joyner, O. J. (1990, February). *Effects of document complexity and organization on learning from hypertext*. Paper presented at the annual meeting of the Eastern Educational Research Association, Clearwater, Fl.

Nielson, J. (1997). *Alertbox: Jakob NielsonUs column on Web usability*. Internet. Available: http://www.usit.com/alertbox/.

Norman, D. A. (1983). Some observations on mental models. In D. Gentner & A. Stevens (Eds.), *Mental models*. Hillsdale, NJ: Lawrence Erlbaum Associates.

Norman, K. L., Weldon, L. J. & Shneiderman, B. (1986). Cognitive layouts of windows and multiple screens for user interfaces. *International Journal of Man-Machine Studies*, 25, 229-248.

Rieber, L. P. & Welliver. P. W. (1989). Infusing educational technology into mainstream educational computing. *International Journal of Instructional Media*, 16(1), 21-32.

Rieber, L. P. (1994). *Computers, graphics, and learning*. Dubuque, IA: Wm. C. Brown.

Rigney, J. (1978). Learning strategies: A theoretical perspective. In H. F. O'Neil (Ed.), *Learning strategies*. New York, NY: Academic Press.

Ross, S. M., Morrison. G. R., & O'Dell, J. K. (1988). Obtaining more out of less text in CBI: Effects of varied text density levels as a function of learner characteristics and control strategy. *Educational Communications and Technology Journal*, 36, 131-142.

Rubinstein, R. & Hersh, H. (1984). *The human factor: Designing computer systems for people*. Burlington, MA: Digital Press.

Salomon, G. & Gardner, H. (January, 1986). The computer as educator: Lessons from television research. *Educational Researcher*, 13-19.

Schneiderman, B. (1997). *Designing the user interface: Strategies for effective human-computer interaction* (Third edition). Reading, MA: Addison-Wesley.

Shneiderman, B. (1992). *Designing the user interface: Strategies for effective human-computer interaction*. Reading, MA: Addison-Wesley Publishing Company.

Smith, D. C., Irby, C., Kimball, R., Verplank, B. & Harslem, E. (1982, April). Design the star user interface. *Byte*, 242-282.

Sweller, J. & Chandler, P. (1991). Evidence for cognitive load theory. *Cognition and Instruction*, 8(4), 351-362.

Sweller, J. (1988). Cognitive load during problem solving: Effects on learning. *Cognitive Science*, 12, 257-285.

Tauscher, L., & Greenberg, S. (1997). How people revisit Web pages: empirical findings and implications for the design of history systems. *International Journal of Human-Computer Studies*, 47, 97-137.

Tombaugh, J., Lickorish, A., & Wright, P. (1987). Multi-window displays for readers of length texts. *International Journal of Man-Machine Studies*, 26, 597-615.

Travers, R. M. W. (1964). The transmission of information to human receivers. *Educational Psychologist*, 2, 1-5.

Turoff, M. (1995). *Designing a virtual classroom*. International conference on computer assisted instruction. National Chiao Tung University, Hsinchu, Taiwan (http://www.njit.edu/njIT/Department/CCCC/VC/Papers/ Design.html).

Weinstein, C. E., & Mayer, R. E. (1985). The teaching of learning strategies. In M. C. Wittrock (Ed.), *Handbook of research on teaching* (3rd Ed.), New York, NY: Macmillan.

Chapter IV

A Ten-Level Web Integration Continuum for Higher Education

Curtis J. Bonk, Jack A. Cummings, Norika Hara,
Robert B. Fischler and Sun Myung Lee
Indiana University, USA

Owston (1997, p. 27) pointed out that, "Nothing before has captured the imagination and interests of educators simultaneously around the globe more than the World Wide Web." Other scholars claim that the Web is converging with other technologies to dramatically alter most conceptions of the teaching and learning process (Bonk & Cunningham, 1998; Duffy, Dueber, & Hawley, 1998; Harasim, Hiltz, Teles, & Turoff, 1995). From every corner of one's instruction there lurk pedagogical opportunities—new resources, partners, courses, and markets—to employ the World Wide Web as an instructional device. Nevertheless, teaching on the Web is not a simple decision since most instructors typically lack vital information about the effects of various Web tools and approaches on student learning. Of course, the dearth of such information negatively impacts the extent faculty are willing to embed Web-based learning components in their classes.

What Web-related decisions do college instructors face? Dozens. Hundreds. Perhaps thousands! There are decisions about the class size, forms of assessments, amount and type of feedback, location of students, and the particular Web courseware system used. Whereas some instructors will want to start using the Web with minor adaptations to their teaching, others will feel comfortable taking extensive risks in building entire courses or programs on the Web. Where you fall in terms of your comfort level as an instructor or student will likely shift in the next few years as Web courseware stabilizes and is more widely accepted in teaching. Of course, significant changes in the Web-based instruction will require advancements in both pedagogy and technology (Bonk & Dennen, 1999). Detailed below is a ten level Web integration continuum of the pedagogical choices faculty must consider in developing Web-based course components.

THE WEB INTEGRATION CONTINUUM

Advances in communications and distributed learning technology have increased the levels and means for incorporating the Web in one's instruction. Instead of lofty promises about world renown researchers coming to your classes via Web-based videoconferencing, this paper will address ways to incorporate the Web in instruction from low-end course advertisement and resource support to high-end shifts in one's teaching practices and institutional offerings. Using this Web integration continuum, instructors can decide on the degree of instructional risk they are willing to take as well as reflect on the risks they have already taken.

To denote the different levels for incorporating the Web in one's instruction, we have designed a ten level Web integration continuum of the pedagogical and technological choices faculty have in developing Web-based course components (see Table 1) (Bonk & Dennen, 1999). In effect, the lower end of the continuum—Levels 1-5—primarily represent informational uses of the Web. For instance, the Web can be a tool used to market courses or share syllabi with potential students and colleagues. In addition, the Web, at times, symbolizes the idea that students need time to explore the vast stores of knowledge in which a field is based. It can also be used as a way to recognize student efforts by creating course legacies or posting previous students' work. The Web can also be used by instructors as a vehicle for posting sample work such as course handouts and supplemental resources. When these student or instructor Web resources are deemed valuable enough, one may decide to repurpose them for instructors and students in similar courses. The repurposing of Web resources, Level 5 of the continuum, may, in fact, be the most exciting and potentially explosive part of Web-based instruction.

At none of these first five levels of our framework is the Web a required component of a course. Instead, the Web might be viewed initially as an information source or place to share resources and prior work. Only when we enter the latter five levels does the Web entail graded components of a class or program. At that point, the atmosphere surrounding Web integration may change since students are held more accountable for their efforts.

Not only are students more accountable at the higher end of the continuum, but there is also a greater time commitment on the part of instructors here. For example, when the Web is no longer just a free information source, instructors have to be more selective in what is linked to their course Web site. They also are charged with updating it and making sure that there are few, if any, unusable or dead Web links. As Web integration moves to Levels 6 and 7, instructors begin to experiment with on-line debates, electronic class discussions, and perhaps even virtual role-play activities.

An instructor in such situations needs to reflect on his or her role. Will you dictate the content covered or will you be a coach or consultant for student learning? The answer here is not particularly easy since it may depend on the task, timing within the semester, and level of students in the class. What makes it even harder is that we lack comprehensive resources regarding how to be a mentor or facilitate student learning on the Web. In response, we have published an initial set of guidelines to scaffold student learning electronically (Bonk & Kim, 1998; Bonk, Malikowski, Angeli, & East, 1998; Bonk, Malikowski, Supplee, & Angeli, 1998) based on the sociocultural work of Gallimore and Tharp (1990) and Collins, Brown, and Newman (1989). While these guidelines provide some brief examples of how to question, offer feedback, structure an electronic task, and push students to articulate and explore, they are just a first step in rethinking the role of the instructor when teaching on the

Table 1. A Continuum of Web Integration in College Courses (Bonk & Dennen, 1999; Rowley, Lujan & Dolence, 1998).

Levels of Web Integration	Description
1. Marketing/Syllabi via the Web	Instructors use the Web to promote course and teaching ideas via electronic fliers and syllabi.
2. Student Exploration of Web Resources	Students use the Web to explore pre-existing resources, both in and outside of class.
3. Student-Generated Resources Published on the Web	Students use the Web to generate resources and exemplary products for the class.
4. Course Resources on the Web	Instructors use the Web to create and present class resources such as handouts, prior student work, class notes and PowerPoint presentations.
5. Repurpose Web Resources	Instructors take Web resources and course activities from one course and, making some adjustments, use them in another.
6. Substantive and Graded Web Activities	Students participate with classmates in Web-based activities such as weekly article reactions or debates as a graded part of their course requirements.
7. Course Activities Extending Beyond Class	Students are required to work or communicate with peers, practitioners, teachers, and/or experts outside of their course, typically via computer conferencing.
8. Web as Alternate Delivery System for Resident Students	Local students with scheduling or other conflicts use the Web as a primary means of course participation, with the possibility of a few live course meetings.
9. Entire Course on the Web for Students Located Anywhere	Students from any location around the world may participate in a course offered entirely on the Web.
10. Course Fits Within Larger Programmatic Web Initiative	Instructors and administrators embed Web-based course development within larger programmatic initiatives of their institution.

Web. Additional inroads into Web-based instruction and pedagogy are vitally needed.

In addition to instructor facilitation, the ten level Web continuum also serves as a reminder that the forms of student participation and interaction are keys to student online success. What forms of interaction are you going to rely upon? Will your students work alone, individually read electronic lecture notes, be placed in small groups, correspond with Web buddies or critical friends, or form satellite interest groups? Perhaps your instructional approach will be one that effectively mixes such techniques.

Careful planning does pay off in on-line learning. In fact, part of the excitement of Web-based instruction is seeing how quickly ideas move to reality. Unlike other arenas of the academy, teaching, especially on-line teaching, provides an immediate sense of accomplishment and a means to exercise one's creativity. The on-line teacher can see the effects of structured student interactions such as the use of debate teams or role play. Not surprisingly, our research confirms that carefully planned out on-line discussions of course readings can significantly impact the depth of processing and help create a sense of a learning community within the regular class (Bonk & King, 1998; Hara, Bonk, & Angeli, in press). Of course, as these online discussions grow beyond a single classroom setting, the need for task clarity and simplicity multiplies (Bonk, Malikowski, Angeli, & East, 1998).

At the top three levels of the continuum, Levels 8-10, the Web is no longer a resource or add-on feature for a course, but, instead, it plays a central role within the course. It is the course! Whereas most students in a course at Level 8 of the continuum are residential, thereby allowing for some face-to-face meetings and informal interactions (see Bonk, 1998; Cummings, 1998), at Level 9 they might be located anywhere on the planet. In contrast, Level 10 involves the coordination of entire Web programs. At this level, instructors need to consider how their course activities, interface, and expectations match with the other courses in the program.

To understand how one's course efforts fit along the ten level continuum, elaboration of each level is provided below along with some course and program examples. This section is divided into Web examples, student issues, and instructional design guidelines. For additional clarification of continuum, the first author's homepage interactively demonstrates each level (see http://php.indiana.edu/~cjbonk).

LEVEL 1: MARKETING/SYLLABI VIA THE WEB

At the lowest level of course integration, the Web can be a marketing tool to promote one's courses and teaching ideas to those in other locales through electronic fliers, syllabi, and announcements. This is the easiest way to start using the Web for educational purposes. Consequently, this form of Web integration is fairly common. For example, Indiana University (IU) has accumulated a fairly extensive list of Web syllabi (http://www.indiana.edu/~courses/). Similarly, the University of Michigan School of Information has compiled a list of faculty course syllabi and placed it online (http://intel.si.umich.edu/cfdocs/si/courses/home/splash.cfm). Third, the UCLA Humanities Department created the E-Campus (http://ecampus.humnet.ucla.edu/). However, the most complete listing of college syllabi is located at the World Lecture Hall (http://www.utexas.edu/world/lecture). As syllabi on display at these locations indicate, there are huge variations in how the Web is used for instruction in higher education. As with traditional forms of college learning, marketing a Web course or an entire degree program requires gaining the attention of potential students and advisors. Prior to advertising the availability of a course, it is necessary to identify and target the appropriate audience for whom the program will be directed. Similar to print or television advertising, the message should be creative and presented with sufficient frequency to capture the attention of the potential student so that he or she will seek additional information on the course or degree program.

For example, after some low technology ratings by Yahoo and others, administrators at UCLA became worried that they did not effectively market their courses. In response, they decided to place the syllabi of all their humanities courses on the Web. However, they apparently used a top-down process that initially lacked faculty buy-in and understanding. In addition, when students were billed separately for this cost, there was extensive dissension and protest. Requiring syllabi and perhaps some lecture notes to be placed in prespecified formats on the Web does little to really enhance student learning. It places administrators in control of faculty, instead of allowing faculty creativity to flourish. In addition, it raises questions regarding who owns the intellectual property that faculty produce for a Web site predesigned by the university, the individual faculty members or the university? Despite efforts by UCLA and other universities, it is hard to locate specific courses offered over the Web, or larger Web-based programs of study, using common Internet search engines. For instance, searching for a course in educational psychology brings many URLs of academic departments, but few hits to courses actually delivered over the Web. To makes matters worse, most of the syllabi culled from such a search are typically created for conventional face-to-face, not on-line, courses. Thus, as with commercial businesses attempting to market goods on the Web, when marketing an on-line course or program, users need to not only find the appropriate course homepage, they also must become interested in pursuing relevant information there.

Cummings, Bonk, and Jacobs (1999) analyzed syllabi of all education courses listed at the World Lecture Hall (http://www.utexas.edu/world/lecture/). Most syllabi posted there were unidirectional with the focus being to transfer information from the instructor to the students. Few courses facilitated multidirectional informational flow from students to the instructor and from practitioners to students as well as extensive peer-to-peer communication within the course.

Based on a content analysis of syllabi found at the World Lecture Hall, Cummings et al. developed a 3 x 3 matrix to describe the communication patterns among instructors, students, and practitioners facilitated by the Web. These syllabi analyses, not surprisingly, revealed that the most common form of communication within this matrix relates to instructors providing information to students (e.g., course objectives, requirements, due dates, topical sequence, and course content, etc.). In contrast to photocopied syllabi, the next most common function of an electronic syllabus was for students to communicate with the instructor. For instance, students could take pre-tests, provide feedback on class sessions, and take quizzes and tests over the Web. More excitingly, perhaps, electronic syllabi share information with practitioners. In return, practitioners may be involved in class discussions and case analyses taking place in electronic conferences that are neither place-based nor dependent on all participants being available at the same time.

Given the above interaction possibilities, it is clear that we can learn about many aspects of Web-based instruction from Level 1 of the Web integration continuum. Just how are our colleagues teaching the same courses we teach? How are they attempting to attract students to their courses? What age or type of student are they targeting? What books, resources, and assessment criteria do they use? How are they incorporating the Web in their instruction? How do other instructors approach the same general content? Answers to such questions in both content heavy courses like introductory psychology classes, as well as advanced seminars on learning and memory, are extremely useful. Level 1 Web integration activities, therefore, appear to offer rich opportunities for instructors to collaborate and exchange ideas. At the same time, the marketing of syllabi also becomes a way to exchange ideas with students, parents, alumni, policy makers, and administrators.

Student Issues: At this initial level, both prospective and current students take advantage of syllabi on the Web. Prospective students have an opportunity to look for courses that would fit their needs as well as understand the expectations for the courses. Current students can also benefit from having syllabi on the Web because they always have access to the updated syllabi.

Instructional Design Guidelines: How should one's syllabi and course information appear on the Web? General guidelines for Web pages should be applied to syllabi. A common mistake is to simply post a word processing document on the Web and then expecting students to scroll though numerous pages of text. Where possible, instructors should deliver Web information in manageable, screen-sized amounts. So, instead of simply translating long passages of text into smaller linear segments, a better idea is to layer the content in levels of depth. For example, the first screen-full of information might be general in nature with links that lead the reader into deeper material at their own volition. Additional levels of material may lead to even more detailed information, to specific examples, or to related information. The key idea here is to present screen-sized (i.e., a paragraph or two) chunks of information at a time and to let users follow their own lines of inquiry. As an option, one could provide a link to a master document for either downloading or printing purposes.

Like all Web pages, one's electronic syllabus should stick to a simple 1-3 color scheme making sure the text is legible, limit use of animation and graphics, avoid distracting background images and blinking text, and develop intuitive navigation tools that always let users know where they are in the site. At a more advanced level, instructors should take advantage of the enriched communication channels of the Web to share their syllabi. For instance, instructors might conduct electronic polls and post the results of these voting practices on the course homepage. Such practices keep the Web site fresh and foster a sense of interactivity and community in the class. Even if you do not have the means for electronic polling, you can still post the results on the Web as well as class announcements, updates, transcripts of real-time electronic chats with guest experts, and other activities. The key is to create a dynamic or changing electronic syllabus that generates student movement inside.

LEVEL 2: STUDENT EXPLORATION OF WEB RESOURCES

At the second level of the integration continuum, the Web is a resource for student exploration both in and outside of class. Instructors provide links to the Web pages relevant to the content of the courses. This use of the Web tends to be a component within many on-line courses such as the typical listing of Web resources in class syllabi, handouts, or activities. For instance, our undergraduate educational psychology course, the "*Smartweb,*" contains a section called "Very Smart Weblinks" that provides Web resources for students to explore (http://www.indiana.edu/~smartweb/links/weblinks.html). Students in the course can also contribute to the list of links by suggesting useful Web sites. Many on-line courses have such types of links for students to explore and instructors to refer to (e.g., see http://www.valdosta.edu/~whuitt/psy702/).

Level 2 use of the Web fosters student exploration and knowledge discovery. Given the surface level learning of most undergraduate survey courses, this instructional technique encourages students (as well as instructors) to explore course material in greater depth and at their own leisure. In addition, using such links as guides, students might pursue areas that have more personal meaning or professional consequences.

Student Issues: Students' knowledge quests need not be totally open-ended. Instead of a pure discovery learning model, it is likely that Level 2 Web integration will most often utilize predesigned Web links or sequences. Like WebQuests at the K-12 level, the Web can provide the resources for a lesson plan. Here, students are guided in their journeys to discover key information from various Web sites such as exploring the Educational Testing Services Web site for vital information on standardized testing or the American Psychological Association (APA) Web site for a description of the 14 extremely popular learner-centered principles from APA.

Instructional Design Guidelines: Educators and corporate trainers might embed these Web exploration activities as a means to display instructional design approaches in action. For instance, Web activities could illustrate concepts and principles related to social learning, discovery, guided, constructivist, and social constructivist theory. In fact, instructors might embed such explorations and then force students to reflect on what learning theories they were addressing in each activity. Or, better still, students might be required to create Web sites that display various instructional approaches in action. Similarly, small groups might compete to create Web-based lessons representing different forms of instruction. There are limitless opportunities for employing Level 2 resources in one's class.

In addition to detailing theory in practice, it is vital to include instructional tools that allow instructors and electronic guests to provide students with lists of URLs that lead to related material. For instance, links to main journals in the field, on-line scholarly papers, and writing styles such as APA or MLA help students understand their field better and become a part of their professional communities. Instructors can ask students to compile similar lists, or add to the one they have already created, and then share these lists with the entire class. Such activities provide instructors with additional resources and also allow students to explore their own interests and volitions.

LEVEL 3: STUDENT-GENERATED RESOURCES PUBLISHED ON THE WEB

At the third level of Web integration, the Web can be utilized by students to generate resources and exemplary products for the class. Instead of returning student-generated papers at the end of a class, instructors can ask permission to publish the best examples on the Web. Hence, Level 3 Web integration can help current students learn the subject matter as well as provide Internet resources for future students.

For instance, the first author has utilized this level of Web integration to post interactive glossaries that students have created for his class as well as links to examples of key concepts, summary pages of topical resources (e.g., distance learning courseware), and school simulation experiences. In each case, his students were happy to share these Web activities and resources; such electronic course materials would have taken weeks or months for the instructor to create (see http://php.indiana.edu/~cjbonk/#three).

College instructors may find a myriad of ways to embed Level 3 Web integration in their classes. Level 3 is useful for at least three reasons. First of all, Web integration at this level motivates students by granting credit for work performed in class. Our experience shows that if students know that the best work will be put on display, they will put more time and effort into their Web products. Second, if such work is exemplary, then the instructor has just gained high quality resources for his or her next class. Keep in mind that in a Web course, modeling is extremely difficult (Bonk, Malikowski, Angeli, & East, 1998; Bonk & Sugar, 1998). At the same time, posting example answers is crucial to overcoming student anxiety about course requirements as well as establishing quality standards. Posting student work is not only a model or example for future students, it is a classroom legacy. The course legacy aspect helps maintain learning communities after a particular unit or semester has ended. Third, publishing student work on the Web reveals to colleagues and peers the range and quality of student learning in one's class.

Student Issues: Instructors and instructional designers must obtain student permission prior to posting their work to the Web, or subsequent dissemination of it. Some students are sensitive to having their work on display to the world. At the same time, current and prospective students find these Web resources informative and helpful in making course-related decisions. Instructors, on the other hand, might be concerned with how they will guard against the pilferage of on-line resources and the direct pirating of ideas. As a result, they must decide whether the display of work on the Web tends to raise the bar for student course performance or amounts to a lowering of standards in favor of wholesale copying and exploitation. As the volume of archived records grows and access is expanded, instructors must become sensitive to the potential for plagiarism. Design of unique assignments should help avoid this problem.

Instructional Design Guidelines: Students can create many types of resources at the third level of Web integration. For example, student profiles can contain information about the student (i.e., interests, e-mail address, personal homepage, etc.) and foster a sense of community among classmates. A second resource, electronic portfolios, might contain all the student work completed thus far over the semester. Classmates and/or the professor (or teaching assistant) could comment on such work. A third resource, student generated Web pages, could serve as reference material for others studying in the field.

In order for students to locate Web resources, instructors need to guide students on how to conduct searches on the Web. Simple search advice, such as Boolean search and the need for caution and patience with dead links and extensive graphics, can be helpful. In addition, instructors can introduce different search engines on the Web and their pros and cons. One of the best Web sites for information on search skills can be found at: http://www.searchenginewatch.com/resources/tutorials.html. Another useful search site is: http://www.calvin.edu/library/ghsearch.htm, while vital Web search training can be found at: http://www.indiana.edu/~tickit/searchengine.htm.

LEVEL 4: COURSE RESOURCES ON WEB

Instructors can also create a set of class resources on the Web for use by current and prospective students. This fourth level of Web integration is an expansion of Level 2 because it not only includes Web resources but also other student resources such as lecture notes, PowerPoint presentations, and instructor guidance and tips.

For instance, the *Bobweb* (a graduate-level course in educational psychology) is a Web site that contains resources and tools to support instruction for a course often taught throughout the State of Indiana using videoconferencing (see: http://www.indiana.edu/

~Bobweb; see Figure 1). This course was created for graduate students and teachers to use in conjunction with a course on *Alternative Instructional Strategies: Critical, Creative, Cooperative, Motivational* (a master's level course). The *Bobweb* Web site affords access to books, handouts, Web links, student information, FAQs about the course, PowerPoint presentations, learner-centered resources, an electronic bulletin board for class discussions, etc. related to critical and creative thinking, motivation, and cooperative learning.

Our Web development team recently designed a slightly different type of course at this level of integration. Instead of a Web site for a local IU course, we developed a set of Web resources for the thousands of students who annually read the introductory educational psychology textbook, "Psychology Applied to Teaching" by Jack Snowman and Robert Biehler. To supplement the text, a team of instructional designers and content specialists from IU worked with Houghton Mifflin Company to create a Web site named "*Insite*." Tools in the *Insite* Web site offer opportunities to access information, reflect on field experiences, construct knowledge, and share knowledge. In the *Insite* Web site, there are weekly activities, course Web links, technology demonstrations, PowerPoint slides, hyperlinked glossaries, student work samples, reflection questions, practice tests, on-line discussions, etc. The *Insite* Web site also provides pedagogical suggestions for using the book, suggestions for using technology in the classroom, and various Web resources. While we list *Insite* as Level 4 integration, instructors might decide to use the *Insite* Web site at higher levels of the Web integration continuum.

Student Issues: The Web allows students to access many resources customized for

Figure 1. The Bobweb *Interface*

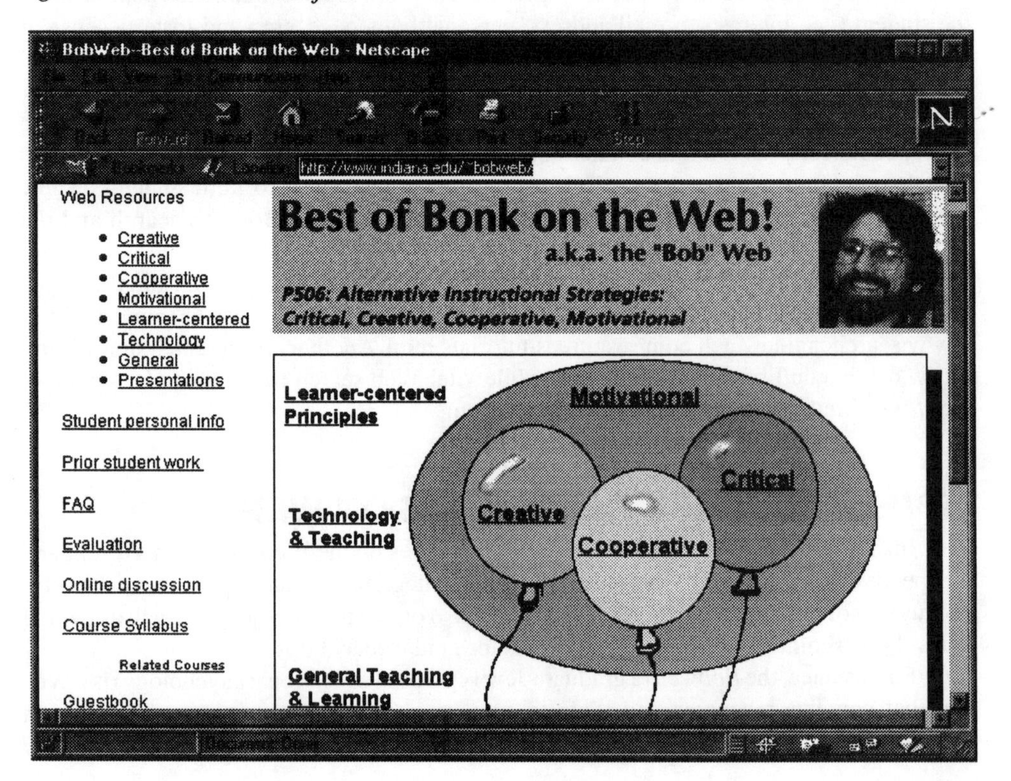

their courses. The advantage of a non-graded Web site is to provide an opportunity for students to freely discuss different issues related to their interests without concerns about subsequent evaluation. For instance, students who meet in a course can electronically continue their discussions about certain pressing issues (e.g., bilingual education or school vouchers).

Instructional Design Guidelines: While the *Bobweb* and *Insite* Web sites are fairly sophisticated Web resources, activities at Level 4 of the Web integration continuum can be relatively easy to design and implement. First, one needs some content. Second, one needs to know someone with Web publishing expertise or find a tool that automates the process. Third, one will have to maintain and update any resources placed on the Web. As a result, instructors should be highly selective regarding what they post to the Web and careful about copyrighted material. Higher education instructors might upload lecture notes, handouts, PowerPoint slides, or surveys. Prior student work might also prove useful, especially if you experiment with innovative tasks and activities. Once posted to the Web, these resources can be used by other instructors teaching the same course at other institutions.

Naturally, students will be discouraged if these course resources are not kept current. Lecture notes, for example, should be posted promptly (i.e, within 24 hours) after the class session. In addition to prompt posting, archived resources like PowerPoint slides or class handouts, should be organized in understandable ways. For example, in calendar navigation formats, students "click" on a particular day (or week) of class and are then presented with all the relevant resources for that day (or week).

LEVEL 5: REPURPOSE WEB RESOURCES

Web resources can be repurposed for use by other instructors and students. At the same time, one can also use materials from colleagues' Web sites to improve the quality of a course and extend the reach of it to students and instructors anywhere in the world.

One Level 5 example is the *Caseweb* site (http://www.indiana.edu/~caseweb; see Figure 2). The *Caseweb* contains cases originally written by students during the field observation in real schools and is intended for undergraduate educational psychology instructors and students around the world (Bonk, Daytner, Daytner, Dennen, & Malikowski, 1999). To develop the *Caseweb*, we repurposed the best cases from over 700 cases that IU students wrote in conferencing on the Web (i.e., *COW*) from 1997-1998 so that others around the world could discuss and debate them. At the present time, there are about 40 cases in the *Caseweb* (two or more for each typical educational psychology chapter) as well as case introductions, sample mentoring and feedback, and a bulletin board system for discussion. Whereas some educational psychology instructors are using these cases as student quizzes, others are using them as points of discussion and reflection.

Student Issues: Those repurposing Web resources must keep student needs in mind. For instance, using case-based scenarios can help change students' perceptions about key course concepts, especially for preservice teachers. Students will learn to become a teacher and think like a teacher through discussions with peers and mentors based on cases presented on the Web. Instead of sitting back and reflecting on instructor lectures, these students can reflect on how concepts emerge in real world settings while noting their personal preferences in electronic conferences. In effect, Level 5 tools provide a vehicle to shift instruction from lectures and didactic instruction, to new resources, partners, courses, and markets.

Instructional Design Guidelines: Level 5 is exciting for instructors since it allows one's teaching ideas to impact students anywhere in the world. It also fosters personal reflection on one's own teaching and learning. In addition to case scenarios, instructors in higher education can develop student surveys and questionnaires, sample tests, testing systems, and class activities. In effect, the Web becomes a tool in which to build resources that can be globally shared with colleagues. Sharing experiences about both traditional and online teaching will likely prove invaluable for novice instructors as well as those with decades of college teaching experience (e.g., see CourseShare.com). Hence, while we think we are repurposing work for others to use in their instruction, we may also be supplying the mental yardsticks for reflecting on one's own teaching performances. Moreover, if each college instructor posted their best instructional resource for teaching to the Web, there would be an amazing wealth of free or inexpensive teaching resources!

There are many caveats for creating resources that could be used anywhere in the world. A potential user should be provided with an opening statement of the purpose and scope of the Web resource or tool. Directions for use should be simple and lucid. Third, suggestions on alternative uses of the resource should be offered. Fourth, there should be a mechanism for sharing with other instructors and students how one is using the tool or activity. Finally, the site should describe how often and to what extent it has been used as well as provide an account of recent activity. When this occurs, new collaborations and partnerships become possible.

In effect, while Levels 4 and 5 represent a wide gamut of Web resources, what distinguishes them from the higher levels of the continuum is that they provide nongraded materials. Once course materials are graded, we move to Levels 6-10 of the continuum.

LEVEL 6: SUBSTANTIVE AND GRADED WEB ACTIVITIES

At the sixth level, the Web is a substantive and graded part of the course experience. For instance, student online discussions about their weekly course readings can significantly impact their depth of processing of the material and help create a sense of a learning community within the regular class (Hara, Bonk, & Angeli, in press). This level of Web use is becoming increasingly popular. For instance, as a result of UCLA "requiring computer Web sites for all of its arts and sciences courses" (Noble, 1998), many courses with computer conferencing or graded online components were launched (http://www.sscnet.ucla.edu/classes/).

During the past two years, the first author was involved in designing one project at Level 6 called TICKIT: *Teacher Institute for Curriculum Knowledge About the Integration of Technology* (http://www.indiana.edu/~tickit) for 25 teachers from five rural schools in Indiana to learn to integrate technology in the curriculum. TICKIT teachers receive six graduate credits while experimenting with technology in their teaching. *TICKIT* projects and teacher training activities to date have included Web quests, Web searching, Web editing and publishing, electronic newsletters, collaborative writing, and digitizing images. The reason this project is listed at Level 6 is that participants in TICKIT are required to contribute to electronic discussions for part of their course grades. During the first year of the project, we employed both *COW* (*Conferencing on the Web*) and *V-Groups* from the

Virtual University for required class discussions. By using these tools, TICKIT teachers engaged in interactive online debates and reactions to course readings.

Student Issues: We enter new and precarious territory when we start discussing graded components of a class that utilize the Web. Students may become more cautious about what they post. They begin to realize that each typewritten message may have an impact on their course grade. Instructors must be sensitive to the potential change in environment. Whereas conventional assignments are typically submitted solely to the instructor, classmates can more easily view assignments posted to a Web conference. Once accomplished, the quality of student work is evident to all. In the paper version, only the instructor is aware of spelling, grammar, and the overall quality of the content.

Our experience shows that without set requirements and points awarded, students, especially undergraduates, may simply decide not to participate. At the same time, it must be recognized that students have many competing activities for their time. Part of the hesitancy to participate is that it may be difficult to know who their classmates and instructors are when learning online. Just where do they get course answers and insights to improve their grades? There are many such serious learning issues that arise when course points and grades are awarded for Web activities and assignments.

Instructional Design Guidelines: Besides student confusion, instructors have daily and moment-to-moment decisions about how best to teach students. Should they rely on Socratic questioning techniques and playing devil's advocate or should they try to give extensive praise and encouragement for student participation? Should they rely on previously canned lecture material or should they push students to explore the Web for similar resources? Should they encourage dialogue among the entire class, foster small-group interaction, or rely on paired activities? As an instructor confronts such questions, one finds a voice on the Web and begins to understand the many ways to utilize the Web in instruction.

At Level 6, a college instructor is not giving up control over his or her course, but is enhancing and extending the course. The graded component not only holds students accountable for their work, but it guarantees that instructor time to create the conference and associated topics is not wasted. Electronic discussions also allow students a chance to digest the extensive material in content-rich classes like history or geology. Thus, with Web discussions and reflections, students might delve deeper into issues of importance and pursue areas of personal relevance. Even traditionally shy students may open up and become bonded with classmates in ways not possible in a traditional classroom setting (Cooney, 1998).

The use of Web-based conferencing tools will change the general dynamic of the regular classroom (Bonk & King, 1998). Using conferencing tools prior to class lecture, students come to class having read the on-line discussions and are more aware of peer positions on issues (Hara, Bonk, & Angeli, in press). Hara et al. found that in a graduate educational psychology class, the assignment of a student to start the discussion and one to end or wrap up the discussion each week fostered interactive discussion and depth to the dialogue. Without such preset starters and wrappers, discussion was disjointed and scattered. Such simple pedagogical interventions like the starter-wrapper technique and various role-play activities, in fact, may determine the success of Web integration. To reduce students' initial anxiety, it is beneficial for students to see models or examples of different roles.

Figure 2. Caseweb *Interface*

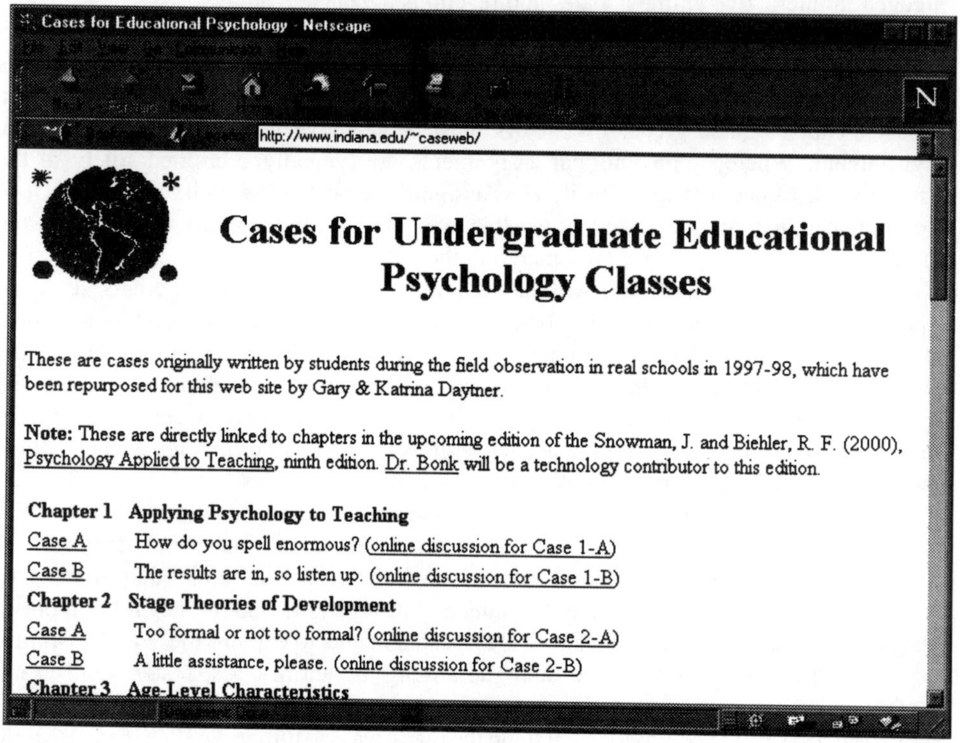

Cases for Educational Psychology - Netscape

http://www.indiana.edu/~caseweb/

Cases for Undergraduate Educational Psychology Classes

These are cases originally written by students during the field observation in real schools in 1997-98, which have been repurposed for this web site by Gary & Katrina Daytner.

Note: These are directly linked to chapters in the upcoming edition of the Snowman, J. and Biehler, R. F. (2000), Psychology Applied to Teaching, ninth edition. Dr. Bonk will be a technology contributor to this edition.

Chapter 1 Applying Psychology to Teaching
Case A How do you spell enormous? (online discussion for Case 1-A)
Case B The results are in, so listen up. (online discussion for Case 1-B)
Chapter 2 Stage Theories of Development
Case A Too formal or not too formal? (online discussion for Case 2-A)
Case B A little assistance, please. (online discussion for Case 2-B)
Chapter 3 Age-Level Characteristics

LEVEL 7: COURSE ACTIVITIES EXTENDING BEYOND CLASS

In Level 7, students communicate with others outside of their class. For instance, student electronic conferencing and course activities can extend beyond one's class to include peers, practitioners, teachers, and experts from other classes and countries. Harasim (1993) states that computer networks make the world more connected. By communicating with other students who are from different schools and countries, students gain multiple perspectives. Fortunately, there are many tools available for such electronic conferencing, such as *Sitescape Forum*, *COW*, *FirstClass*, *Caucus*, *WebCrossing*, and *Lotus Domino*.

For instance, we have used COW for the past five semesters to foster student interaction with peers and experts around the world. In helping with teacher education field reflections, the Web serves as a safe harbor for preservice teachers to try out instructional ideas and reflect on their early field experiences with students from other classes and universities around the world (Bonk, Malikowski, Angeli, & East, 1998). In addition, we have used *COW* for chapter discussions, small-group work, and other reflections in the *Smartweb* undergraduate course mentioned below. We have also created mentoring programs between graduate and undergraduate students and fostered interactions among practicing teachers.

The *COW* project recently evolved into *The Intraplanetary Teacher Learning Ex-*

change (TITLE). TITLE is a Web activity wherein preservice teachers at IU are discussing their early field experiences with peers at universities in Finland, Korea, Peru, Texas A&M, University of South Carolina, and students in the Cultural Immersion Program at IU. Using COW, these preservice teachers are generating case situations on the Web, while getting feedback from students and practicing teachers around the globe. Here, we are researching the forms of electronic mentoring. In particular, we are interested in how to extend discussion, engage students in critical thinking, and encourage them to justify their reasoning.

One graduate level project at IU within Level 7 involves Jack Cummings' creation of an electronic journal that allows experts in the field of school psychology, as well as practitioners and students, the chance to comment directly on recent publications (see http://www.indiana.edu/~ejournal/). Each article published in this journal serves as a starting activity for discussion on such topics as assessment, consultation, intervention, and prevention/health promotion. The ultimate purpose of Web use here is to stimulate dialogue among a learning community of school psychologists.

Student Issues: The advantage of activities at Level 7 is that students will gain the opportunity to learn from each other. No longer is the teacher the center of the classroom. Instead, students can learn from exchanging ideas with people from different cultures. Given this new environment, it is important to document just how electronic conferencing can help students explore a myriad of ideas from multiple perspectives. Just how do students begin to create shared meaning?

Instructional Design Guidelines: At Level 7, Web integration brings your students to the world and the world to your students. Not only can undergraduate preservice teachers go online to ask questions of practitioners and peers, these professionals can ask questions of your students and offer timely advice. As indicated, conferencing tools can enhance field experiences within higher education courses such as auditing, safety management, or social work. Having expert mentors might also help with team projects or proposals as well as with initiation into professional organizations and internships (Cummings, Bonk, & Jacobs, 1999).

When fostering cross-classroom collaboration at Level 7, instructional designers must consider the predominant language of the participants while simultaneously allowing for conversations among native speakers of other languages. In the *TITLE* conference, for instance, we recently created a "Spanish only" conversation originally intended for students and faculty from Peru. However, this conference area soon became a place for students in the United States to practice their Spanish.

LEVEL 8: WEB AS ALTERNATE DELIVERY SYSTEM FOR RESIDENT STUDENTS

At Level 8, the Web is typically used to make course instruction asynchronous or "anyplace, anytime." Here, local and residential students with time conflicts (e.g., working parents or those with performance careers) can sign up for a Web-based class. Since the target audiences at this level are primarily students living on-campus, instructors can assume that the students have access to vital information, such as libraries and computer labs, from their respective universities. For example, the *Smartweb*, mentioned earlier, relies on common campus e-mail and file sharing systems (see http://www.indiana.edu/

~smartweb).

The *Smartweb* is an elaborate undergraduate educational psychology class we have developed complete with student electronic portfolios, weekly chapter activities, small group work, discussion groups, reflection papers, avatars, peer commenting and interaction capabilities, Web link suggestions, personal profiles, administrivia, cafes, syllabus, agenda, etc. (see Figure 3). Since we began this project three years ago, there has been minimal lecturing in the *Smartweb*; instead, we have emphasized a myriad of instructional strategies and extensive student-student social interaction online.

In addition to the *Smartweb*, the World Lecture Hall lists two other educational psychology courses that appear to be at this level of Web integration. Of course, with Level 8 courses likely to proliferate in the next few years, it is crucial for the instructors of these courses to communicate ideas and success stories with each other. The *Insite* Web site, mentioned earlier, as well as a newer Web site we are developing called "Courseshare.com" are places wherein success stories or summaries of best practices will accumulate.

Student Issues: Web courses at Level 8 have several clear advantages and disadvantages for students. On the one hand, it is convenient for students to take courses online because they do not have to go to physical classrooms. However, on-line courses also require students to be self-disciplined and self-motivated. Procrastination is a significant dilemma in courses taught totally online since instructors have fewer opportunities for physically reminding students of due dates and collecting completed assignments. The parallel issue here is that online learning forums can quickly overwhelm students. Since most Web instruction and task submission processes are foreign to them, many students will use this as a crutch if allowed to by the instructor. The key advantage at Level 8 is that students are typically on campus and, accordingly, can seek the instructor out for help and guidance if needed. In addition, the instructor can hold formal meetings or informal lunches with students to touch base with them and offer advice.

Instructional Design Guidelines: Instructors need to motivate students to keep them in on-line courses. Since students cannot see instructors physically, they need to feel connected with their instructors. To reduce dropouts, Bonk and Cummings (1998) suggest that it is necessary to effectively use both public and private forms of feedback. For instance, instructors might use public feedback for official announcements but private feedback like e-mail to encourage student work and to build personal relationships with individual students. Instructional designers might create new Level 8 tools not only for offering varied and specific course feedback, but also for fostering interpersonal relationships and shared knowledge in a community of learners. Another way for online communities to form while keeping students informed of course tasks and schedules is to assign everyone in class an e-mail pal, critical friend, or Web buddy from within the class (or from another class). These "critical friends" might provide weekly feedback on each other's work and keep peers up-to-date on tasks coming due.

LEVEL 9: ENTIRE COURSE ON THE WEB FOR STUDENTS LOCATED ANYWHERE

The ninth level of Web integration involves teaching an entire course on the Web to students located off campus and around the world. This kind of course offers opportunities

Figure 3. Smartweb *Interface*

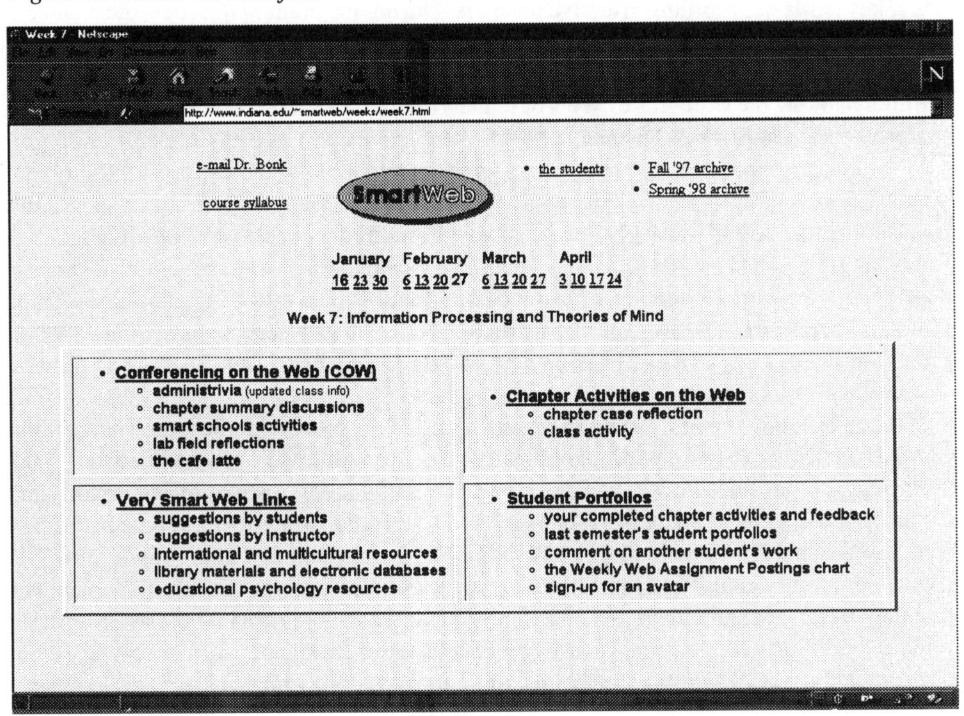

for students who cannot be physically on campus to actually study with other students in the class (e.g., Owston, 1997). There are many examples of this level including courses at Michigan State University's Virtual University (http://www.vu.msu.edu/), Technology-Assisted Lifelong Learning at Oxford University (http://www.conted.ox.ac.uk/intall.html), and Taming the Electronic Frontier (http://www.virtualschool.edu/98a/).

At IU, Professor Kathleen Gilbert has developed and taught a Level 9 course for graduate or undergraduate credit related to death and dying called "Grief in the Family Context" (see http://www.indiana.edu/~famlygrf/). Since students from Hawaii to Israel enroll in this course, the sun never sets on it. Here, students are expected to utilize technologies such as Web browsers, Web-based conferencing, e-mail, and tools for sending and receiving files. Similarly, Dr. David Perry at IU offers a graduate level educational psychology course called "Learning and Cognition in Education'' to students throughout the planet. Web resources, computer conferences, electronic syllabi, course schedules, and lecture notes can be found at his Web course site (see http://education.indiana.edu/~p540/webcourse/index.html).

Clearly, Level 9 Web course opportunities, as with every level of the continuum, are on the rise. It seems plausible that student learning at Level 9 will be the marker by which online learning will be judged. Hence, the collection of data and reports on student learning at this level is now vital.

Student Issues: Level 9 offers unique opportunities for students to learn with peers at other locales and in different time zones. At Level 9, students can share course knowledge and become good friends with students they may never meet. Through such socially shared knowledge, teacher education students might build perspective-taking and interpersonal skills, key skills in becoming effective teachers. During the coming decades, the chance to share knowledge and ideas across such distances is bound to impact courses in international business, teacher education, and healthcare. Such global collaboration and dialogue is definitely among the strengths of Web-based learning (for a list of Web instruction benefits and problems, see Bonk & Dennen, 1999).

Of course, when Web courses are offered to students around the world, the typical norms for operating a course are no longer in effect. Many questions arise. Should instructors provide daily, weekly, monthly, or bimonthly feedback? Will peer feedback be required? If so, when? What scoring or evaluation systems will be in place? Will students get written or electronic feedback? How detailed will it be? Will exams be proctored or somehow supervised? How can an instructor verify that a certain individual actually generated various work? Each decision here will have significant ramifications in terms of student learning.

Instructional Design Guidelines: Instructional design guidelines are increasingly complex as we move to the upper edges of the continuum. At Level 9, instructional designers must begin to consider how to develop tools for establishing a sense of community and fostering student engagement in the learning process. Equally interesting, some instructors who now teach courses with minimal Web integration might team up to offer a joint Web course across university settings. Some instructors might combine pieces of Web courses that they have separately developed to jointly offer cross-institutional courses. Similarly, some accrediting bodies in areas such as teacher education, business, and medicine may start recommending various Web-based courses to schools receiving marginal or failing reviews.

LEVEL 10: COURSE FITS WITHIN LARGER PROGRAMMATIC WEB INITIATIVE

The tenth and final level involves embedding Web-based course development efforts within larger programmatic initiatives of a university, department, or courseware company (Rowley, Lujan, & Dolence, 1998). Traditional universities with programmatic efforts in distance learning include the Ohio University MBA Program—The Ohio University MBA Without Boundaries (http://mbawb.cob.ohiou.edu/), the University of Illinois' Master's Degree in Library and Information Science program (http://alexia.lis.uiuc.edu/gslis/leep3/index.html#head), IU's Master's Degree in Language Education (http://education.indiana.edu/~disted/masters.html), and Drexel University's Master of Science in Information Systems (http://www.cis.drexel.edu/aln). Well known for profit institutions and commercial organizations in Web-based learning include the University of Phoenix (http://www.uophx.edu/), Walden University's Master's Degree in Educational Change and Technology Innovation (see http://www.waldenu.edu/), and Western Governors University (http://www.wgu.edu). Those seeking more information might visit the Yahoo site that lists universities providing distance education courses for both kinds of organizations (http://dir.yahoo.com/Education/Distance_Learning/Colleges_and_Universities/).

Beyond the U.S., such cyber or virtual universities are becoming very popular in countries such as Korea and the entire Pacific Rim. One of the underlying rationales for this Web-based instruction boom in Korean educational institutions is to expand the accessibility of quality instruction to people enrolled in different universities. This trend is spurred by a new educational law called "credit bank system," a policy to grant a degree based on the amount of credits a student registers in his/her credit bank regardless of the school in which he or she is enrolled.

For example, there is the Korea Virtual University or "Cyber UNIV," a consortium of large urban universities in Korea such as Chunnam University, Ewha Women's University, Kyung Hee University, Kwanghoon University, and Hannam University. This consortium is offering students Web-based instruction possibilities (see http://cyber.chonnam.ac.kr/kvu/index.html). One of advantages of this united Cyber UNIV is that it provides students with a variety of choices of courses offered by different universities and professors as well as special nondegree or certificate programs in such areas as information management technology. A second example of this Web-based instruction boom in Korea is found at Seoul National University. Seoul National University (see http://www.snu.ac.kr/engsnu/index.html) has created the Virtual Campus (see http://snuvc.snu.ac.kr/) to provide a uniform platform for all Internet-based courses.

Without a doubt, the range of institutions offering entire programs on the Web is proliferating. In fact, Internet companies, university consortia, and other services are emerging to administer these programs. It is conceivable that teacher education institutions or for-profit Internet businesses might try to locate the best Web courses for different aspects of an undergraduate degree in teaching. Exactly how these large-scale consortia will affect higher education remains unclear.

Student Issues: As entire college programs become available over the Web, students will benefit in a number of ways. First of all, students can more directly compare the courses, course requirements, faculty, costs, and instructional opportunities at different universities. Instead of paying for courses on a piecemeal basis, students might discover the true costs of the courses leading to their degree. Second, they will begin to focus beyond obtaining knowledge in individual courses and perhaps reflect on how various courses might fit within an overall scheme of study. They will better appreciate the sequencing of certain courses and the planning required for completion of their degrees. Third, students will be able to explore particular course and program Web pages and make better guesses as to which instructors go the extra mile in their teaching. Recent issues of the *Chronicle of Higher Education* indicate that students are already accessing Web sites that document and compare on-line course offerings at different institutions. Finally, on-line programs benefit students by providing a cohort of peers on the Web. When this occurs, students should have more shared knowledge from which to post statements and ideas.

Of course, all institutions are faced with many new decisions regarding what to charge students in on-line programs of study (e.g., in-state or out-of-state fees). New policies about course fees, instruction, course management, and advertising will significantly impact student online learning. Naturally, students will benefit if there is some instructor and course stability. Students are the big losers when instructors decide that they can no longer handle the workload of teaching on the Web. Along these same lines, what if students get really turned on by the instructional approaches of one Web instructor but other instructors simply transport lecture notes to the Web? Clearly, how students are treated before, during, and after the Web experience, will determine the long-term as well as the short-lived players in on-line learning.

Instructional Design Guidelines: In order to provide entire programs on the Web, carefully planned curricula are necessary. Getting a degree is different from randomly taking available online courses. Thus, students and their advisors need to carefully plan the curriculum that fits individual student needs. This kind of support becomes crucial to successful Web-based degree programs. In addition, instructors teaching within on-line programs must consider how their course fits within a common on-line interface. They need to consider whether course expectations, format, sequencing, and grading criteria will be similar across on-line courses.

REFLECTION ON THE LEVELS

It is vital to think deeply about the level of your Web integration efforts. Each decision about course design has long-term implications for student attitudes, social interaction, and overall learning. The ten level Web integration continuum provides an initial step for thinking about the degree to which you can incorporate the Web in your teaching and learning settings. Will you utilize the Web for nongraded activities or experiment with one of the top five levels of the continuum? Perhaps you will do both.

Once you have determined the level at which you will embed Web activities in your teaching, you will need to decide on the instructional strategies that might make the Web effective (Bonk & Dennen, 1999; Bonk & Reynolds, 1997). What types of creative thinking techniques will foster students' generative processes? For example, you might try brainstorming ideas on the Web or using computer conferencing and chat tools to free up student inhibitions. Besides student divergent processes, you will want to include opportunities to foster critical thinking and evaluation skills. One might structure electronic debates on key issues seen in the field with forced compromise positions, or, if there are specific course readings, reading reactions might encourage students to defend ideas, analyze the credibility of sources, draw appropriate conclusions, and distinguish relevant from irrelevant information—all vital critical thinking skills.

Web instructors might also embed cooperative learning or team-oriented activities such as having assigned "critical friends" or e-mail pals in the course respond to one's work in a private conference. Using other cooperative learning methods, such as jigsaw or group investigation, can force students to contribute pieces to an on-line conference or assignment, thereby fostering teamwork and collaboration skills (Bonk, 1998). As Bonk and Dennen (1999) point out, templates of such pedagogical activities are too often ignored in the development of Web courseware, where glitzy technology with prespecified formats is the norm.

In addition to instructional strategies, instructors need to reflect on how they will use the Web to enhance learning from a learner-centered perspective (Bonk & Cummings, 1998; Bonk & Reynolds, 1997). In linking their 12 recommendations to different aspects of the 14 learner-centered principles from APA, Bonk and Cummings (1998) begin an important next step in Web instruction—to frame Web-based instruction from psychologically sound learning theory.

In their recommendations, they point out how groups can form on the Web, what the Web encourages or nearly mandates for instructors, and how to create psychologically safe learning environments on the Web. For instance, embedding student choice in activities is a way to foster intrinsic motivation within the course and build on one's learning strengths. In addition, students need clear task structuring and immediate feedback in a Web course.

Unlike traditional instruction, on-line students are expecting feedback on every post they submit. In a traditional class, the instructor may only call on a few students to get their answers, but on the Web, everyone contributes. Establishing peer mentors or buddies effectively reduces the amount of work an instructor has to do in these environments.

Finally, as good teachers do in traditional classrooms, Bonk and Cummings point out that Web instructors need to find ways to vary the forms of electronic mentoring and apprenticeship. For instance, at any point in instruction, one can now incorporate peer mentoring, practitioner mentoring, cross-cultural mentoring, or self-reflection. Given the variety of instructional methods now possible, instructors should not simply recreate their lectures on the Web. Some direct instruction is fine and valuable at the appropriate times, but Web instructors need to find ways to question, praise, advise, and push students to explore and reflect.

NEXT STEPS

There has been an explosion of instructional ideas and courses on the Web during the past few years as well as new funding opportunities for creating courses with Web components. As a result, it is relatively easy to find examples of Web-based instruction at each of the ten levels of Web integration. Whether one teaches college courses in educational psychology, anthropology, or knowledge management, some form of Web-based instruction can be incorporated. It is our hope that frameworks like the integration continuum provide a means to reflect on and make sense of all the changes that Web instruction fosters.

We are moving ahead on several fronts here. First, we are continuing to fine-tune and expand the various courses that we are already teaching on the Web. Second, we hope to expand upon our initial attempts to create *The Intraplanetary Teacher Learning Exchange* (TITLE). If we do, tens of thousands of students from around the world will be discussing their early field experiences and offering each other advice on how to handle various dilemmas. Third, as indicated earlier, we are developing new Web-based learning tools such as those in INSITE as well as those in Courseshare.com. Fourth, we are creating an electronic course packet for an on-line educational psychology reader from Bell and Howell. Those four developments and others along the way will place us in a position to test tools along the entire Web integration continuum.

Clearly college instructors have many options for Web-based instruction. It is likely that such options will only increase in the foreseeable future. Think about what you can do to make sense of these options. Think about what your intended goals are before determining the degree of Web integration or types of courseware tools employed. Think about how you will be rewarded within your institution as well as personally before you start. Finally, think about the range of people who might gain from your Web efforts. What new resources, partners, courses, and markets await? What new students might you teach? If we plan how to use the Web as a pedagogical device now, student learning will hopefully be more relevant, exciting, and powerful in the future. Just where in the Web are you?

REFERENCES

Bonk, C. J. (1998, April). *Pedagogical activities on the "Smartweb": Electronically mentoring undergraduate educational psychology students*. Paper to be presented at the American Educational Research Association annual convention, San Diego, CA.

Bonk, C. J., & Cummings, J. A. (1998). A dozen recommendations for placing the student at the center of Web-based learning. Educational Media International, 35(2), 82-89.

Bonk, C. J., & Cunningham, D. J. (1998). Searching for learner-centered, constructivist, and sociocultural components of collaborative educational learning tools. In C. J. Bonk, & K. S. King (Eds.), *Electronic collaborators: Learner-centered technologies for literacy, apprenticeship, and discourse* (pp. 25-50). Mahwah, NJ: Lawrence Erlbaum Associates.

Bonk, C. J., Daytner, K., Daytner, G., Dennen, V., & Malikowski, S. (1999, April). *Online mentoring of preservice teachers with Web-based cases, conversations, and collaborations: Two years in review*. Paper presented at the American Educational Research Association (AERA) annual convention, Montreal.

Bonk, C. J., & Dennen, V. P. (1999). Teaching on the Web: With a little help from my pedagogical friends. *Journal of Computing in Higher Education*, 11(1), 3-28.

Bonk, C. J., & Kim, K. A. (1998). Extending sociocultural theory to adult learning. In M. C. Smith & T. Pourchot (Ed.), *Adult learning and development: Perspectives from educational psychology* (pp. 67-88). Lawrence Erlbaum Associates.

Bonk, C. J., & King, K. S. (1998). Computer conferencing and collaborative writing tools: Starting a dialogue about student dialogue. In C. J. Bonk, & K. S. King (Eds.), *Electronic collaborators: Learner-centered technologies for literacy, apprenticeship, and discourse* (pp. 3-23). Mahwah, NJ: Lawrence Erlbaum Associates.

Bonk, C. J., Malikowski, S., Angeli, C., & East, J. (1998). Case-based conferencing for preservice teacher education: Electronic discourse from the field. *Journal of Educational Computing Research, 19*(3), 267-304.

Bonk, C. J., Malikowski, S., Supplee, L., & Angeli, C. (1998, April). *Holy COW: Scaffolding case-based "Conferencing on the Web" with preservice teachers*. Paper presented at the American Educational Research Association (AERA) annual convention, San Diego, CA.

Bonk, C. J., & Reynolds, T. H. (1997). Learner-centered web instruction for higher-order thinking, teamwork, and apprenticeship. In B. H. Khan (Ed.) *Web-based instruction*, Englewood Cliffs, NJ: Educational Technology Publications.

Bonk, C. J., & Sugar, W. A. (1998). Student role play in the World Forum: Analyses of an Arctic learning apprenticeship. *Interactive Learning Environments*, *6*(1-2), 1-29.

Collins, A., Brown J. S., & Newman S. E. (1989). Cognitive apprenticeship: Teaching the crafts of reading, writing, and mathematics. In L. Resnick, (Ed.), *Knowing, learning, and instruction: Essays in honor of Robert Glaser* (453-494). Hillsdale, NJ: Lawrence Erlbaum Associates.

Cooney, D. H. (1998). Sharing aspects within *Aspects*: Real-time collaboration in the high school English classroom. In C. J. Bonk, & K. S. King (Eds.), *Electronic collaborators: Learner-centered technologies for literacy, apprenticeship, and discourse* (pp.26 3-287). Mahwah, NJ: Erlbaum.

Cummings, J. A. (1998, April). *Promoting academic discourse with the web*. Paper to be presented at the American Educational Research Association annual convention, San Diego, CA.

Cummings, J. A., Bonk, C. J., & Jacobs, B. (1999). *Twenty-First century syllabi: Dynamic tools for promoting interactivity*. Unpublished manuscript, Indiana University, Bloomington, IN.

Duffy, T. M., Dueber, B., & Hawley, C. (1998). Critical thinking in a distributed environment: A pedagogical base for the design of conferencing systems. In C. J. Bonk, & K. S. King (Eds.), *Electronic collaborators: Learner-centered technologies for literacy, apprenticeship, and discourse* (pp. 51-78). Mahwah, NJ: Erlbaum.

Gallimore, R., & Tharp, R. (1990). Teaching mind in society: Teaching, schooling, and literate discourse. In L. C. Moll (Ed.). *Vygotsky in education: Instructional implications of sociohistorical psychology*. New York: Cambridge University Press.

Hara, N., Bonk, C. J., & Angeli, C. (in press). Content analysis of online discussion in educational psychology courses. *Instructional Science*.

Harasim, L. M. (1993). Networld: Networks as social space. In L. M. Harasim (Ed.), *Global networks: Computer and international communication*, (pp. 15-34). Cambridge, MA: MIT Press.

Harasim, L., Hiltz, S. R., Teles, L., & Turoff, M. (1995). Learning networks: A field guide to teaching and learning online. Cambridge, MA: MIT Press.

Noble, D. F. (1998). Digital diploma mills: The automation of higher education. [Online]. Available: *http://www.firstmonday.dk/issues/issues3_1/noble/index.html*

Owston, R. D. (1997). The World Wide Web: A technology to enhance teaching and learning? *Educational Researcher, 26*(2), 27-33.

Rowley, D. J., Lujan, H. D., & Dolence, M. G. (1998). *Strategic choices for the academy: How demand for lifelong learning will re-create higher education*. San Francisco: Jossey Bass.

Chapter V

Implementation Considerations for Instructional Design of Web-Based Learning Environments

Mercedes M. Fisher
Marquette University, USA

INTRODUCTION

Today's technology is delivering greater access of current information and knowledge for instructional use. The introduction of the Internet has brought forth a wide variety of educational possibilities for teaching and learning; however, experience with these opportunities has yet to occur for the great majority of teachers. In order to prepare students for success in the next century, all teachers must have the motivation, knowledge, and skills needed to use Web-based resources for improved teaching and learning in both face-to-face and on-line settings. Planning for effective use of the Internet can impact students' ability to communicate and interpret information in and out of the classroom. Understanding and supporting teachers as they begin this journey is an important area that requires further exploration.

As Kurshan and Dawson (1992) acknowledge, the growth of the Internet and telecommunications is changing the nature of today's classroom. As new communications technologies link more computers into a worldwide network, the walls of the classroom are, metaphorically speaking, coming down. In effect, teachers are finding that with relatively modest investment of time and money, they can create "global classrooms" in which the world and its peoples become an integral part of a student's learning environment. Teachers of the 21st century will, therefore, have to anticipate the impact that technological advancement may have on school systems and be prepared to implement solutions that maximize learning while minimizing complexity (Kurshan & Dawson, 1992).

This seamless network of information has had tremendous implications on the way we think about and use technology in our schools. Today's teachers must learn how to develop and employ these resources to meet students' needs. The growing infusion of information technologies into the home and school demands that teachers know how to access and retrieve information, as well as how to use it discriminantly in their teaching (Harris, 1995).

Educators must increasingly push for contextualized learning experiences, sustained by technology, or perhaps technology-based environments.

The best illustration of this phenomenon and its impact on the educational system is the traditional encyclopedia and how it is being replaced with the integrated technology of the Internet. The Internet has created new paradigms, which allow us to teach and learn collaboratively. In this new paradigm of education, students require rich learning environments that are supported by well-designed resources and curriculum developed by teachers for use on the Internet (Harris, 1995). Subsequently, teachers need training in how to develop and employ these resources to meet student needs.

The integration of information technologies into academic and training institutions requires developing new pathways to information. Teacher educators must be challenged to use the Internet to make an interconnected set of educational services and partnerships a reality for teachers. Much of learning is analogous to holding up our open hands to catch information as it passes by. Our purpose more properly lies in the meaningful learning experiences that can be made from the information. Schools need to be promoting a range of approaches for students to communicate and make meaning through resources on the Internet. Since Web-based education will play at any speed, it acts as a "safety net." Teachers no longer have to worry about students grasping every concept as it is taught in the classroom because the Web-based education can go home with them and learning can take place outside the classroom.

According to Pugalee and Robinson (1998), it is the teacher who is the most important factor in creating an appropriate environment for maximizing student learning with the Internet. It is how the teacher structures the experiences for students and answers questions that will ultimately determine its educational effectiveness. Good instructional design of Web-based education dramatically improves what teachers can deliver to students and enhances learning outcomes. On the contrary, generally poor outcomes are almost always the result of poorly designed instruction. The first principle is, different learning objectives require different instructional strategies (Bills, 1997). It all begins with instructors providing a clear course structure.

The growing trend of computer technology in the classroom makes it imperative that educators move toward the best designs for instruction that we can create. As Web-based instruction is rapidly increasing in our educational system, and more and more educators are utilizing its great potential in their teaching, there is the need for designing some guidelines for the structure of Web-based instruction (Vafa, 1999). This chapter is aimed at helping teachers design and deliver on-line activities by providing a process to create Web-based instruction through the analysis of the key design elements of structure, authentic assessment, and interactivity.

Though there is only a brief history of research on this new phenomenon, a review of previous findings on the topic of curriculum design for Web-based teaching will be discussed. Then the chapter will test these theoretical perspectives against a real-world application through the analysis of the emergence of a Web-based program at Marquette University. Since educators constantly learn from the favorable experiences of other teachers and students, an analysis of this program will hopefully help educators design continuously improving on-line courses. More specifically, it should help facilitate curriculum design and presentation delivery, primarily through the identification of instructional alternatives that educators may wish to use. These options can assist other teachers in developing an awareness and knowledge of on-line teaching capabilities available for use in their teaching. Results from Marquette's Web-based courses will be evaluated in terms of their success in supporting clearly designed performance outcomes, interactive instructional strategies, and authentic assessment. Examples are also included that describe problems teachers experienced with the courses and suggested solutions for incorporation into future staff-development for Web-based education.

BACKGROUND

Much has been written about the use of the Internet in society. The general consensus is that the Internet is valuable but few have attempted to uncover the aspects that make it valuable within education. The Internet allows students to gain insight by interacting with raw data. The process of converting data into insight is through asking questions. By searching for answers to their questions, students begin to observe patterns in the data. It is through this process of observing patterns and asking continuous questions that allows students to derive meaning from the data and convert it into information. In essence, students are subjecting the data to tests in order to find patterns to bring data to the information level. What they do with the information brings them to the insight level. It results in students not only acquiring the information but also thinking about what they are going to do with it (Harris, 1995). The Internet gives students the opportunity for communication, collaboration, and student-centered learning; however, the technology tool (i.e., the Internet) is secondary. It is the higher level learning and independent thinking that is of primary importance.

With the Internet, teachers tend to shift their style of teaching from didactic to a more project-based approach in which students ask questions, investigate, and act. This is typically done by structuring group projects where members in different geographic locations have a common goal to reach or problem to solve. The Internet offers the promise of suspense and true discovery because it empowers students to collect data and sort it in new ways until they develop insight and acquire new knowledge.

The process for setting up project-based learning is a student-centered, hands-on approach. Students analyze their research and decide whether or not it is credible for others to see and use it. The role of the teacher is that of a good interface which facilitates meaningful connections for the students (Harris, 1995).

This approach is reflected in the three primary levels of learning that occur through Web-based education. Initially, students are learning to use a specific Web site on a specific bookmark list. At this stage, learning is not conceptual; however, as students progress, they learn how to use a Web browser. This second level allows them to learn the rules of the process. Only at the highest level, which is seldom reached, does the student learn actual content (i.e. reading, writing and arithmetic).

At Levels I and II, students do not focus on content because they spend their time solely on the aspects of presentation. Only when students reach Level III does the learning make an impact. If students reach Level III their work is generally better and more creative, resulting in them taking more risks and working longer. The ramifications of the Internet require teachers to build a different kind of classroom. They must not focus exclusively on curriculum or Web sites but rather a blending of the two in order to transfer information which will teach students to obtain knowledge and practice basic skills on their own.

In the traditional classroom, teachers usually first decide what essential skills students have already acquired in order to accomplish a task. These types of classrooms utilize mastery models, which completely define the performance of specific tasks. Mastery models require lots of repetitive practice, feedback, and evaluation until students acquire 100% of skills. Though mastery models will remain in dangerous professions, such as lifesaving and the military, we will see less and less of it in the future because it is based on all students having demonstrated all the necessary skills.

This is a sort of backward thinking for Web-based education. As teachers, we tend to teach with technology in the order in which students perform tasks; however, the chronology of steps for performing a task does not necessarily match the conceptual hierarchy. The last step in the conceptual hierarchy should come first. An overview is a key concept to the learner. The student needs an understanding of outcomes to construct a cognitive map in their mind that they can use as a reference. When this cognitive mapping is accomplished, students will capture what is most powerful in a particular type of learning activity and communicate it in such a way as to encourage the creation (not replication) of individualized, context-appropriate environment for greater learning (Harris, 1999).

There is an important role in supporting students or presenting examples of what instructors see as good or best practice. It represents realistic examples, projects that have been put into action in authentic settings successfully, that relate to quality planning for other types of activities. One method is "reverse shaping" where teachers get students off the ground by showing them the end product. For example, before explaining the details of using word processing software to format a document, a teacher might show a completed newsletter to the class. If learners do not see the map, they tend to get confused and lost in the learning process. This type of structure gives shape and strength to the actual learning activity, but is flexible according to an individual student's preference, past experience and expertise (Harris, 1999). Reverse shaping goes against the type of structure of the traditional classroom environment which treats students as if they are passive recipients of information, and offers all students the same lecture, presentation, or explanation (Gifford, 1997).

Once the student has been given an overview, the teacher should give the student as much control as possible through unguided practice. Teachers often find that students will process the content and generate their own information. Students are most engaged when they are processing the content and teaching it to someone else because just as teachers must take action themselves before professional development can occur, true knowing comes from doing. Teaching and learning are inextricably intertwined. A thought which does not result in action is nothing much. Teachers must create effective and engaging spaces for Internet-supported learning (Harris, 1999). Therefore it is imperative to get students involved in small group exercises that allow them to teach each other instead of listening to the teacher through the entire instruction.

The intent of instruction is to have students involved in the learning process rather than merely learning to use or adapt to technology delivering the instruction. Because Web-based instruction has so many variables that differ from traditional instruction, consideration must be given to approaches framing the design of the instruction so that successful learning can occur (Downs, Carlson, Repman, & Clark, 1999).

The successful design of Web-based instruction relies on the ability to transmit or send the essential information that the learner needs in order to acquire the skills or knowledge required of the content. The challenge for the designer becomes one of facilitating the delivery of the content to maximize the potential of the Internet so that the majority of the learners successfully acquire the skills or content (Downs, Carlson, Repman & Clark, 1999). As Gifford (1997) states, "Successful designing of Web-based instruction allows an organization to deliver powerful, effective, efficient and flexible computer-mediated instructional materials in disciplinary areas where instructors and their students require more individualized support. And as validated in the findings by Wood and colleagues, Web-based environments can be used to facilitate critical reflection (Wood, Stevens, McFarlane, Peterson, Richardson, Davis & LeJeune, 1998). The end result ultimately being enhanced student production and efficiency.

BUILDING QUALITY STRUCTURES FOR CREATING WEB-BASED LEARNING ENVIRONMENTS

Structure

Structure is the instructional strategy that provides the framework for the learning activity. It promotes more meaningful learning and consequently facilitates the application of learned information to real-world situations. The framework shows students how the content relates to what they have previously learned. As found by Bills (1997), structure becomes the advance organizer and is the "hat rack" to facilitate the encoding of internal schema for the lesson content. When this structure is in place, students have the requisite schema into which new information can be integrated. Meaningfulness in interaction comes about when the student accesses the appropriate schema from memory. The context for the response is the advanced organizer. Structure brings meaningfulness to interactivity. The provision of structure promotes meaningful learning in students and can lead to achieving successful outcomes. In fact, Bills found in his research that the mean for the structure interactivity group was higher than the mean for the non-structure interactivity group (Bills, 1997). In addition, structure tends to incorporate into the disciplinary materials cognitively rich representations (Gifford, 1997).

In translating successful teaching strategies from a classroom environment to the Internet, a framework can address such issues as the following:

- Clearly designed performance outcomes
- Interactive instructional strategies
- Student-centered learning environments that considers cooperative learning styles
- Collaborative on-line discussions
- Environments for group process and support
- Innovative course projects
- On-line assessment (Fisher, 1998)

The model has to concentrate on the instructional use of technology and independently generated projects for appropriate and effective teaching applications because it is the needs of the students that drive instruction, not the tools we use. As noted by Quinlan when she wrote on the framework for beginning a Web-based lesson, the strategies that an instructor develops have to weigh Web use against all other resources, otherwise the alluring nature of the Web detract from serious academic inquire (Quinlan, 1996). Web-based resources and projects are one tool for authentic demonstration of what a student has learned. It can be a very powerful tool or just another tool of banal assessment as described in the article, "Why Should Assessment Be Based on a Vision of Learning?" A Web page with a slide show, or a desktop published pamphlet that only has students restate what they know with fancy text and graphics is not more meaningful than a paper and pencil task. However, it may spur some students to go beyond the minimum because of its motivational factor. Just as with any other assignment or project given in class that is to demonstrate genuine understanding, it is necessary to design the Web-based project so that students are asked to use higher level thinking skills. In considering multiple intelligences and authentic assessment, the use of Web-based technology needs to be seen as one component that has great potential to engage and empower learners. In some cases it may be the medium for the final presentation such as a slide show. In other cases, it may be the tool used to enhance and ease musical composition, research, design projects, and communication beyond the classroom, but it is not necessarily the medium of the final product such as a dance or dramatic performance. In addition, it is important to note that there is a need for the structure to be consciously processed and flexible because specific activity structures are often limited regarding tools and resources that are available for their implementation (Harris, 1999).

Assessment

A critical component of structure is assessment. Often teachers attempt to grade students' work only to find that the assessment criteria are vague and the performance behavior overly subjective? Newer and improved on-line assessments have tended to take the form of rubrics.

The rubric is an authentic assessment tool, which is designed to simulate real-life activity where students are engaged in solving real-life problems. It is a formative type of assessment because it becomes an ongoing part of the whole teaching and learning process. Students themselves are involved in the assessment process through both peer and self-assessment. As students become familiar with rubrics, they can assist in the rubric design process. This involvement empowers the students and as a result, their learning becomes more focused and self-directed. Rubrics are an effective assessment tool in evaluating student performance in areas which are complex and vague. Students have a better idea of what is expected in terms of specific performance. For example, it is now commonly recognized that achievement is best ensured within a climate of clear expectations and where students are encouraged to take active roles. Stakeholders are given clear information about student assessment and instructional objectives. Teachers clarify their goals, expectations, and focus (Pickett, 1999). The primary advantages of using rubrics in assessment include:

- Allowing assessment to be more objective and consistent
- Forcing the teacher to clarify criteria in specific terms
- Showing the student how their work will be evaluated and what is expected
- Promoting student awareness of the criteria used in assessing peer performance
- Providing useful feedback regarding the effectiveness of the instruction
- Providing benchmarks against which to measure and document progress (Pickett, 1999)

Rubrics can be created in a variety of forms and levels of complexity. However, they all contain common features which focus on measuring a stated objective (performance, behavior, or quality), using a range to rate performance, and containing specific performance characteristics arranged in levels indicating the degree to which a standard has been met (Pickett, 1999).

These methods allow the student to show the instructor that they have mastered the desired course outcomes. The new model of technology-mediated instruction should provide assessment and support methods that both mirror and measure students' abilities to solve problems or perform tasks under simulated "real-life" situations. For example, if we want students to communicate effectively in writing, the authentic way to assess them is to evaluate actual samples of their writing. This provides designers the opportunity to "fine tune" the instruction, making sure that it is focused in the right direction. It also serves as an instrument to review the design (Downs, Carlson, Repman & Clark, 1999).

Assessment modifies the role of each element of instruction so that the individual needs of the student are addressed. It gives students better access to more learning resources, when they need them and at the level they require. Instructors can leverage scarce and valuable resources—including their expertise and their time—and gain more flexibility in the allocation of resources within their department (Gifford, 1996).

In addition, the new model of technology-mediated instruction has to reflect environments for group process because it is a teacher-guided, learner-centered approach that takes advantage of the combined strengths of the instructor, the learner, and multimedia to create an individualized learning environment and increased student academic achievement (Gifford, 1996).

Assessment performances are day-to-day activities that can be engaging demonstrations of students' abilities to grapple with central challenges of a discipline in real life contexts. Ideally, these performances become an integral part of the instructional cycle. Feedback provided by the teacher and peers is intended to help students assess their strengths and weaknesses. Performances are provocations of what needs to be learned and extensions of what is learned to help push the student to the next level of performance. Performances become tools for reflection on learning accomplished and learning deferred.

Interactivity

The third design element of Web-based education to be discussed involves interactivity. Effective collaboration in on-line environments provides the student the means of being actively involved in the learning activity. It results in learner-centered instruction, improves student attitude towards learning, and gives the student the opportunity of having personal interaction with both the instructor and other learners (Bills, 1997). According to Matthews (1997), active learning has been shown to be most effective when the learner is engaged. Technology, when used well, can tailor the instruction and learning experience. As students become more involved in their learning, they assume greater responsibility for that learning. Engaged learning empowers students to establish their own learning goals and explore appropriate resources in order to research real-life issues that are meaningful to them. It is multidisciplinary in nature and provides an atmosphere in which teachers serve as guides, coaches, facilitators, and 'co-active' learners.

As Kim Song (1998) has found, when teachers participate as 'co-active' learners, it stimulates students' interest in content and induces them to direct their learning. As students have more materials available to them in exciting and innovative ways, they are more likely

to learn on their own. Instead of having an instructor tell them where to access information and what to do, students are more likely to share with the instructor what they have found and how much information is available. They are more likely to continue their education and training through the Internet (Song, 1998).

The Internet provides many opportunities for interactivity and engaged learning by enabling students to work cooperatively with one another. Interacting with virtual classmates and instructors makes learners creative and thoughtful. As reported in Kim Song (1998) students assert that taking part in an Internet-based course program engenders a higher set of skills, particularly the ability to communicate. Successful cooperative groups depend on each member taking an active role in assuring that the peer collaboration works efficiently and effectively with each member "pulling their own weight." This helps facilitate peer collaboration in the on-line learning environment. Similar to what Bourdeau & Bates (1997) discovered regarding distance learning, collaboration between students is an essential component of the activities of participants involved in Web-based education. Participants have to join forces in order to learn more. It recognizes the importance of peer relationships in establishing a climate of learning. Students need to understand and demonstrate social skills required for working collaboratively on the Web, such as; trust, acceptance, support, communication, and diplomacy (Bourdeau & Bates, 1997). It forces group members to value the role of peers in promoting each other's learning and recognize the importance of peer relationships in establishing a climate of learning in both face-to-face and on-line learning environments.

The instructor's role in the cooperative group is highlighted as a means to facilitate maximum sharing of information and knowledge among the students rather than to control the delivery and pace of the content. In line with the thoughts of Shale (1990), instructors have to assess the students' activities and the adequacy of their knowledge in using technology for learning and providing feedback. The way this type of "co-active" learning can accelerate student performance is by, first, stimulating learners' interest in learning the content. Secondly, it gives learners access to what they need when they need it. This, in turn, helps learners engage in useful forms of cognitive processing and supports the application of new knowledge or skills to real-life situations.

In addition, the determination of the context which learning will take place should also be considered. Learning can either be a solitary experience or it may include group interaction. Group interaction is enhanced by Web-based instruction because learners have the option of selecting collaboration because of shared interest rather than shared geography (Downs, Carlson, Repman & Clark, 1999).

A REAL-WORLD STAFF-DEVELOPMENT COURSE MODEL: MARQUETTE UNIVERSITY AND MILWAUKEE PUBLIC SCHOOLS

Over the past two years, my colleagues at Marquette University and I have been designing and delivering on-line staff-development for middle-school teachers. Our model reflects the evolution of a staff-development course entitled, "Using Technologies for Instruction and Assessment." This on-line course has delivered over 250 new students to Marquette University for staff-development. The Marquette University School of Educa-

tion, in a partnership with Milwaukee Public Schools (MPS), has developed a collaborative learning environment utilizing the Internet and Lotus LearningSpace. The current model of the course features activities that demonstrate clearly designed performance outcomes and authentic assessment, as well as interactive instructional strategies that create a student-centered learning environment, which maximizes cooperative learning (Fisher, 1998).

Initially, professors of educational technology and curriculum development at Marquette University, along with four Milwaukee Public School teachers, met on a regular basis to review curriculum design and instructional delivery. The main issues identified included: (a) how to improve teaching and learning for middle-school teachers and students; (b) how to foster exemplary instructional practices; (c) how to assist delivery of staff-development to teachers through Web-based learning environments; and (d) how to share application solutions that enable schools to develop new ways of conducting teacher training in the network computing world (Fisher, 1998).

We decided to modify an existing course entitled "Current Topics in Instruction: Technological Applications of Curriculum & Instructional Design." This course was relevant, up to date, and a course preference for many inservice teachers. It had been offered to in-house graduate students and off-campus professionals for face-to-face staff-development. The on-line version of the course is intended to serve as a prototype for other School of Education courses offered online through Marquette University, as well as other universities across the country for staff-development.

The on-line course consists of 13 modules each entitled, as follows: (1) Getting to know each other and Lotus Notes LearningSpace, (2) Action research, (3) Foundations of assessment design, (4) Equity and fair use (i.e., copyright), (5) Video conferencing, (6) E-mail, (7) Internet resources, (8) Presentation managers, (9) Multimedia applications, (10) Desktop publishing, (11) Animation, (12) Introduction to portfolio options, and (13) Technology exhibition and celebration. Previous "face-to-face" course examples have been incorporated into the on-line course to illustrate teaching practices, student involvement, and specific projects.

Within each module, the format is similarly designed: Learner Objectives, Content Outline, Readings, Tools for Instruction and Assessment, Basic Design Guidelines, Links to Instructions for Software Programs, Project Option (i.e., assignment), Due Dates, Course Room Discussion, and Project Rubric. The identical format has created a routine that has provided for a set of steps for teachers to execute. This has enabled teachers to complete assignments over the course of the entire semester (Fisher, 1998).

Consistent with the findings of Collis (1992) and Harassim and Johnson (1986), before going online, the teachers have to be provided with an accurate description of the system, the task, requisite skills and knowledge required, and the expected benefits of the program. The first class of the course has been conducted in a face-to-face setting to discuss these parameters. Also during this class, the middle-school teachers have been asked to read the descriptions of different roles that members of each group need to assume – summarizer, technician, and facilitator. Next, the instructors have assigned the teachers to groups of seven to eight members each; therefore, each role has been the responsibility of at least two teachers in order to allow flexibility in regards to individual time commitment. Once in their groups, the teachers have discussed and decided who assumes which roles. For example, the summarizer will be asked to summarize the discussion for the week and place it in the discussion area for all class members to see and send group comments, projects, and

assignments to the instructor on behalf of the entire group (Fisher, 1998). When fellow group members ran into technical problems, the technician was the person available for extra assistance, encouragement and advice. The technician was the person most knowledgeable about hardware and software questions, problems, and shortcuts. The technician also worked with the course technical support team. The facilitator encourages group members to participate, informs the instructor of any problems the group is experiencing and helps those who need extra support (Fisher, 1999). Consistent with Willis (1992), teachers found it useful to have a "real" person available locally if they had special needs; and instructors were kept apprised of teachers interest and progress, as well as provided instant guidance in answering questions (Willis, 1992).

The first step of course redesign involved the categories of Learner Outcomes and Content Outline, which have been presented sequentially in each module. The teachers have made lists of all the tasks they have wanted their students to perform. The middle-school teachers have learned the procedural generalization in the on-line course. An example from the seventh module can be seen below (Figure 1). To incorporate discovery learning techniques, we have challenged teachers by providing rich instructional project models from previous classes so students can see the bigger picture or end product. This has allowed comparison to a standard, indicated need for improvement, and helped specify the assignment of a grade.

Project-based learning has been a primary approach, including assignments involving projects, products, and learning practice. This type of course is effective for teaching the processes of designing projects for the classroom that integrate technology and will transfer to new skills that the middle-school teachers can use in their own classrooms. Students are given a variety of resources to explore, including on-line sources, and they progressively work up to harder projects. Thus far, the students' feedback has indicated that the projects

Figure 1: Learner Outcomes

The learner will:

1) Identify research tools available on the Internet to support instruction and aid student learning.
2) Demonstrate knowledge of developing research and communication by creating partnership projects, or group activities and classroom application activities.
3) Develop a broader understanding of the use and potential of the Internet.

After reading about the skills needed to effectively use the Internet as a research tool, it's time to try your hand at teaching your middle-school students how to do an Internet search using the search engine(s) of your choice.

Procedure:

1) Select a topic to research (make it one you are currently teaching about).
2) Introduce Internet Research to your students.
3) Assign a mini-Internet Research activity related to the topic you selected in #1.
4) Observe and take notes.
5) Record your observations and reflections.

have enhanced understanding and have been a valuable part of the courses.

We have found that students have wanted procedures or a streamlined approach with instructions for how to use such resources. Also, it would be helpful to be able to download "How to use" video demonstrations of processes on different applications highlighting key skills. This would help them develop procedural generalizations. Since content has been taught through the use of models and project examples, the teachers were expected to develop relevant content examples. Subsequently, the teachers have been better able to recreate and adapt instructional models with the necessary practice.

The role of assessment has been incorporated into each module of the on-line course in the form of rubrics. The rubrics have provided for improved participation, guidance and clarity. Assessment rubrics include the evaluation of submitted projects, class participation in on-line discussions, on-line electronic journal entries, and the learning practice that students send to the instructor by submitting them within the course site. An example of the assessment checklist from the *Internet Resources* project can be seen in Figure 2.

Rubrics have improved student performance in our on-line courses. Teacher feedback indicates that they have been user friendly, clear and concise. They have served as advance organizers to guide project experiences. They helped students focus on teacher expectations and examples have shown teachers how to meet the expectations outlined in the rubrics. In addition, they have been more able to reflect and improve their own work and evaluate the

Figure 2: Rubric for the Internet Resources Project

Criteria

Key: M= Mastery D=Developing U=Unacceptable

Learning Objectives
___ Use precise verbs to specify expected level of thinking and performance.
___ Address district exit requirements.
___ Are performance based.
___ Address individual differences and learning styles.

Content
___ Subject matter is accurate.
___ Applies to current instructional principles, and appropriate assessment practices.
___ Project is appropriate to learning outcomes.
___ Project is interactive.
___ Easy to follow instructions for students.
___ Project design encourages critical thinking.
___ Project ensures active participation by students.

Project Rubric (Student Assessment)
___ Criteria sufficiently measures the outcomes.
___ Criteria appropriate to level of middle-school student.
___ Criteria clearly allows student/peer/teacher assessment.

works of peers.

Below is one teacher's reflection concerning the use of rubrics for her middle-school students:

> After processing the reading assignments in Module 3 and talking with some of my on-line group members, I see how I might have pursued certain learning tasks differently as a teacher. Recently I did a unit on how scientists determine the atomic mass of an element listed in the periodic table. I presented the students with cookies that had different numbers of dark and white chocolate chips on them. Using a rubric to guide the lesson, I might have presented the determination of atomic mass with four levels of performance. With the background information that white chips are protons and dark chips are neutrons, a rubric might be in place to guide the student through the process of determining atomic mass. For example:
>
> - D Grade (25 points)—First criterion: The students identify the number of protons of their atom (i.e., Cookie).
> - C Grade (50 points)—The students calculate the mass number (number of protons and neutrons) of their atom (i.e., cookie).
> - B Grade (75 points)—In addition to fulfilling the first and second criteria, the students determine the relative percent of cookie isotope abundance. (How many times each type of cookie atom appears in the group.)
> - A Grade (100 points)—After completing criteria one, two and three, the students apply their understanding of relative abundance by calculating the average atomic (cookie) mass of the element represented by the group.

In the above example, the use of rubric underscores problem-solving as a building process whereby there is something to be gained by taking that first step. Once the first step is taken, momentum is there to move on to the next level. Success leads to success. Instead of going down in defeat by striving for too much from the onset, which can be pretty threatening to some, students often set themselves up for success by initially aiming for the more easily attainable option. Then, in reaching this goal, they can extend themselves to the next level of success without being overwhelmed by the fear of failure.

The use of rubrics not only helps students process chemistry concepts, but it also serves the students in that they begin to understand themselves better (i.e., intrapersonal skills). This results in fine-tuned personal management skills. So, in addition to fulfilling aspects of K-12 curriculum, the student is working to internalize the use of rubric as a positive feedback mechanism in various problem-solving situations. Once the students realize that the rubric does not necessarily have to be teacher imposed—it can be self-imposed with even more significant and meaningful outcomes—they are well underway to becoming a self-actualized learner.

Rubrics are very powerful tools to guide students, especially those who do not have well-developed internal loci of control. The rubric has been a means of making them aware of the step-wise or building process involved in any problem-solving endeavor. As teachers guide student learning and problem-solving by specifying criteria for levels of performance, and by consistently using them as an inherent part of the course structure, students become skilled in more than just the subject area. They develop intrapersonal management skills that will serve them for the rest of their lives.

Though rubrics have been successful in our on-line courses thus far, testing has been a different story. We have not tried on-line testing because we could not successfully get students to respond to on-line baseline surveys or course evaluations in the "Assessments" area of the WWW-based course support system. We have had very low return rates on both. Additional concerns for testing online included confidentiality, security, and proof that participants do their own work. Specifically, we did not want to have "open-note" tests or require students to come to campus for testing. So for now we have decided to avoid the on-line testing feature. As the on-line program progresses, we plan on studying not only our successes with current assessment strategies but also our failures in order to learn from our mistakes and continually improve the use of the course-support site for alternative assessment strategies.

Overall, assessment has made it easier for students to understand the instructor's expectations and it has allowed an opportunity for instructors to evaluate the students' work and enabled students to evaluate each others'. However, it also has been just as important to the instructors. In our on-line course, assessment has been used as a reflective tool to help the instructors see where they are with students. The rubrics have essentially provided the foundation for detailed feedback on different aspects of projects. It has allowed students to reference weaknesses in projects by pointing out specific criteria and guidelines, thus, saving valuable time for the instructors. Too often, teachers are proud when one or two students do exceptionally well on a test; however, the louder message should be that the remaining students were not effectively reached. The experience from the on-line course has strengthened the commitment of the instructors toward cooperative assessment and learning.

For the instructors, the major hurdle in teaching the course was how to design a learning environment that encouraged participation, thus, differentiating itself from being solely a correspondence course by creating a sense of community greater than what is seen in traditional face-to-face environments. This has been accomplished through the on-line discussions that enabled students to share personal experiences that relate to course topics. This type of interaction motivated the students to continue when faced with problems or with curriculum-development challenges in there own work. (Fisher, 1998).

One of the most difficult issues an instructor faces when creating on-line learning environments is deciding on the amount of student-to-student and student-to-instructor interaction that is needed. For this reason discussions were structured in cooperative groups which are individually accountable. Similar to the experience of Collis (1992), there has been strong enthusiasm among the teachers who actively participated in the on-line learning. Even though the teachers in these groups have been very dependent on the instructors at the start, they have become more independent as they move through the course work (Collis, 1992).

Like Schlechter (1990) the teachers who actively participated in cooperative groups demonstrated an ability to generate a greater diversity of ideas, more reflective thinking, and increased creative responses for applying and integrating technology and curriculum. And, as with Flynn (1992), this course demonstrated that this approach was preferred to individual learning since the learning objective was information transfer and skills acquisition.

Also, a unique forum for group discussion utilizing Lotus LearningSpace and an on-line "Course Room" where students can share ideas, edit shared documents, insert graphics, link to new documents or graphics and make links to other Web sites was established. In this environment, students created a dynamically evolving information base of ideas, facts, insights, goals, plans, and solutions to school-related issues. This is where course participants have consulted one another to discuss topics and assignments. The "Course Room" has enabled the teachers to ask questions and have discussions either publicly or privately as they wish. During these discussions the teachers quickly have identified a need to develop and use communication conventions and protocols to interact clearly and minimize misunderstanding in their on-line transactions with others. The "Course Room" has acted as the virtual database that has allowed the middle-school teachers to interact with their classmates and instructor as required by the course.

However, before actually going online on their own, two face-to-face, in-house class orientations have been necessary. Using the Internet resources in the campus lab, the teachers initially establish communication with the instructor by accessing the course and then the e-mail option in Lotus LearningSpace. The first two face-to-face sessions have included both interpersonal and on-line exercises for the teachers, such as creating profile pages and doing interactive exercises. A discussion assignment has been given that instructs the teachers to go to the "Course Room" using their computers at school and begin to participate in a discussion about the face-to-face classroom. Teachers have used interactive course elements instead of static Web pages. Here the teachers have exchanged ideas and information with other group members and the instructors.

Through these first face-to-face sessions, the teachers usually begin to feel more "secure" because someone is there to help them get through it initially. The intent is to provide the teachers with experience in moving around the virtual space that hosted their course. They are also provided with hard copies of the course syllabus and technology-use instructions for such tasks as: "Submitting Assignments", "Reading Assignments," "Roles and Responsibilities for Cooperative Group Members," "Emergency Guidelines," "Computer and Network Requirements for LearningSpace," "Tips for Taking a Course Online," a list of mentors for the course, and a list for the Technical Support team with contact information.

Two areas that are also addressed during the initial sessions were mentoring and technical-support information. Mentors are past participants familiar with the on-line course who provided tutoring and advice about course-related experiences. The students explored course topics and questions through electronic mentoring via e-mail with the mentors, advanced student volunteers having greater expertise. In Marquette's case, mentors have supported the continuous professional development and provided ongoing support for the middle-school teachers in the school district even after the course was completed. At this time, members of the previous class were invited to campus to demonstrate and explain the individual and team projects. At the end of the course, students presented their projects and explained how they integrated technology into the assessment of communication skills in ways that enhanced student learning. This approach helped to promote a sense of belonging and students indicated that it provided a sense of closure for the course to them.

Identifying what technical support is available for students and how to contact them for assistance has been invaluable. The technical-support people in the program had taken the course previously, so they were familiar with potential technical challenges for new participants. They helped with any technical issues teachers had related to the course. Several past-participants volunteered initially and then a network has evolved among them for technical support.

The Marquette University help desk helped reduce instructor time for visiting each student at their respective schools to help with technical problems and student frustrations. The "help desk" provides technology support to class participants via electronic mail and telephone. The first hurdle in teaching our course was connectivity. In this instance, connectivity is meant as the ability to access the server and the course in a timely fashion. In the first three weeks, the teachers asked the majority of the technical questions. Examples of common problems students encounter are: Java script errors, problems with submitting files to the course site, handling various WWW-browser error messages, difficulties with the MPS school networks (for example, caused by idiosyncrasies in the school connections), and other technical issues students had related to the course. In addition, instructors were more effective at handling teacher concerns and needs by receiving ideas or problems from them before they held on-line office hours each week.

The importance of covering these issues in the face-to-face classes cannot be emphasized enough in helping the teachers to reach a proper comfort level. This is reflected in one student's post-course comments below:

> When I first attended an Internet class, I was scared, since my level of knowledge and interest in the technology is minimal. It was as if I was learning to drive a car: afraid of an accident and getting lost (Internet express and behind the wheel), go slow/drive cautiously, limit distractions/stay focused (no radio, soda), need for a license/password, and the possibility of abusing the privilege and having it suspended or revoked.

It is interesting to note that once a comfort zone was approached, and in most cases established in the use of WWW-based courses, intuitive learning strategies seem to emerge and even drive the development of course projects. Students began changing the characteristics of new strategies. Those strategies, in turn, changed the way the students created projects for the classroom, which, in turn, will influence how much of the innovation will be used in practice.

As with Bourdeau and Bates (1997), interactivity for increased effectiveness was not only practiced between the teachers, and between teachers and the instructor, but also between the students and the instructional material. Teachers have multidimensional interactions, such as; teachers and activities (i.e., group discussions); teachers and learning resources like animation, video, and slide shows; teachers sharing ideas with other teachers (i.e., research); as well as, teachers and the instructor (i.e., assignment feedback). They have solved problems and worked together in a manner similar to a cooperative group approach from their respective schools.

Consistent with findings of other research (Collins and Murphy, 1997; Rohfeld and Heimstra, 1995), teachers have acknowledged that the "Course Room" discussions would have been less productive and more difficult without having first established rapport with other group members in a face-to-face setting (Collis and Murphy, 1997). Cooperative groups depended on each member taking an active role in assuring that the group functions efficiently and effectively with each member "pulling their own weight." Similar to what Bourdeau and Bates (1997) discovered regarding distance learning, collaboration between students has been an essential component of the activities of participants in the course; participants have had to join forces in order to learn more.

Discussions can be open to all course participants, restricted to members of a small cohort group, or private; however, each teacher is required to provide feedback as part of the course. We have found that requiring participation is a good way to ensure equal participation because each middle-school teacher has to do his or her part.

To implement the discussion, the instructor posted opening questions in the topic discussions. These questions typically encouraged students to take a position on an issue and reflect on classroom experience. In the discussion each student was required to post an initial response to a topic question and respond to at least two topic threads related to other students' initial responses for each discussion. Each topic discussion was "live" for two weeks. It became clear that whenever a WWW-based discussion tool was used — a listserve, chatroom, forum, or CourseRoom (i.e. a database interface in *Lotus LearningSpace*) — discussion guidelines were necessary.

Class interaction has been vital. The course's interactive curriculum has allowed for meaningful teaching applications in formal and informal educational settings. This model has enabled the middle-school teachers to assess the application of learned skills and concepts in authentic settings. The teachers have learned not only the facts but also how to express their knowledge and ideas with these tools. We found that they have needed these hands-on learning opportunities in projects they try out in the schools. In several modules, we have asked students to share strategies and solutions to specific classroom issues with other students, such as Internet Resources (see Figure 4).

There is a need for cooperative learning group discussions in many Web-based

Figure 3

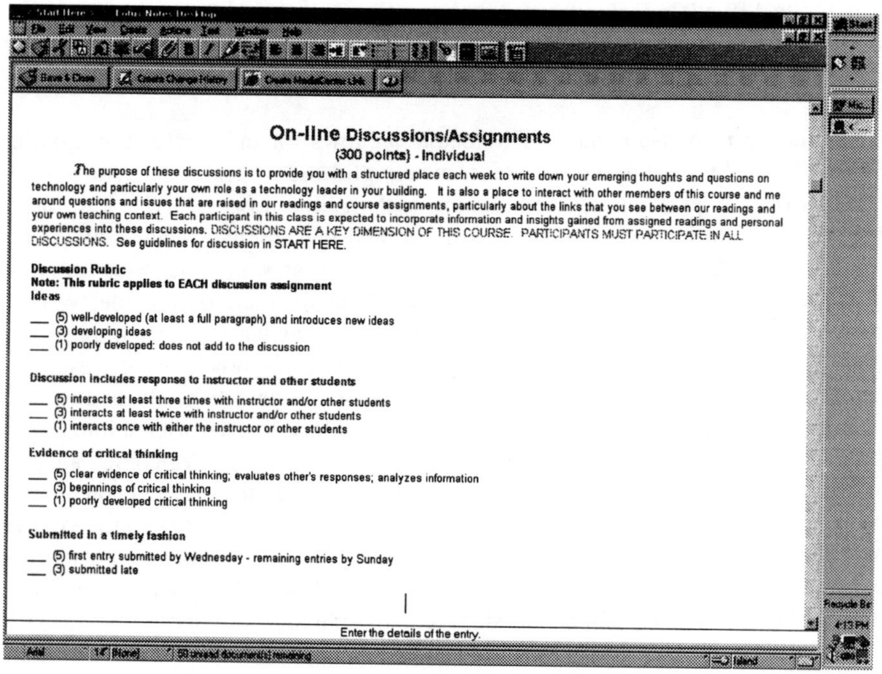

On-line Discussions/Assignments

(300 points) - Individual

The purpose of these discussions is to provide you with a structured place each week to write down your emerging thoughts and questions on technology and particularly your own role as a technology leader in your building. It is also a place to interact with other members of this course and me around questions and issues that are raised in our readings and course assignments, particularly about the links that you see between our readings and your own teaching context. Each participant in this class is expected to incorporate information and insights gained from assigned readings and personal experiences into these discussions. DISCUSSIONS ARE A KEY DIMENSION OF THIS COURSE. PARTICIPANTS MUST PARTICIPATE IN ALL DISCUSSIONS. See guidelines for discussion in START HERE.

Discussion Rubric
Note: This rubric applies to EACH discussion assignment
Ideas

___ (5) well-developed (at least a full paragraph) and introduces new ideas
___ (3) developing ideas
___ (1) poorly developed: does not add to the discussion

Discussion includes response to instructor and other students

___ (5) interacts at least three times with instructor and/or other students
___ (3) interacts at least twice with instructor and/or other students
___ (1) interacts once with either the instructor or other students

Evidence of critical thinking

___ (5) clear evidence of critical thinking; evaluates other's responses; analyzes information
___ (3) beginnings of critical thinking
___ (1) poorly developed critical thinking

Submitted in a timely fashion

___ (5) first entry submitted by Wednesday - remaining entries by Sunday
___ (3) submitted late

Enter the details of the entry.

Figure 4: CourseRoom Assignment

Internet Resources: Share Your Project Ideas

After completing this Module on Internet Resources, share with us your ideas and experiences about using one or more of the technologies introduced in this module in the classroom. What have you either tried or seen that works? What are your ideas about effectively using Internet resources in the classroom? Share what you learned!

activities. Students have claimed that this was probably the most crucial element in the success of a group. The teachers have learned to explore and examine the curriculum within groups rather than just as individuals. The new learning groups have been found to reduce isolation and lack of sustained support experienced by teachers in their own schools. Nonetheless, before we created the discussion rubric many of our first course on-line discussions appeared somewhat meaningless. Much of the initial feedback from the teachers indicated uncertainty to whether or not they had reached the correct answers. Because of this problem, it is imperative that the on-line discussions are structured well. The teachers wanted lively conversations that more closely resembled face-to-face discussion. Another student's comment helps illustrate this point:

> I conceptualized more interactions during discussions, stemming from initial comments, of about a paragraph or two long, then everything flowing from there. It is a little difficult to feel connected in the on-line discussions. I am still getting used to the format and feel...because I wanted to get my work done early and I cannot because I am waiting around to read other responses to comment to.

The delay in response or lack of immediacy allows for more reflection time and thought making the follow-up responses more meaningful and content-loaded; however, as is apparent from the previous teacher comment, there is a downside. Though on-line conversations tend to be very thought provoking and can involve much more critical thinking than one might get in a traditional classroom, you can sometimes wait days to get a reply to your discussion. If we are going to make on-line interaction available, we might have many frustrated teachers on our hands, especially if they want feedback right away.

A solution to the dilemma of immediacy lies in designing how teachers respond to discussions. One approach that has worked in our course has been to establish a detailed, step-by-step procedure. Besides the preview in the initial face-to-face orientation, instructions have been pasted in the course "Announcements" section and "Welcome Pages." In the initial discussion, teachers have been more successful when they related comments to their reading assignments. Teachers must ask themselves, "How can you apply what you have read and learned?" Teachers should try to enter comments into assignments a few days before they are due to allow the discussion to "take off." Also, it has proven important to check out the rubrics and assignments first, before completing the work.

Even with good topics, teachers wrote last-minute entries, so a valuable discussion often gets going just before the due date. This has not been the instructor's fault, since early entries have been encouraged. The most successful possibility thus far has been for discussions to require one response by Wednesday of the first week and the second response by the end of the following week.

A tactic that has proven effective in delivering desired outcomes is providing feedback about the progress of teacher learning early and often. A common comment from teachers in the course has been that the frequent feedback has been a good motivator and has kept many participants logging on. In addition, the types of questions are important. As with any other educational activity, it is how one structures and answers questions that will determine the educational effectiveness of the Internet (Iseke-Barnes, 1996). Instructors need to listen in on group discussions and offer advice. Try to get the student to think a little further or view a subject from a different angle. Instructors should try to respond to all initial comments by students in discussions and ask questions in responses to students to encourage discussion at a deeper level. On-line courses need better questions because one does not have those subtle nonverbal cues that exist in the face-to-face classroom. Inquiry into authentic questions generated from student experiences is a central strategy for teaching online. In our case, teachers have used e-mail outside the course to tell each other what they really feel if the questions have been too tightly written or have not allowed them to explore controversial aspects of topics. We have points awarded in our rubric for being positive in an assignment requesting opinions. The teachers have disagreed with requesting opinions as criteria for an assignment. We were thinking more about mutual respect; however, in a face-to-face classroom, teachers would be required to address and answer questions, give details and examples, or rationale for their answers. The on-line questions have not always been able to inspire reflective thought. The instructor has not always been able to encourage or challenge the teachers the same as in a face-to-face class. As a result, we sometimes have had to accept superficial lower level responses to online assignments.

Another issue to consider is the type of groups one structures. Past participants in the course have claimed their worst experiences in groups came from working in groups they themselves formed, therefore, our process to allow the instructors to assign teachers to groups. We often pair up teachers at the same schools in groups, when possible. We have found that establishing "school partners" — putting students geographically close to each other in the same group — provides an environment for "local" support. It has also proven a good idea to allow teachers to sit in their groups during the face-to-face orientation sessions.

Each semester has required innovative restructuring of groups. After teaching the course several times, we have found discussion groups numbering seven or eight have worked best. Smaller groups often lack resources and larger groups have difficulty working together due to logistical conflicts. Our experience has been that the less teacher-controlled, the more indepth discussion occurred. The middle-school teachers began to explore and examine the power of their ideas. Their "voice" is what matters. It is their summaries of the instruction that have helped instructors to see if the teachers were "getting" the questions.

The instructor's role was to facilitate maximum sharing of information and knowledge among the teachers rather than to control the delivery and pace of the content. In line with the thoughts of Shale (1990), instructors had to assess the teachers' activities and the adequacy of their knowledge in use of technology for teaching in order to be able to provide feedback to teachers and create a proper environment that would generate peer feedback (Shale, 1990). One example of this was when teachers shared their ideas about potential uses of technology for teaching and the result when they implemented their ideas in their classrooms. The instructors not only provided feedback to each teacher's ideas and projects but also created an environment to generate peer feedback (Fisher, 1998).

Promoting interaction through the development of on-line course discussion requires the instructor to reconsider the relationship between students, the instructor, and the curriculum. Many of our students think electronic conversations are more reflective and less competitive than real-time classroom discussions. The electronic asynchronous format facilitates a balanced input of ideas from people participating in the conversation and diminishes the chance that the conversation will be dominated by one of the participants. In this respect, electronic conversations offer an advantage to groups of individuals who might feel threatened by verbal interaction that takes on a competitive edge. Many students feel that this format for electronic conversations inherently makes the forum more equally accessible to all.

FUTURE TRENDS

The on-line course at Marquette has proven to be a process of continuous learning and improvement. There are a number of areas yet to be explored. Characteristics of Web-based education that work best in classrooms have yet to be completely determined, but they must extend beyond the classroom because training no longer ends in the classroom.

One design issue that cannot be overlooked is that of acceptance. Though live instruction is still optimal for teaching complex concepts, technology presents new challenges. Today students want and expect Web-based education coming at them from various multisensory modes (i.e., visual, audio, digital, etc.). Will students accept instruction if they don't see glitz? Another key consideration in the success of an effective online course is how attractive are the instructional features. Boshier, Mohapi, Moulton, Qayyum, Sadownik, and Wilson (1997) at the University of British Columbia evaluated 127 courses taken over the Internet. They found that the aesthetic standards of an online course can be as important as the content and skills it is expected to convey. The study looked specifically at the on-line courses according to how a student enrolled in each course might respond (Schweizer, 1999). "We paid attention to the feeling and tone of the course, not just the content and teaching process," said Boshier. He went even so far to say that, the appearance "can make or break" an online course (Schweizer, 1999). Additional research is necessary in this area, however, it is safe to say, we must pay attention to the visual appeal and "feel" of our course if we expect to maximize student learning online." (Boshier, Mohapi and Moulton, 1997).

The following are examples of relevant instructional design features and some specific questions teachers should ask when investigating potential Web-based resources for teaching via the Internet:

- Are Web pages easy to read with appropriate spacing between lines?
- Are icons easily identified?
- Are there links to Web sites for online readings?
- Are the images of high quality (text, charts, pictures, videotape, multimedia, models, etc.)?
- Is audio included? Can the audio be turned on or off?
- Are small well-designed video bytes included that illustrate concepts being presented?

- Does the Web site incorporate good information display and organization strategies?

Learning is as much a social as an individual activity. Learners need to access, combine, create, and transmit data as necessary. This will determine design requirements and indicate the need to build a system that supports this form of learning, both formal and informal (Bates, 1998). The process should build peer support and relationships within the class, as well as encourage interaction with the instructor and provide performance feedback early in the course

As a final thought, it is suggested that future research focus on types of teacher characteristics that are conducive to success in Web-based courses. Examples of such research might include finding out (a) how students organized themselves, (b) how students structured their time, or (c) how students went about completing their assignments for on-line course work (Fisher, 1998). Some guidelines we found to be helpful and might aid students in the future include:

- Do all of your work in a word processor and save it. Then paste it into the on-line course so you do not lose your work if the server kicks you off line.
- Finish your assignments early and expect network congestion to slow you down, making it a little nerve racking if you are getting done just in time.
- The best time to go online is early in the morning or late at night. So when you do get online, you can just copy and paste your assignment into the right place and be done in minutes.
- When attaching or uploading assignments, expect this process to take a long time. Turn off screen savers because sometimes they might interfere with uploads. If at all possible, attach and upload assignments from your school if you are on a T-1 line.
- Practice navigating around in cyberspace the first week. It makes the rest of the class much easier.
- Expect everything to take longer than you planned.
- Bookmark your site.
- Do not be afraid to ask for help from either the instructors or others in your group.
- Have fun with your on-line discussion responses; otherwise people reading them will have boring comments in response to you.

As noted by Scott (1996), although historically there has been a far greater emphasis on the development of new technological applications, there has been little written regarding the implementation of technology within the realm of higher education. We still do not know if these Internet activities show up systematically in teachers' future instruction because we lack studies that examine the integration beyond design and that measure the effect on student performance. These concerns are significant because schools need to be promoting a range of approaches for students to communicate and make meaning through the resources on the Internet (Scott, 1996).

CONCLUSION

Somehow when information is seen on the Web, many students find it more relevant to the real world, even though the identical information might be found in a book in the library. The Internet brings every subject area at educational levels from primary to doctorate available to the user with immediate access. Multimedia is there for access to music, theater, art, and in content related clips. It provides learning experiences that support subject matter and makes learning more meaningful to students. Access to the Internet in the classroom is like a doorway to the world but the instructor needs to do a fair amount of preliminary work in the lesson prior to actually going online. The better the activity is structured the more effective it will be. Finding a project that involves Internet use is fairly easy. Finding a project that fits your setting means looking at several factors: time frame, availability of the Internet, and the amount of work that can be done independently.

It is suggested that the most effective use of the Internet in the classroom is to incorporate it as a source of information used to augment the regular lesson. A specific example of this can be found in a lesson on Federal Government and the election process. In addition to class lectures and assigned readings from the text, students can view predetermined sites that contained Real Audio and Video clips from the candidates. They can also conduct independent research using various mainstream news Web sites to discover what the media was saying about the candidates in various parts of the country. Students can further demonstrate their learning by analyzing the source of the information and providing a brief written paper in which they summarize articles found on the Web.

To create the teacher's role as instructional technology facilitator, the teacher must first understand the capabilities and possibilities of technology. One of the successes of this Lotus LearningSpace program was in the context of training. We hoped that the teachers' struggles and accomplishments with the on-line technologies would help them rethink teaching and learning. We were unprepared, however, for the dramatic examples of reflective practice that our teachers displayed. Collectively, they began to see the shortcomings of many instructional practices used in their school and were able to integrate new outcomes, assessment models, and apply new strategies for instructional technology. Through their experiences, we were reminded that technology is only a tool and is only as effective as the ideas and applications of those who deal with the technological challenges facing us all. Overall our teachers understood that good teaching is the key and that technology is only one of many useful hooks that can be used to capture the learner. The middle-school teachers believed they had the knowledge and the skills to improve instruction and assessment for their students; therefore, technological change became reality.

The examples contained within this paper describe the problems students have experienced with on-line design and delivery and the solutions that have led to current on-line courses and future staff-development. The Internet is opening up a new world for both teachers and students that continues to change the face of teaching and learning, and provides greater access to current information and knowledge. Putting a powerful communications tool into the hands of students is just beginning to produce exciting results.

We have seen an evolution in the beliefs of teachers using the Internet for teaching students. Faculty needs to begin to learn the uses and implications of this new teaching tool. When students and faculty start using the Internet, they will understand and benefit from its potential advancements. Educators need to feel competent to facilitate and guide students in their journey through their own training experiences. Internet experiences in teacher training are beneficial yet currently limited. If we require high standards of our educators, they must receive the preparation, support, and ongoing training they need to meet our demands. These training experiences should aid in the dissemination of new and innovative uses of Internet technology that will have a positive impact on current teaching practices, including those taught in teacher preparation programs. Further research in this area will prove instrumental in generating awareness of optimum resources and strategies for integrating use of the Internet in the classroom and dramatically improving what teachers can deliver to students.

ACKNOWLEDGMENTS

I thank Fr. Emanuel Udo and the Milwaukee Public School teachers for their timely and thoughtful help with this project. Portions of this chapter are drawn from the course entitled, *Using Technology for Instruction and Assessment*, developed by Mercedes Fisher, Heidi Schweizer, and Joan Whipp, Marquette University.

REFERENCES

Bates, Anthony (1998). Educational Multi - Media in a Networked Society Conference IT in Education & Training.

Bills, Conrad G. (1997). *Effects of Structure and Interactivity on Internet-Based Instruction.* Paper presented at the Interservice/Industry Training, Simulation, and Education Conference, Orlando, FL.

Boshier, R., Mohapi, M., & Moulton, G. "Best and Worst Dressed Web Courses: Strutting Into the 21st Century in Comfort and Style". *Distance Learning Education: An International Journal*, Vol.18. No.2, 1997.

Bourdeau, J., & Bates, A. (1997). Instructional design for distance learning. In S. Dijkstra, M. N. See, f. Scott, and R.A. Tennyson (Eds.), *Instructional design: International Perspectives*, Vol. 2, Solving instructional design problems. Mahwah, NJ: Lawrence Erlbaum Associates.

Collins, M. P., & Murphy, K. L. (1997, August). *Reducing conversational chaos: The use of communications in instructional electronic chats.* Paper presented at the 13th Annual Conference on Distance Teaching & Learning, WI: Madison

Collis, B. (1992). Supporting educational uses of telecommunication in the secondary school: Part II. Strategies for improved implementation. *International Journal of Instructional Media.* 19(2), 97-109.

Downs, E.; Carlson, R.D; Repman, J.; & Clark, K. (1999) Web-based Instruction: Focus on Learning. *Technology and Teacher Education Annual*, Association for the Advancement of Computing in Education, Charlottesville, VA, 773-779.

Fisher, M. (1998) " Using Lotus LearningSpace for Staff-development in Public Schools" *Journal of Interactive Learning Research*, 9 (3/4) .

Fisher, M. (1999). Lotus LearningSpace: A WWW Strategy for Growth. *International Journal of Educational Telecommunications*, 5 (4).

Flynn, J. L., (1992). Cooperative learning and gagne's events of instruction: A syncretic view. *Educational Technology*. 53-60.

Gifford, Bernard (1997). *From Theory to Practice: The Odyssey of the Distributed Mediated Learning Model.* Paper presented at the American Association for Higher Education, Washington, D.C.

Gifford, Bernard (1996). *Mediated Learning: A New Model of Networked Instruction and*

Learning. Paper presented at the Educom '96 Information Technology: Transcending Traditional Boundaries, Philadelphia, Pennsylvania.

Harasim, L., & Johnson, E. M. (1986). *Educational applications of computer network for teachers/trainers in Ontario.* Toronto: Ontario Department of Education. (ERIC Document Reproduction Service No. 276 398).

Harris, J. (1999). *Designing Curriculum-Based Telecomputing Using Activity Structures and Action Sequences*. Technology and Teacher Education Annual, 1999, Association for the Advancement of Computing in Education, Charlottesville, VA, 637-642.

Harris, J. (1995). "Knowledge-making in the Information Age: Beyond Information Access." *Learning and Leading with Technology*, October.

Iseke-Barnes, J., (1996). Issues of educational uses of the Internet: Power and criticism in communications and searching. *Journal of Educational Computing Research*, 15 (1),

Kulieke, N., Baker, J. Collins, C., Fennimore, T., Fine, C., Herman, J., Jones, B.F., Raack, L. & Tinzman, M.B.(1990). *"Why Should Assessment Be Based on a Vision of Learning*?" from Pathways to School Improvement Internet Server. NCREL, Oak Brook.

Kurshan, B., & Dawson, T. (January 1992). The global classroom: Reaching Beyond the walls of the school building. *Technology & Learning*, 48-51..

Matthews, R. (1997). *Guidelines for Good Practice: Technology Mediated Instruction*. Paper presented at the Acedemic Senate for California Community Colleges, Sacramento, CA..

Pickett, N. *Rubrics for Web Lessons*. Trinton Project; School of Education; San Diego State University; San Diego, California. Date of last revision March 31, 1999. [Online]. Available: http://edweb.sdsu.edu/triton/july/Rubrics/Rubrics_for_Web_ Lessons.html [Access date May, 1999].

Pugalee, D.K., & Robinson, R. (1998). A study of the impact of teacher training in using Internet resources for mathematics and science instruction. *Journal of Research on Computing in Education*, 31(1), 78-88.

Quinlan, L. (1996). The Digital Classroom. *Tech trends* [online], xx. Available: http://columbia.digiweb.com/~achar95/staff/laurie.html/

Rohfeld & Heimstra (1997, August). *Cooperative groups on-line*. Paper presented at the 11th Annual Conference on Distance Teaching and Learning. WI: Madison.

Schlechter, T. M., (1990). The relative instructional efficiency of small group computer-based training. *Journal of Educational Computing Research*. 6(3), 329-341.

Schweizer, H. (1999). *Spinning Your Web Classroom.* Allyn & Bacon, 91.

Scott, R. (1996). *Managing technological change in higher education*. In Shona Cameron (Ed.), ALT C 96: Integrating technology into the curriculum. Conference program and abstracts of the Association for Learning Technology Conference. 3rd. Glasgow, Scotland, (ERIC Document Reproduction Services No. ED 416 836).

Shale, D. (1990). Toward a reconceptualization of distance education. In I. M. Moore (Ed.). *Contemporary issues in American distance education*. NY: Pergarnon.

Song, James Kow Kim (1998). *Using the World Wide Web in Education and Training*. Conference IT in Education & Training.

Vafa, Shahrzad (1999). Web-based Instruction and Motivation: Some Useful Guidelines for Educators. *Technology and Teacher Education Annual, 1999*, Association for the Advancement of Computing in Education, Charlottesville, VA, 1900-1904.

Willis, B. (1992). From a distance: Making distance learning effective: Key roles and

responsibilities. *Educational Technology*. 35(6), 35-37.
Wood, Victoria L.; Stevens, Ellen; McFarlane, Terry; Peterson, Kim; Richardson, Karen; Davis, Robert; LeJeune, Noel (1998). *Faculty Development Workshop: Critical Reflection in a Web-Based Environment.* Paper presented at the Society for Information Technology & Teacher Education International Conference, Washington, D.C.

Chapter VI

Theory Supporting Design Guidelines for Web-based Instruction

Dorothy Leflore
North Carolina A&T State University, USA

More and more universities are turning to Web-based instruction in order to accommodate a larger student population. Much of the coursework available online follows the traditional packet type system that has been available for printed correspondence courses. The major difference has been synchronous and asynchronous communication, not just between the instructor and students but among the students. However, learning can be enhanced if attention is given to how the material to be learned is presented and how students are required to interact with and interpret the material. Learning theories can be used to provide sound guidelines for designing a variety of presentation modes and student activities online. Examples provided later in this chapter come from an on-line course in Learning Theories at North Carolina A & T State University which was designed and taught by Karen Smith-Gratto.

A primary theory to consider is Gestalt theory because the main focus of Gestalt theorists was to explore perception and its relationship to learning. Smith-Gratto and Fisher (1998-99) stated "The screens rely heavily on the 'visual perception' of the learner" (p. 3). Consequently, the Laws of Perception should be the foundation for visually designing and evaluating the Web-based instructional page. Some of the Laws of Perception that would be beneficial in designing Web-based instructional pages are figure-ground contrast, simplicity, proximity, similarity, symmetry, and closure. In addition to the Laws of Perception, Gestalt theory can also provide guidance in the development of activities for students to engage in during the Web-based learning experience. While modern cognitive theory is in some respects an outgrowth of Gestalt theory, there are differences that can be exploited to provide additional approaches to Web-based instruction.

There are several approaches from cognitive theory that can be used to help design what appears on the Web-based instructional page and help design student interactions. Cognitive mapping or webbing, concept attainment activities, and use of motivational graphics, animations and sounds are ways that cognitive theory can substantially contribute to the instruction.

In addition to Gestalt and cognitive theory, constructivism can be drawn upon to create Web-based instructional activities that require students to approach learning in different ways. Guidelines for developing Constructivist based activities require that students be given active and engaging tasks that require more than minimal intellectual involvement. Examples of such tasks include student development of models and metaphors to explain what they are learning. Students can be provided with demonstration simulations that are not explained. Students are then required to explain what happened within the demonstration and construct definitions and explanations based upon what they observed. In addition to these types of activities, students can be required to participate in on-line problem solving activities both alone and with other students.

GESTALT THEORY

In applying the theory of perception to screen design, figure-ground relationship must be considered.

Figure-ground contrast deals with the concept that the foreground of a visual needs to be distinct from the background. This is often violated on screens seen on the Web. Backgrounds often contain patterns or color, which cause the text to fade into the background making the text difficult to read. This aspect of Gestalt theory tells us that the text or graphics should have sufficient differences to make the separation of the information to be learned easily accessed by the learner.

Kohler (1947) and Koffka (1935) theorized that individuals unconsciously try to simplify what they perceive based upon expectations that are formed because of previous experiences. When a complex visual is used, the viewers will simplify the visual into a form that they can understand (Smith-Gratto & Fisher, 1998-99). Since viewers do this it would be more efficient to simplify the graphic when it is introduced then gradually add the complexity so that the learner may build up to the complexity required. The path from simple to complex can help prevent learners from misinterpreting the visuals provided. The principle of simplicity indicates that when visuals are used in Web-based instruction, the visuals should avoid the inclusion of distracting visual content. The visual should be unambiguous and easily interpreted by the learner; otherwise the content will be more difficult for the learner to understand.

Proximity is another aspect of Gestalt theory that can help with the design of Web-based instruction. It is easier for learners to understand that different text or graphic elements go together if these elements are placed close together. Text used to explain a graphic or as a label for parts of a graphic should be close by the graphic or part of the graphic to which the text refers. There should be no ambiguity or learners may perceive the text as referring to something other than what was intended.

The Law of Similarity states that people will group things together that have a similar appearance. Since this is the case, learners need to be aided in the recall of information by focusing their attention to the key concepts in a visual field (Kohler, 1947). This can be done in Web-based instruction by highlighting, animation, use of contrasting colors, or other techniques for calling attention to an item within the visual display. If the elements in a graphic are all the same style, the graphic will be seen as a whole. In order to call learners' attention to specific elements of the graphic, different colors, flashing of the specific element of concern, or other means of differentiation should be employed. This concept applies to text also. However, too many differences on one screen of information will make it difficult for learners to focus on the desired information. These techniques should be used to emphasize key words or key aspects of a graphic, rather than large segments of information.

The Law of Closure indicates that individuals will try to interpret incomplete graphics or text based on past experience. Incomplete graphics should be avoided because learners will spend time trying to make meaning rather than learning from the information that is presented. For example, if a series of dotted lines are used and the general shape is circular, individuals will fill in the space between the dots and say that the dots represent a circle. Individuals tend to fill in areas based upon their previous experience and will interpret what is perceived accordingly. Individuals seek to bring meaning to what is perceived and will force meaning on information that is perceived as incomplete. During instruction, incomplete information can lead to a misunderstanding of the information presented.

When designing activities for instruction on the Web, how individuals make meaning should be considered. Either individuals obtain meaning directly from the information or they impose patterns on the information in order to give the information meaning (Kohler,1947). However, individuals learn more readily when meaning is attached to information (Kohler, 1947; Koffka, 1935). Therefore, how individuals will respond to the presentation of material should be considered and the design should facilitate "meaning-making".

Gestalt Theory Guidelines

1. When designing Web-based instruction, make sure that the background does not interfere with the clarity of the information presented on the foreground.
   Example. Figure 1 shows a good example of a balanced screen design incorporating the basic principles of Gestalt theory. The background and foreground contrast is very clear so that the learner easily decodes the text and figures.
2. Use simplified graphics to introduce new information. If the concept is one that requires complexity, start out with the simplified version and gradually add the complexity.
   Example. As can be seen in Figure 2, the complex concept of Information Processing Theory is presented in a simple graphic format so that students can get an overall view of the concept on which to build.
3. When designing the layout of the computer screen, place related information together so that the learner will automatically group the information together as a unit rather than as separate elements.
   Example. In Figure 1, the navigation and sound controls are placed on one side of the screen and the textual instruction is on the other side. This layout groups like information (or in this case information and tools) which makes it easier for the learner to discern the function of each section.
4. Use color, animation, flashing, or other means to draw attention to key phrases in text or key areas in graphics.
   Example. Giving an example of animation or flashing is not possible on the printed page, but the use of bolding text on the printed page can be used to focus the learners'

attention.

5. When designing the instruction, use visual information and textual information that allows the learner to concentrate on the information rather than using time to make meaning because the information is incomplete.
   Example. Figure 2 provides textual information that focuses the learner's attention to the complete concept presented by the graphics, rather than trying to figure out what the graphics mean.
6. When introducing a new topic, vocabulary that is unique to the content being taught should be introduced by using common terms. Avoid the use of jargon, until the concepts have been introduced in basic terms. Once a concept has been introduced in basic terms, introduce the appropriate term so that learners do not have to struggle to make meaning.
   Example. In the on-line course cited here, information processing theory was introduced by using the concepts represented by the graphics in Figure 2. These concepts are commonly understood by students, and students can relate to the experience of seeing something, thinking about it, and recalling what was observed at a later time. This of course is a simplified view of the theory and the simplified view built upon as instruction proceeds.

COGNITIVE THEORY

There are several approaches from cognitive theory that can be used to help design what appears on the Web-based instructional page. Cognitive mapping or webbing, concept attainment activities, activation of prior knowledge, and use of motivational graphics, animation, and sounds are ways that cognitive theory can substantially contribute to the instruction.

Webs, graphic organizers, and outlines are forms of cognitive mapping. Individuals build frameworks or schemas to help them understand the world (Piaget, 1954). While each person's schema will be different, we can provide some structure to help guide students' schema formation. Taba (1962) states that when individuals develop concepts, they reorganize existing concepts when the existing concepts interact with the new experience. Therefore, a cognitive map of some sort would be appropriate at the beginning of a Web-based lesson. Visual referents are one way to help show relationships that exist between the elements of the content students are expected to learn (Reiber, 1994). Webs and graphic organizers are visual referents that fulfill the function suggested by Reiber. Overviews of information and relationships among the elements of the content are easily shown using webs and graphic organizers. They are often constructed by enclosing text in geometric shapes and connecting the shapes by means of lines. This technique provides a pictorial view of how concepts students are expected to learn are related. These organizers can help students understand complex concepts and the subconcept relationships among elements that contribute to their overview of the complex concept. While outlines are not visual referents in this sense, they do provide an overview of information and can be used in a similar manner. While use of outlines, webs, and graphic organizers is presented under cognitive theory, their use is also supported by Gestalt theory because they provide a whole view of the information at one time.

Concept development is another aspect of cognitive theory that can be used in Web-

Figure 1. Gestalt Principles for Screen Design

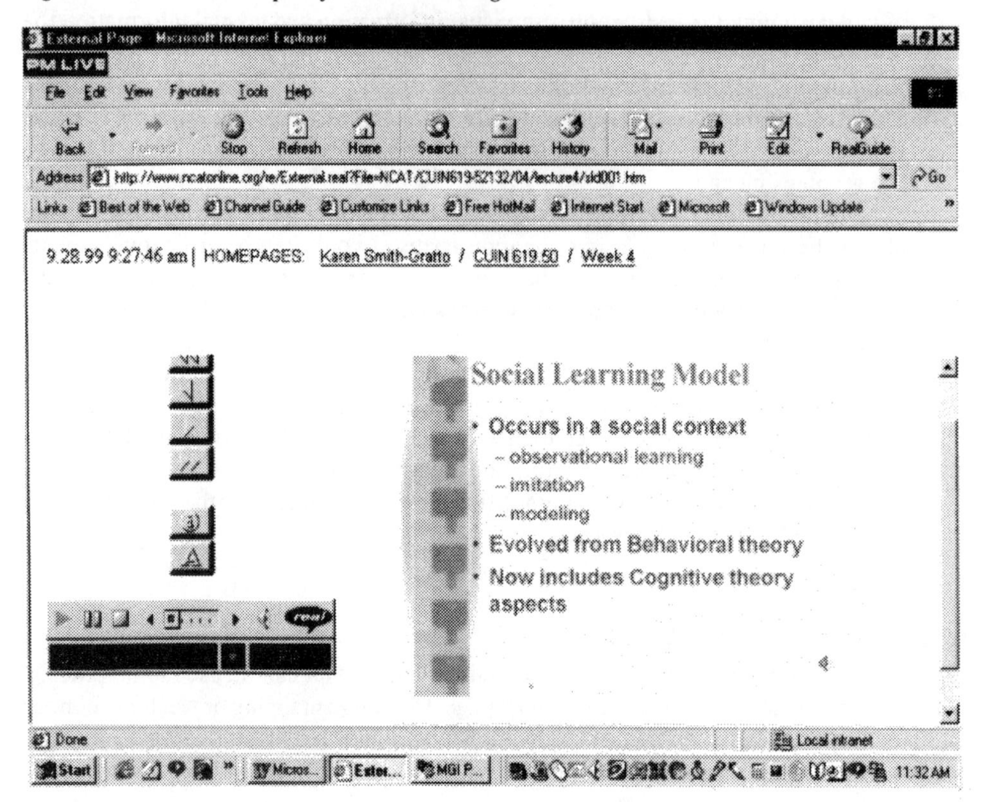

based instruction. Concept attainment is an interactive process (Bruner, Goodnow, and Austin, 1956). Individuals are provided with examples and non-examples of a concept so that the characteristics of the concept become evident to the learner. Learners form hypotheses about the definition of the concept until the definition is reached (Bruner, Goodnow, and Austin, 1956; Hodges, 1986). This process involves the learners in examining the features of a concept and organizing and reorganizing their understanding until they detect and define a pattern. Smith (1989) postulated that concepts help individuals classify things into different categories. This classification of information into different categories enables an individual to remember and learn information.

Nelson and Pan (1995) used Hypercard in the elementary classroom to present examples and non-examples to elementary science students. Students were asked to develop hypotheses to define the concept. As students were shown new examples and non-examples, the students were asked to refine their hypotheses until the class had reached a consensus about the concept. The hypotheses were further checked using more examples and non-examples. When students agreed on one hypothesis, they were asked to write a definition of the concept and to provide more examples and non-examples of the concept.

The method used by Nelson and Pan (1995) could be adapted for use during Web-based instruction. Students could be asked to participate in small groups, which could be communicated in "real-time" by using chat rooms, asynchronous by using e-mail, listservs

Figure 2. Simplified Graphics for Complex Concept Presentation

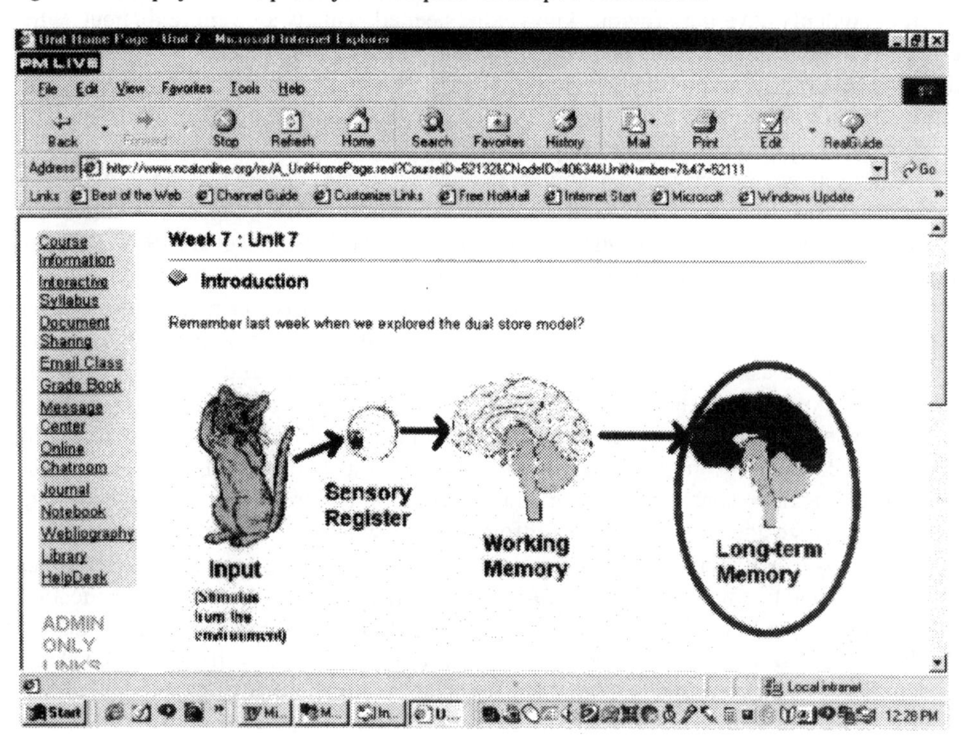

or threaded discussions. Regardless of the communication methods, students would be given a list of examples and non-examples to refer to when discussing hypotheses. If students were working in a synchronous manner, they would contact the instructor and give the hypothesis that the group had discussed. The instructor would then provide the next list of examples and non-examples. Once all groups had a hypothesis they were satisfied with, they would join in an entire class on-line chat and discuss the similarities and differences between their hypotheses and refine them. Each group would then break into small chat rooms to create a definition for the concept and the concept would be posted. Each group would also be asked to provide further examples and non-examples for the whole class. If the activity is done asynchronously, students could use e-mail for small groups and post their hypotheses on a listserv, or in a threaded discussion. After all groups have submitted a hypothesis, the instructor would place the new examples and non-examples on the Listserv and the process would continue until each group had provided a definition and a list of examples and non-examples.

The activation of previous knowledge is another way in which cognitive theory can be applied to Web-based instruction. Ausubel and Robinson (1969) state that new material should be related to the individual's existing cognitive structures. The individual's existing schema or pattern of the information is built from previous experiences. By activating students' previous knowledge, new information is more meaningful and easier to learn. Often in the classroom, instructors ask questions to activate previous student knowledge. In addition to student answers, instructors watch student body language in order to determine whether students have the previous knowledge needed. This is a bit more difficult when using Web-based instruction. Instructors cannot perceive the students' body language; therefore, alternatives need to be explored. Since we cannot see body language during on-line instruction, when we ask questions to activate prior student knowledge, more emphasis must be placed on student responses.

Connected to the activation of student knowledge is the concept that individuals learn better if new information is meaningful to them. Several theorists suggest that individuals learn more effectively when the information is meaningful (Ausubel et al., 1978; Bower & Clapper, 1989; Mayer, 1996). Individuals are able to store and retrieve information better, if that information has meaning for them. Indeed, this cognitive principle goes back to experiments by Kohler (1947) and Koffka (1935). Both theorists cite experiments in which individuals were asked to memorize lists of nonsense syllables and lists of meaningful words. The experiments showed that individuals memorized meaningful lists more easily than the nonsense lists. Ausubel and Robinson (1969) believe that rote memorization prevents individuals from forming wholes that can help them remember the material. Therefore, it is important to make sure new information is introduced in a way that helps students organize and connect the new information to what they already know.

One way to activate students' previous knowledge is to create a series of questions and create a program that will evaluate the variety of possible student answers. These questions should be designed to allow students to type in brief answers. Possible student answers would be checked. While not all student answers could be accounted for, many could. Those student answers not accounted for would be branched to another question for those students to answer and be checked to see if previous knowledge has been activated. While this is not the best method, careful planning can help it be successful.

Another way to activate previous student knowledge during Web-based instruction is to place a question on a Listserv and have students respond. This will enable the instructor to evaluate the previous knowledge of the students. In order for this to be successful, each student would need to be required to respond to the question. Using chat rooms would be more difficult because not all students in a class size group would be able to respond.

Another method that has been used in the classroom to activate previous student knowledge and help students to organize information in a meaningful way is the advance organizer (Ausubel et al., 1978). The advance organizer provides students with an overview of a new topic. This can include connections to previously learned material. Sometimes, new information is not clearly organized and students have difficulty when they try to organize the information (Ausubel et al., 1978; Zook, 1991). Therefore, the use of advance organizers can be used, both to activate prior student knowledge and to help students organize new information. For Web-based instruction an advance organizer could be made using a sound file or as text on the screen. Normally, an advance organizer would not be used when questions are used to activate prior knowledge or when graphic organizers, webs, or outlines are used to introduce new material.

Web-based instruction is rich in its ability to use motivational graphics and animation, and sound. According to Gagne's Instructional Events (1985), gaining students' attention is an important part of any instructional sequence. Graphics, animation, and sound can help us to do so. Under normal circumstances, the ideal is to provide graphics and animation that forward the instruction, but when using them to peak the students' interest latitude is appropriate. Indeed, Rieber (1994) states that graphics can increase both extrinsic and intrinsic motivation in a learning situation. For example, if we were providing instruction about the human heart on the Web, we might begin the instruction with an animation of a beating heart that has a beating sound. Sound can be used to alter the learning environment in small ways. For example, an animated title can carry a whooshing sound to capture attention. Remember, however, that too much use of graphics, animation, or sound to gain attention will become a distraction for the learner.

Guidelines for Cognitive Theory

1. Provide students with elements that help them structure and organize the information they are expected to learn. Starting the on-line lesson with a cognitive map, Web, outline, or list of objectives can do this.
   Example. In the on-line course used as an example within this chapter, the instructor uses a list of objectives each week. The following is from the course:
   Objectives
   Students will:
   1. Compare and contrast classical and operant conditioning.
   2. Define the following terms in relation to classical conditioning: extinction; spontaneous recovery; stimulus generalization; stimulus discrimination; higher-order conditioning; sensory preconditioning
   3. Define the following terms in relation to operant conditioning: reinforces; reinforcement; free operant level; baseline; terminal behavior; extinction; superstitious behavior; shaping; chaining; positive reinforcement; negative reinforcement; punishment stimulus control; stimulus generalization; and stimulus discrimination.
   4. Describe the factors that influence the effectiveness of reinforcement.
   5. Compare and contrast the different schedules of reinforcement.
   6. explain why reinforcement doesn't work.
   7. Apply the principles of classical conditioning theory to the analysis of learning situations.
   8. Apply the principles of operant conditioning theory to the analysis of learning situations.
   9. Analyze learning situations and choose the theoretical basis for explaining the events.

   (Online Learning Theories course – North Carolina A & T State University; Dr. Karen Smith-Gratto)
2. When appropriate use a concept development activity. To facilitate this, place students in small groups and have an appropriate list of examples and non-examples prepared in advance. Decide whether students will do the activity synchronously or asynchronously. If students will be completing the activity asynchronously, be sure to set deadlines for each part of the activity.
3. Decide how you will activate your students' prior knowledge.
   a. If you are going to use programmed questions, be sure to have other people help you create a list of possible student answers to each question. Your list of questions should have enough variety to lead to the prior experiences of your students. This will entail a great deal of thought because, generally speaking, in Web-based

instruction you will have less knowledge about your individual students than you would about students you meet with in a traditional classroom.

Example. IN Figure 2, the statement above the graphics required students to recall what they had learned the previous week. This is a simplified example because the instructor knew what was covered in the previous lessons.

b. If you are going to have students use a Listserv or Threaded Discussion to respond to questions, make sure you set deadlines to insure that all students take part before beginning the new instruction.

Example. The following quote is from the on-line Learning Theories class. Notice that the instructions include deadlines.

> **Threaded Discussions (20% of grade)**: You will need to take part in the threaded discussions. During these discussions, you must respond at least twice to the topic at hand. **TAKE RISKS**. While I will monitor the quality of your responses, the grading will be focused on participation and evidence that you are grappling with the concepts under discussion. I don't expect all of your responses to be 'brilliant', but I do expect thoughtful participation. Sometimes you won't understand something under study, I expect you to use the threaded discussion to help you clarify your own understanding. Many times other students have the same question that you have and discussing it will help everyone gain a better understanding.
>
> *(On-line Learning Theories course – North Carolina A & T State University; Dr. Karen Smith-Gratto)*

c. Instead of using questions to activate prior knowledge for every on-line lesson, use advance organizers. Make sure you provide a clear structure for the information and include elements of what students have previously learned so that they can connect the new knowledge to it.

Example. Some of the Introductions to weekly lesson in the Learning Theories course use advance organizers. An example of one follows.

> **Introduction**
>
> The antecedents of modern cognitive theory developed in reaction to behaviorism. As you will recall from the chapters on behavioral theory, the early theorists stated that humans and animals learned in the same way. Early behaviorists also stated that only external behaviors indicated learning. As with everything, there were disagreements. As you will notice Tolman remains within the behavioral theory context but develops some changes within his theory to reflect cognitive elements. Even though Tolman does this he is still considered a behavioral theorist. The earliest theory considered to be wholly cognitive is Gestalt theory. In fact, it is often considered the grandfather of modern cognitive theory. This week we will lay the foundations for a closer look at cognitive theories.
>
> *(On-line Learning Theories course – North Carolina A & T State University; Dr. Karen Smith-Gratto)*

4. Motivational graphics, animation and sounds should be used with discretion when planning a Web page. Where possible use graphics, animations and sounds that are related to the content being taught. It is not necessary to use graphics and animations or sounds with each Web page or lesson.

Example. Figure 2 represents an example of motivational graphics; the graphics present the concept to be learned in a "cute, funny" way that focuses the learner's attention on the concept to be learned.

CONSTRUCTIVIST THEORY

Another theoretical base that we can draw from to design Web-based instruction is Constructivist theory. Constructivist theory has several characteristics that are easily adapted for Web-based activities. Some of these characteristics include: learner construction of meaning; social interaction to help students learn; and student problem-solving in "real world" contexts.

Von Glaserfeld (1989) states that learners construct their own meaning based on their experiences. This is related to schema development as defined by Piaget (1954). Each individual has a unique mental structure which allows the individual to make meaning from their experiences.

We can help students understand their structures and connect their experiences by making the process of connecting what they are learning a conscious one. In other words, a Web-based lesson can include activities that require students to create their own graphic organizers, webs, or outlines. Since students are unique one from the other, they should be allowed to choose the form this activity will take. Some students may create a Web, others an outline. The important point is that students participate in an activity which allows them to create an external structure that reflects their internal conceptualization of the topic. With the authoring programs available for Web design, we can provide students with the on-line tools for using geometric shapes, lines, text, and even color to structure their work. This allows the student both the freedom and the responsibility for organizing their understanding of the content.

Constructivism also supports social interaction during the learning process. While individuals perceive and understand the world in different ways, there are overlaps in understanding which are created through social interaction. Social interaction provides mediated interpretations of experiences and much of what is learned about the world is dependant upon communication among individuals (Vygotsky, 1981). Language is a primary tool for creating and mediating meaning for the individual. In addition, Vygotsky supports the idea that language is key in problem solving. Meanings are mediated and require that individuals interact and exchange ideas so that some commonality of understanding can be achieved for a given concept. Indeed, the social interaction is actually adding to the students' experiences.

In Web-based instruction this can be accomplished through the use of chat rooms, e-mail, and listservs and threaded discussions. Students can be provided with questions and activities that must be completed by groups rather than individuals. The Web actually is an improvement over normal group-based activities because what each student does is published in some way. This means that an instructor can actually see who has taken an active part in the process. Normally, when students in the classroom participate in this type of activity, some skate by without contributing to the group. Within Web group work it becomes obvious which students are not participating and the instructor can address it with the individual. Because this is the case, social interaction in this modality is actually an improvement over class group work. A word of caution: the instructor must monitor the interactions and intervene to make sure that the students are accomplishing a suitable depth of discussion and exploration. Left to their own devices, students will often touch the surface of a subject and avoid "thinking" too deeply. Just as instructors use Socratic questioning in a classroom, instructors need to do so online.

In order for meaningful learning to occur, students must address "real-world" problems (Duffy & Jonassen, 1991). "Real-world" problems have many contexts and are more easily addressed if multiple viewpoints are explored. When students deal with authentic problems, it helps them to construct highly developed schema that contributes to an increased ability to solve problems (Bednar et al., 1992; Brown et al., 1989). Students can gain experience and address problems in different ways during Web-based instruction. Web-based instruction, if used properly, lends itself very well to involving students in "real world" problem-solving.

Web-based instruction can enhance student experience by including the use of simulations. There are two types of simulations that can be useful in building concepts and broadening experiences. The two types work in different ways.

One type of simulation allows students to observe an event. The event could involve a variety of things with which students are unfamiliar and, therefore, provide students with experience with the phenomena. This method has been recommended for use with lecture/ computer presentations (Smith-Gratto & Leflore, 1998). For example, a simulation of the process of cell division could show a student how the cell division occurs. In order to make this type of simulation work effectively under constructivist theory, the instructor should use the simulation as an introduction without explaining the phenomena. The Web-based instruction should tell students that they would be observing animation and that they will be expected to explain what they observed. How much information is given up front to the student and what the student is asked to do in relation to the simulation will depend on the simulation used. While this is not directly related to the problem-solving aspect of constructivism, it does address the structuring of knowledge by the student. Indeed, this type of activity could be directly linked to the one in which students use graphic organizers or webs to structure what they are learning. Instead of using expository text, students could create a structure, which shows the links they observed and how the links were connected together as they viewed the simulation.

The other type of simulation more accurately involves students in the process of problem solving. Under constructivist theory, this would involve addressing "real-world" situations. For example, students studying hotel management would participate in the running of a hotel. This would involve students addressing problems that could occur in a hotel in every area of management from staffing to fiscal concerns. Usually, these types of simulations are quite complex and require a high learning curve. When using complex problem-solving simulations make sure the students understand how to work within the simulation. Clear directions and time to learn how to use a simulation are needed.

Another way to involve students in "real-world" problem solving is to assign a choice of problems for students within the content area addressed. Once students choose a problem, the Web offers is a variety of tools for students to use to research their problem. Students can access databases and other kinds of Web sites. In addition to this students can contact experts within a field. Jonnasen (1990) suggests that the use of tools, such as databases, help individuals construct their knowledge in authentic ways. Using these tools students have the opportunity to explore a variety of viewpoints and obtain different kinds of information

Figure 3. Frame Assignment that is a form of Cognitive Mapping.

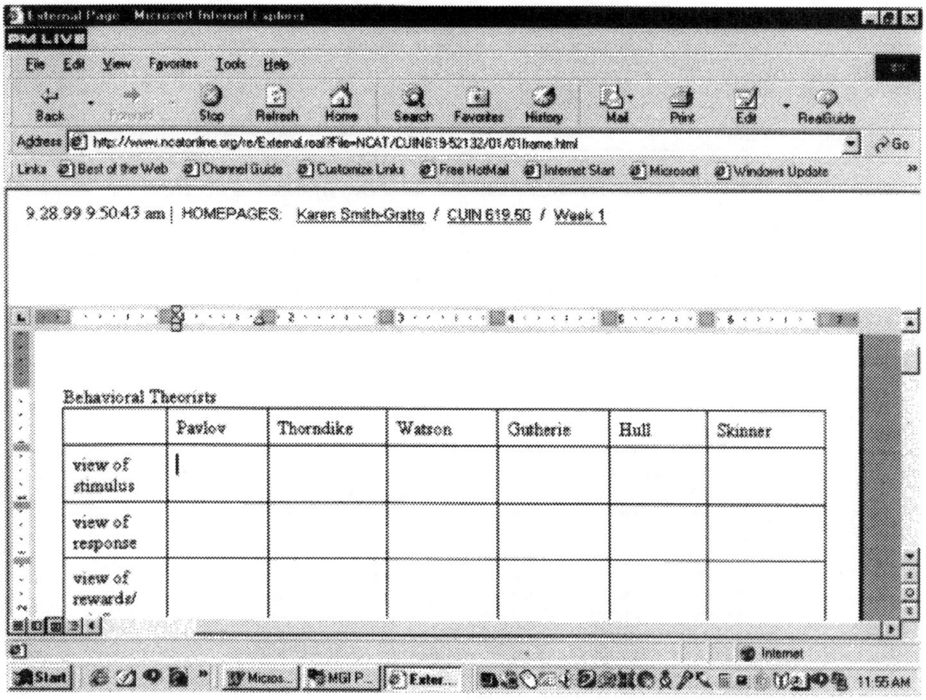

Behavioral Theorists

	Pavlov	Thorndike	Watson	Gutherie	Hull	Skinner
view of stimulus						
view of response						
view of rewards/						

related to their problem. Since students can use chat rooms, e-mail, listservs or threaded discussions to communicate with each other, the social interaction aspect of constructivist theory can be incorporated. Additionally, if students are working on a problem-solving simulation, such as the hotel example given earlier, the use of research tools on the Web could easily be incorporated. When using this approach to authentic problem solving, students will need to be able to use the Web tools available. This might require instruction on how to conduct searches on the Web, how to evaluate information on Web sites, and how to access on-line databases. Students should be encouraged to use additional resources, which may not be found on the World Wide Web.

Guidelines for Constructivist Theory

1. Plan activities that require the learner to construct meaning from the information presented. Have students construct a graphic organizer, Web, or outline. If requiring a graphic organizer or Web, make sure tools for combining text and graphics are available for student use.
   Example. Figure 3 provides an opportunity for students using the frame to produce an explicit example of how they are interpreting and making meaning from the content they are expected to learn.
2. Include activities that allow students to communicate with others. Monitor student

Figure 4. Example of Threaded Discussion (similar to Listserv Assignments)

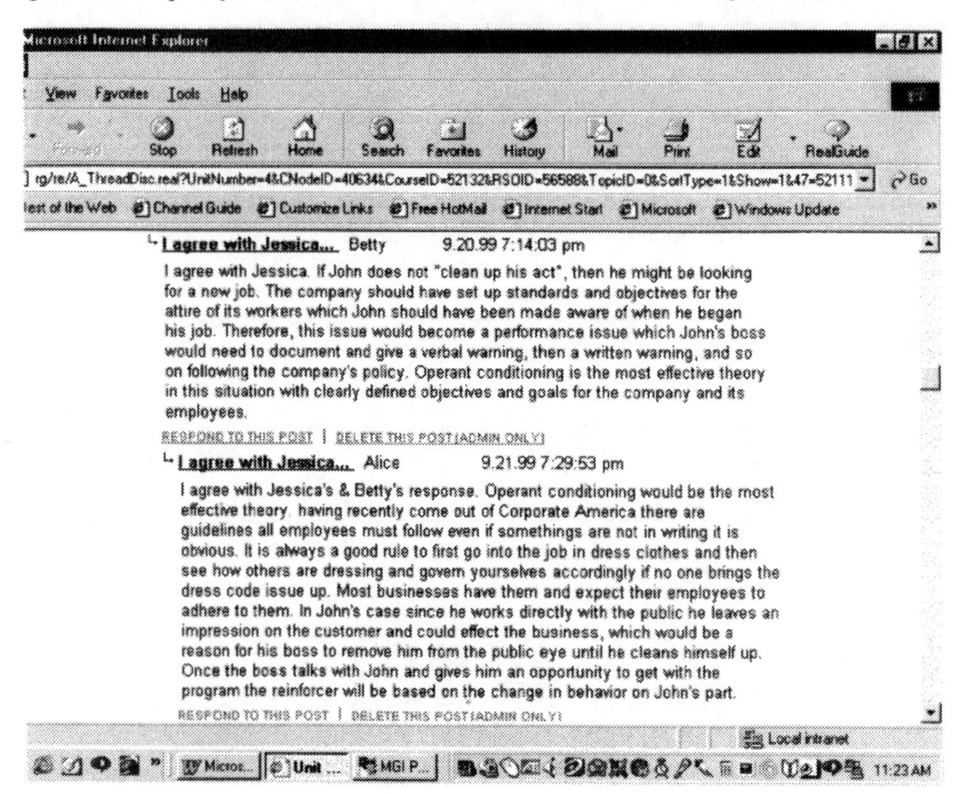

interactions and provide students with guidance in the order to obtain an appropriate depth to the discussion.

a. When using on-line chat capabilities, have students provide summaries periodically or drop in on the chat rooms and monitor the student interactions.
b When having students use e-mail, have them e-mail summaries of their discussions on a regular basis.
c. The easiest way is to have students interact on a listserv or threaded discussion. The ongoing discussion can be easily followed and guidance provided throughout the student exchanges.

Example. Figure 4 is an example of the use of a threaded discussion among students. Note how they expanded upon the discussion of the original discussion presented. This provides an opportunity for students to clarify meaning and understanding and gain greater depth in exploring concepts.

3. Where appropriate provide students with the opportunity to engage in authentic problem-solving activities.
   a. If problem-solving simulations are used, make sure directions for use are clearly understood by the students. Plan to include time for students to learn how to work within the simulation program. Have students provide periodic reports so that they are kept on track. Having students report enables the instructor to provide guidance

when it is needed by the students.

b. When students choose authentic problems within the content area, make sure students know how to use the appropriate on-line tools. Also have students provide a plan of action. This will provide a starting point for monitoring student work. Students should also provide the instructor with periodic reports. The reporting allows the instructor to more readily guide the students when guidance is needed.

Example. In the Learning Theories course, the instructor provides case studies for students to analyze, to discuss, and to solve common classroom/learning problems. Note that the instructor gave specific instructions to the students about the use of on-line tools for problem-solving as a group. In addition, the instructor provided specific items to address in the answers. Since this was an early assignment the students needed scaffolding to approach this type of problem.

Case Study:

You will complete this as a group and forward the completed assignment as an attachment. I suggest that you discuss it in your group and plan your answer. Next create a file as an attachment and send to all members in the group. Refine your written answer as a group and send it to me via e-mail as an attachment.

You must do the following in your answer:

1. State how you would handle the situation.
2. Give the theoretical base for your answer—why you are doing what you are doing in relation to the situation according to the theory base you chose.
3. Use appropriate terms from the theory base - e.g. extinction.
4. Use good writing—Well-constructed paragraphs, correct grammar, spelling, and punctuation.

A teacher is experiencing difficulty with a student. The student has never handed in a homework assignment. The student's parents have been notified and they say they are too busy to monitor their child's homework. What would you suggest that the teacher do to get this child to do homework?

(Online Learning Theories course – North Carolina A & T State University; Dr. Karen Smith-Gratto)

CONCLUSION

The World Wide Web offers many opportunities for providing instruction, but as with other delivery methods, we must consider the best forms for the instruction. Learning theory should be applied to create on-line learning environments that provide effective and efficient instruction. Very often we have let the technology drive the way instruction is presented. It is time to carefully consider how we construct on-line learning. While we have used computers to provide instruction in the past, very often the use of multimedia techniques and hypermedia access have taken precedence over sound instructional planning.

It has been suggested in this chapter that activities for on-line learning can be derived from learning theory. The guidelines provided here should be used with careful thought. When planning on-line instruction, it is important to know what the instructional goals and objectives are. Once it has been established what is expected of the students, the appropriate on-line activities can be designed. While the three general theoretical areas presented here have aspects in common, each can provide guidance. In this chapter, cognitive theory and constructivist theory have been used primarily to design learner activities, and Gestalt theory has been primarily used to address screen design issues.

REFERENCES

Ausubel, D. P., Novak, J. D., & Hanesian, H. (1978). *Educational psychology: A cognitive view*. (2nd ed.) New York: Holt, Rinehart & Winston.

Ausubel, D. P., & Robinson, F. G. (1969). *School learning: An introduction to educational psychology*. New York: Holt, Rinehart and Winston, Inc.

Bednar, A. K., Cunningham, D., Duffy, T. M., & Perry, J. D. (1992). Theory into practice: How do we link?. In Duffy, T. M., & Jonassen, D. H. (Eds.), *Constructivism and the technology of instruction*. Hillsdale, NJ: Lawrence Erlbaum.

Bower, G. H., & Clapper, J. P. (1989). Experimental methods and cognitive science. In M. I. Posner (Ed.), *Foundations of cognitive science*. (pp. 245-300). Cambridge, MA: The MIT Pres.

Bower, G. H., & Hilgard, E. R. (1981). *Theories of Learning*. Englewood Cliffs, NJ: Prentice-Hall, Inc.

Brown, J. S., Collins, A. & Duguid, P. (1989). Situated cognition and the culture of learning. *Educational Researcher, 18*, 32-42.

Bruner, J. S., Goodnow,J. J., & Austin, G. A. (1956). *A Study of Thinking*. (3rd ed.). New York: John Wiley & Sons.

Duffy, T. M., & Jonassen, D. H. (1991). Constructivism: New implications for technology? *Educational Technology, 31*(5), 7-12.

Hodges, D. L. (1986, October). *How the use of cognitive psychology findings can raise the productivity of computer-assisted instruction*. Paper presented at the 1986 Conference of the League for Innovation in the Community College, Miami, FL.

Jonassen, D. H. (1990). Thinking technology: Toward a constructivist view of instructional design. *Educational Technology, 30* (9), 32 - 34.

Koffka, K. (1935). *Principles of Gestalt psychology*. (5th ed.) London: Foutedge & Kegan Paul Ltd.

Kohler, W. (1947). *Gestalt psychology: An introduction to new concepts in modern psychology*. New York: Liveright Publishing Corporation.

Mayer, R. E. (1996). Learning strategies for making sense out of expository text: The SOI model for guiding three cognitive processes in knowledge construction. *Educational Psychology Review, 8*, 357-371.

Nelson, M., & Pan, A. C. (1995). Concept attainment model: A viable component for elementary science curriculum. *Technology and Teacher Education Annual, 1995*. Charlottesville, VA: Association for the Advancement of Computing in Education.

Piaget, J. (1954). *The construction of reality in the child*. New York: Basic Books.

Reiber, L. P. (1994). *Computers, graphics, & learning*. Madison, WI: Brown & Benchmark.

Smith, E. E. (1989). Concepts and induction. In M. I. Posner (ed), *Foundations of cognitive science*. (pp. 501-526). Cambridge, MA: The MIT Press.

Smith-Gratto, K. (1999). *Learning Theories*. On-line course from North Carolina Agricultural and Technical State University, Greensboro, NC. *Note: Cannot be accessed without login and password.

Smith-Gratto, K., & Fisher, M. (1998-99). Gestalt theory: A foundation for instructional screen design. *Journal of Instructional Technology Systems, 27.*(4),361-371

Smith-Gratto, K., & Leflore, D. (1998, November). *Using learning theory to improve computer presentations.* Paper presented at the 1998 Computers on Campus Conference, Myrtle Beach, SC.

Taba, H. (1962). *Curriculum development: Theory and practice.* New York: Harcourt, Brace & World, Inc.

Von Glaserfeld, E. (1989). Cognition, construction of knowledge, and teaching. *Synthese, 80*, 121-140.

Vygotsky, L. S. (1981). The genesis of higher mental functions. In J. V. Wertsch (Ed.), *The concept of activity in Soviet psychology.* Armonk, NY: Sharpe.

Zook, K. B. (1991). Effects of analogical processes on learning and misrepresentation. *Educational Psychology Review, 3*, 41-72.

Chapter VII

ID and HCI: A Marriage of Necessity

Jared Danielson, Barbara Lockee and John Burton
Virginia Tech, USA

Several years ago a professor at a large research institution prepared to deliver her first on-line course. The activities had been planned meticulously, the software to be used had been tested, and hopes were high. One week after the course started, the professor in frustration pulled students back into the classroom and delivered the course in its traditional format. The problem? The students were unable to figure out how to use the software.

This story highlights the need to design Web-based learning experiences that are user-friendly, as well as instructionally sound. While most instructional developers acknowledge the importance of the systematic design process for effective mediated learning experiences, many fail to recognize the necessity to include interface design as a component of that process. Many instructional designers believe that if one can design instruction, one can design anything, including intuitive and easy-to-use Web-based programming. The field of human-computer interaction has evolved over the past 20 years as a discipline of its own, with principles and practices based on empirical research. Though similar to the process of instructional design, interface design is a separate endeavor with its own procedures and outcomes, and is essential to producing good instructional software. In this chapter we will describe how interface design can be integrated into the traditional instructional design process, thereby helping to ensure the overall effectiveness of the final product.

BACKGROUND

In general, design is a complex problem-solving activity that is often treated as a fairly straightforward, structured, or well-defined endeavor but is, in fact, very much an unstructured, "fuzzy, " or ill-defined one (Reitman,1965). As such, design problems typically have rather unclear starting conditions and a rather large (if not infinite) number of "moves" from the unclear starting state to the equally unclear goal state. Interface design is about solving the problem of humans interacting with computers. Information systems and applications designers want the user to be able to access the systems they design to solve user problems as opposed to working through the interface as a separate set of problems to be solved in order to access the tools or information they are seeking.

Instructional designers are accustomed to seeing the instructional design process as a series of stages that inform each other through feedback loops. Instructional design models (Dick and Carey, 1996; Romiszowski, 1981; Gustafson and Powell, 1991) contribute to this perception. In general, instructional design is seen to have the following components:

Conduct front-end analysis
- Learners
- Instruction
- Context

Construct performance objectives
Develop assessment instruments
Develop instructional strategies
Develop instruction
Conduct formative evaluation of instruction
Revise instruction
Conduct summative evaluation

While the intricacies of instructional design frequently require a great deal of overlapping and repeating of the stages presented above, it is frequently useful to think of these processes in a somewhat linear fashion. The authors submit that at each stage of the instructional design process, there are related interface design procedures. This chapter will follow the instructional design process, suggesting at each step along the way concurrent interface design considerations which, if addressed, will improve the final instructional product. We will draw heavily from Hix and Harton's "Designing User Interfaces" (1993) as we discuss the interface design processes and concepts to be considered. However, there are a number of good texts dedicated to the design of interfaces which might be referred to by the interested reader as well (Beyer and Holtzblatt, 1998; Carroll, 1995; Grudin, 1994; Moran and Carroll, 1996; Wasserman and Shewmake, 1982; Whiteside, Bennett, and Holtzblatt, 1988).

Before diving headlong into our discussion, we also wish to point out that an essential part of the instructional design process involves the selection of media. This chapter ignores that process, assuming that if the reader has chosen to read a chapter on usability and instructional design in a book dedicated to Web-based instruction, this decision has already been made. We also realize that there are instances in which the medium is prescribed long before the problem is presented to the instructional designer, and that in such instances, the media selection process is not ideal from the designer's perspective. Regardless of how the reader has reached the point of Web-based instruction, it is our hope to provide insights to create more user-friendly on-line courses.

INSTRUCTIONAL DESIGN AND INTERFACE DESIGN

The Front-End Analysis

In instructional design, we generally begin with an analysis that considers needs, tasks, learners, instruction and context. At this point, issues specific to the interface must be considered as well. These interface design issues can also be considered in terms of needs, learners, instruction, and context.

Needs Analysis

What must the user be able to do with the finished system? What, in a general sense, will it accomplish? Often, in addition to teaching, instructional software provides course and grade-related information, acts as an administrative communication medium between teacher and students, allows the teacher to track student progress, and more. The possible "non-instructional" needs of the end users are boundless, and will not all be discovered through a traditional analysis of instructional "needs".

Task Analysis

With Web-based instruction, learners will almost always be required to perform non-instructional tasks involving interaction with the computer which were not tasks identified or created by the designer. For example, learners engaged in Web-based instruction always have to perform a variety of tasks related to connecting to the network which are not part of the instruction. Such tasks should be considered as part of the task analysis procedure.

Learner Analysis

In instructional design we are accustomed to analyzing learners in terms of the basic demographics of the learner group, as well as the ability of individual learners to perform prerequisite learning tasks. We must also consider how well learner characteristics, abilities, and/or attitudes match the proposed delivery mechanism. Learners should be analyzed in terms of their ability to perform the tasks identified in the previously described task analysis procedure. Are there specific interface requirements or prescriptions that are learner-based? Are the learners most familiar with a particular computer platform? Are conventions of menus and file systems familiar to them? For example, one course designer recently tested an instructional applet which required use of a specific version of a particular browser to run properly. Anticipating that students would not be able to figure out what browser was required on their own, the designer posted an html "help" file advising students of the browser and platform requirements. What the designer did not foresee, however, was that many students did not know how to tell what browser (much less what browser version) they were currently using. A more detailed learner analysis addressing the students' abilities to perform this non-instructional task could have saved time and resulted in a more useful help page.

Functional Analysis

A functional analysis describes what the system will do (Hix and Hartson, 1993). A functional analysis serves two important purposes from the perspective of the instructional/ interface designer. First, it facilitates communication with the person who will actually be implementing the software. Such interchange is important because it is easy in the design of instructional software to take certain functionality for granted. For example, when assignments are submitted via paper, the teacher has all the information submitted by the student at his or her disposal automatically. However, when instructional work is completed and submitted via the Web, the information collected from the student must be predetermined and specified. Designing and implementing software that does not track any student-related information is a far different (and easier) task than designing and implementing software that allows students to resume a task where they left off, turn in assignments, and compare their final score with all other final scores in the class. Seemingly "small" system requirements that are transparent to the user and assumed by the designer are very significant and time consuming from the perspective of implementation.

Second, a functional analysis clarifies what, in terms of the interface, must be designed. Computer-based instructional systems frequently are expected to do much more than deliver the screens and interactions directly related to the instructional tasks. If, for example, the system will allow users to print a record of what they did at the end of each instructional session, an interface for specifying how the learners will communicate when and what they want printed must be designed. Similarly, if a teacher will use the system to track and note student progress, it cannot be assumed that the teacher "side" of the software will not require the same quality of interface design required by the learner side. The ease of performing these "peripheral" tasks will certainly affect the overall effectiveness and acceptance of the instructional software.

Task/Function Analysis

Hix and Hartson (1993) stress the importance of doing a task/function "allocation" – i.e., determining what tasks will be performed by the system and which tasks will be performed by the learner. In general, it is best to have learners perform essential learning tasks, while leaving as many of the other tasks as possible to the system. For example, if an on-line course requires that daily "journal entries" be submitted electronically by each student, there are a number of ways the related tasks might be delineated. A design which places most of the burden for this transaction on the system might allow the student to type or paste an entry into a field in a browser window and click a "submit" button whereupon the submission would be saved to a database which sorted entries by student, date, and time. A design which places more of the burden on the student and teacher might require the use of e-mail for the submission. A design placing most of the burden on the student might require the student to use an FTP client to copy the submission to a folder on a server. A task/function analysis early in the development process can prevent unnecessarily funneling the learners' limited cognitive resources to irrelevant tasks.

Other Contextual Factors

Many practical considerations affect the interface design. What resources are available for the project? Can the money allocated to the project reasonably be expected to support a sophisticated or cutting-edge design? Can the available bandwidth support the design? Does the design require computing power that goes beyond what most learners' computers will be able to handle? In some cases, a less-than-ideal design might be decided upon in the interest of feasibility based on an analysis of such contextual factors.

THE DESIGN PROCESS

In the overall process of instructional design, the "design process" (where specific decisions about the instruction are made) generally follows the front-end analysis. In Instructional Design this is the point at which performance objectives, assessment instruments, and strategies are generally determined. Related interface design decisions must be made at this point. These procedures are described as follows.

Conceptualizing the Design

As the instructional strategy is being determined, decisions are made as to how the learner will interact with the instructional program. At this point, perhaps more than at any other, the instructional and interface designs become one. In Web-based instruction, the interface is the embodiment of the instructional strategy. Before selecting such strategies, though, it is recommended that course developers refer to some established interface guidelines. Hix and Hartson (1993) dedicate the better part of a very good chapter to reviewing general guidelines. A good instructional interface will only require learners to struggle with remembering or figuring out planned and designed instructional problems. Learner time and effort dedicated to navigating between pages, entering irrelevant text, wading through unnecessary interactions, or waiting for extraneous flashy sounds, images, or animations can reasonably be expected to interfere with learning outcomes. A well-conceived interface design, then, will make everything but performing the learning tasks as transparent as possible.

Interface decisions at this point generally address the order in which information will be presented, how the screen will be laid out, what colors schemes will be used, what general navigation schemes will be employed, etc.

Detailed Design

In practice, the detailed design of the interface will emerge from and possibly merge with the conceptualization of the instructional design. The two processes are discussed separately; however, because it is frequently advantageous to make overall, conceptual design decisions before launching into a full-scale, detailed design.

The importance of a detailed interface design lies in the fact that every aspect of a program will be designed at some point. Any decisions not specified in the usability design will probably be made on the fly by whomever implements the software. For this reason, a detailed design, while seeming tedious at first, will save time and likely lead to a better product in the long run. This design will include a detailed graphic of each screen in the software, with accompanying text descriptions of all screen components including buttons, images, menus, graphics, etc. This document should be detailed enough that the person implementing the design does not have to do any guesswork. Anything that matters to the designer should be spelled out precisely. Appearance issues should be clearly specified including the exact content of the text on frames, buttons, and menus; button and menu placement; image size and placement; whether windows will be scrolling or static; and color schemes.

Navigation and other user interaction with Web pages should also be very clear. Specify whether a required mouse click is a single click or a double click. If objects are to be dragged and dropped, specify how they will affect the objects around them when they are moved. Specify text size, color, and special attributes. If the Web-based program can use system defaults with particular aspects of the interface, specify that, too. Sometimes it is possible to save time and space, while still communicating effectively by relying on convention. For example, the designer might specify a "Windows"-type menu titled "File" with "Open" and "Close" menu items, and leave it to the programmer to fill in any details. However, it is better to be too specific than to be not specific enough. For example, one interface designer completed a design that called for the ability to highlight and delete certain objects. The designer assumed that the delete or backspace keys would be used to delete the objects once they were highlighted. When the implemented program was returned for testing, however, it was discovered that the programmer had implemented the design so that the "escape" key deleted the objects. This innocent communication failure resulted in lost time for both the designer and programmer.

User Action Notation (UAN) described by Hix and Hartson (1993, 1997) is one technique for ensuring that the proposed user interaction is thoroughly communicated. This notation specifies exactly what the user does to interact with the interface in painstaking detail. UAN requires some learning and is a little cumbersome in practice – probably too much so for specifying an entire interface. However, it is thorough and unambiguous, and could prove useful for complicated interactions. A basic familiarity with UAN or a similar technique is also likely to provide someone new to interface design with a picture of the kinds of important interface details that might easily be overlooked.

DEVELOPMENT OF OBJECTIVES AND ASSESSMENT INSTRUMENTS

Instructional designers are accustomed to determining objectives and designing evaluation methods and tools for assessing learning outcomes. In Web-based instruction, similar objectives, methods, and tools should be applied to assessing the effectiveness of the interface. In general, the course developer needs some way to decide if the interface is effective independent of learning outcomes. A bad interface design can nullify a tool built on the most sound instructional design principles.

Hix and Hartson (1993) propose the use of usability specifications and accompanying benchmark tasks for guiding evaluation. Creating benchmark tasks and usability specifications is very much like using the "ABCD" (Audience, Behavior, Condition, Degree) method for creating performance objectives in instructional design. Benchmark tasks specify the "B" component, or the behavior that must be performed. These behaviors are a series of tasks meant to represent all possible user interactions with the proposed Web interface. If one were writing benchmark tasks for testing the usability of a word processor, for example, one might have a benchmark task that required users to create a new document and name it "My Letter." Another benchmark task might require the user to indent a paragraph, and another might require printing a document. Clearly, there would be hundreds of benchmark tasks associated with the evaluation of a complex piece of software like a word processor.

If benchmark tasks represent the behavior component of usability evaluation, the usability specifications represent the "degree" component. Hix and Hartson (1993) use a usability specification table to record the usability specifications, as well as the outcomes of the evaluation as seen in the sample table (Table 1).

The usability attribute column in Table 1 refers to the aspect of the performance that

Table 1. Usability Specifications

Usability Attribute	Measuring Instrument	Value To Be Measured	Current Level	Target Level	Observed Results
#1 Initial Performance	"Save a File" per benchmark 1	Length of time taken to successfully complete task	11 SEC	22 SEC	
#2 Number of Errors Observed	"Save a File" per benchmark 2	Number of errors observed while performing the task	N/A	<1 Error	

is to be measured. The measuring instrument usually refers to a benchmark task, though it might also indicate some other instrument such as a questionnaire. Each value to be measured (third column) with its accompanying target level (fifth column) is roughly analogous to a "degree" component of a behavioral objective. The current level indicates how well the task can be accomplished with a competing product (or with the current product if it is being improved). When the evaluation is conducted, one table is used for each participant to record the outcomes of each usability attribute for each benchmark task as specified.

Guidelines

Evaluation of user performance based on usability specifications provides the best overall indicator of interface effectiveness. However, it is worth deciding early on to compare an interface design with existing guidelines. Many norms of "good" and "bad" design have already been determined through costly and time-consuming research, which it would seem unadvisable to replicate unnecessarily on a tight budget and timeline. Hix and Hartson (1993) have a very good summary of such guidelines and references to many more.

THE DEVELOPMENT PROCESS

In computer-based instruction, the instructional and interface designs are implemented together during the development (implementation) process. However, there are several techniques that, if followed during the early stages of development, can make the implementation process quicker, easier, and less expensive.

The Paper Prototype

A paper prototype is a set of screens and menus, built on paper, and designed to support the benchmark tasks described earlier (Hix & Hartson, 1993; 1997). A person designated as the "computer" runs the prototype as the participant in the evaluation performs the benchmark tasks. The participant can use a pencil or paper-based mouse and keyboard to "click" or "double-click" on buttons and menu items, or to enter text into text fields. The process for evaluating the paper prototype is the same as the normal interface evaluation process described in the evaluation section of this chapter, and employs the usability specifications table. Using a paper prototype to discover major usability problems can save hours of coding time.

Rapid Prototyping

Similar to the use of the paper prototype, rapid prototyping involves creating quick temporary screens that are not fully functional, but allow testing of the interface with potential learners. Just as is the case with the paper prototype, rapid prototyping makes it possible to test an interface relatively quickly and inexpensively.

FORMATIVE EVALUATION

Instructional designers are accustomed to performing formative evaluations. Several familiar formative evaluation models (Dick & Carey, 1996; Tessmer, 1993) prescribe a four-part evaluation procedure employing expert reviews, one-to-one evaluations, small group evaluations, and field trials. Revision occurs throughout this entire process. The interface evaluation procedure is a similar one. It can employ the same four parts and can occur at literally the same time as the instructional evaluation while using the same participants. However, the tools and aims of the interface evaluation are slightly different from those used to measure learning outcomes.

The Benchmark Tasks and Usability Specifications

At the point of the formative evaluation, the course developer should have already identified tasks for evaluation (benchmark tasks) and performance goals (usability specifications). To test the interface, participants are observed performing each benchmark task. During this time, each learner's performance as gauged by the usability attributes previously decided upon (such as time taken to complete a certain task and number of mistakes for first-time use) are recorded. Descriptive data should also be recorded, particularly when learners encounter "critical incidents" — moments at which it is difficult or impossible for them to know what to do next. In one-to-one and small group sessions learners can provide immediate feedback concerning what they do and do not like. These sessions can be video or audio taped.

Remember that while learning outcomes are also being measured based on the designated performance objectives, the situation should be set up in such a way that performance due to interface design and performance due to instructional design can be separated. Perhaps the easiest way to accomplish this goal is to give participants trivially easy learning tasks at the initial stages of the interface evaluation. If the learners cannot perform the benchmark tasks with very easy learning tasks (i.e., content for which they already know the "answers"), chances are that the performance problems lie in the interface design. A healthy dialog with participants will also help indicate whether the instructional aspects of the program or the interface of the program are at the heart of the difficulty students are having. Note that there are times when the instructional and interface factors can have a confounding effect on each other. Interactions that are "easy" with easy learning tasks might suddenly seem more complex when more of a learner's attention is being consumed by a difficult learning task. For this reason tests which gradually increase in learning difficulty might provide an optimal evaluation of both instruction and interface.

The Pilot Test

Hix and Hartson (1993) recommend doing a simple pilot test of an evaluation *before* the expert review process to avoid paying experts for information that could have been gleaned more economically without them.

THE REVISION PROCESS

The instructional and interface design processes merge once again during revision, as this is essentially a second (or third or fourth) pass at implementation. There are many methods for weighing the benefits of certain revisions against the costs. Hix and Hartson (1993) provide an intuitive and useful scheme for determining the costs/benefits of implementing changes resulting from the formative evaluation.

SUMMATIVE EVALUATION

The purpose of a summative evaluation, of course, is to determine whether or not a program was effective, for the purposes of decision making. In this sense, it probably matters little to decision-makers whether or not the program succeeded or failed because of instruction or interface. Chances are that to succeed, both will have to be well-designed. However, an evaluation that can point to success or failure factors due to interface design or instructional design can prove very useful for future endeavors.

WHEN INTERFACE DESIGN AND INSTRUCTIONAL GOALS ARE AT ODDS

Recently, when evaluating a Java-based instructional tool designed to help clinical pathology students learn to classify and synthesize clinical laboratory data, the authors ran across a situation in which the instructional and interface designs seemed to be at odds. The program design required students to enter, from memory and spelled correctly, data abnormalities with names like "thrombocytosis" and "hyperaminotransferasemia". One interface design expert on the team immediately called the rest of the team to task contending that requiring text entry is a bad idea in general, and represents a clear violation of human memory limitations guidelines. She suggested that the interface could be made much more usable if it provided students with a pull down menu of possible choices, or, better yet, had the system simply provide the names of the data abnormalities for the students. During usability testing, a variety of participants made the same suggestion. After all, some contended, the purpose of a computer is to make one's job (in this case, homework) easier. While apparently correct from a usability standpoint, the suggested change would have undermined the instructional objectives, which involved (among many other things) the students' ability to produce the data abnormality names from memory. The feature remained in the software. The lesson to be learned is that there are times at which instructional and interface design objectives seem to be at odds. Naturally, our job as instructional designers is to help people learn, and as a result, the software we produce will create cognitively difficult situations. We will put loads on human memory and problem solving. The power of interface design, however, is that it allows us to ensure that the effort involved in using the software we design is planned and productive toward the accomplishment of the learning objectives.

FUTURE TRENDS

The future of interface design for Web-based instruction is as uncertain as the future of the Web itself. Increased bandwidth and system capabilities will permit more "natural" interfaces through such devices as virtual environments with increasingly more fidelity, voice recognition systems that "understand" our questions and directions, etc. These developments may make the work of the instructional designer more like it was before computers and the Web: designing for "familiar" systems of delivery found in classrooms prior to the microcomputer revolution. More likely is that what is "familiar" will become something far different in the future than it is today. In the same way that walking to school may be good exercise but not necessarily the most relevant part of learning science, interface systems based on the reality of today will likely be equally cumbersome.

Almost certain is that interfaces will become more standard across all applications. Short term, standards will continue to be the result of monolithic software giants who enforce their own look and feel across all their applications with a goal toward integrating separate pieces in larger wholes and decreasing user learning curves as a reward for brand loyalty. Smaller developers will have to go along to survive. Long term, in the area of courseware, groups like the Learning Management Alliance have developed common units and "wrappers" such that businesses can buy some training/instruction from one vender, some from another, and have them operate under an instructional management system produced by yet a third company. Initially proposed by NETg and now embraced by a score of major software producers in education and training, the standards define the smallest "chunk" of technology based training (TBT) to be an objective, activity, and assessment. These chunks or learning objects are then "wrapped" with a code that give the code for the object as well as the pre and post requisites, suggested modules, units, etc. Objects can be mixed and matched. Obviously, for notions like this to succeed, not only do objects and wrappers have to be standardized to permit efficient management, interfaces will have to be standardized to prevent the users from having to relearn navigation, tool selection, etc., while moving unit to unit. Such standards will take most, if not all, interface decisions out of the local arena where small units are designed.

CONCLUSION

The strong emphasis on the acknowledgment of interface design in Web-based instruction may lead the readers to believe that they as course developers must become proficient in yet another arena regarding computer-based learning. While the authors have stressed the necessity to integrate human-computer interface principles into on-line courses, we believe an issue of practicality exists. As mentioned earlier in the chapter, the HCI field has its own experts and literature base; it is not necessary for all instructional designers to develop yet another expertise. Simply knowing basic interface design concepts will go far in the creation of effective Web-based instruction and the facilitation of learning in this electronic environment.

REFERENCES

Beyer, H. & Holtzblatt, K. (1998). *Contextual design: Defining customer-centered systems*. San Francisco: Morgan Kaufman.

Carroll, J.M. (1995). *Scenario-based design: envisioning work and technology in system development*. New York: John Wiley and Sons.

Dick, W., & Carey, L. (1996). *The Systematic Design of Instruction*. (Fourth ed.). New York: Harper Collins.

Grudin, J. (1994). Groupware and social dynamics: Eight challenges for developers. *Communications of the ACM*, 37(1), 92-105.

Hix, D., & Hartson, H. R. (1993). *Developing user interfaces: Ensuring usability through product and process*. New York: John Wiley & Sons, Inc.

Hix, D., & Hartson, H. R. (1997). Usability engineering course packet: CS 5714: Fall 1997. Blacksburg, VA: Virginia Tech.

Gustafson, K. L., & Powell, G. C. (1991). *Survey of instructional development models with an annotated ERIC bibliography* (Information Analyses- ERIC Clearinghouse Products (071) — Reference Materials — Bibliographies (131) ED 335 027). Syracuse, NY: Syracuse University.

Moran, T.P. & Carroll, J.M. (1996). *Design rationale: Concepts, methods and techniques*. Mahwah, NJ: Erlbaum.

Romiszowski, A. J. (1981). *Designing instructional systems*. London: Kogan Page.

Smith, P. L., & Ragan, T. J. (1999). *Instructional Design*. (Second ed.). Upper Saddle River, NJ: Merrill/Prentice-Hall

Tessmer, M. (1993). *Planning and conducting formative evaluations:*
Improving the quality of education and training. London: Kogan Page.

Wasserman, A.I. & Shewmake, D.T. (1982). Rapid prototyping of interactive information systems. *ACM Software Engineering Notes, 7*, 171-180.

Whiteside, J., Bennett, J., & Holtzblatt, K. (1988). Usability engineering: Our experience and evolution. In M. Helander (Ed.), *Handbook of Human-Computer Interaction*. Amsterdam: North Holland.

Chapter VIII

Preparing Tomorrow's Teachers to Use Web-Based Education

Deborah L. Lowther, Marshall G. Jones and Robert T. Plants
University of Memphis, USA

The potential impact of the World Wide Web (WWW) on our educational system is limitless. However, if our teachers do not possess the appropriate knowledge and skills to use the Web, the impact could be less than positive. It is evident, then, that our teachers need to be prepared to effectively use these powerful on-line resources to prepare our children to thrive in a digital society. The purpose of this chapter is to discuss the impact of Web-based education on teacher education programs by addressing the following questions:

- How is the World Wide Web impacting education?
- Are teacher education programs meeting the challenge of producing certified teachers who are capable of integrating meaningful use of technology into K-12 classrooms?
- What is expected of teacher education programs in regards to technology and Web-based education?
- What knowledge and skills do preservice teachers need to effectively use Web-based education?
- What instructional approaches should be used to prepare preservice teachers to use Web-based education?

BACKGROUND

How is the World Wide Web impacting education?

The World Wide Web (WWW) may be the most important development in educational technology in our lifetimes. It represents an enormous increase in communications bandwidth over anything we have seen in the past. Increases in communications bandwidth often provide for dramatic changes in civilization (Ferren, 1996). The link between the creation of the printing press and the Renaissance in western Europe is one strong example of this. Ferren holds that the Web, or more generally the Internet, is the most recent significant increase in communications bandwidth. He suggests that society as we know it will soon become society as we have only begun to imagine it. But the future is not yet here. The current rush to conduct education and training on the Web is at best ill-advised and at worst could create a backlash of the disillusioned masses when the Web in its current state fails to deliver the magic educational bullet everyone expects (Harmon & Jones, in press).

The Web will be incredibly valuable for education in the future. It can also be valuable today if used appropriately. Perhaps more so than any new technology, the WWW has become an integral part of our society. Barnard (1997) states that the extensive development of the world's telecommunications infrastructure has put powerful tools into the hands of educators. This is only true if the educators know how to use and to take full advantage of the vast potential of the Web in education (Duchastel, 1997). We are suggesting here that in order for teachers to take advantage of the Web today, and to get in on the ground floor for future use in education, they must be prepared, and be prepared properly. Access to the Internet is essential, yet pointless without preparation. Teacher education programs must move today to prepare teachers to use the WWW effectively in the classroom. But the WWW, while a powerful technology, is still a technology, and teacher education programs do not have a strong history of preparing teachers to use technology in the classroom.

ISSUES AND PROBLEMS

Are Teacher Education Programs meeting the challenge of producing certified teachers who are capable of integrating meaningful use of technology into K-12 classrooms?

A 1999 national survey completed by 416 teacher education institutions addressed the above question of whether or not new teachers will be prepared to teach in a digital age (Moursund & Bielefeldt, 1999). The survey investigated coursework in instructional technology, faculty ability and use of technology, facilities, field experiences, and the skills of graduates. The results indicated that, in general, most institutions had adequate access to technology, although many classrooms were not equipped for digital presentations or Internet usage. Most institutions also reported that their teacher education programs (TEP) required students to complete a stand-alone computer class, but that technology was not consistently integrated into other courses or field experiences. Specifically, the results indicated that although 75% of the field experience classrooms had access to technology, less than half of the student teachers were required to integrate technology into their practice lessons, and less than half of the cooperating teachers were able to model the use of computers. These results are consistent with a 1996 review of literature on technology use in teacher education programs which revealed that most programs offer coursework in instructional technology, but it is infrequently tied to field experiences, curriculum, or student teaching (Wilis & Mehlinger, 1996).

Since the data from the previously mentioned studies indicate that effective use of technology is not modeled by faculty throughout the TEP, two concerns are raised. The first concern is related to data from the Moursund and Bielefeldt (1999) study which indicated that the ability of preservice teachers to integrate technology into their future classrooms is correlated with whether or not technology was integrated into coursework other than the computer literacy class. The second concern relates to the work of Barron and Goldman (1994) which suggests that if preservice teachers are expected to integrate the use of technology into their instruction when they enter the classroom, it is important that TEP faculty model its appropriate use because teachers tend to teach as they were taught. Therefore, if the goal of TEPs is to graduate students who can successfully integrate technology into the curriculum, it is critical that TEP students experience the use of technology not only in the basic computer course but throughout the entire program.

When TEPs were examined in relation to Web-based education, results also indicate that students are not receiving adequate preparation to effectively use this resource when they become teachers. In 1997, the American Association of Colleges of Teacher Education (AACTE) surveyed its member institutions about the use of technology and discovered that faculty in teacher education programs do not typically utilize the Web as a resource for students in their classes (Persichitte, Tharp, & Cafferella, 1997). Along the same lines, the National Council for Accreditation of Teacher Education (NCATE) formed a task force to investigate the use of technology in teacher education programs and found that technology had little impact on the teaching practices of faculty. As a result, one of the task force recommendations was that TEPs should place a stronger emphasis on the use of telecommunications or Web technologies, particularly as a means to disseminate exemplary practices of technology use between preservice and practicing teachers (National Council for Accreditation of Teacher Education, 1997). A similar recommendation was given in the Moursund and Bielefeldt (1999) report, indicating that it would be beneficial for preservice teachers to use the Web as a means of collaborating with technology mentors. Again, these studies suggest that our future teachers do not seem to be receiving the types of experiences necessary to fully utilize opportunities offered through Web-based education. If our TEP faculty do not model effective use of Web-based education, how can our new teachers learn to competently use the Web in their K-12 classrooms to assure that our students will be productive in this digital society?

What is expected of teacher education programs in regards to technology and Web-based education?

The opening section of this chapter demonstrates the pervasiveness of the World Wide Web and its impact on our society. Therefore, it is only natural to assume that our K-12 schools should prepare students to use the Internet in an effective manner. In an effort to accomplish this goal, the International Society for Technology in Education (ISTE) along with NCATE and several other educational organizations developed a series of technology standards. Two of the standards are of particular interest for this chapter: The National Educational Technology Standards (NETS) for K-12 Students and the Foundations in Technology for All Teachers: Foundation Standards.

The NETS is comprised of six categories of technology foundation standards for K-12 students: basic operations and concepts; social, ethical, and human issues; technology productivity tools; technology communication tools; technology research tools; and technology problem-solving and decision-making tools (ISTE, 1998). Included with the standards are suggestions for how and when to integrate the standards into the K-12 curriculum, and performance indicators that require students to go beyond just knowing about technology to being able to use it in realistic contexts (Thomas & Knezek, 1999). A goal statement included on the opening page of the *National Educational Technology Standards for Students* summarizes the challenge that faces our teachers:

> Our educational system *must* produce technology capable kids. To live, learn, and work successfully in an increasingly complex and information-rich society, students must use technology effectively. Within a sound educational setting, technology can enable students to become:
> - capable information technology users
> - information seekers, analyzers, and evaluators
> - problem-solvers and decision-makers
> - creative and effective users of productivity tools
> - communicators, collaborators, publishers, and producers
> - informed responsible, and contributing citizens

How can we expect our K-12 students to meet the NETS when our K-12 teachers cannot, themselves, meet these standards? It is for this reason that the ISTE Recommended Foundation in Technology for All Teachers: Foundation Standards have been generated. These standards indicate that teachers must first have a general understanding and capability with technology, that they should use technology to enhance both their professional and personal life, and that they should be able to effectively integrate technology into their curriculum. Specific details of these three areas are given below.

> *Basic computer/technology operations and concepts*—[Teacher] Candidates will use computer systems to run software; to access, generate and manipulate data; and to publish results. They will also evaluate performance of hardware and software components of computer systems and apply basic troubleshooting strategies as needed.
>
> *Personal and professional use of technology*—[Teacher] Candidates will apply tools for enhancing their own professional growth and productivity. They will use technology in communicating, collaborating, and conducting research, and solving problems. In addition, they will plan and participate in activities that encourage lifelong learning and will promote equitable, ethical, and legal use of computer/technology resources.
>
> *Applications of technology in instruction*—[Teacher] Candidates will apply computers and related technologies to support instruction in their grade level and subject areas. They must plan and deliver instructional units that integrate a variety of software, applications, and learning tools. Lessons developed must reflect effective grouping and assessment strategies for diverse populations (ISTE, 1999).

An examination of the NETS and Foundation Standards reveals that the Web is an integral component in almost every standard. Therefore, it is critical that today's teacher education programs be modified to ensure that graduating students possess the essential knowledge, skills, and understanding needed to effectively use Web-based education in a setting that fosters growth and learning.

SOLUTIONS AND RECOMMENDATIONS

What knowledge and skills do preservice teachers need to effectively use Web-based education?

As can be seen in the technology standards, today's teachers must not only know how to use computers, but they must also know how and when to effectively integrate them into their curriculum. This section briefly highlights four areas related to what teachers need to know and be able to do to integrate Web-based education into a K-12 curriculum. The section begins with a description of the different levels of Web-based education. This is followed by a discussion of information literacy and technical skills needed for an educator to take advantage of the World Wide Web. Both of these areas also include a chart which lists specific skills and a rationale for why the skill is needed. The section ends by emphasizing that teachers need to achieve a level of technological competence which enables them to understand how and be able to meaningfully integrate Web-based education into their teaching practices.

FIVE LEVELS OF WEB USE

When faced with either the prospect or requirement of using the Web in education, many people assume that they are being asked to create an on-line environment that will be a stand alone, self-sustaining educational product. While this may be the goal of some environments, it need not be the goal of all. Harmon and Jones (in press) suggest five levels of use of the Web common in schools, colleges, and corporations. These levels represent a continuum from basic occasional use to advanced continual use. We feel that these levels go a long way towards helping teachers understand how the Web might be used in the classroom. Each level provides for particular uses and classifications of interaction between the students and teachers, and between the humans and the technology. Table one defines and summarizes each of the levels.

The use of any of these levels will require particular skill sets on the part of the teacher and the student. We are not advocating that everyone be at Level 5. In point of fact, Level 5 may not be appropriate for many teacher education programs, and we would certainly question the wisdom of putting a traditional K-12 class completely on-line. On the other hand, we do not think people should be staying at Level 0 either. Somewhere in the middle is where the future of the Web in the K-12 classroom lies. In order to work in these areas, skills are needed. It is not necessary that one become a Web master to use the Web in the classroom, but it is necessary that one understands the need for a particular set of skills. In an attempt to reach technological competence (Lowther, Bassoppo-Moyo, & Morrison, 1997), educators and students need to concentrate on developing both information literacy skills and technology skills.

INFORMATION LITERACY AND RESEARCH SKILLS

One of the most common ways to use the Web in the classroom is as a research tool. Students are given topics to study, some guidelines for the finished product, and then sent on to the Internet to do the research. Much time has been spent teaching teachers library skills, and much time is spent by teachers passing these skills on to their students. Information literacy is similar to library skills. It refers to the set of skills used to mine the vast wealth of information on the Internet. While many refer to the WWW as the "information superhighway," it can also be seen as the information junk pile.

There is no inherent organization to the Internet. While domain names can tell you some things, i.e. that ".com" is a Web site on the commercial side of the Internet, or that ".edu" is on the educational side of the Internet, the Internet does not have a classification scheme. Search engines may help you find information, but many people need help in making the search engine work. Finding information is only the beginning. When we find it, then we have to decide whether or not to use it. Even the name of the site can be deceiving to a user. Frequent Internet users have had the experience of a domain name not reflecting, or in some cases intentionally masking, the content of the site.

Good information exists—so does bad information, and information that is inflammatory, insulting, degrading, and in some cases, just plain wrong. The Internet does not have a regulatory body. There is not, at the basic level, someone who will tell you that you can or cannot put up a Web page. Web sites such as the Drudge Report (http://www.durdgereport.com) can publish whatever they please. In some cases the information may be true. In others it is not. It is the responsibility of the user to make good decisions on what to do with the information that is found. We need to become good consumers of information. We need to know where to shop for it, and how to decide if the information is worth using. Table 2 suggests information literacy skills that teachers will need and a rationale for using them.

TECHNOLOGY SKILLS

Teachers need to develop technical skills to enable them to use the Web effectively. There is a core set of skills that people need to be able to use the Web in education. Simply having access to the Web is not enough. A teacher needs the skills to manage the Web. For every level suggested by Harmon and Jones (in press), a teacher would need basic Hyper Text Markup Language (HTML) skills to create information. Building Web pages using HTML is not particularly difficult. While we do recommend that people be able to read and understand HTML, we don't suggest that all pages be created by writing the codes by hand.

HTML is a set of commands that provide basic formatting to the text. The simplest example would be creating a bold word. In a word processor, to create a bold word, you simply type the word, click on the B in the menu, and the word is bold. There are HTML editors, programs that generate HTML code for you, that will simulate this familiar environment. However, what the HTML editor does to the word is place the correct codes before and after the word. So if you wanted to have the word"dog" displayed in bold, the word would look like this in HTML: <B> dog <\B>. Being able to write the codes is not as important as being able to understand what they mean. The technical skills in creating Web pages are not that significant, but understanding how the pages work is very important.

These skills need to be taught instead of hard-core HTML programming. Table 3 presents a list of skills needed, and the rationale for teaching them.

TECHNOLOGICAL COMPETENCE

As described in the sections above, it is essential that preservice teachers understand the five different levels of Web use and possess the information literacy and technology skills needed to integrate Web-based education into their classes. However, the information and skills alone are not enough to achieve effective and meaningful integration, because the preservice teachers must go beyond basic computer literacy to achieve a level of technological competence (Lowther, Bassoppo-Moyo, & Morrison, 1997).

One critical component of technological competence is for teachers to have an understanding of the relationship between basic computer functions and student learning. This understanding assists teachers in planning appropriate student use of computers. To do this, the teacher needs to be familiar with specific computer functions - as they relate to

Table 1. Levels of WWW use in education. (From Harmon and Jones, in press).

Level of Web Use	Description
Level 0 No Web Use	The default level. Implies no Web use at all.
Level 1 Informational	Providing relatively stable information to the student typically consisting of instructor placed items such as the syllabus, course schedules, and contact information. This sort of information is easily created by the instructor or an assistant, requires little or no daily maintenance, and takes up minimal space and bandwidth.
Level 2 Supplemental	Provides course content information for the learner. May consist of the instructor placed course notes and other handouts. A typical example would be a PowerPoint presentation saved as an HTML document and placed on the Web for students to review later.
Level 3 Essential	The student cannot be a productive member of the class without regular Web access to the course. At this level the student obtains most, if not all of the written course content information from the Web.
Level 4 Communal	Classes meet both face-to-face and online. Course content may be provided in an on-line environment or in a traditional classroom environment. Ideally, students generate much of the course content themselves.
Level 5 Immersive	All of the course content and course interactions occur online. Does not refer to the more traditional idea of distance learning. Instead, this level should be seen as a sophisticated, constructivistic virtual learning community.

learning. For example, if you examined a Web environment some of the basic functions could be to enter key words to search for information, click on hyperlinked words to access related information (maybe in the form of video/sound clips, animation, or text), manipulate graphics (3-D virtual tours), etc. If you examined email, the functions would include entering and manipulating text, responding to messages, etc. If you examined a database, one basic function would include being able to alphabetically or numerically sort sets of information, and in a like manner, graphically charting data in multiple formats would be a function of spreadsheets. Once the teacher understands how to reduce a computer application down to its basic functions, she can then determine how that function can be used to enhance learning. For example, how can hyperlinks within a Web environment best be used to help students learn. Or, how can the sort feature on a database best be used to help students understand patterns and trends found within a set of information they pulled from the Web?

Too often students learn technology for the sake of learning technology without realizing its potential to solve problems and assist in understanding. For example, if teachers have students randomly place their art projects on the Web, the result is one more, soon to be out-dated site with information that has limited usefulness. But if teachers understand that creating a Web site is not what is important, but rather, that the significance lies in the collaborative student research and planning which underlies the displayed information, *then* student learning would indeed be enhanced from creating a Web presence.

To further explain, technological competence can be described as the understanding and ability to know when and how to create a classroom culture in which students use computers in a productive way that results in positive social and cognitive outcomes. Papert (1998) describes these learning environments as ones "...where there'll be diversity of learning paths, diversity of teaching methods, [and] diversity of subjects to be learned (p. 6)." A further description by Ryba and Anderson (1993) demonstrates the complexity and fluency of effective computer environments:

> Each learning culture is different. The culture emerges in its own way through the interaction of the people and how they use computers. The learning culture is not something that can be defined in textbook terms. It has as much to do with social engagement and sensitivity toward others as it has to do with intellectual and academic development. For this reason, we believe that equal importance should be placed on social and cognitive development within the computer environment (p. 5).

In summary, technologically competent teachers understand that learning *about* technology is not the primary goal, but rather, it is learning how to use technology as a tool to enhance learning and communication that is of primary interest (Duffield, 1997; Kovalchick, 1997; Lowther et al. 1997). This competence enables teachers to draw upon their knowledge of how people learn and interact to create successful and productive educational environments. Table 4 provides a summary of the basic components of technological competence.

Table 2. Information Literacy Skills

Information Literacy Skill and Description	Rationale
History of the Web. *A brief overview of what the Internet is & how it got started.*	The Internet has a unique history. Teachers need to understand, at a non-technical level, the infrastructure of the Internet to help them understand the dynamic nature of the Internet and its unique culture.
Reading an Internet address. *How to identify a server and a particular domain.*	The difference in whether or not an Internet address ends in ".com" or ".gov" can be extreme in many cases. Being able to read an Internet address is one tool to help you understand the reliability of the site. Recognizable domain names, such as **http://cnn.com** or **http://espn.com** represent known entities. Information is likely to have been more painstakingly researched. Additionally, the ability to read an Internet address will help you as you begin to create Web sites. Knowing that the "/" represents a folder will be quite significant in developing Web materials later.
Browser skills. *Understanding how to configure your web browser, and use its functions.*	One concern of having the Internet available to K-12 students is that they will access "inappropriate" content. Every Web browser allows for tracking of users that teachers may use to go back and look at where a student has been. The browser's cache will store images on the hard drive of the computer. Knowing this exists provides the teacher with a method of keeping tabs on what is happening on the computer. Other important tools exist in the browser as well. Knowing and understanding them will help prepare teachers for WWW use in the classroom.
Search Skills. *Finding and using a search engine and being able to broaden or limit a search.*	Internet search engines have made it much easier to search for information. In order to use them effectively, teachers will need to understand and employ Boolean operators to help narrow or broaden a search. Teachers need to understand what an Internet search is and how to help students in starting and finishing a search.
Evaluating Information. *Making value decisions on information.*	This is a difficult skill to teach. While other skills may have demonstrative tasks associated with them, evaluating information doesn't. The ability to distinguish between accurate and inaccurate information is a lifelong skill that many struggle with daily. E-mail boxes are filled with virus hoaxes that many thought to be true, and Pierre Salinger, an experienced journalist, can attest all too well to the fact that information that looks true is not always true. Teachers need to be aware that false information exists, and be prepared to check information carefully before use.
Bookmarking. *Marking interesting web sites so that you can go back to them easily later.*	Bookmarks need to be classified and organized. Many new Internet users find themselves with long lists of Web sites in their bookmark menu. Learning how to organize these and classify them can help you find information later. Teachers can classify bookmarks by curriculum, by grade level, or even by individual student needs.
Downloading. *Moving a file from a server to your computer.*	Technically speaking, downloading off the Web is not hard. If it is possible to download, all you need to do is click on the download link and it will come. However, teachers do need to be aware of the dangers of downloading unknown files, and how to capture images and text that may not be marked as downloadable.

What instructional approaches should be used to prepare preservice teachers to use Web-based education?

When you examine what preservice teachers need to know and be able to do to create learning cultures in which technologies, such as Web-based education, are meaningfully integrated, it is evident that a broad spectrum of competencies are required.

This makes it difficult to prescribe a set of instructional approaches that would be appropriate for all TEPs. We can, however, offer some guidelines and suggestions to consider when structuring TEP coursework that will prepare preservice teachers to use Web-based education and other technologies. Below is a description of the following methods: simulated K-12 technology classrooms; modeling; observing/participating in technology settings; learning technology skills; and reflective practices. A summary of the approaches and guidelines for use are found in Table 5. The final section discusses learning theories.

Simulated K-12 technology classrooms—Lowther and Morrison (1998) advocate that it is critically important for teachers to experience using the computer as a tool in simulated K-12 classrooms. . For example, a social studies methods course could be held in a classroom with five student computers that have access to the Internet. The instructor tells the students that they are to assume the role of ninth grade students who want to determine if there are differences in the numbers and types of natural disasters according to location. The students are divided into five groups, with each group being assigned to a computer, and each group is assigned to work with students from a different county. The task is for the class to build a Web site that compares natural disasters from different countries.

This approach enables teachers to experience, firsthand, how the use of computers can result in deeper processing of information, how collaboration enhances problem-solving situations, how the teacher's use of guidance and questioning results in more student responsibility and greater learning, how to manage students using computers, and how to handle technical difficulties during class time. The knowledge and skills gained can only occur through these types of hands-on experiences.

Modeling As can be seen, an integral component of using simulated K-12 settings is for the TEP faculty to model the behaviors that preservice teachers will be expected to implement in their classes. If simulated classrooms are not available, TEP faculty can model the desired behaviors in regular classrooms. Modeling is an effective approach for demonstrating technology skills, but more importantly it is useful for demonstrating facilitation skills. Tapscott (1999) indicates that as a facilitator, "...the teacher acts as consultant to the teams, facilitates the learning process, and participates as a technical consultant on the new media" (p. 11). Being in a class that has the faculty assume the role of a facilitator is often a new experience for preservice teachers, thus the modeling experience will give students a reference to draw upon when they begin to use facilitation in the future. Modeling is considered to be a critical component of teacher education programs if the programs want to graduate teachers who are prepared to use technology (Barron & Goldman, 1994; Duffield, 1997; Faison, 1996; Moursund & Bielefeldt, 1999).

Observing/participating in technology settings— Since, again, most preservice teachers have not had direct experience with learning in a technology setting, it is helpful for them

Table 3. Technology Skills

Skills and Description	Rationale
Disk management. *The ability to identify and access particular files, folders (directories), and disk drives.*	Disk management is a common, but too often not taught, skill. Linking pages together and placing pictures on Web pages requires skill in placing and finding specific files. Posting Web pages requires skill in accessing servers and copying files back and forth. Teachers need to be able to do these things in order to be independent creators of basic materials. Without these skills, they must rely on technicians to do these things for them.
Graphics creation and editing. *The ability to use capture & modify images. Facility with scanners, digital cameras, & image manipulation software is required.*	Pictures are an integral part of Web pages. Teachers need to be able to move student work from paper to the Web. They do not need to be commercial quality graphic artists, but they do need to be able to save images into a format that can be used on the Web. Basic experience with scanning and digital cameras will provide a strong background for teachers to do more later.
Code Stealing. *The ability to find,* analyze, *and employ existing code.*	Stealing code, or "viewing the source" of a Web page is quite common. People see something they like, then look at how it was done in HTML. If they can analyze how it was done, then they may be able to replicate it. This relates to the need to understand basic HTML.
HTML. *The ability to recognize code and use a Web editor to create Web pages.*	Unless you have a staff of people to create pages to your specifications, most people will need to learn to create pages themselves. It is essential that teachers can create basic pages and post them on the Internet.
Visual Literacy. *The ability to read the message of an image, and to create layouts that are appropriate and visually pleasing.*	Pages that are well designed are easier to look at and easier to use. Teachers need to be able to create pages that are both.

to be exposed to this type of environment. Brown and Henscheid (1997) recommend that students both observe and participate in classrooms where technology is being used. The observation component allows students to learn and grasp new insights in a non-threatening manner because observing does not require the demonstration of technology skills. The participation component is handled as an open invitation to assist or interact with students during a lesson when the preservice teachers feel comfortable and are interested. If this approach is used, care needs to be taken when choosing the teachers that will be observed to ensure that they implement the desired uses of technology.

Learning technology skills —When Ritchie and Baylor (1997) teach their preservice teachers new technology skills, they use a three-part process. They begin by demonstrating the new skill while the students observe, thus allowing them to create mental models of the process to be learned. This is followed by the students using a job aid, with step-by-step procedures, to learn the technology skill. After the students achieve a level of comfort and proficiency, they apply this new skill in an educational context to reinforce how the skill can enhance learning.

Kovalchick (1997) on the other hand, teaches new technology skills within the context of a simulated K-12 lesson. The technology is taught as needed to achieve specific instructional goals. For example, if the desired student outcome is for students to understand the relationship between barometric pressure and weather conditions, they would be taught how to copy weather data from the Web and place it into a spreadsheet. Both of these tasks are quite simple, and only require a minor amount of technological skill. The students do not need to know how to conduct Web searches, how to create book marks, or the history of the Web to complete what is required for this particular learning task. But rather, the students learn specific computer skills that are needed at that time to help them grasp the meaning of a concept. They learn that the Web has up-to-date information that is easily transferable to other applications. They also learn that spreadsheets help to display information in ways that assist in understanding. As mentioned earlier, the goal is not learning technology skills, but rather to learn with the use of technology.

Reflective practices —Kovalchick (1997) suggests that preservice teachers must consider technology from both a user/learner and a user/teacher perspective. She advocates that preservice teachers should compile a technology portfolio to assist with understanding these two roles. The portfolios are used as a method of self-reflection and therefore, self-evaluation, in that the students must reflect on each piece that is to be included. The students address three areas for each piece of work: first they assess the quality of the work, then they describe why it should be included, and finally, the students discuss how they could use the

Table 4. Technological Competence

Component	Description
Goes beyond computer literacy	√ Computer literacy = how to operate a computer √ Technological competence = how to use the computer-as-a-tool to enhance learning
Understand the relationship between basic computer functions and student learning	√ Identifying basic computer functions (sorting, calculating, creating tables, charts, drawing, searching, etc.) √ Matching the function to intended student outcomes √ Using the function to process information and thus enhance learning
Understand when and how to create an environment for effective technology use	√ Determine when it is appropriate to integrate technology √ Determine the appropriate method for integration √ Determine how to create a classroom culture that results in positive social and cognitive outcomes

technology represented to assist student learning. She advocates that student learning is supported through the use of technology portfolios in four ways:

- promoting metacognitive development
- fostering a sense of self-efficacy
- modeling instruction and learning
- guiding critical inquiry and advocacy (p. 33)

Learning theories—It would be quite easy to advocate that our teacher education programs adopt current, successful learning theories and instructional methodologies, such

Table 5. Instructional Approaches

Approach	Guidelines
Simulated K-12 Technology Classrooms	A simulated K-12 technology classroom environment should contain the following: √ Classroom has from 3-6 computers √ Preservice teachers assume role of K-12 students √ Lesson in problem-based √ Lesson involves collaboration √ Students experience rotation between activities √ Students experience using the computer-as-a-tool √ Students experience solving technical problems
Modeling	TEP faculty model the following while in the simulated K-12 setting: √ teacher as facilitator √ management of student rotation between activities √ solving technical problems
Observing/Participating in Technology Settings	Observations √ Non-obtrusive means to experience K-12 students using technology √ Non-threatening because technology skills are not needed to observe Participation √ Occurs in an open/comfortable environment √ Preservice teachers assist when their skills and capability match the need
Learning Technology Skills	Two approaches to choose from: √ Teach technology skills first, then teach how to integrate technology into coursework √ Teach technology skills as needed while using technology-as-a-tool to learn
Reflective Practices	Reflective practices (e.g., a technology portfolio): √ Promote metacognitive development √ Foster a sense of self-efficacy √ Model instruction and learning √ Guide critical inquiry and advocacy

as constructivism (Bruner, 1960, 1966, 1973, 1986, 1990), anchored instruction (CTGV, 1993), cognitive apprenticeship (Brown, Collins, & Duguid, 1989), or multiple intelligences (Gardner, 1993). However, when trying to decide how to discuss the applicable theories, it became evident that this one chapter could not begin to address the needed content. So, we decided to share a couple of examples of how others have addressed the multitude of instructional approaches advocated by these theories.

Since, as was mentioned earlier, preservice teachers need to acquire such a variety of competencies to use technology and Web-based resources in an effective manner, it is obvious that multiple approaches need to be used to accomplish this goal. For example, when you look at the types of information that is needed, you see that teachers have to learn hands-on technical skills and routine procedures such as programming with HTML as well as learning how to facilitate a classroom setting that has student groups creating Web sites. It is because of this diversity that some teacher educators have found it beneficial to incorporate the use of a behaviorist, cognitivist, and constructivist approach when teaching preservice teachers to use technology (Ritchie & Baylor, 1997; Duffield, 1997; Smaldino & Muffoletto, 1997).

Campbell (1999), on the other hand, wanted to identify a common set of conceptual frameworks that could effectively be used with Web-based instructional environments. To do this, she investigated several learning theories and principles and identified six common conceptual frameworks: multiple representations of reality, authentic tasks; real-world, case-based contexts; fostering reflective practices; knowledge construction; and collaborative learning. The key elements of each framework and suggestions for appropriate use are in Table 6.

FUTURE TRENDS

Negroponte (1995) speculates on a digital age where technology becomes so sophisticated that it will know our wants and needs and adapt for us. If this view becomes a reality then a teacher could build profiles for every student, send a "bot" onto the Web and have it retrieve individualized information for every student in the classroom. This is possible.

But while many people speculate on the future of the Web in education, the only real constant we can prepare for is change. Bandwidth and the computing power will increase, and with this increase will come changes in how we access information. Predicting the future does not seem to be as important as being prepared for it. And being prepared for the future of technology means getting started on it today. There truly is no silver bullet that will cure all our problems with education, but it does appear that the future of access to information will be on a global network such as the Internet. It is time that we prepare ourselves today so that we may be ready for the future. Teachers need to be prepared for not only the technical aspects of the Web in education, but for the pedagogical aspects as well. Our recommendation for the future is tied very closely with our view of the future. Both are outlined in this chapter with the following admonition: get started today.

CONCLUSION

If you return to our original questions regarding the impact of the WWW on education, the current status of TEPs, and how to prepare preservice teachers to effectively utilize this

Table 6. Six conceptual frameworks for creating web-based instructional environments.

Framework	Key Elements	Use when...
Multiple representations of reality	• learner experiences reality from another perspective • a reflective component requires re-construction of experience • the learner's values and experiences are legitimated	• goal is development of different perspectives • there is an element of curiosity • too complex • a reflective component is important
Authentic tasks	• anchored instruction • real contexts and tasks	• task can be related to the real world of practice • content domains are affective or psychomotor • cognitive apprenticeship is sought
Real-world, case-based contexts	• cognitive apprenticeship • lateral thinking • story-based	• instruction based on simulating real practice (e.g. flight simulators) • rich repository of expert stories available • access to a coach or facilitator
Fostering Reflective Practices	• access to experts/facilitators • questioning own practice	• the process is important • learners would benefit from conversation with others • instruction is effectively based • learners have access to a facilitator
Knowledge Construction	• situated learning • social interaction is key	• learners are to arrive at a new point of view • problem-solving is a goal • personal knowledge base includes incidental • knowledge on which to build • there are opportunities for dialogue in groups
Collaborative Learning	• negotiation through conversation • interdependency, accountability to peers	• learners will work in small groups • a product is to be created • to teach social/communicative skills • when the content is complex

Source: http://www.atl.ualberta.ca

emerging resource, it is evident that the WWW has the potential to dramatically change K-12 classrooms. However, it is also clear that the impact has not yet been realized and therefore our education system must adopt new approaches to address the issue.

The Moursund and Bielefeldt, (1999) study revealed, most of today's teacher education programs are not meeting the challenge of graduating teachers that meet the current ISTE and NCATE technology standards. We have proposed that this challenge be addressed from several different perspectives. First, both the TEPs and the preservice teachers need to be able to identify at which level they intend to utilize the Web— from no use to immersive use—recognizing that the level of use may vary with different classes and circumstances. Integrating the WWW into a curriculum also requires the attainment of information literacy and research skills, as well as specific technology skills. But, again, as mentioned earlier, the attainment of basic knowledge and skills "about" how to use the WWW is not enough to ensure that teachers can use it to effectively impact learning. Therefore, the goal of TEPs should not be to prepare teachers that are only computer literate, but to prepare teachers that are technologically competent. This will require TEPs to incorporate new instructional approaches which include: engaging preservice teachers in simulated K-12 settings that have the TEP faculty modeling behaviors that will be expected of teachers in future classrooms; times to observe and participate in K-12 technology settings; learning basic computer skills and how to create integration lessons; and reflective practices. The TEP also needs to demonstrate how to incorporate the key conceptual frameworks that support Web-based instructional environments: multiple representations of reality, authentic tasks, real-world contexts, reflective practices, knowledge construction, and collaborative learning.

If Teacher Education Programs meet these challenges and begin to engage preservice teachers in technology-rich environments that model the support and interactions necessary for learning to occur, the teachers will then better be able to create learning cultures in which "...children can use ... technology as a constructive medium to do things that no child could do before, [and] to do things at a complexity that was not previously accessible to children" (Papert, 1998, p. 5).

REFERENCES

Barnard, J. (1997). The world wide Web and higher education: The promise of virtual universities and online libraries. *Educational Technology, 37* (3), 30 -35.

Barron, L. C. & Goldman, E. S. (1994). "Integrating technology with teacher preparation. In Barbara Means (Ed.) *Technology and Education Reform.* San Francisco: Jossey-Bass, pp. 81-110.

Brown, J.S., Collins, A. & Duguid, S. (1989). Situated cognition and the culture of learning. *Educational Researcher, 18*(1), 32-42.

Brown, G. & Henscheid, J. (1997). The toe dip or the big plunge: Providing teachers effective strategies for using technology. *TechTrends, 42*(4), 17-21.

Bruner, J. (1960). *The Process of Education.* Cambridge, MA: Harvard University Press.

Bruner, J. (1966). *Toward a Theory of Instruction.* Cambridge, MA: Harvard University Press.

Bruner, J. (1973). *Going Beyond the Information Given.* New York: Norton.

Bruner, J. (1986). *Actual minds, possible worlds.* Cambridge, MA: Harvard University Press.

Bruner, J. (1990). *Acts of Meaning*. Cambridge, MA: Harvard University Press.

Campbell. K. (1999). *The Web: Design for Active Learning. Academic Technologies for Teaching*. At http://www.atl.ualberta.ca (accessed May, 1999).

Cognition and Technology Group. (1990). Anchored instruction and situated cognition. Educational Researcher,19 (6), 2 - 10.

Cognition and Technology Group at Vanderbilt. (1993). Anchored instruction and situated cognition revisited. *Educational Technology, 333*), 52-70.

Duchastel, P. (1997). A Web-based model for university instruction. *Journal of Educational Technology Systems, 25* (3), 221 -228.

Duffield, J. A. (1997). Trials, Tribulations, and Minor Successes: Integrating technology into a preservice teacher preparation program. *TechTrends, 42*(4), 22-26.

Faison, Christy L. (1996). Modeling instructional technology use in teacher preparation: Why we can't wait. *Educational Technology, 36* (5), 57 - 59.

Ferren, B. (1996). There's no bits like show bits. Plenary session United States Air Force Academy conference "Education in the information age. Colorado Springs: CO.

Gardner, H. (1993). *Multiple intelligences: The theory in practice.* New York, NY: Basic Books.

Harmon, S. W. & Jones, M. G. (1999). The five levels of Web use in education: Factors to consider in planning an online course. *Educational Technology,* 36(6), 28-32.

International Society for Technology in Education (ISTE) (1998). *National Educational Technology Standards for Students.* Eugene, OR: ISTE and Milken Exchange on Education Technology.

International Society for Technology in Education (ISTE) (1999). *ISTE recommended Foundations in Technology for all Teachers.* Located at: http://www.ISTE.org/standards/NCATE/found.html (accessed May, 1999).

Kovalchick, A. (1997). Technology portfolios as instructional strategy: Designing a reflexive approach to preservice technology training. *TechTrends, 42*(4), 31-36.

Lowther, D. L. & Morrison, G. R. (1998). The NTeQ model: A framework for technology integration. *TechTrends, 43*(2), 35-38.

Lowther, D. L., Bassoppo-Moyo, T., & Morrison, G. R. (1997). Moving from Computer Literate to Technological Competent: The Next Educational Reform. *Computers in Human Behavior, 14*(1), 93-109.

Moursund, D. & Bielefeldt, T. (1999). *Will new teachers be prepared to teach in a digital age? A National Survey on Information in Teacher Education.* Santa Monica, CA: Milken Exchange on Education Technology.

National Council for Accreditation of Teacher Education, Task Force on Technology and Teacher Education, (1997). *Technology and the New Professional Teacher: Preparing for the 21st Century Classroom.* Washington, DC: Author. (Also available at http://www.ncate.org/projects/tech/TECH.HTM.)

Negroponte, N. (1995). *Being Digital.* New York: Alfred Knopf Inc.

Papert, S. (June 2, 1998). Child Power: Keys to the New Learning of the Digital Century. Speech given at the 11th Colin Cherry Memorial Lecture on Communication Imperial College: London. Available at http://www.ConnectedFamily.com/frame4/cf0413seymour/recent_essays/cf0413_cherry_2.html (accessed May, 1999).

Persichitte, K. A., Tharp, D. D. & Cafferella, E. P. (1997). The use of Technology by Schools, Colleges, and Departments of Education 1996. Washington, DC: American Association of Colleges of Teacher Education.

Ritchie, D. & Baylor, A. (1997). Teaching with technology: Finding a workable strategy. *TechTrends, 42*(4), 27-30.

Ryba, K. & Anderson, B. (1993). *Learning with computers: Effective teaching strategies.* Eugene, OR: International Society for Technology in Education.

Smaldino, S. & Muffoletto, R. (1997). The educational media experience in teacher education. *TechTrends, 42*(4), 37-40.

Tapscott, D. (1999). Educating the Net Generation. *Educational Leadership, 56*(5), 7-11.

Thomas, L. G. & Knezek, D. G. (1999). National educational technology standards. *Educational Leadership, 56*(5), 27.

Willis, J. W. & Mehlinger, H. D. (1996). Information Technology and Teacher Education in J. Sikula, T. J. Buttery, & E. Guyton, (Eds.) *Handbook of Research on Teacher Education (2nd edition).* New York: Simon & Schuster Macmillan, pp. 978-1029.

Chapter IX

Developing Web Pages as Supplements to Traditional Courses

Cleborne D. Maddux and Rhoda Cummings
University of Nevada, Reno, USA

There has been a recent explosion of interest in distance education. On college and university campuses, this interest owes much of its life and vigor to (a) a belief by university faculty that technology may be able to improve instruction, and (b) the sudden realization by university administrators that distance education is producing large sums of money and has the potential to produce much more.

In higher education, the World Wide Web (WWW) has come to be one of the most popular service delivery vehicles for distance education efforts. At first, most sites were created primarily for courses delivered *entirely* over the Web. More recently, many Web sites are being created by individual instructors as supplements to their more traditionally delivered, on-campus courses.

Currently, many thousands of Web sites are dedicated to higher education courses, and the number of such sites is increasing rapidly. This rapid increase has resulted in publication of many course-related pages that are less than ideal in both pedagogical and technical terms. This problem is especially acute for those pages that are supplementary to traditional courses, since there are seldom support services available for instructors who wish to design, create, and maintain such pages. Consequently, individual instructors are typically "on their own" with regard to planning, producing, and maintaining such pages.

In contrast, institutional technical and pedagogical support is often provided for developers of Web sites intended for use in courses delivered primarily or exclusively by distance education, since such efforts are often assigned to a special unit such as an extension department or a department of continuing education. These units often employ or retain both technicians and subject matter specialists to assist in the development of course-related Web pages. Although this does not guarantee a quality product, some of the more obvious problems faced by individual instructors are sometimes avoided.

The lack of support for instructors of traditional on-campus courses who wish to create and maintain supplementary Web sites is unfortunate because good supplementary pages can be highly beneficial to both professors and students. While useful pages can be developed by professors who have some simple knowledge and skills related to the Web, poor pages are often the result of efforts by neophytes who lack such prerequisites.

The purpose of the present chapter is to present aids and cautions for higher education instructors who wish to produce Web pages as supplements to their courses. It is hoped that the suggestions found here will improve the quality of such pages and their usefulness to both learners and teachers.

BACKGROUND

There is little argument that the demand for distance education is increasing rapidly. In fact, there are estimates that as early as 1997, the global market for technology-based learning was already $6 billion, and that it will increase to at least $26 billion by the year 2005 (Canadian Telework Association, 1998).

McIsaac and Gunawardena (1996) suggest that distance education is currently the fastest growing form of education in the U.S. and across the globe, and is now universally considered an important part of mainstream education. Some experts have suggested that this phenomenon is so important that "We are clearly looking at a paradigm shift in educational practice" (Trilling & Hood, 1999, p. 10). It remains to be seen whether distance education will actually bring about such a paradigm shift. However, there is no denying that it is having profound and diverse effects on faculty in higher education. Dillon and Granger (1998, para. 12) suggest, for example, that "Distance education today has exceeded the mere concerns of time and space and is forcing us to question some of our most basic approaches to teaching and learning."

Universities and colleges around the world are now scrambling to provide on-line courses, many of which make use of the World Wide Web for all or part of course delivery. In addition, professors everywhere are increasingly providing Web sites that supplement traditional undergraduate and graduate courses (LeJeune, 1998; Maddux, Cummings, & Torres-Rivera, 1999).

An indication of the extent of interest in the Web for course-related use is that a recent search using the AltaVista search engine (http://www.altavista.com/) and the search string "syllabus" produced over 1.6 million "hits!" An informal examination of the first 200 of these sites shows that most are related to higher education classes of one type or another. Narrowing the search string to include only those sites that deal with "Web," "university," and "instruction" still resulted in over 177,000 identified Web sites.

Like all course materials, Web-based course materials vary in quality. It almost goes without saying that high-quality educational pages must be carefully planned, developed, and maintained. However, even a casual scanning of available Web sites reveals that such care has not been taken with many existing pages. *In fact, the Web is littered with higher education course-related pages that are technically and/or pedagogically flawed.* Perhaps this should not surprise us, since, as Crossman (1997) has pointed out, the Web, like life itself, is full of "incredible amounts of trivia, misinformation, bad manners, hostility, stupidity and other vagaries of mankind" (p. 22). However, he goes on to suggest that the Web, with all its problems, has the potential to become the most comprehensive communication system ever developed. We agree, and further suggest that it has the potential to become the single most important and most positively transformational influence in modern education.

Before we can realize such a lofty goal, however, it is essential to improve the overall quality of course-related Web sites. A great many of the most common problems with existing sites could have been avoided if the instructors who designed and developed them had been aware of some of the common pitfalls of course-related Web page design and maintenance, and how to avoid such problems.

THE NEED FOR CAREFUL PLANNING

Although it is easy to suggest the need for careful planning before developing course-related Web pages, it is much more difficult to specify exactly how such planning should occur. Planning strategies will vary depending on the personality, cognitive style, and preferences of individual instructors. Of course, the same is true of planning for any creative endeavor and may explain why the planning advice found in textbooks on creative writing is notoriously varied, contradictory, and almost universally ignored by writers. For example, although developing a written outline works well for some authors, others say this strategy has never been of any value to them. Web designers are equally varied in their approach to planning. Some, such as Boling and Frick (1997), specify a detailed design sequence to be carried out and tested on paper before a single electronic file is created. This sequence contains the following steps:

- create holistic, paper prototypes very early in the process;
- test the prototypes on the actual people who will use your site;
- revise your design; and
- then build the site on the computer. (p. 320)

These authors go so far as to enter each bit of planned information on a separate notebook card, punching holes in the cards and placing them in a binder. Links from one card (page) to the next are simulated with lettered tabs, and the test subjects simulate choosing a link by flipping to the card of choice.

Other strategies include formal flowcharting (usually preferred by traditional programmers), the use of storyboards or checklists, sketching out a plan using the author's own idiosyncratic notation, or thinking through the organization in advance without committing anything to paper.

Although research does not provide us with evidence for the superiority of any of the above methods, practical experience suggests that it is a mistake to simply begin to create Web pages without advance planning of some kind. (We also have found that very large Web sites necessitate some form of advance *written* planning.) In general, we suggest that authors of course-related Web sites use whatever organizational planning strategy works best for them, and we offer the following questions to help guide their thinking:

1. *What elements of the class will be placed on the Web?* There are many choices available. Some examples include syllabi, handouts, enrichment material, sample quizzes, solutions to homework problems, chat rooms, tests, and lecture notes. As we talk to students on an informal basis, we have found that the single element students say they want most on the Web is daily lecture notes.
2. *How can students access the Web material if they do not have a home computer with an Internet connection?* Students should be told about available campus labs that will

be open for their use and they should be provided with telephone numbers and a schedule of open hours for each of these.

3. *Is there help available for students who are not familiar with the Internet and the Web?* Students should not be simply "thrown into" Web use with no instruction or orientation. We have found it helpful to develop a series of hands-on modules to familiarize students with the use of E-mail, common Web browsers, search engines and directories, and other basic information technology hardware and software. These modules are distributed on paper at the beginning of classes for which we provide supplementary Web pages, and they are also available on the class Web site. In addition, students should be provided with institutional help desk numbers and told whether or not various campus labs provide proctors, part of whose job description includes helping users.

There are many guides and tutorials on how to plan Web sites and Web pages. Many are available on the Web itself. To find these, interested readers should go to AltaVista at http://www.altavista.com/ and type the following search string (including the quotation marks):

"planning a Web"

A recent AltaVista search (http://www.altavista.com/) using these key words produced over 1100 "hits." We are always reluctant to provide actual URLs to specific Web sites because of the possibility that they will quickly become obsolete. However, a quick AltaVista search will always turn up many good current Web sites. The following are only a few planning sites we have found helpful and that we believe stand a good chance of remaining active for a long period of time:

1. Planning a Web-Based Course—http://www.dl.vt.edu/main2/webbasedcourse/index.htm
2. ECAT: Planning a Web Site—http://ag.arizona.edu/ecat/Web/overview.html
3. Designing a Web Page - http://chen.ncpesp.uri.edu/design/Default.htm
4. In and Out of the Classroom—Planning a Web Site - http://agent.microsoft.com/education/curric/fp98/planning.htm
5. Web Based Course Presentation—http://www.edtech.vt.edu/DL/Main2/webbasedcourse/index.htm
6. Creating a Storyboard—http://psrtec.clmer.csulb.edu/Composer_Tutorial/part2.html
7. Web Page Planning Worksheet—http://firstdesign.com/worksht.htm
8. Planning a Web Site—http://www.slais.ubc.ca/courses/libr559a/902/eriko/html8.htm
9. Creating Good Storyboards for the World Wide Web—http://www.public.iastate.edu/~nielandj/webarticle4.html
10. Hands-On Web Design—http://icl-server.ucsd.edu/~kirsh/Practical/index.html

LEARN AN EDITOR OR HTML?

Web pages must be created in a simple markup language that evolved from the notation system editors placed on manuscripts when they were sent to the printer. This markup language is called *Hypertext Markup Language* (HTML). HTML is very simple and easy to learn, although there are some subtle nuances to master. However, various freeware, shareware, and commercial computer programs have been developed that allow page developers to create Web pages with little or no knowledge of HTML.

This sounds good. After all, why spend the time and exert the effort needed to learn something new if it is not necessary to do so? However, the decision to learn HTML or to use an editor is not as clear-cut as it sounds. *We have found that a mastery of basic HTML is absolutely essential for Web authors, although we also recommend use of a variety of HTML editors for certain specific tasks.*

The problems with editors are related to the way they work. Regardless of the specific program, these editors allow users to somehow specify what they want the page to look like, and editors then convert the user-entered material into HTML. In the course of this conversion or translation process, users will encounter several problems or difficulties. The first is that there is no such thing as an HTML editor that operates on a true "what you see is what you get" (WYSIWYG) basis. In other words, when the editor translates into HTML what the author has entered through some other means, there are invariably differences between the way the original content appeared in the editor and the way it appears when a browser displays it.

Another problem is that editors that are simple and easy to learn quickly are not very powerful and will not permit the user to make use of all of the features available on the Web. Conversely, sophisticated, powerful editors are complicated and are difficult to learn to use well.

These problems present obvious dilemmas. Because there is no such thing as a WYSIWYG editor, users who want to take full advantage of Web features and capabilities must also know HTML so that they can "tweak" the editor-produced code when it does not produce pages that look and perform exactly as intended. Similarly, the most powerful HTML editors are difficult and time-consuming to use. In fact, they are so complex and difficult to learn that it is debatable whether it might be as fast or faster to learn HTML itself.

Our experience has convinced us, and most experts agree, that serious Web authors need to learn HTML (Groves, 1997; Musciano & Kennedy, 1998). After they have mastered both basic and advanced features of the language, they will probably then want to learn to use one of the more sophisticated editors such as MicroSoft's *Front Page*. However, no currently available editor can completely substitute for direct skill in writing HTML. Meyers (1999) addresses this topic and gives the following three reasons for learning HTML rather than depending totally on editors:

1. Editors cannot keep up with rapidly changing HTML standards.
2. All editors have many idiosyncrasies, and complete control over Web pages requires skill with HTML.
3. Some of the most sophisticated and exciting capabilities such as cgi scripts, Active X controls, etc. require knowledge of HTML in order to use them.

Even authors who have written books on how to use specific HTML editors usually emphasize the importance of also learning HTML itself. Zimmerman (1999), whose book is on the use of Microsoft's FrontPage Editor, puts it like this:

> Although FrontPage creates the HTML code for the user, it is still important to learn the HTML code itself. This is because even the best WYSIWYG editor can't cover all the HTML tags. New HTML tags are created on a frequent basis and students learn that they can type in the tags directly in the FrontPage editor.

> By understanding the code that is automatically generated by FrontPage, students better understand how to implement new code on their own. (p. iii)

There are many ways to learn HTML. There are scores of excellent books on the topic. We particularly like Musciano and Kennedy (1998), Groves (1997), and Meyers (1999). The latter two of these volumes are aimed at those who will be creating educational Web pages. In addition, it is quite practical to use the Web itself to learn HTML. There are hundreds of sites whose purpose is to teach HTML to users. These can be found by using the following AltaVista (http://www.altavista.com/) search string, including the quotation marks:

"learn html"

In addition, we permanently maintain five hands-on modules designed to teach HTML to teachers. Links to these modules can be found at http://unr.edu/homepage/maddux/prog/sylcp411.html#modules.

SPECIFIC TIPS ABOUT CONTENT

Unfortunately, even experts in HTML may produce poor quality, course-related Web pages. The following list of recommendations (some applying only to home pages and others to all pages on the site) would, if followed, go a long way toward rectifying some of the most common problems:

1. All pages should contain complete identifiers including university, department, college, course name and number, catalog description, abbreviation, semester or quarter and year, and name of instructor. These identifiers should appear on every page in the site, not simply on the homepage, since many users will find their way to such pages through a search engine.
2. All homepages should contain a one-paragraph statement of the purpose of the site. Such a statement will help "Web surfers" determine whether the page is what they are looking for, and will help the author of the page maintain his or her focus as the page is created. In addition, course objectives should be stated.
3. All homepages should contain a statement of the role of the course in the overall program, prerequisites, and any other administrative information.
4. All homepages should contain a list of required and recommended textbooks and other needed material.
5. All homepages should contain a list of course requirements with full descriptions, and, where appropriate, links to sample student projects or products from previous semesters or quarters.
6. All home pages should present a full description of grading criteria.
7. All home pages should contain a list of links to recommended sites related to course content.
8. All homepages should contain a link to the homepage of any professional or student organizations related to course content.
9. All pages should contain a link to the university or college page and to departmental pages.
10. All pages should contain a list of credits for any graphics used on the page.
11. All pages should contain a footer including at least the university name and logo, URL

of the page, another "date last modified" line, and e-mail link to the instructor.

12. All pages should contain the up-to-date telephone number and office hours of the instructor and a hot link to the instructor's e-mail address. The link should be the actual e-mail address so that users whose browsers are not configured for e-mail can write the address down for use later when they open their e-mail programs.
13. All pages should contain a "last updated" line that displays the date the page was last modified. There are many simple javascript programs that can be copied from the Web and placed into the HTML code. These programs will automatically display the date that the page was last modified. There are countless variations of this little program that typically consist of only four or five lines. To find them, go to AltaVista (http://www.altavista.com/) and type +"javascript" +"last updated" (including the plus signs and the quotation marks). At the time of this writing, this search string produced more than 65,000 "hits."

   There are a growing number of sites on the Web that provide free javascript programs that can be copied verbatim and embedded in HTML code to perform specialized tasks. To find these sites and browse through the available scripts, use the following AltaVista search string including the quotation marks:

   "free javascript"

   The last time we did this, we obtained more than 1600 "hits."
14. Home pages should display a "hit counter" to keep track of the number of times the page is viewed. This is useful in helping to determine whether students are actually using the site. There are many sites on the Web that will provide free counters. The site provides the code needed to display the counter, and authors copy the code and paste it into the HTML for their page. Hundreds of these can be located by going to AltaVista (http://www.altavista.com/) and typing "free counters." Here are the names and URLs of only a few of those sites that we have used in the past:
    a. WebCounter Usage Page—http://www.digits.com/usage.html
    b. Escati—http://www.escati.com/free-services.htm
    c. WebTracker—http://www.fxweb.holowww.com/tracker/adduser.shtml
    d. XOOMCounter—http://www3.pagecount.com/
    e. Cam's Java Web Hit Counter—http://counter.bloke.com/
    f. Site-Stat's Free Counter—http://www.site-stats.com/
    g. LBINet Counters—http://www.nealcomm.com/c40000/index.htm
16. All pages should contain a link back to the home page so that users who find the page through a search engine can access that home page.
17. Pages employing frames (a Web device that causes pages to display two or more windows at a time) should always include the code to enable users who dislike frames to view a non-frames version of the page.
18. Since different browsers differ in the way they interpret HTML, authors should view their pages on the Web using as many different browsers as possible to ensure that the pages are competently displayed in all. At a minimum, authors should view their pages on Netscape Communicator and Microsoft's Internet Explorer, since these are the two most popular browsers.
19. Authors should update pages regularly, at least weekly, if not daily. If the content of Web pages does not change, students will soon stop visiting. There are many free javascript programs that will cause a "javascript alert" to appear whenever anyone

visits the site. The alert appears in a special box when the site is accessed and users must click an "OK button" before they proceed. The message displayed can be changed daily in only a minute or two. Alternatively, there are also free javascript programs to display scrolling marquees with easily changeable messages. (See suggestion #13 above for how to find such free javascript programs.)

20. Instructors should reply to all e-mail messages promptly. Students will stop e-mailing if they feel they are "talking to themselves."
21. Instructors should ask each class to evaluate the course Web site and to provide suggestions for improvement that will benefit future students.

FUTURE TRENDS

We learned long ago not to try to predict future developments in information technology in education, especially if it involves the Internet. One of many amazing statistics about the Web is that when President Clinton took office, there were only 50 pages on the Web, while today there are well over 500 million pages to be found there. The amazing growth of the Web was not predicted by any of the futurists we know of. In fact, most often the futurists' predictions about information technology have paled beside the actual developments.

We could talk about the future of dynamic HTML, cascading style sheets, compressed video, and other technical innovations. But we suspect the future will again prove to be even more revolutionary and more exciting than anything we might choose to highlight. However, we do think it safe to predict that the Web will continue to increase in importance in education at all levels and particularly in higher education. We are also willing to predict that the debate over quality control of Web-based learning will continue to grow. However, we do not know how best to ensure that the quality of distance education is as high as possible. We do think that faculty and administration in the nation's colleges and universities should stop debating whether or not distance education should be implemented. Whether we like it or not, distance education is probably here to stay. It is unlikely that we could prevent its continued growth even if we tried. Therefore, the best thing we can do at the present time is to pitch in and try to make it work as best we can.

CONCLUSION

Distance education is growing rapidly in higher education. On most campuses, there is little, if any, institutional support for instructors who wish to develop Web pages to supplement traditional, on-campus courses. Because of the newness of the Web and the lack of institutional design or development support, many course-related Web pages are of poor quality. To improve this situation, instructors need to engage in careful planning before beginning to produce Web pages. Large Web sites probably require some form of written plan involving such things as flowcharts, storyboards, or checklists. Careful attention should be given to the purpose of the proposed site, student access to the Web, and technical assistance for students who experience difficulty accessing and using the site. Instructors can find assistance in planning on the Web and should learn HTML even if they plan to use an HTML editor. There are a number of specific suggestions that could be used to improve the quality of Web pages. Although it is impossible to predict the future of the Web in higher education, it is probably safe to say that the demand for distance education will continue to increase. Since we could probably not prevent the future increased importance of the Web in distance education, we should focus on improving the quality of course-related Web pages and the entire distance education experience for both students and instructors.

REFERENCES

Boling, E., & Frick, T.W. (1997). Holistic rapid prototyping for Web design: Early usability testing is essential. In B. H. Khan (Ed.), *Web-based instruction* (pp. 319-328). Englewood Cliffs, NJ: Educational Technology Publications.

Canadian Telework Association (1998). *Distance education.* Nepean, Ontario, Canada. Author. [WWW document]. URL http://www.ivc.ca/part10.html

Crossman, D. M. (1997). The evolution of the World Wide Web as an emerging instructional technology tool. In B. H. Khan (Ed.), *Web-based instruction* (pp. 19-23). Englewood Cliffs, NJ: Educational Technology Publications.

Dillon, C., & Granger, D. (1998). Guest editorial. *The American Journal of Distance Education*, 12(1). Retrieved May 21, 1999 from the World Wide Web: http://www.ed.psu.edu/ACSDE/ed121.html

Groves, D. (1997). *The Web page workbook: Academic edition.* Wilsonville, OR: Franklin, Beedle & Associates.

LeJeune, N.F. (1998). *Learner-Centered strategies in Web-based instruction for adults.* [WWW document]. URL http://ouray.cudenver.edu/~nflejeun/lcstrategies.htm

McIsaac, M.S. & Gunawardena, C.N. (1996). Distance Education. In D.H. Jonassen, ed. *Handbook of research for educational communications and technology: a project of the Association for Educational Communications and Technology*. 403-437. New York: Simon & Schuster Macmillan.

Maddux, C.D., Cummings, R., & Torres-Rivera, E. (1999). Facilitating the integration of information technology into higher-education instruction. *Educational Technology, 39*(3), 43-47.

Meyers, P.F. (1999). *The HTML Web classroom.* Upper Saddle River, NJ: Prentice Hall.

Musciano, C., & Kennedy, B. (1998). *HTML: The definitive guide* (3rd. ed.). Sebastopol, CA: Oreilly & Associates.

Trilling, B., & Hood, P. (1999). Learning, technology, and education reform in the knowledge age or "We're wired, webbed, and windowed, now what?" *Educational Technology, 39*(3), 5-18.

Zimmerman, P.H. (1999). *Web page fundamentals with FrontPage*. Indianapolis, IN: Macmillan Computer Publishing.

Chapter X

Theoretical and Practical Considerations in the Design of Web-Based Instruction

Susan M. Miller
Texas A & M University-Commerce, USA

Kenneth L. Miller
Grayson Place Consulting, USA

INTRODUCTION

The intended audiences for this chapter are (a) individuals who design and develop Web-based instruction in any setting (i.e., university faculty, instructional developers in medical, business and government settings), and (b) graduate students in the fields of instructional design, educational technology, and educational psychology.

The purposes of this chapter are to:

- describe three unique features of the Web environment relevant to instruction: structure, media, and communication capabilities;
- explore the role of epistemology in the design of instruction: relationships of epistemology to cognitive learning theories, Web technologies and practice;
- examine five factors that influence the design of Web-based instruction: theoretical orientation, learning goals, content, learner characteristics, and technological capabilities;
- recommend ten issues for Web course developers to consider as they design Web-based instruction;
- discuss four factors that will affect the future of Web-based instruction: efficacy studies, technological advances, pressures of competition and cost containment, and professional responses to market influences.

UNIQUE INSTRUCTIONAL FEATURES OF THE WORLD WIDE WEB

Web-based instruction uses hyperlinking and communication capabilities that are time and place independent (Jonassen, Davidson, Collins, Campbell, & Haag, 1995). These characteristics apply to on-line courses in both education and corporate settings. Designing instruction for on-line delivery requires consideration of this complex learning environment. The associative, nonlinear, and hierarchical *structure* of the Web, enhanced *media* capabilities, and a variety of synchronous and asynchronous *communication* opportunities are unique features of the Web that influence instruction (Ayersman, 1995b; Jonassen, 1991, 1993; McGuire, 1996; Yang, 1996). Although discussed separately below, these features are interrelated. For example, constructivists view the web's nonlinear and associative structure as a way for students to express and reflect understanding of a topic as they collaboratively build knowledge. In turn, collaboration requires sophisticated and supportive communication and performance tools (i.e., Computer Supported Communication Work tools as noted in Jonassen, et al., 1995; Mayes, 1999).

Structure

There is unanimous agreement that the hypermedia structure of the Web is associative, nonlinear, and hierarchical with unrestricted hyperlinking capabilities (e.g., Ayersman, 1995b; Jonassen, 1991, 1993; McGuire, 1996; Wilson & Jonassen, 1989; Yang, 1996). This structure can be thought of as "mimicking" the associative, nonlinear, hierarchical structure of memory (Jonassen, 1991).

The semantic network model of memory proposes a representation system constructed of nodes (i.e., propositions or concepts) that are meaningfully connected or linked (Jonassen, 1991, 1993; Lanza, 1991; McGuire, 1996; Vrasidas, 1996). Concepts relate to other concepts in a nonlinear and hierarchical fashion forming a net-like organization of memory (Jonassen, 1991; Lanza, 1991). This structure is reflected in the net-like organization of the Web where nodes are linked in an associative, nonlinear, and hierarchical fashion. Larger configurations of associations can be assembled that reflect a schematic model of memory. A schema consists of associative connections that represent a larger body of knowledge, that is, what one knows about "something." Schemata interrelate to form the structure of memory and learning involves the reorganization of these cognitive structures (Jonassen, 1991; McGuire, 1996). Although consensus exists on the correspondence between cognitive models of memory and the structure of the Web, differences have emerged in the applicatin of this similarity to the design of instruction.

Media

Use of the term "hypermedia" instead of "hypertext" in describing the structure of the Web reflects the "multimedia" nature of information that is available (Yang, 1996). The Web structure is not comprised solely of links among text documents or parts of text documents (Jonassen, 1991; Vrasidas, 1996), but of a range of media such as illustrations, pictures, animation, video, and sound. The "media" component of hypermedia enables representations of real-world contexts that produce authentic learning situations. Technological advances (e.g., second generation hypertext systems and browsers, alternate link types, distributed architecture, audio and video streaming technologies, [see Hill, 1996]) make possible representations that are accurate and realistic: qualities required for some learning tasks (Marshall & Hurley, 1996).

Communication

The Internet affords a variety of synchronous communication (e.g., chat, video conferencing, instant messaging, whiteboard) and asynchronous communication (bulletin boards, shared databases, embedded questions) technologies (Jonassen, et al., 1995; McManus, 1995; Schneider, 1994; Warschauer, 1997). When content is delivered at a distance, one form of communication is that which occurs between the content and the learner (see discussion in Miller & Miller, 1999; Wagner, 1997). Differences in instructional approaches are reflected in differing degrees of interactivity embedded in the learning environment.

Literature in computer mediated communication (CMC) typically identifies three communication configurations: instructor to groups of learners (i.e., one to many), between instructor and individual students (i.e., one to one), and among students (i.e., many-to-many) (Warschauer, 1997). Choice of communication modalities depends upon instructional theory, learning goals, type of content, learner characteristics, and availability and skill in using collaborative technologies (Miller & Miller, 1999).

These three features of the Web—hyperlinking *structure*, realistic and enhanced *media*, and synchronous and asynchronous *communication* capabilities—converge to make the Web a unique learning environment. McGuire (1996) suggested that development of these technologies may have heralded another revolution in learning, rivaling the influences of earlier technologies such as the written alphabet and printing press (see discussion in McGuire, 1996, on whether this is the third or fourth such revolution). In the case of Web-based instruction, technology may be driving instructional theory and practice. This possibility has prompted considerable professional discourse (e.g., Jonassen, 1991, 1993; Jonassen, et al., 1995; Wilson, 1999; and see similar comments regarding technology and hypertext in Spiro, Feltovich, Jacobson, & Coulson, 1995).

EPISTEMOLOGICAL CONSIDERATIONS

Epistemology and Cognitive Learning Theories

Epistemology is the branch of philosophy concerned with the nature of knowledge, and thus with questions of reality and truth (Cronin, 1997; Duffy & Jonassen, 1992). The latter half of this century has witnessed a shift from objectivist to constructivist epistemological perspectives (Cooper, 1993) and this shift has influenced instructional practices and use of Web technology.

The objectivist paradigm posits knowledge (i.e., reality/truth) as separate from and external to the knower. As an external entity, knowledge has structure that can be known objectively (Cronin, 1997) in "terms of entities, properties, and relations" (Duffy & Jonassen, 1992, p. 2). Objects and events (i.e., reality, knowledge) have inherent meaning that exists whether or not an individual has awareness of them (Driscoll, 1994). Objectivists acknowledge that personal experiences and bias hinder accurate perceptions of reality. Therefore, perceptions of reality are inevitably distorted (Driscoll, 1994; Duffy & Jonassen, 1992). The point is that, given the appropriate means (i.e., the scientific method), accurate perceptions of reality can be achieved (Bednar, Cunningham, Duffy, & Perry, 1992). Translated to education, the task of instruction is to symbolically represent external knowledge (i.e., reality) so that the learner can accurately acquire its meaning (Duffy & Jonassen, 1992).

The paradigmatic assumptions of constructivism are in distinct contrast; knowledge (i.e., reality, truth) is not external and objective, but is a subjective construction. Constructivists acknowledge the existence of an external reality, but one that can only be known subjectively (Duffy & Jonassen, 1992). Learners actively interpret reality, bringing to bear existing cognitive structures in the process of assimilating new information (Fosnot, 1992). Thus, reality and truth are relative (i.e., constructed), not absolute (i.e., objective) (Cronin, 1997). As learners engage in new experiences, cognitive structures change, bringing new interpretations (re-interpretations) of reality (Fosnot, 1992). Although often presented as promoting a totally relativistic view of reality (Driscoll, 1994), constructivism is saved from this untenable state by the process of consensus (Heylighen, 1997). Consensus is achieved either through internal congruence of understanding and knowledge, or through social negotiation with others (Heylighen, 1997).

As the objectivist paradigm that provided its support came under attack, one casualty of the epistemological revolution was behaviorism. There is general agreement that the re-emergence of cognition as psychology's legitimate field of study occurred in the mid-1950s. A convergence of forces and events (i.e., the rise of computer and communication sciences, and dissatisfaction with behaviorism) fueled this change. The return to the cognitive perspective took place on two fronts: information processing theory and constructivism. Information processing theory dominated the field of cognitive psychology, and consequently instructional theory and practice, until growing criticism of its objectivist assumptions supported the rise of constructivism in the 1990s (Cronin, 1997; Dole & Sinatra, 1998; Jonassen et al., 1995; Reynolds, Sinatra, & Jetton, 1996; Wilson, 1999).

Epistemology and Technology

Although beliefs about knowledge, reality, and truth may seem ephemeral and remote to the instructor laboring to design effective on-line instruction, epistemological beliefs are ultimately at the center of the instructional process (Bednar, et al., 1992). Epistemology informs learning and instruction theories that, in turn, suggest applications of Web technologies.

Designing theory-driven instruction requires an understanding of teaching and learning processes. As noted by Shermis (quoted in Bartasis & Palumbo, 1995) "... Effective teaching requires that one possess a theory of learning, a body of conceptual tools concerning the definition of learning and beliefs about how learning takes place ... But what must also be realized is that any learning theory presupposes a philosophical position" (p. 2). Thus, epistemological questions are important to designers of instruction, for whom learning and instructional theories are tools of the trade. In turn, decisions about how technology is used in the learning process are directly connected to beliefs about the learning process (Bartasis & Palumbo, 1995; Cooper, 1993; Mayes, 1999). For example, *presentation*, *representation*, and *construction* are frequently mentioned as three uses of hypertext environment that are influenced by different theoretical approaches (Nelson & Palumbo, 1992, in Yang, 1996; also see Ayersman, 1996). Prescriptive instructional approaches based on information processing theory are associated with presentation and representation, and constructivist theory is associated with construction (Ayersman, 1995b, McGuire, 1996, Yang, 1996).

Epistemology and Practice

The unique features of the Web create a learning environment that is at once complex and poorly defined. This ambiguity has yielded two types of responses by developers of on-line instruction. One approach is atheoretical. Technology is used "ad hoc" because it is available (Jacobson, 1994, p. 142). In this context, on-line instruction typically consists of placing course components such as the syllabus, lecture notes, and course schedule on the Web, while providing opportunities for some type of communication among course participants. This approach is supported by professional articles of the "how to" genre. This literature consists of recommendations regarding course elements (e.g., syllabus, lecture notes) and communication tools (e.g., email, bulletin board), as well as advice on practical activities (e.g., check links, limit text scrolling).

A second response to opportunities afforded by the web's associative structure, enhanced media, and communication features is decidedly theoretical. The correspondence between the web's structure and that of human memory has focused attention on knowledge representation as sine qua non. This raises epistemological questions: is knowledge external and knowable as objectivists claim, or is knowledge subjectively constructed as constructivists purport? Answers to these questions suggest corresponding learning theories: objectivist information processing theory versus constructivist learning approaches.

The ad hoc approach to course development undervalues both the capacity of Web technology for teaching and learning and the processes by which teaching and learning occur. The authors recommend that developers of Web-based instruction choose a theoretical approach. The starting point, however, is not selection of the "right" theory, but awareness that instructional practices should be grounded in theory. This occurs through the "systematic implementation of processes and procedures that are rooted in established theory and research in human learning" (Hannafin, Hannafin, Land, & Oliver quoted in Wilson, 1999). The result is congruence between practice and theory. Technologically based strategies should reflect theoretical underpinnings (Jacobson, 1994), with the caveat that some strategies can be used to achieve different purposes depending upon context (Wilson, 1997). An example of congruence is the inclusion of contextual factors and learner directed goals in constructivist-based instruction, or the use of strategies that gain learner attention and aid encoding in instruction based on information processing theory (Wilson, 1999). Selecting a "correct" theoretical framework is secondary to implementing instructional strategies consistent with a given theoretical orientation (see discussions in Bednar et al., 1992; Wilson, 1999).

Abdicating adherence to a single theoretical approach for one that requires only congruence between theory and practice leaves unanswered the question of how to proceed. This is a reasonable question to ask before undertaking development of on-line instruction. Wilson (1999) proposed an eclectic, "problem or practitioner-centered" (p. 5) approach to strategy selection where theory "informs" but does not constrain practice. Jonassen (1999) recommended incorporating objectivist and constructivist views as part of designer's repertoire. The authors advocate flexibility, moderation, and rationality in selecting learning theory for Web-based instruction, with an ever-vigilant focus on congruence between epistemological beliefs and practice.

FACTORS THAT INFLUENCE THE DESIGN OF WEB-BASED INSTRUCTION

Adopting an effective approach to on-line instruction for a given situation should be guided by the following factors: (a) theoretical orientation, (b) learning goals, (c) content, (d) learner characteristics, and (f) technological capabilities. Relationships among these factors to on-line instruction are examined in the remainder of this section. Emphasis is placed on theoretical issues.

Factor One: Theoretical Orientation

Information Processing Theory

Information processing theory reflects the "mind as computer" metaphor and the study of humans as information processors (Westbury & Wilensky, 1999). The focus is on descriptions of mental structures and processes that account for representations of knowledge (Anderson, Reder, & Simon, 1995; Reynolds et al., 1996). Reflecting objectivist assumptions, this approach reduces the mind to basic elements (i.e., structure, processes) and delineates the mechanisms of knowledge acquisition (Gallager, 1979).

There are two primary implications of this theoretical approach for instruction. Descriptions of human information processing (supported by empirical data) are translated into instructional strategies designed to result in effective and efficient processing (Bednar et al., 1992). Presentation of content involves using prescriptive strategies based on understanding how learners encode, process, and retrieve information. For example, strategies include activation of prior knowledge, hierarchical sequencing of content, and use of analogies to connect new with existing knowledge (see Hoffman, 1999, Encyclopedia of Educational Technology for other examples). Use of these strategies assumes that content (i.e., knowledge) has an external existence, and that its properties and structure can be known. The implication is that appropriately designed instructional strategies aid acquisition of knowledge (McGuire, 1996).

The second implication of information processing theory for instruction is that accurate representations of knowledge (i.e., expert's knowledge structure) will increase the likelihood that learners accurately acquire information. This implication is seen in the representational use of hypertext (Ayersman, 1995b; McGuire, 1996). However, McGuire noted Jonassen's caution that arranging a hyperlinking structure to reflect the "semantic structure of a subject-matter expert" (p. 257) does not guarantee accurate acquisition of the same structure by the learner. Influences of this theoretical paradigm can be seen in Gagne's Events of Instruction, Merrill's Component Display Theory and Instructional Transaction Theory, and Reigeluth's Elaboration Theory.

The task for designers of Web-based instruction is to integrate the theoretical assumptions and instructional implications of information processing theory and the unique features of the Web: hyperlinking *structure*, enhanced *media*, and synchronous and asynchronous *communication* capabilities. These considerations are addressed in the following paragraphs.

Structure: From the perspective of instructional theories based on information processing theory, the correspondence between the associative, non-linear, hierarchical, hyper-linking structure of the Web and postulated mental structures (i.e., semantic network, schemata) and processes (i.e., encoding, retrieval) provide opportunities to achieve the presentation and representation instructional goals noted above (Vrasidas, 1996). This associative and hierarchical structure permits development of more precise and elaborate instructional strategies (e.g., organizational and participation strategies). The web's unique hyperlinking structure (i.e., associative, non-linear, and hierarchical linking) can be arranged to provide more accurate representations of experts' knowledge structures (Wilson & Jonassen, 1989).

Media: These advantages are also evident with regard to the use of media in Web-based instruction. A range of media (i.e., illustration, animation, video, 3D) are available that enhance presentation strategies and provide more accurate descriptions, thereby increasing the likelihood that learners will acquire accurate representations of knowledge. Incorporating media in on-line instruction is restricted by technical issues such as bandwidth, as well as variability in the capabilities of computers used by learners. The capability to use a variety of media to present and represent knowledge in ways that are realistic and accurate will increase as technological tools, applications, and capacities become more sophisticated (e.g., virtual words, video streaming) (Vivid Studios, 1999).

Communication: One way of conceptualizing interactivity is communication between the learner and content (Miller & Miller, 1999). This type of interactivity is a component of prescriptive presentation strategies. The type and degree of interactivity that is prescribed depends upon the underlying cognitive processes involved in the learning task. For example, different levels of interactivity are required for memorization than for problem solving because different cognitive processes are utilized.

According to the objectivist paradigm, learning is a matter of knowledge acquisition. The role of the expert (i.e., instructor or program) is to transmit knowledge to the learner, whose job it is to receive or acquire it (Jonassen, 1991). As noted in Miller and Miller (1999), primary communication configurations associated with this paradigm are one-to-many (instructor to groups of students) and one-to-one (between the instructor and individual students). Communication tools that permit an instructor to present information (one-to-many) include posting information to a bulletin board, and using audio and video conferencing tools. Communication strategies that permit students to ask questions of an instructor and for an instructor or provide feedback to a student (one-to-one) include email and instant messaging tools. Use of a discussion forum provides opportunities for learners (many-to-many) to discuss content, express their understanding, and receive feedback from other learners on the accuracy of this understanding.

Constructivism

Constructivism is an epistemological approach (Wilson, Teslow, & Oshman-Jouchoux, 1995), although the same term is applied to learning and instructional theories. As observed by Fosnot (1992), constructivism as "a theory of 'knowing' and a theory about 'coming to know'" (p.168) is robust. However, its translation as a valid theory of instruction has not yet been established.

According to Jonassen et al. (1995), a constructivist approach to instruction requires an understanding of how learners make meaning so that learning environments can promote knowledge *construction*. Instruction does not involve prescriptive presentation strategies or accurate knowledge representation found in objectivist based approaches. The constructivist canopy encompasses a variety of views on how learning occurs (Perkins, 1992; Reynolds, et al., 1996). Instructional approaches include cognitive apprenticeship (Brown, Collins, & Duguid, 1989), anchored instruction (Cognition and Technology Group at Vanderbilt, 1990), and Cognitive Flexibility Theory (Spiro et al., 1995). The following three implications of constructivism for instruction are common to most approaches; an instructional environment must provide for (a) collaboration, (b) diverse perspectives, and (c) authentic context (derived from Bednar et al., 1992; Cronin, 1997; Jonassen, 1999; Wilson, Jonassen, & Cole, 1993).

Collaboration is a process by which meaning is constructed, thus collaboration is the cardinal element of constructivist instruction (Cronin, 1997; Jonassen et al., 1995; Hein, 1991; McGuire, 1996; Warschauer, 1997; Wilson et al., 1993). Constructivist approaches are designed to foster conversation and collaboration among learners, as this is the process by which learning occurs.

Building consensus requires expression of multiple and divergent perspectives and the ability of learners to explore, discuss, and integrate differing views (Jonassen, 1999). Several activities are involved in this process. Content is not prespecified; instead learners are presented a content domain and are then expected to explore and "go beyond" what is given. In doing so, learners view the subject matter from different perspectives and engage in conversations and disagreements with other learners. Understanding develops through analysis and reflection, and activities must be provided that foster these processes (Jonassen, 1999). Combined, these activities imply a high degree of learner control in the instructional process.

Constructivism suggests that knowledge is constructed as individuals make meaning of their experiences. Knowledge only has meaning in context. Thus, instruction includes presentations of real-world problems in authentic contexts that facilitate collaboration (Jonassen, 1999; Wilson, et al., 1993). Learning in the "real world" involves guidance from experts and strategies such as modeling, coaching and scaffolding provide the necessary cognitive support (Hannafin, Land, & Oliver, 1999; Jonassen, 1999; Wilson et al., 1993).

The task for designers of Web-based instruction is to integrate constructivist theoretical assumptions, instructional implications, and the unique features of the Web: hyperlinking *structure*, enhanced *media*, and synchronous and asynchronous *communication* capabilities. Constructivists view these features in terms of helping learners *construct* unique knowledge representations. These considerations are addressed below.

Structure: The rise of constructivism as an instructional force has occurred simultaneously with technological advances in the delivery of instruction, first in closed hypertext environments, and more recently, in the open environment of the Internet. The associative, hyperlinking, and nonlinear structural features of the Web environment are viewed by constructivists as a means for learners to build their own representations of knowledge, rather than as a structure that can model an expert's knowledge representation (Ayersman, 1995b; McGuire, 1996; Yang, 1996). This translates into learner control of linking capabilities and content sequencing. Since making meaning is an individual process, learners differ in how they use the hyperlinking structure (McGuire, 1996). Learners, however, especially novice learners, may not have sufficient metacognitive and domain knowledge to effectively use the Web either to locate resources or to strategically integrate information (Jonassen, 1999; Locatis, Letrourneau, & Banvard, 1989).

Media: Where objectivists incorporate media (i.e., animation, video, 3D) in on-line instruction as a way to provide enhanced presentation and representation of content, constructivists use media to construct realistic learning environments and provide realistic problem-solving situations (Ayersman, 1995b; Jonassen, 1991, 1993; McGuire, 1996; Yang, 1996). Hannafin et al. (1999) noted the plethora of media available on the Web, although the very number ("millions of source materials," p. 126) makes location of relevant material difficult. Some learners do not possess adequate knowledge or skills to make effective decisions when using the Web to locate material (Ryder & Wilson, 1996). Jonassen (1999) recommended restricted and guided use of the Web by learners with insufficient skills to operate successfully in a constructivist learning environment.

Communication: Constructivists view collaboration as "communities of learners" (Bielaczyc & Collin, 1999; Jonassen, 1999), and the Internet provides a wealth of communication tools that support this many-to-many communication mode (Hannafin, et al., 1999). Learners can use basic synchronous communication modes such as conferencing, chat rooms, and whiteboards to engage in conversation and collaboration (Jonassen, et al., 1995; Warschauer, 1997). Asynchronous communication technologies (e.g., bulletin boards) permit time for learners to reflect, which is an essential step in building meaning and knowledge. Collaboration is further promoted by technologies such as decision support systems, and computer-supported intentional learning environments (CSILEs) that enable learners to construct knowledge databases (Jonassen, 1999; Jonassen et al., 1995; Schneider, 1994; Wagner, 1997).

Factor Two: Learning Goals

Considerations of learning goals overlap with those of other factors (i.e., theory, content, learner characteristics, technological capabilities) discussed in this chapter. For example, *learning goals* influence structuring of content, but *content* also influences learning goals. Wilson (1985-86) observed "As a general rule, the overall organizing structure of a course should reflect the primary goals of the course" which, in turn, is mediated by "subject matter characteristics" (p. 143).

Theory and *learning goals* are closely related. In the objectivist paradigm, the goal of learning is knowledge acquisition. Much of the attention given to the analogous structures of the Web and human information processing centers on the "added value" that Web-based instruction offers. This "added value" is a learning environment that supports enhanced representation of expert knowledge and presentation of cognitively-based strategies that can increase accurate knowledge acquisition. From the constructivist perspective, the goal of learning is construction of meaningful knowledge (i.e., understanding). The added value that the Web offers is a structure that permits expression of learners' evolving comprehension.

These different epistemological views and different uses of the Web environment have resulted in sweeping, and somewhat inaccurate, characterizations regarding learning goals associated with prescriptive theories. Prescriptive instructional theories include strategies for learning outcomes ranging from memorization to problem solving, although they are often criticized as promoting "acquisition-only" learning outcomes (Merrill, 1992). This latter view is not shared by all cognitive theorists. For example, Reigeluth (1999) stated that Elaboration Theory was appropriate for acquisition of complex cognitive tasks and skills, understanding, and comprehension (e.g., problem solving, problem-based and situated learning tasks) (p. 433). He noted that a primary instructional goal is the creation of well-developed and stable cognitive structures (i.e., schemas) that can scaffold advanced learning. This description shares some commonalties with the goals of Cognitive Flexibility theory, which include higher-ordered thinking skills, expert knowledge, and flexibility in solving complex problems. Cognitive Flexibility Theory was designed to be used with learners at the stage of acquiring "advanced knowledge" (Spiro et al., 1992).

Different learning goals require different instructional approaches. Although proposing "understanding" (i.e., "knowledge in thoughtful action," p. 95) as an important learning goal, Perkins and Unger (1992) pointed out that not all learning must involve understanding or complex thinking skills. Sometimes, the goal is memorization (e.g., multiplication tables). Effective instruction requires identification of learning goals matched with an appropriate instructional approach.

Factor Three: Content

Considerations regarding the role of content overlap with those of other factors (i.e., theory, goals, learner characteristics, technological capabilities) discussed in this chapter. *Theory* and *content* are closely related. Theory influences how content is structured (prescriptive sequencing versus learner control of sequencing). Content structure (well structured versus ill-structured knowledge domains) influences the choice of instructional strategies.

Theory influences content structure in two ways. The theoretical orientation of the course designer and/or the theoretical perspective in which course design is grounded (i.e., information processing theory or constructivism) influences the: (a) relationship between Web structure and content structure, and, concomitantly, (b) selection of specific instructional theories (e.g., Elaboration Theory, Cognitive Flexibility Theory). These influences are elaborated below.

Instructional approaches grounded in information processing theory use the associative, non-linear structure of the Web to represent the content's associative and non-linear structure (i.e., the expert's conceptualization of the subject matter). Of course, representing the expert's cognitive structure is no guarantee that it will be of direct use to novice learners, who may lack necessary knowledge to make sense of connections understood by the expert (Locatis, et al., 1989). Thus, acquisition of content also involves presentation strategies. For example, one strategy is to "teach content structure explicitly" (Wilson, 1985-86, p. 141) through use of graphic organizers, diagrams and organization of text (Locatis et al., 1989; Wilson, 1985-86; Wilson & Jonassen, 1989).

Reigeluth's Elaboration Theory (1999) is a prescriptive instructional theory based on Ausubel's cognitive description of learning, but is associated with objectivist prescriptive strategies (Winn, 1992). Elaboration Theory uses a top-down approach; sequencing the essence of the content is presented in an epitome and then elaborated upon at greater levels of specificity. Two sequencing strategies are: (a) content is organized from simple to complex or from general to detailed, and (b) learners are guided to integrate successively complex new content with content previously presented (House & Miller, 1997). This theory has been frequently mentioned as an approach compatible with closed hypertext environments (Jonassen, 1986; Locatis, et al., 1989; Wilson, 1985-86). However, it is also applicable to the open environment of the Web. Within-course linking permits simple-to-complex elaborations (i.e., from an epitome to sublevels), and successive integration of content (i.e., summarization and synthesis strategies). External links provide access to subject matter resources. Depending upon course goals and learner abilities, designers can incorporate greater learner control of external hyperlinking opportunities, while at the same time maintaining control of sequencing at the macro-level. One of the authors has used this approach to sequence on-line courses.

In contrast, constructivism emphasizes content in terms of learners' growing knowledge about the subject matter. Content is introduced in authentic contexts, such as case studies or as real-world problems (Wilson & Jonassen, 1989). Learners seek resources to address the presenting instructional problem or case. They access content in a way that is meaningful to them; therefore, sequencing varies as learners build unique knowledge structures (McGuire, 1996). It is this high degree of learner control over sequencing that differentiates constructivist learning from instruction based on information processing theory. However, as discussed in the next section, *Learner Characteristics*, it is the extent to which learners should control the learning environment that poses the greatest problem for developers of Web-based instruction.

Learners vary in their ability to integrate associative and nonlinear content (Hannafin et al., 1999). Thus, placement, frequency, and consistency of linking opportunities are important determinants of a meaningful learning experience (Locatis et al., 1989). Prescriptive theories (i.e., Elaboration Theory) provide guidelines that enhance the likelihood that hyperlinking results in successful learning outcomes. However, most constructivist approaches involve more global, non-prescriptive strategies (i.e., modeling). Cognitive Flexibility Theory is a constructivist-based approach for sequencing closed hypertext environments that can provide direction for structuring Web-based courses. This theory uses a case-based format. Three strategies guide sequencing: (a) content is sequenced from complex to complex, (b) content is presented using a variety of complex and "irregular" cases, and (c) learners are guided to view these varied cases from multiple perspectives (i.e., sequencing "criss-crosses" the content) (Spiro, Feltovich, Jacobson, & Coulson, 1992).

As noted above, not only does theory drive course structure, but also the type of knowledge domain (i.e., well structured versus ill-structured content) influences selection of instructional theories. Cognitive Flexibility Theory was designed for ill-structured domains. Spiro, et al. (1992) identified the following two characteristics of an ill-structured domain: each case is complex and can be viewed from multiple perspectives ("concept- and case-complexity"), and apparently similar cases involve irregular features ("across-case irregularity") (p. 60). Examples of ill-structured content areas are history and literature; well-structured domains include mathematics and engineering (Spiro et al., 1992). Other instructional approaches are better suited for well-structured content areas such as: Merrill's Instructional Transaction Theory (Merrill, 1992; 1999) and Reigeluth's Elaboration Theory (Winn, 1992).

Factor Four: Learner Characteristics

Two problems that limit the effective use of hypertext environments are unrestricted learner control of sequencing and lack of learner ability to meaningfully integrate unstructured information (Jonassen, 1991; Grabowski & Curtis, 1991). Reviews on learner control in hypertext environments consistently report evidence that learner control does not result in improved learning. Novice learners are especially vulnerable; in some instances learning decreased under conditions of learner control (Ayersman, 1995a; Chen & Rada, 1996; Large, 1996). One result of unrestricted learner control is that many learners become "lost-in-hyperspace" (Park & Hannafin, 1993, p. ; Weller, Repman, Lan, & Rooze, 1995; Wilson,

& Jonassen, 1989) and engage in "wild goose chases" (Gay, Trumbull, & Mazur, 1991, p. 190). In addition to navigational issues, learners often fail to make sense of information they locate. Simply navigating the hyperlinked structure of the Web does not ensure that learners comprehend the underlying structure of subject matter, make appropriate connections among concepts, or build appropriate understandings of subject matter (Park & Hannafin, 1993; Weller, et al., 1995).

Course developers must consider learner characteristics if they are to create effective instruction. This principle applies in all learning environments, but has unique implications for Web-based courses. In addition to usual considerations such as students' ages, developmental levels, and abilities, Web-based course developers should also consider the following *categories* of learner characteristics: (a) cognitive characteristics, (b) motivation, (c) knowledge, and (d) social context. Although characteristics within these categories are not unique (i.e., some characteristics may apply to more than one category), the categories provide a useful framework for understanding the interaction between learner differences and use of the Web as a learning environment.

Cognitive Characteristics

Cognitive characteristics include (a) epistemic beliefs, (b) cognitive styles, (c) spatial ability, (d) metacognitive skills, and (e) learning styles. Epistemic beliefs are defined as learners' assumptions about how learning occurs (Jacobson, Maouri, Mishra, & Kolar, 1996). Findings from a study by Jacobson and Spiro (reported in Jacobson et al., 1996; Jacobson & Spiro, 1994) suggest a congruence between epistemic beliefs and effective use of the unlimited hyperlinking structure of the Web. These researchers found that students who held "simplistic" epistemic beliefs preferred well-structured presentations, learned less in a hypertext environment, and demonstrated less skill in a transfer situation than did students who viewed learning with "...complexity, flexibility, and nonlinearity..."(p. 4).

Cognitive styles are "preferred, consistent, individual characteristics in organizing and processing information" (Chen & Rada, 1996, p.129). One cognitive style that has relevance to hypertext learning environments is field dependence/independence. This cognitive style is defined as a tendency to approach problem solving in a global (i.e., undifferentiated) rather than analytical manner. Field dependent learners attend to environmental features and cues that are salient, but irrelevant, to learning tasks. This cognitive style inhibits the ability of such learners to reorganize perceptions. Conversely, field independent learners are not distracted by dominant but irrelevant features, which improves their ability to organize (and reorganize) perceptions required for learning (Burton, Moore, & Holmes, 1995). As a consequence, field-independent learners are at an advantage in using hypertext environments (Ayersman, 1995a; Burton, et al., 1995; Chen & Rada, 1996; Hsiao, 1997) because of their abilities to organize information in the unstructured atmosphere of hyperspace (Weller, et al., 1995).

Other cognitive styles that may have relevance in a hypermedia learning environment include (a) scanning (narrow versus wide focus on detail), (b) constricted versus flexible control (abilities to filter distractions and focus attention), (c) leveling versus sharpening (variations in memory), (d) reflection versus impulsivity (rate of idea generation and response), (e) conceptual differentiation/integration (ability to categorize), and (f) risk taking versus cautiousness (in means selected to achieve goals) (some of these styles were suggested by Messick, as noted in Burton, et al., 1995; Grabowski & Curtis, 1991).

Grabowski and Curtis (1991) suggested that individuals who are risk-takers, extreme scanners, high conceptual integrators, and who demonstrate flexible control should enjoy and perform well in a learner-controlled, hypermedia environment. Because cognitive styles also influence values, attitudes, and social interaction, Web-based course developers must carefully consider their influence on selections of instructional theory, learning goals, type of course content, and communications options.

Spatial ability involves the capacity to accurately perceive, represent, and cognitively manipulate representations (Kellogg, 1995). Based on three studies included in their meta-analysis of hypertext literature, Chen and Rada (1996) found a relationship between high spatial ability and efficient use of the hypertext environment. Low spatial ability learners, however, were aided by the use of graphical organizers. The researchers concluded that "based on the synthesized findings, spatial ability influences the processes of interaction with hypertext more directly than individual differences such as cognitive styles, field dependency, or learning styles" (p. 147).

Metacognition is the "awareness of one's own knowledge and the ability to understand, control, and manipulate individual cognitive processes" (Osman & Hannafin, 1992, p. 83). Learners with a high degree of metacognitive skill can monitor their learning, and strategically employ learning strategies. They are aware of what they need to know and can employ techniques that will help them to acquire knowledge. Because metacognitive demands are lower for highly structured learning environments than for loosely structured environments (Park & Hannafin, 1993), course developers can select appropriate learning goals and tailor instructional activities to accommodate learners with different levels of metacognitive skills.

Learning styles refer to behaviors that indicate how a person learns (Gregorc, 1979). Kim (1997) reported findings by Ellis, Ford, and Wood, which revealed that serialists and holists performed differently on a recall task in a hypertext environment. However, the role of this learning style on performance was minimal. Ayersman (1996) concluded that evidence does not support differences in hypertext performance based on learning styles, citing methodological flaws that hinder generalizability of findings. The influence of learning styles on hypertext performance continues to be of interest, but research findings to date reveal the need for more rigorous research.

Motivation

Motivation is a particularly important learner characteristic because of its reciprocal effects on performance in hyperspace. Jonassen and Wang (1993) noted that the most important determinant of learning is probably "awareness, acceptance, and understanding of the required task or learning outcome" (p. 5). Grabowski and Curtis (1991) adapted Keller's model of motivational design to identify four motivational factors that influence learning in hypermedia environments: "(1) interest in or attention to the information and the technology; (2) perceived relevance of the information; (3) self-confidence in the ability to access and use the information; and, (4) resulting satisfaction from successful access to and usefulness of the information" (p. 10). Chen and Rada (1996) reported findings by Nielsen that users' motivation was one of three factors associated with the use of hypertext. Although these findings reveal that motivation affects performance in hypermedia environments, well-designed hypertext instruction (Wilson & Jonassen) and the use of hypertext as a learning tool can also enhance motivation (Becker & Dwyer in Ayersman, 1996).

Given the reciprocal influences of motivational factors and performance in Web-based learning environments, developers should first insure that instruction is well designed. They should further insure that learners: a) understand the rationale for Web-based course offerings, b) possess skills to effectively use Web technologies in order to access required information and, c) comprehend the relevance and value of learning both technological skills and specified course content.

Knowledge

In order to successfully navigate hypermedia environments, users must possess sufficient knowledge and study skills (Gay et al., 1991). Not surprisingly, unfamiliarity with hypertext imposes significant limitations on its use, especially in open learning environments (Jonassen & Grabinger, 1993). Chen and Rada (1996) reported research conducted by Nielsen, which revealed "expertise for required tasks" (p. 128) as one of three factors associated with the use of hypertext. Kim (1997) reported findings by Marchionini et al. which revealed that both subject matter experts and information searching experts retrieved more information more quickly in a hypertext system than did a novice group. Ryder and Wilson (1996) pointed out that "the power of Internet resources remains latent to those without the skills to use them" (p. 6). They also stated that "the immediate overriding constraint of the Internet" (p. 6) was the limited number of people who could use the Internet as readily as they could a library.

These comments suggest the existence of widespread deficits in Internet knowledge and skills required for successful performance in Web-based courses. They further reveal potential remediation strategies. At the outset of instruction, course developers should assess learners' knowledge and skill levels with regard to study habits, computer literacy (e.g., hardware, software, technological issues), and the Internet (e.g., connections to service providers, Web browsers, search engines, communications tools). Results of these assessments should be used to design within-course training interventions if identified deficits are not excessive. For students who demonstrate significant knowledge and skills deficiencies, referrals to remedial courses are recommended.

Social Context

The social context of learning refers to environmental conditions that may facilitate deeper understandings of subject matter through collaboration with others (typically peers). Social context as a learning variable gained prominence as an outgrowth of Vygotsky's work on the social construction of knowledge, which suggested that learners become immersed in the intellectual lives of people in their environments. Scaffolding with others, both experts and fellow learners, provides the foundation for learning (Weller et al., 1995). Hypertext environments may also provide scaffolding opportunities. Weller et al. (1995) cited Crook, who extended the notion of peer to include hypermedia-based instructional software as a "kind of human partner in joint activity" (p. 453).

The popularity of collaborative learning models and their emerging use in hypermedia-based instructional environments appear to suggest strategies for Web-based course developers. Those who adopt a constructivist theoretical framework will incorporate learning goals, instructional activities, and communication options that require collaboration among learners. However, research on the effectiveness of collaborative learning in hypermedia-based learning environments has produced equivocal findings (Weller et al.,

1995). In a study of the effects of social context on learning from hypermedia-based instruction (Weller, et al., 1995) found that, regardless of assignment to collaborative or individual learning groups, high ability students learned more effectively from this type of instruction than less talented subjects.

Social context may be an important factor in the design of Web-based courses. However, more research is needed to make this determination (Windschitl, 1998). Until findings are more conclusive, instructional designers should not assume that building collaborative course components will enhance learning.

Factor Five: Technological Capabilities

The future of Web-based instruction will be shaped, in large measure, by advances in communication, Internet, and Web technologies. As government agencies deregulate the communications industry, companies will merge in an effort to generate financial resources necessary for building fiber optic and cordless digital infrastructures. With so much profit potential, new companies will emerge to stake claims in the ongoing digital revolution. Increased competition will drive down costs of communications services even as technological advances enhance quality and speed of delivery. Integrated telephone, television, and Internet resources will be available via the World Wide Web (LinkLore, 1996). All of these changes will influence what, how, when, and where learning occurs.

Advances in Web technologies will enhance the capabilities of browsers, servers, and project management and communication tools (Vivid Studios, 1999). Increased Internet speeds will enable Web browsers to integrate live audio and video, interactive multimedia presentations, and large three-dimensional models of objects, "...and even entire worlds, that can be manipulated and navigated however the user wishes" (LinkLore, 1996, p. 1). Web servers will provide enhanced database connectivity, virtual reality environments tht can be shared, and distributed object services, that may replace Web browsers. Sophisticated Web-based project management and communications tools will promote user interaction and collaboration. Improved versions of these tools will enable users to share document publishing and videoconference from their desktops (Vivid Studios, 1999).

Despite these forecasts, most technological advances that will occur in the next century have yet to be conceived. This is particularly true with regard to communications, Internet, and Web-based technologies. Although humans are limited in predicting what these changes will be, they can be certain that technology will continue to evolve. Consequently, keeping abreast of these changes will be critical to the design of effective Web-based instruction. Most advancements will have applications for courses developed from either cognitive processing or constructivist theoretical frameworks. However, the majority will facilitate interactivity and shared learning experiences, hallmarks of a constructivist approach. Armed with such knowledge, course developers will be able to create increasingly sophisticated learning experiences consistent with both theoretical perspectives and the capabilities afforded by emerging technologies.

RECOMMENDATIONS

The authors believe that instructors who plan to develop Web-based courses should carefully consider the following 10 points.

1. Review relevant research to determine the effectiveness of pedagogical approaches and instructional techniques used in existing Web-based courses.
2. Understand similarities and differences between/among current and emerging epistemological orientations.
3. Delineate a personal epistemological orientation and related instructional techniques —apprehend how they will affect development of your Web-based course.
4. Assess your level of technological expertise as well as your desire and ability to acquire technological knowledge and skills needed to offer Web-based instruction.
5. Determine learning goals (vs. instructional goals) for the course.
6. Identify the nature of course content (e.g., ill-structured vs. well-defined domains) to be offered.
7. Consider learner characteristics (e.g., cognitive characteristics, motivation) that affect their ability to utilize Web-based instruction.
8. Decide whether it would be more judicious to offer a Web-based or traditional classroom course based on considerations of all factors identified above.
9. Acquire technological expertise (e.g., networking capabilities, authoring/course development software) necessary to offer Web-based courses.
10. Adopt instructional theories and theory-congruent techniques that have been demonstrated, through research, to be effective in the delivery of Web-based instruction.

WEB-BASED INSTRUCTION IN THE TWENTY-FIRST CENTURY

Much is unknown and unknowable about the future of Web-based instruction in higher education. However, factors that will affect this future can be identified. The following four are likely to play crucial roles: efficacy studies, technological advances, pressures of competition and cost containment, and professional responses to market influences.

In its analysis of research on the effectiveness of distance learning in higher education, the Institute for Higher Education Policy (1999) questioned the overall quality of research used in many studies that support this approach. The Institute concluded that the shortcomings of these studies rendered "many of the findings inconclusive." Windschitl (1998) criticized the inadequacy of substantive research on learning derived from Web-based projects. He identified several research questions that have not yet been studied, but which would provide important data for those involved in Web-based teaching: "Are [special classroom activities and collaborative projects based on the use of the World Wide Web] helping students, and, if so, how? How is the introduction of this technology changing pedagogical practices?" (p.28). These articles suggest that, despite its embrace by many administrators and faculty, much remains unknown about the effectiveness of Web-based instruction. Consequently, the future of this approach in academe will be written, in part, by the results of efficacy studies that reveal its actual value as a teaching and learning tool.

Intimately tied to this future will be developments in Web technologies. As discussed above, advancements in the Internet as well as Web-based hardware and software (Marshall, & Hurley, 1996; Schneider, 1994; Vivid Studios, 1999) will yield tools substantially different from those in use today. Browsers will offer more sophisticated media handling options and Web servers will be able to provide increasingly complex services. Project management and communication tools will simplify information exchange and opportunities for learner collaboration (Jonassen et al., 1995; Vivid Studios, 1999) Many instructors who currently offer on-line courses welcome such advances because they facilitate delivery of content-rich courses that offer fast and efficient hypermedia, hyperlinking, and communication capabilities. If research supports the efficacy of Web-based instruction and if these promising new technologies come to fruition, it seems probable that instructors and course developers will adopt them.

Web-based instruction is a considerably cheaper alternative to traditional classroom offerings. Not only are fewer instructors needed to reach a larger number of students, but also are fewer classroom buildings, residence halls, and support staff necessary. Asynchronous course offerings enable students anywhere to complete requirements anytime. Savings to universities in faculty and staff salaries, new building costs, and maintenance expenditures are enticing many administrators to require their institutions to offer Web-based courses. As more colleges and universities develop on-line courses and degree plans, competition for students will increase. Such competition, combined with declining needs for expensive infrastructures, may produce dramatic declines in student enrollments at many of the nation's 3,600 accredited institutions. Such developments could foreshadow fundamental changes in both the physical landscape and concept of higher education in the United States.

Politicians, the media, and educators have generally hailed Internet technologies as essential educational tools in the twenty-first century. Noble (in Margolis, 1998) pointed out that while these technologies may promote the transformation of colleges and universities in North America, the driving force behind this conversion is market capitalism. Margolis (1998) argued that as higher education is commodified by the adoption of Internet-based training, universities will be forced to implement reforms necessary for their survival in a global market. These reforms include: (1) downsizing faculty, (b) reducing the need for physical infrastructures, (c) paring research costs and charging for support services, and (d) eliminating tenure and evaluating faculty performance on economic criteria.

These market influences prompted Hammonds, Jackson, DeGeorge and Morris (1997) to remark that higher education is "retreating from the ideals of liberal arts and leading-edge research…it is behaving more like the $250 billion business it has become" (p. 96). Noble (in Margolis, 1998) warned that such influences will "...fundamentally alter and possibly destroy a great democratic higher education system" (p. 8). As Internet technologies and Web-based instruction reshape higher education, university faculty and administrators will be forced to grapple with the effects of market forces imposed by use of these technologies. To the extent that the wired university "commodifies" higher education and threatens its raison d'être in a democratic society, so will its utility be diminished.

CONCLUSIONS

The "best" theories and practices of Web-based instruction have not been identified, nor are they likely to be in the near future. High demand and limited knowledge have generated atheoretical approaches of questionable value. Rapid developments in Web technologies, difficulties in adapting learning theories to Web-based instruction, and theoretical bias have all hampered this search. Only well-designed studies that incorporate meaningful research questions and rigorous methodologies will provide answers that lead to "better" instructional designs.

Consequently, Web-based course developers must stay abreast of research on the efficacy of theoretical approaches and instructional practices. Findings should inform and shape theoretical preferences and design strategies. By adopting empirically-derived instructional approaches, developers can create theory-based courses that incorporate theory-congruent strategies for achieving particular learning goals. Such courses may offer different types of content in alternative ways to meet different learners' needs through the use of diverse Internet technologies. If these goals can be accomplished, the promise of Web-based instruction may be realized.

REFERENCES

Anderson, J. R., Reder, L. M., Simon, H. A. (1995). *Applications and misapplications of cognitive psychology to mathematics education* [On-line]. Available: http://act.psy.cmu.edu/personal/ja/misapplied

Ayersman, D. J. (1995a). Effects of knowledge representation format and hypermedia instruction on metacognitive accuracy. *Computers in Human Behavior, 11* (3-4), 533-555.

Ayersman, D. J. (1995b). Introduction to hypermedia as a knowledge representation system. *Computers in Human Behavior, 11*(3-4), 529-531.

Ayersman, D. J. (1996). Reviewing the research on hypermedia-based learning. *Journal on Computing in Education, 28* (4), 500-525.

Bartasis, J., & Palumbo, D. (1995). *Theory and technology: Design considerations for hypermedia/discovery learning environments* [On-line]. Available: http://www.cl.uh.edu/INST5931/Discovery_Learning.html

Bednar, A. K., Cunningham, D., Duffy, T. M., & Perry, J. D., (1992). In T. M Duffy & D. H., Jonassen (Eds.), *Constructivism and the technology of instruction* (pp. 17-34). Hillsdale, NJ: Lawrence Erlbaum.

Bielaczyc, K., & Collin, A. (1999). Learning communities in classrooms: A reconceptualization of educational practice. In C. M. Reigeluth (Ed.), *Instructional-design theories and models: A new paradigm of instructional theory, Vol.II* (pp. 269-292). Mahwah, NJ: Lawrence Erlbaum.

Brown, J. S., Collins, A., & Duguid, P. (1989). Situated cognition and the culture of learning. *Educational Researcher, 18* (1), 32-42.

Burton, J. K., Moore, M., & Holmes, G. A. (1995). Hypermedia concepts and research: An overview. *Computers in Human Behavior, 11* (3-4), 345-369.

Chen, C., & Rada, R. (1996). Interacting with hypertext: A meta-analysis of experimental studies. *Human Computer Interaction, 11*, 125-156.

Cognition and Technology Group at Vanderbilt. (1990). Anchored instruction and its relationship to situated cognition. *Educational Researcher, 19* (6), 2-10.

Cooper, P. A. (1993, May). Paradigm shifts in designed instruction: From behaviorism to cognitivism to constructivism. *Educational Technology*, 12-19.

Cronin, P. (1997). *Learning and assessment of instruction* [On-line]. Available: http://www.cogsci.ed.ac.uk/~paulus/Work/Vranded/litconsa.htm

Dole, J. A. & Sinatra, G. M. (1998). Reconceptualizing change in the cognitive construction of knowledge. *Educational Psychologist, 33* (2/3), 109-128.

Driscoll, M. (1994). *Psychology of learning for instruction.* Boston: Allyn and Bacon.

Duffy, T. M, & Jonassen, D. H. (1992). Constructivism: New implications for instructional technology. In T. M Duffy & D. H. Jonassen (Eds.), *Constructivism and the technology of instruction* (pp. 1 - 16), Hillsdale, NJ: Lawrence Erlbaum.

Fosnot, C. (1992). Constructing constructivism. In T. M Duffy & D. H. Jonassen (Eds.), *Constructivism and the technology of instruction* (pp.167-176), Hillsdale, NJ: Lawrence Erlbaum.

Gallagher, J. P. (1979). Cognitive/information processing psychology and instruction: Reviewing recent theory and practice. *Instructional Science, 8*, 393-414.

Gay, G., Trumbull, D., & Mazur, J. (1991). Designing and testing navigational strategies and guidance tools for a hypermedia program. *Journal of Educational Computing Research, 7* (2), 189-202.

Grabowski, B. L., & Curtis, R. (1991). Information, instruction and learning: A hypermedia perspective. *Performance Improvement Quarterly, 4* (3) 2-12.

Gregorc, A. F. (1979). Learning/teaching styles: Potent forces behind them. Editorial. *Educational Leadership*, 234-236.

Hammonds, K. H., Jackson, S., DeGeorge, G., & Morris, K. (1997, December 22). The new university. *Business Week, 3558*, 96-102.

Hannafin, M., Land, S., Oliver, K., (1999). Open learning environments: Foundations, methods, and models. In C. M. Reigeluth (Ed.), *Instructional-design theories and models: A new paradigm of instructional theory, Vol.II* (pp. 115-140). Mahwah, NJ: Lawrence Erlbaum.

Hein, G. (1991). *Constructivist learning theory: The museum and the needs of people* [On-line]. Available: http://www.exploratorium.edu/IFI/resources/constructivistlearning.html

Heylighen F. (1997). *Epistemological constructivism* [On-line]. Available: http://pespmc1.vub.ac.be/construc.html

Hill, G. (1996). *Extended linking facilities for the WWW* [On-line]. Available: http://www.ecs.soton.ac.uk/~gjh/ht96pospaper.html

Hoffman, B. (Ed.). (1999). *Encyclopedia of educational* [On-line]. Available: http://edweb.sdsu.edu/eet/

House, G., & Miller, S. M. (1997). Reigeluth's Elaboration Theory of instructional design applied to Web-based course development. *Proceedings of the Fifth Annual Distance Education Conference.* Center for Distance Learning Research, Texas A & M University.

Hsiao, Y. (1997). *The effects of cognitive styles and learning strategies in a hypermedia environment: A review of the literature* [On-line]. Available: http://www.edb.utexas.edu/mmresearch/Students97/Hsiao

Jacobson, M. J. (1994). Issues in hypertext and hypermedia research: Toward a framework for linking theory-to-design. *Journal of Educational Multimedia and Hypermedia, 3*(2), 141-154.

Jacobson, M. J., Maouri, C., Mishra, P., & Kolar (1996). Learning with hypertext learning environments: Theory design, and research. *Journal of Educational Multimedia and Hypermedia, 5*(3/4), 239-281. [On-line]. Available: http://lpsl.coe.uga.edu/jacobson/papers/JEMH96/JEMH96.html

Jacobson, M. J., & Spiro, R. J., (1994). *Learning and applying difficult science knowledge:*

Research into the application of hypermedia learning environments. (Second year progress report.) [On-line]. Available: http://www.lpsl.coe.uga.edu/jacobson/papers/NSF.Annual.Report.94/Jacobson-NSF94.html

Jonasssen, D. H. (1986). Hypertext principles for text and courseware design. *Educational Psychologist, 21* (4), 269-292.

Jonassen, D. (1991). Hypertext as instructional design. *Educational Technology Research and Development, 39(1)*, 83-92.

Jonassen, D. (1993). Changes in knowledge structures from building semantic net versus production rule representations of subject content. *Journal of Computer-Based Instruction, 20*(4), 99-106.

Jonassen, D. (1999). Designing constructivist learning environments. In C. M. Reigeluth (Ed.), *Instructional-design theories and models: A new paradigm of instructional theory, Vol.II* (pp. 215-239). Mahwah, NJ: Lawrence Erlbaum.

Jonassen, D., Davidson, M., Collins, M., Campbell, J., & Haag, B. B. (1995). Constructivism and computer-mediated communication in distance education. *The American Journal of Distance Education, 9* (2), 7-26.

Jonassen, D. H., & Grabinger, R. S. (1993). Applications of hypertext: Technologies for higher education. *Journal of Computing in Higher Education, 4* (2), 12-42.

Jonassen, D. H., & Wang, S. (1993). Acquiring structural knowledge from semantically structured hypertext. *Journal of Computer-Based Instruction, 20* (1), 1-8.

Kellogg, R. T. (1995). *Cognitive psychology.* Thousand Oaks, CA: Sage.

Kim, K. S. (1997). *Effects of cognitive and problem-solving styles on information-seeking behavior in the WWW: A case study* [On-line]. Available: http://www.edb.utexas.edu/mmresearch/Students97/Kim/

Lanza, A. (1991, October). Some guidelines for the design of effective hypercourses. *Educational Technology,* 18-22.

Large, A. (1996). Hypertext instructional programs and learner control: A research review. *Education for Information, 14*, 95-106.

Linklore Internet Marketing Guide. (1996). *What will the Web do tomorrow* [On-line]. Available: http://linklore.com/mktg/mktg3b.shtml

Locatis, C., Letourneau, G. & Banvard, R. (1989). Hypermedia and instruction. *Educational Technology Research and Development, 37*(4), 65-77.

Margolis, M. (1998). Brave new universities. *First Monday* [On-line], 3_5. Available: http://www.firstmonday.org/issues/issues3_5/margolis/index.html

Marshall, A. D., & Hurley, S., (1996). The design, development and evaluation of hypermedia courseware for the world wide Web. *Multimedia Tools and Applications, 3*, 5-31.

Mayes, J. T. (1999, March 18). *Commentary: Impact of cognitive theory on the practice of courseware authoring* [On-line]. Available: http://www.icbl.hw.ac.uk/ctl/mayes/paper12.html.

McGuire, E. G., (1996). Knowledge representation and construction in hypermedia environments. *Telematics and Informatics, 13* (4), 251-260.

McManus, T. (1995). *Special considerations for designing internet based instruction* [On-line]. Available: http://ccwf.cc.utexas.edu/~manus/special.html

Merrill, M. D. (1992). Constructivism and instructional design. In T. M Duffy & D. H. Jonassen (Eds.), *Constructivism and the technology of instruction* (pp. 99-114). Hillsdale, NJ: Lawrence Erlbaum.

Merrill, M. D. (1999). Instructional Transaction Theory (ITT): Instructional design based on knowledge objects. In C. M. Reigeluth (Ed.), *Instructional-design theories and models: A new paradigm of instructional theory, Vol.II* (pp. 397-424). Mahwah, NJ: Lawrence Erlbaum.

Miller, S. M., & Miller, K. L., (1999). Using instructional theory to facilitate communication in Web-based courses. *Educational Technology and Society* [On-line], 2 (3). Available: http://ifets.gmd.de/periodical/vol_3_99/miller.html

Osman, M. E., & Hannafin, M. J. (1992). Metacognition research and theory: Analysis and implications for instructional design. *Educational Technology Research and Development, 40* (2), 83-99.

Park, I., & Hannafin, M. J. (1993). Empirically-based guidelines for the design of interactive multimedia. *Educational Technology Research & Development, 41* (3), 63-85.

Pask, G. (1976). Styles and strategies of learning. *British Journal of Educational Psychology, 46*, 128-148.

Perkins, D. N. (1992). Technology meets constructivism: Do they make a marriage? In T. M Duffy & D. H. Jonassen (Eds.), *Constructivism and the technology of instruction* (pp. 45-55). Hillsdale, NJ: Lawrence Erlbaum.

Perkins, D. N., & Unger, C. (1999). Teaching and learning for understanding. In C. M. Reigeluth (Ed.), *Instructional-design theories and models: A new paradigm of instructional theory, Vol.II* (pp. 91-114). Mahwah, NJ: Lawrence Erlbaum.

Reigeluth, C. M., (1999). The Elaboration Theory: Guidance for scope and sequence decisions. In C. M. Reigeluth (Ed.), *Instructional-design theories and models: A new paradigm of instructional theory, Vol.II* (pp. 425-453). Mahwah, NJ: Lawrence Erlbaum.

Reynolds, R. E., Sinatra, G. M., & Jetton, T. L. (1996). View of knowledge acquisition and representation: A continuum from experience centered to mind centered. *Educational Psychologist, 31* (2), 93-104.

Ryder, M., & Wilson, B., G. (1996, February). *Affordances and constraints of the internet for learning and instruction.* Paper presented at the meeting of the Association for Educational Communications Technology, Indianapolis, IN. [On-line]. Available: http://www.cudenver.edu/~mryder/aect_96.html

Schneider, D. (1994). *Teaching and learning with internet tools: A position paper* [On-line]. Available: http://tecfa.unige.ch/edu-comp/edu-ws94/contrib/schneider/schneide.fm.html

Spiro, R. J., Feltovich, P. J., Jacobson, M. J., & Coulson, R. L. (1992). Knowledge representation, content specification, and the development of skill in situation specific knowledge assembly: Some constructivist issues as they relate to Cognitive Flexibility Theory and hypertext.. In T. M Duffy & D. H. Jonassen (Eds.), *Constructivism and the technology of instruction* (pp. 121-128), Hillsdale, NJ: Lawrence Erlbaum.

Spiro, R. J., Feltovich, P. J., Jacobson, M. I. & Coulson, R. L. (1995). *Cognitive flexibiliy, constructivism and hypertext: random access instruction for advanced knowledge acquisition in ill-structured domains* [On-line]. Available: http://www.ilt.columbia.edu/ilt/papers/Sprio.html

The Institute for Higher Education Policy. (1999). *What's the difference?: A review of contemporary research on the effectiveness of distance learning in higher education* [On-line]. Available: http://www.ihep.com/difference.pdf

Vivid Studios. (1999). *Future trends* [On-line]. Available: http://www.go-digital.net/vivid/future.html

Vrasidas, C. (1996). *A systematic approach for designing hypermedia environments for on-line courses* [On-line]. Available: http://seamonkey.ed.asu.edu/~mcisaac/emc523old96/work/research/vrasidas.html

Wagner, E. D. (1997). Interactivity: From agents to outcomes. In T. E. Cyrs (Ed.), *Teaching and learning at a distance: What it takes to effectively design, deliver and evaluate programs: No. 71: new directions for teaching and learning* (pp. 19-26). San Francisco: Jossey-Bass.

Warschauer, M. (1997). Computer-mediated collaborative learning: Theory and practice. *The Modern Language Journal, 81*(4) 470-480.

Weller, H. G., Repman, J., Lan, W., & Rooze, G. (1995). Improving the effectiveness of learning through hypermedia-based instruction: The importance of learner characteristics. *Computers in Human Behavior, 11* (3-4), 451-465.

Westbury, C., & Wilensky, U. (1999, September 24). *Knowledge representation in cognitive science: Implications for education* [On-line]. Available: http://www.tufts.edu/cm/papers/cogsci

Wilson, B. G. (1985-86). Using content structure in course design. *Journal of Educational Technology Systems, 14* (2), pp. 137-147.

Wilson, B. (1997). *Reflections on constructivism and instructional design* [On-line]. Available: http://www.cudenver.edu/~bwilson/construct.html

Wilson, B. (1999). *The dangers of theory-based design* [On-line]. Available: http://www.cudenver.edu/~brent_wilson/dangers.html

Wilson, B. G, & Jonassen, D. H. (1989). Hypertext and instructional design: Some preliminary guidelines. *Performance Improvement Quarterly, 2* (3) 34-39.

Wilson, B. G., Jonassen, D. H., & Cole, P. (1993). Cognitive approaches to instructional design. In G. M. Piskurich (Ed.), *The ASTD handbook of instructional technology* (pp. 21.1-21.22). New York: McGraw-Hill. [On-line]. Available: http://www.cudenver.edu/~brent_wilson/training.html

Wilson, B., Teslow, J., & Osman-Jouchoux, R. (1995). The impact of constructivism (and postmodernism) on ID fundamentals. In B. B. Seels (Ed.), *Instructional Design Fundamentals: A review and reconsideration* (pp. 137-157). Englewood Cliffs NJ: Educational Technology Publications. [On-line]. Available: http://ouray.cudenver.edu/~jlteslow/idfund.html

Windschitl, M. (1998). The WWW and classroom research: What path should we take? *Educational Researcher, 27* (1), 28-33.

Winn, W. (1992). The assumptions of constructivism and instructional design. In T. M Duffy & D. H. Jonassen (Eds.), *Constructivism and the technology of instruction* (pp. 177-182), Hillsdale, NJ: Lawrence Erlbaum.

Yang, S. C. (1996, November-December). Designing instructional applications using constructive hypermedia. *Educational Technology*, 45-50.

Chapter XI

Using Situated Learning as a Design Strategy for Web-Based Learning

Ron Oliver and Jan Herrington
Edith Cowan University, Australia

Many writers argue for a place for the use the new educational technologies from the perspective of IT management (e.g., Holt & Thompson, 1998). This form of reasoning sees a technological, rather than educational, imperative as leading the move to embrace learning technologies. The technological imperative sees the need and place for information technologies in education being based on such organisational factors as opportunity, competition and efficiency. When such imperatives are driving change, the applications of learning technologies are more likely to be made through additive strategies which see existing strategies and methods being complemented by technology-oriented initiatives. Many writers argue for more integrated approaches which have the potential to redefine and transform the more fundamental aspects of teaching and learning (e.g., Collis,1997), that is, a pedagogical imperative.

Teachers are using the Web for a variety of reasons and the extent and scope of the usage differs significantly. A majority of current Web-based learning environments have evolved from face-to-face teaching programs in the additive form described above. Typically the first step in the evolutionary process is the creation of an electronic form of existing course content. This content usually takes the form of HTML with hyperlinks to related information within and beyond the immediate course. An added feature is often a communicative element enabling interactions between learners and the teacher. What is characteristic in much of this development is the absence of any particular Web-based instructional design. The purpose of this paper is to explore a possible Web-based instructional design model that seeks to make optimal use of the opportunities and advantages of the Web as a learning environment and which can return enhanced learning outcomes.

WEB-BASED INSTRUCTIONAL DESIGN

The majority of learning theories guiding technology-based instructional design today are based on constructivist principles which value the role of an active learner in the learning process working with information to derive meaning and understanding. In contemporary computer-based learning environments, activities are often embedded in curriculum sequences, so that computers become a learning partner, rather than a medium for direct instruction or a generic tool. The logic and reason behind this application of the technology stems from the need for effective learning tools not to represent the world to the learner but to assist the learner in building meaningful, personal interpretations and representations of the world (Jonassen, Mayes & McAleese, 1993).

There are several strong theoretical foundations to guide instructional design for the Web-based learning environment. For example, Spiro, Feltovich, Jacobson & Coulson (1991a) argue that there are special requirements for attaining advanced learning goals given the impediments associated with ill-structured features of knowledge domains. They describe the value of a criss-crossed landscape, multiple dimensions of knowledge representation, an d multiple interconnections across knowledge components—all elements of learning that care readily supported by hypertext domains and communication facilities of the Web. Jonassen & Reeves (1996) use the term *cognitive tools* to describe computer-based learning applications which assist learners in representing their own knowledge of the external world. Cognitive tools when used appropriately can engage learners in higher order thinking and learning providing opportunities for the acquired knowledge to be generalised to new and alternative problem spaces and contexts.

Until the invention of schools, nearly all formal knowledge and skill was transferred through apprenticeships (Collins, 1988). In the 1980s, teachers and researchers in education began to investigate the notion of apprenticeships and to try to distinguish those characteristics which were critical to its success. Their aim was to begin the process of developing a theoretical perspective for learning based on the apprenticeship model. Brown, Collins and Duguid (1989) were the first to use the ideas to produce a proposal for a model of instruction that has implications for classroom practice. In their model of situated cognition, Brown et al. (1989) argue that meaningful learning will only take place if it is embedded in the social and physical context within which it will be used.

We have previously used the concepts of situated cognition and situated learning as successful design strategies for technology-based multimedia and it has strong prospect for application in Web-based learning. Situated learning as a model of instruction has grown out of a general theoretical shift within the educational community from 'behavioral to cognitive to constructivist' learning perspectives (Ertmer & Newby, 1993, p. 50). It provides strong contexts for learning and is strongly supported in a Web-based environment by the information and communication capabilities of the technology.

Situated Cognition and Web-Based Instructional Design

Our previous research (Herrington & Oliver, 1995; 1998) identified nine discrete characteristics as critical elements in designing learning environments based on the principles of situated cognition and situated learning. The identification of these characteristics was enabled through a distillation of the extant literature describing this learning theory and those closely related to it. Through this process we developed a set of guidelines which could be used to inform instructional design processes associated with operationalising the situated learning elements for computer-based learning environments. In the following section, the nine elements are described and descriptions are provided of the ways in which each can be incorporated into computer-based learning materials.

1. ***Authentic contexts***

Situated learning environments reflect the ways in which the knowledge and learning outcomes are to be used in the real-life settings beyond the classroom. For this reason, a situated learning environment needs to provide an arena which preserves the complexity of the real-life context with 'rich situational affordances'. From a design viewpoint, the setting needs to provide learners with a variety of resources reflecting different perspectives and to incorporate a structure which does not fragment or overly simplify the environment (Brown et al., 1989; Collins, 1988; Gabrys, Weiner, & Lesgold, 1993; Harley, 1993; Moore et al., 1994; Palincsar, 1989; Resnick, 1987; Winn, 1993; Young, 1993).

2. ***Authentic activities***

The learning activities that are designed for situated learning must have real-world relevance. This relevance can be achieved by the development of ill-defined rather than the more commonly used prescriptive activities. Authenticity is enhanced through the use of a single complex task to be investigated by students rather than a series of fragmented tasks. In some instances it is useful to create opportunities for students to define for themselves the tasks and the sub-tasks required to complete an activity. Authentic tasks require a sustained period of time for investigation and need to provide learners with the opportunity to detect relevant information from among that which is irrelevant. Such tasks can often be integrated across subject areas reflecting the complexity and ill-structured nature of most real-life problems (Brown et al., 1989; Cognition and Technology Group at Vanderbilt (CTGV), 1990a; Griffin, 1995; Harley, 1993; Resnick, 1987; Tripp, 1993; Winn, 1993; Young, 1993).

3. ***Access to expert performances and the modelling of processes***

In real-life settings, learners often learn through interactions with those who are more experienced and with experts. Such interactions provide learners with access to expert thinking and modelling processes. Often learners learn through interactions with other learners with different levels of expertise and the opportunity for the sharing of narratives and stories. The design of situated learning environments benefits from the development of instructional activities involving the observation of, and participation in, what are ostensibly real-life episodes (Collins, 1988; Collins et al., 1989; Lave & Wenger, 1991; Resnick, 1987).

4. ***Multiple roles and perspectives***

This fourth characteristic of situated learning stems from the depth of the knowledge that is gained from access to different perspectives and representations of the material that is to be learned. This form of learning activity is characterised by learners having to deal with information presented from various points of view or being given the opportunity to express different points of view through collaboration. Alternatively it is encouraged when learners are given the opportunity to immerse themselves within the learning environment through multiple investigations within a resource base sufficiently rich to sustain repeated examination (Bransford et al., 1990; Brown et al., 1989; CTGV, 1990a; CTGV, 1993; Collins et al., 1989; Lave & Wenger, 1991; Spiro, Feltovich, Jacobson, & Coulson, 1991a; Spiro, Feltovich, Jacobson, & Coulson, 1991b; Young, 1993).

5. ***Collaborative construction of knowledge***
Much of the learning that occurs outside the walls of formal institutions takes place through activities and tasks that are addressed and attempted by a group rather than an individual. Collaborative learning requires the organisation of learners into pairs or small groups and involves appropriate incentive structures for whole group achievement. Whereas previously many computer-based learning environments were deliberately designed for individuals working in isolation, situated learning environments are characterised by activities with learners learning with, and from, one another in cooperative and collaborative ventures (Bransford et al., 1990; Brown et al., 1989b; CTGV, 1990a; Collins et al., 1989; Resnick, 1987; Young, 1993).

6. ***Reflection to enable abstractions to be formed***
Reflection is a learning strategy that encourages and enables students to consider and deliberate on both their learning and learning processes. It is facilitated by tasks and contexts with high degrees of authenticity. In computer-based settings, it is facilitated when students are able to return to any element of the program if desired, and to act upon the outcomes of their reflections. Other strategies that can be used to encourage reflection include providing learners with the opportunity to compare themselves with experts and with other learners in varying stages of accomplishment (Brown et al., 1989b; CTGV, 1990a; Collins, 1988; Collins et al., 1989; Resnick, 1987).

7. ***Articulation to enable tacit knowledge to be made explicit***
A learning strategy that is closely allied to reflection is articulation. Articulation is critical to situated learning environments to make explicit the knowledge which has been gained. The purpose of the articulation is to create inherent, as opposed to constructed, opportunities for the learners to explain their understandings and constructed meanings. The tasks that are required to create the appropriate contexts for articulation are complex and involve collaborative groups, which enable first social then individual understanding. Strategies often used for this purpose include the public presentation of arguments by learners, an activity requiring articulation and defence of students' ideas and their learning (Bransford, et al., 1990; Collins, 1988; Collins et al., 1989).

8. ***Coaching and scaffolding by the teacher at critical times***
Situated learning settings often provide distinct roles for teachers as facilitators and coaches for the learners. In these roles the teachers are able to provide different forms of support for learning, particularly support in the form of scaffolding. The forms of design strategy that have been used for this purpose include the use of complex, open-ended learning environments where no attempt is made to provide intrinsic scaffolding and coaching. In such settings more able partners in collaborative environments are often able to assist others with scaffolding and coaching. Often designers of situated learning settings involving computer-based applications create opportunities

for articulation by requiring the teacher implementing the program to provide coaching and scaffolding assistance for a significant portion of the period of use (Collins, 1988; Collins et al., 1989; Griffin, 1995; Harley, 1993; Resnick, 1987; Young, 1993).

9. ***Authentic assessment of learning within the tasks***
The final characteristic of situated learning involves the ways in which the learning outcomes are assessed and evaluated. Many writers have argued the need for authentic assessment, assessment which is characterised by fidelity of context where students have the opportunity, as they would in real life, to be effective performers with their acquired knowledge, and opportunities to craft polished performances or products. Authentic assessment requires significant student time and effort in collaboration with others and, as with authentic learning activities, requires complex, ill-structured challenges that involve judgment and a full array of tasks with the assessment seamlessly integrated with the activity. Authentic assessments have multiple indicators of learning and require attention to the validity and reliability of the measures to enable appropriate criteria for scoring varied products (McLellan, 1993; Young, 1993; Young, 1995).

SITUATED LEARNING THROUGH WEB-BASED ENVIRONMENTS

Many writers are now suggesting design guidelines for those planning to develop on-line courses (e.g., Duschatel, 1997; Wild & Quinn, 1997; Berge, 1998; Collis, 1998). As one would expect, the advice is very broad and covers all aspects of instructional design from methods to integrate new technologies to on-line learning to potential assessment strategies. The plethora of advice being offered is often difficult to digest and apply due to the vast differences in the scope, extent and depth of the guidance provided. We can use the nine elements of situated learning as guiding principles to develop design strategies for Web-based learning by discretely considering their impact on the design and selection of the content, the learning activities and the learning supports. The following sections discuss how these factors can guide Web-based instructional design.

In our previous research into the design of effective technology-based learning environments, we developed a framework which identified and distinguished between the critical elements. Our research identified discrete roles for the three principal components: the learner; the multimedia materials and the teacher implementing the course (e.g., Oliver, Omari & Herrington, 1998a; 1998b).

More recently our research and development with Web-based learning materials has led us to refine the components of the model described in Figure 1 to more accurately reflect the changed and varying roles for stakeholders in on-line and Web-based learning environments (e.g.. Oliver & Omari, 1999; Oliver, 1999). The original model was used to describe elements in a classroom-based learning environment and while many of these are present in on-line settings, slight but important differences do exist. For example, in on-line settings, the technology plays an important role in providing an array of resources for the learners, but the resources are not confined to multimedia and Web-based materials alone. In designing Web-based learning, teachers are required to develop learning activities and learning strategies that incorporate the various resources in ways that cause the learners to attend to the materials and to be cognitively engaged in their dealings with them. The role of the teacher in Web-based environments is also changed. In on-line settings the teacher's role becomes less direct and is often described as that of a facilitator and coach, given that they have to provide support in less evident forms than that usually provided by the classroom teacher. The revised model for describing situated learning in Web environments still contains the nine elements described earlier but these are now integrated across the whole learning environment and are less focused on the particular participants (Figure 2).

There are many ways in which the principles of situated learning can be applied to the design of Web-based learning settings. Situated learning can be achieved to some degree by the inclusion of any of these elements in a learning setting. The challenge for designers is to explore how all the nine elements might be incorporated so that they can act together to support student learning. While the constituent elements suggest the forms of learning resources, learning activities and learning supports that are needed, designers have considerable scope in the ways in which they apply these principles. One strategy that we have used successfully to embrace situated learning in Web-based environments is that of problem-based learning.

Problem-Based Learning

Problem-based learning is a curriculum approach which helps the learner frame experience as a series of problems to be solved and where the process of learning unfolds through the application of knowledge and skills to the solution of real-world problems, often in the contexts of real practice (Bligh, 1995). It supports learning through goal-directed activity situated in circumstances which are authentic in terms of the intended application of the learned knowledge. Problem-based learning and the use of authentic tasks have become an alternative to more content-oriented approaches to education. Problem-based learning builds on experiences and empirical findings that students learn more from a problem-oriented task than from a fact-oriented one. At the same time problem-based

Figure 1. The constituent elements of situated learning in interactive multimedia

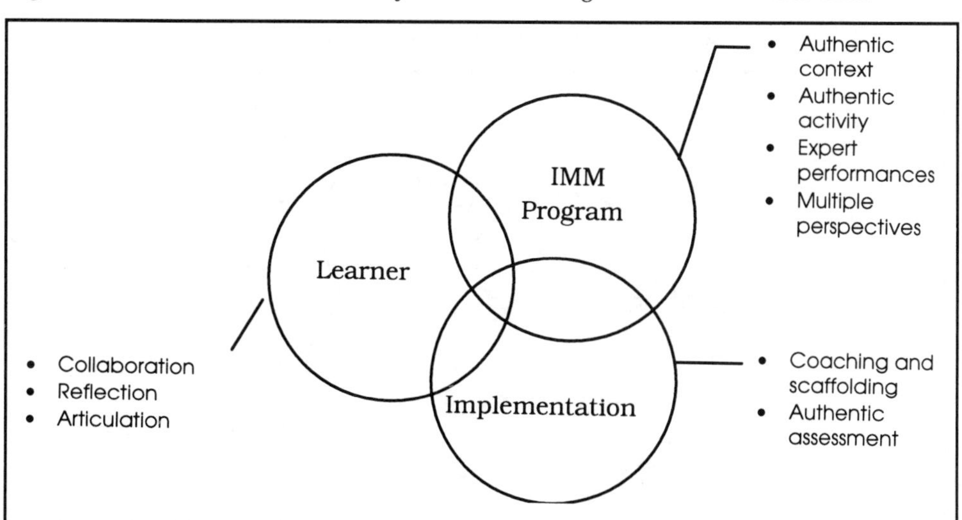

learning environments are frequently reported to increase student motivation, to develop their critical thinking skills and deepen their understanding of significant content (Sage & Torp, 1997).

Promoting learning through problem-based activities provides considerable scope for designers looking to employ situated learning as a design strategy in their Web courses. It facilitates learners solving authentic problems which reflect the way in which the learned information will be used outside classroom settings. Authentic problems tend to be ill-structured with multiple solutions. Students are able to use a multitude of perspectives in the problem solution, and many solutions exist for the problem. This form of learning, it is argued, can provide better forms of learning transfer between the university setting and the workplace, as well as enhancing students' abilities to continue to learn beyond the classroom setting (Herrington & Oliver, 1998). It is this potential which often motivates the use of problem-based learning and exploration of the factors which influence its success.

Problem-based learning has become very popular in university programs across a range of courses including business, education and science. In medicine and biology, for example, learners are often required to deal with large amounts of information in ways which reflect the forms of practice for which they are training. Whereas in traditional courses students would have been exposed to the information in such activities as lectures and workshops, in problem-based environments students are required to use the information in meaningful ways as they will be required when they graduate (e.g., Prawat, 1993; Fenwick & Parsons, 1998). Such forms of learning draw heavily on communication and collaboration among learners. The context in which the activity takes place has a strong influence on the forms and types of learning achieved (Vernon, 1995).

Problem-based learning can be supported well through Web-based technologies by virtue of the information access and cognitive support which they can provide. Use of the Web provides access to a raft of information and resources that can be used in the problem solution. The conferencing capabilities of the WWW also add considerably to its capacity to support problem-based learning. Learners using electronic conferencing can establish a sense of community among themselves and teachers can become more accessible to

Figure 2. The constituent elements of situated learning for Web-based learning

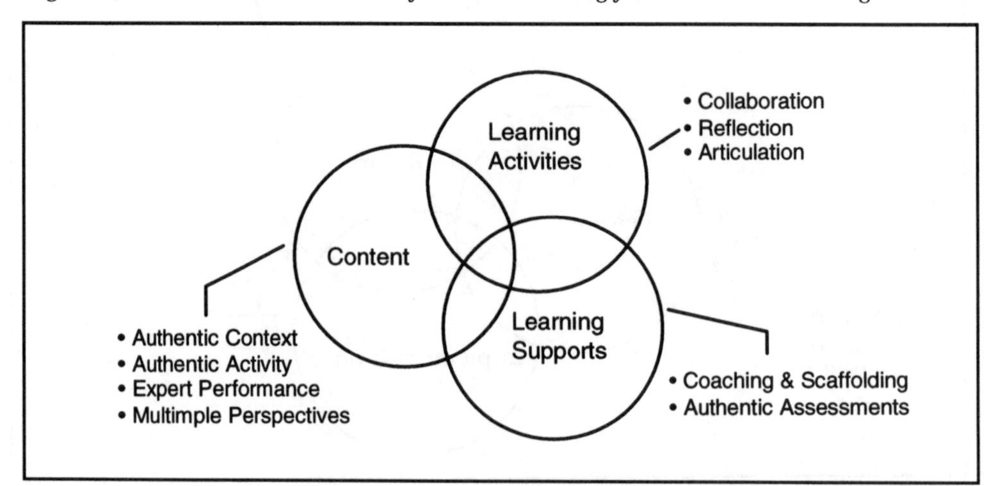

learners. The same applications can return disadvantages in some ways. Increased electronic communication can limit the capacity of teachers to deal with students. In electronic conferencing, the content of the discussion can be poor and not all topics relevant to the courseware may be discussed. A number of researchers are now exploring ways to support technology-based teaching and learning and in particular to support computer conferencing and asynchronous communication (e.g.. Masterton,1998).

At our university we have been exploring the use of problem-based learning as a design strategy for Web-based learning for several years now. The problem-based learning creates a powerful setting to create a situated learning environment. The following sections describe one such example and illustrate the various elements and components of the teaching.

RONSUB: A PROBLEM-BASED LEARNING ENVIRONMENT

The format we chose for our Web problem-based learning environment was a set of learning activities based around a weekly problem-solving activity. We developed a Web-based learning system, RonSub, to manage and coordinate these activities. The system enables students in a course to be arranged into workshop groups of about 20 students. Within each workshop, students are formed into smaller groups of four or five for the problem-based activity. Each of these small groups is required to develop a solution to a weekly problem, an activity that necessitates them to explore the topic, locate relevant information and resources, consider the various options and outcomes and to create a response which is informed and well argued. The solution is posted through the Web to a bulletin board and accessible to other students in that workshop. Once posted, solutions are then read and assessed by both the tutor and other groups in the workshop, an activity that requires students to read the solutions of about four other groups and to consider the arguments and information presented. From one week to the next, a record is kept by the system of the marks received by each group for their problem solution and at the end of the

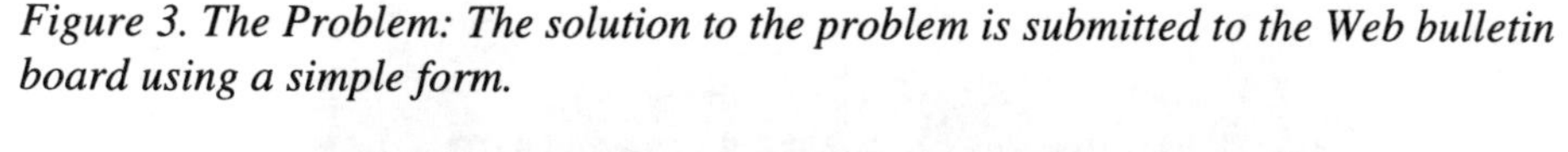

Figure 3. The Problem: The solution to the problem is submitted to the Web bulletin board using a simple form.

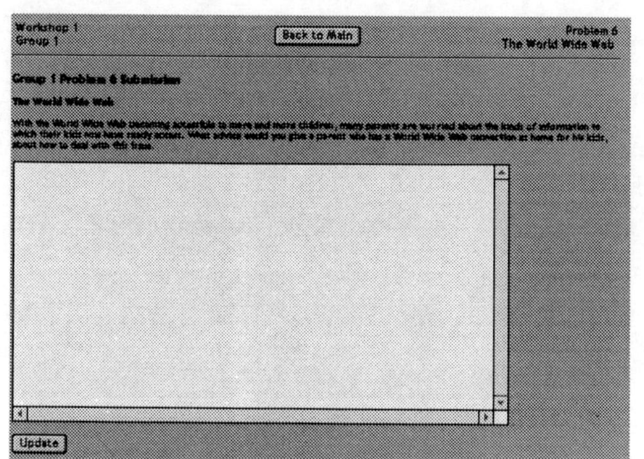

course, this cumulative mark can be used in the students' assessment.

The following section describes the main features of the RonSub system which was developed according to this specification. The screens provide examples of the electronic environment developed for the course and the forms of interaction supported in a typical week for both students and their teachers.

The weekly problem is given in the on-line course notes along with a number of initial references and information sources, both online and in print. Students are expected to read the various sources and consider an appropriate solution. The students can then meet together to plan their problem-solving strategies; many, however, prefer to use e-mail for this purpose. The Web problem-based learning environment is controlled by a menu system which is password protected and provides closed access to students within the various workshops to the system. The students work together to solve the problem, some collecting information, others analysing the problem setting and considering the options. A solution is developed with a word limit of 250 words. The students pass this between themselves to polish and refine it. At the end of the week, the solution is posted (Figure 3).

The Web provides many supports for the problem-solving process in the form of resources and tools for communication and collaboration. Once the solution has been posted, the members of a group can then see the solutions posted by others in their workshop. Students are required to read the solutions of others and to choose the best solutions from the other groups.

The learning system supports peer assessment through a simple voting mechanism, the results of which are uploaded into the system database. In each workshop, the group which receives the most votes achieves a score of 5, the second group receives 4 and all other groups which have submitted a solution receive 3 marks. The tutors of each workshop can now mark the solutions of their groups. In this instance, the tutors give marks out of 5. When all groups have been scored by their peers and their tutors, the marks for the activity can be

Figure 4. Assessing the Problem Solutions: The Coordinator and Tutors can view the overall results for all Groups and Workshops.

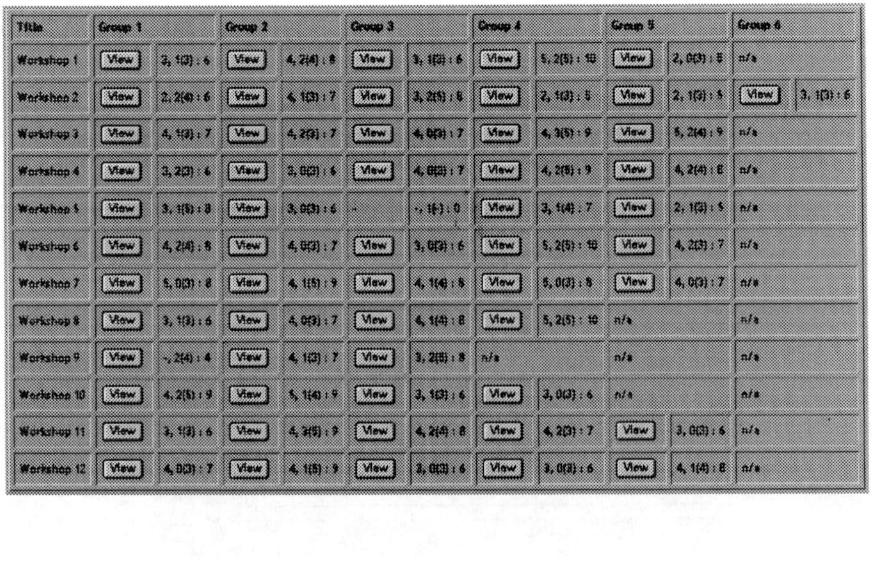

Title	Group 1		Group 2		Group 3		Group 4		Group 5		Group 6	
Workshop 1	View	3, 1(3) : 6	View	4, 2(4) : 8	View	3, 1(3) : 6	View	5, 2(5) : 10	View	2, 0(3) : 5	n/a	
Workshop 2	View	2, 2(4) : 6	View	4, 1(3) : 7	View	3, 2(5) : 8	View	2, 1(3) : 5	View	2, 1(3) : 5	View	3, 1(3) : 6
Workshop 3	View	4, 1(3) : 7	View	4, 2(3) : 7	View	4, 0(3) : 7	View	4, 3(5) : 9	View	5, 2(4) : 9	n/a	
Workshop 4	View	3, 2(3) : 6	View	3, 0(3) : 6	View	4, 0(3) : 7	View	4, 2(5) : 9	View	4, 2(4) : 8	n/a	
Workshop 5	View	3, 1(5) : 8	View	3, 0(3) : 6	-	-, 1(-) : 0	View	3, 1(4) : 7	View	2, 1(3) : 5	n/a	
Workshop 6	View	4, 2(4) : 8	View	4, 0(3) : 7	View	3, 0(3) : 6	View	5, 2(5) : 10	View	4, 2(3) : 7	n/a	
Workshop 7	View	5, 0(3) : 8	View	4, 1(5) : 9	View	4, 1(4) : 8	View	5, 0(3) : 8	View	4, 0(3) : 7	n/a	
Workshop 8	View	3, 1(3) : 6	View	4, 0(3) : 7	View	4, 1(4) : 8	View	5, 2(5) : 10	n/a		n/a	
Workshop 9	View	-, 2(4) : 4	View	4, 1(3) : 7	View	3, 2(5) : 8	n/a		n/a		n/a	
Workshop 10	View	4, 2(5) : 9	View	5, 1(4) : 9	View	3, 1(3) : 6	View	3, 0(3) : 6	n/a		n/a	
Workshop 11	View	3, 1(3) : 6	View	4, 3(5) : 9	View	4, 2(4) : 8	View	4, 2(3) : 7	View	3, 0(3) : 6	n/a	
Workshop 12	View	4, 0(3) : 7	View	4, 1(5) : 9	View	3, 0(3) : 6	View	3, 0(3) : 6	View	4, 1(4) : 8	n/a	

Table 1. Elements of situated learning with supporting on-line activities and affordances.

Learning Elements	System Features
Authentic contexts	• content presented in ways reflecting intended use • the problems give relevance and meaning to the coursework
Authentic activities	• real-life problems are presented to the learners • problems require open-ended inquiry • the problems are non-structured learning activities
Expert performances	• sample solutions are provided to guide learners in problem-solving processes • access to Web sites of experts and experienced others add to the information sources
Multiple perspectives	• access to multiple Web sites for information • a variety of media sources, e.g. print, video • groupings provide different perspectives • best solutions present alternative perspectives
Collaboration	• group-based activities encourage collaboration • the open-ended problems require group-based decision making
Reflection	• the open-ended questions require definition and description • peer assessment necessitates reflective processes
Articulation	• group-based problem solving requires students to create solutions to open-ended problems • summarised solutions necessitate articulation and explanation of learning
Coaching and scaffolding	• Students are supported by other group members • materials are available to model problem-solving processes • e-mail access to tutors provides learner support
Authentic assessment	• Assessment strategies assess the processes of learning as well as the products • peer-assessment ensures students became critical reviewers of others' work

viewed. The system shows students the results for each problem solution in a graphical form.

The program chooses the best solutions from each workshop, based on the marks achieved, and creates a page which students can view. In this way, students can see the solutions of students from other workshops and consider other alternative to the problem, a useful activity to encourage reflection. The course coordinator and tutors use a different menu system to gain access to the data from the learning system. They can view the results for each group and can see the results across all the workshops (Figure 4).

The Components of the Web-Based System

The problem-based learning setting that we developed for our students was designed to include the constituent elements of situated learning. In some instances, the on-line setting facilitated the inclusion of these elements as natural parts of the learning environment while in other instances their presence had to be achieved through careful and deliberate instructional design. In the finished product, it was evident that the problem-based learning setting was able to provide the necessary framework and structure for learning that we were seeking. Table 1 shows the various elements within the on-line learning environment and their relationship to the situated learning elements described earlier. The table clearly shows the capacity of a problem-based environment to create the necessary conditions for implementing a situated learning setting and exemplifies the elements that are more easily incorporated. The flexibility of the Web as a learning tool, however, makes it possible to supplement the learning environment in many ways to provide for those elements that are least evident.

The problem-based learning environment that we have described is but one example of how a situated learning strategy can be applied using the Web. We developed a customised setting that met our needs and the needs of our learners. Other teachers will necessarily make entirely different decisions and create quite different settings depending on the needs of their courses and their learners. What we have tried to illustrate in this example is that the Web offers many opportunities for teachers and designers, and many of these opportunities provide strong support for developing environments that incorporate the various elements of situated learning.

SUMMARY AND CONCLUSIONS

This paper has described the concept of situated learning and discussed how it can be used to guide the design of Web-based learning. It provides an example of a Web-based situated learning environment developed by the authors in a university setting. The setting incorporated a problem-based learning environment supported by a customised on-line system which managed and coordinated the problem-solving activities of the students. The problem-based learning activity was organised around small collaborative groups within with a larger cohort. There are other examples of situated learning being used as a guiding principle for Web-based design. Pennell et al. (1997) provide an excellent example of yet another design strategy for implementing this form of learning on the Web.

There are many ways to create Web-based learning environments and the example described in this chapter is quite different to those that are typical today. Typical Web-based learning environments tend to revolve around course content presented and delivered in an electronic format (e.g., Dehoney & Reeves, 1998). The design of such environments is often the same as the design of conventional environments and the Web is used as a presentation medium for the content to be delivered and learned. In the example described in this paper, the focus of the design and development was towards a Web-based setting to engage and motivate learners to explore, inquire and reflect on information and content. The bulk of the effort and activity in the design of the environment was towards creating engaging learning activities and learning supports. Very little time and effort was given to the development of Web-based content.

When the effectiveness of the learning setting is considered, there appear to be many advantages to be derived from the learning setting we have described. From a theoretical perspective, there are quite powerful learning advantages to be achieved from activities that are undertaken in these circumstances. Situated learning supports student learning in many ways and in particular it supports the knowledge construction as distinct from knowledge transmission. The value of situated learning has been demonstrated clearly in classroom settings through empirical research (e.g., Brown et al., 1989). Its effectiveness has also been demonstrated in computer-based learning environments (e.g., Herrington & Oliver, 1998). Web-based learning presents new opportunities for exploring yet other applications of this powerful learning strategy and our current research is focused on discovering the learning enhancements achieved through applications in this medium.

Using situated learning as a design strategy for Web-based learning enables teachers to craft learning activities that take advantage of the unique opportunities and affordances of the Web. The Web is a powerful medium with many attributes for learning. It provides a vast source of information for learners. It provides many opportunities for communication and collaboration. It provides learners with access to a variety of learning tools and the means to apply these tools for knowledge construction. Using design strategies such as situated learning in the development of Web-based learning environments provides teachers with the means to pedagogically re-engineer their existing courses to ensure that the maximum learning benefit can be obtained from use of this medium. Each of the discrete constituent elements in the situated learning model is a powerful adjunct to learning and this paper has shown that the Web provides a learning medium in which all the elements can be combined into a single learning environment.

REFERENCES

Berge, Z. (1998). Guiding principles in Web-based instructional design. *Education Media International, 35*(2),

Bligh, J. (1995). Problem-based learning in medicine: an introduction. *Post-Graduate Medial Journal, 71*(8), 323-326.

Bransford, J.D., Sherwood, R.D., Hasselbring, T.S., Kinzer, C.K., & Williams, S.M. (1990). Anchored instruction: Why we need it and how technology can help. In D. Nix & R. Spiro (Eds.), *Cognition, education and multimedia: Exploring ideas in high technology* (pp. 115-141). Hillsdale, NJ: Lawrence Erlbaum.

Brown, J.S., Collins, A., & Duguid, P. (1989). Situated cognition and the culture of learning. *Educational Researcher, 18*(1), 32-42.

Cognition and Technology Group at Vanderbilt. (1990a). Anchored instruction and its relationship to situated cognition. *Educational Researcher, 19*(6), 2-10.

Cognition and Technology Group at Vanderbilt. (1990b). Technology and the design of generative learning environments. *Educational Technology, 31*(5), 34-40.

Cognition and Technology Group at Vanderbilt. (1993). Anchored instruction and situated cognition revisited. *Educational Technology, 33*(3), 52-70.

Collins, A. (1988). *Cognitive apprenticeship and instructional technology* (Technical Report 6899): BBN Labs Inc., Cambridge, MA.

Collins, A., Brown, J.S., & Newman, S.E. (1989). Cognitive apprenticeship: Teaching the crafts of reading, writing, and mathematics. In L.B. Resnick (Ed.), *Knowing, learning and instruction: Essays in honour of Robert Glaser* (pp. 453-494). Hillsdale, NJ: LEA.

Collis, B. (1997). Pedagogical reengineering: A pedagogical approach to course enrichment and redesign with the WWW. *Educational Technology Review, 8*, 11-15.

Collis, B. (1998). WWW-based environments for collaborative group work. *Education and Information Technologies, 3*, 231-245.

Duchastel, P. (1997). A motivational framework for web-based instruction. In (B. Khan, (Ed.), *Web-based Instruction*. New Jersey: Englewood Cliffs.

Ertmer, P.A., & Newby, T.J. (1993). Behaviorism, cognitivism, constructivism: Comparing critical features from an instructional design perspective. *Performance Improvement Quarterly, 6*(4), 50-72.

Fenwick, T., & Parsons, J. (1998). Boldly solving the world: a critical analysis of problem-based learning as a method of professional education. *Studies-in-the-Education-of-Adults, 30*(1), 53-66.

Gabrys, G., Weiner, A., & Lesgold, A. (1993). Learning by problem solving in a coached apprenticeship system. In M. Rabinowitz (Ed.), *Cognitive science foundations of instruction* (pp. 119-147). Hillsdale, NJ: Lawrence Erlbaum Associates.

Griffin, M.M. (1995). You can't get there from here: Situated learning, transfer and map skills. *Contemporary Educational Psychology, 20*, 65-87.

Harley, S. (1993). Situated learning and classroom instruction. *Educational Technology, 33*(3), 46-51.

Herrington, J., & Oliver, R. (1995). Critical characteristics of situated learning: Implications for the instructional design of multimedia. In J. M. E. Pearce, A (Ed.), *ASCILITE'95 - The 12th Annual Conference of the Australian Society for Computers in Learning in Tertiary Education*. Melbourne: University of Melbourne.

Herrington, J., & Oliver, R. (1998). Using situated learning and multimedia to promote higher-order thinking. In T. Ottmann & I. Tomek (Eds.), *Proceedings of EdMedia and EdTelecom, 1998* (pp. 565-570). Charlottesville, VA: AACE.

Holt, D., & Thompson, D. (1998). Managing information technology in open and distance higher education. *Distance education, 19*(2), 197-227.

Jonassen, D. & Reeves, T. (1996). Learning with technology: using computers as cognitive tools. In D. Jonassen (Ed.) *Handbook of Research for Educational Communications and Technology*. New York: Macmillan.

Jonassen, D., Mayes, T., & McAleese, R. (1993). A manifesto for a constructivist approach to uses of technology in higher education. In T. Duffy, J. Lowyck, & D. Jonassen (Eds.), *Designing Environments for Constructivist Learning* (pp. 231-247). Berlin Heidelberg: Springer-Verlag.

Lave, J., & Wenger, E. (1991). *Situated learning: Legitimate peripheral participation*. Cambridge: Cambridge University Press.

Masterton, S. (1998). Computer support for learners using intelligent educational agents: the way forward. In Chan, T., Collins, A. & Lin, J. (Eds). *Global Education on the Net: Proceedings of the 6th International Conference on Computers in Education*. China Higher Education Press Beijing and Springer Verlag, Heidelberg. (pp 211-219).

McLellan, H. (1993). Evaluation in a situated learning environment. *Educational Technology, 33*(3), 39-45.

Moore, J.L., Lin, X., Schwartz, D.L., Petrosino, A., Hickey, D.T., Campbell, O., Hmelo, C., & Cognition and Technology Group at Vanderbilt. (1994). The relationship between situated cognition and anchored instruction: A response to Tripp. *Educational Technol-*

ogy, 34(10), 28-32.

Oliver, R. (1999). Exploring learning strategies for on-line teaching and learning. *Distance Education,* 20(2), 240-254.

Oliver, R. & Omari, A. (1999). Using on-line technologies to support problem-based learning: Learners' responses and perceptions. *Australian Journal of Educational Technology, 15*(1), 58-79.

Oliver, R. & Omari, A. & Herrington, J. (1998a). Investigating implementation strategies for WWW computer-based learning environments. *International Journal of Instructional Media, 25*(2), 121-138.

Oliver, R. & Omari, A. & Herrington, J. (1998b). Exploring student interactions in collaborative World Wide Web comuter-based learning environments. *Journal of Educational Multimedia and Hypermedia, 7(2/3)*, 263-287.

Palincsar, A.S. (1989). Less charted waters. *Educational Researcher, 18*(5), 5-7.

Pennell, R., Durham, M., Ozog, C., & Spark, A. (1997). Writing in context: Situated learning on the Web. In R. Kevill, R. Oliver, & R. Phillips (Eds.), *What Works and Why: Fourteenth Annual Conference of ASCILITE*, (pp. 463-469). Curtin University, Western Australia: Curtin University of Technology.

Prawat, R. (1993). The value of ideas: Problems versus possibilities in learning. *Educational Researcher,* August-September, 5-16.

Resnick, L. (1987). Learning in school and out. *Educational Researcher, 16*(9), 13-20.

Sage, S., & Torp, L. (1997). What does it take to become a teacher of problem-based learning? *Journal of Staff Development, 18*, 32-36.

Spiro, R.J., Feltovich, P.J., Jacobson, M.J., & Coulson, R.L. (1991a). Cognitive flexibility, constructivism, and hypertext: Random access instruction for advanced knowledge acquisition in ill-structured domains. *Educational Technology, 31*(5), 24-33.

Spiro, R.J., Feltovich, P.J., Jacobson, M.J., & Coulson, R.L. (1991b). Knowledge representation, content specification, and the development of skill in situation-specific knowledge assembly: Some constructivist issues as they relate to cognitive flexibility theory and hypertext. *Educational Technology, 31*(9), 22-25.

Tripp, S.D. (1993). Theories, traditions and situated learning. *Educational Technology, 33*(3), 71-77.

Vernon, D. (1995). Attitudes and opinions of faculty tutors about problem-based learning. *Medical Education, 23,* 542-558.

Wild, M., & Quinn, C. (1997). Implications of educational theory for the design of instructional multimedia. *British Journal of Educational Technology, 29*(1), 73-82.

Winn, W. (1993). Instructional design and situated learning: Paradox or partnership. *Educational Technology, 33*(3), 16-21.

Young, M.F. (1993). Instructional design for situated learning. *Educational Technology Research and Development, 41*(1), 43-58.

Young, M.F. (1995). Assessment of situated learning using computer environments. *Journal of Science Education and Technology, 4*(1), 89-96.

Young, M.F., & McNeese, M. (1993). A situated cognition approach to problem solving with implications for computer-based learning and assessment. In G. Salvendy & M.J. Smith (Eds.), *Human-computer interaction: Software and hardware interfaces* . New York: Elsevier Science Publishers.

Chapter XII

A Case Study of Lessons Learned for the Web-Based Educator

Kay A. Persichitte
University of Northern Colorado, USA

Like many instructors in higher education, I have found myself increasingly pressed to respond to demands for courses delivered with alternative technologies. This pressure is particularly dramatic today given the expanded access to and use of the Internet (NCES, 1997; NTIA, 1997). Web-based learning environments (WBLEs) are clearly the contemporary instructional "innovation of choice" in higher education. Feeling an obligation to extend my own professional preparation in this area, as well as a desire to determine the *real* issues associated with learning and teaching on the Web, I have ventured forward with a variety of WBLE experiences. This chapter is a case study description of my rookie experience teaching in an on-line environment that was custom designed to focus on learner and pedagogy issues found in the contemporary literature.

BACKGROUND

The experience described here is contextualized by a number of relevant factors. Comments, recommendations, and solutions provided in this chapter are based primarily on my experiences as the designer and instructor for a course delivered mostly online. A traditional, face-to-face meeting started the class, and there were two compressed video sessions held mid-semester. The importance of establishing a baseline community for learners in WBLEs cannot be over estimated. Throughout the semester, students seemed much less anxious about the limitations of the delivery systems because they felt a sense of community with other students and the instructor. The compressed video sessions were included primarily for exposure to that distance delivery system, but inadvertently contributed to an opportunity for community renewal and sharing for the students.

I have a variety of recent (development and pedagogical) experiences with WBLEs that have contributed to my academic and practitioner knowledge base. My area of professional preparation is in instructional design and distance education. Much of my work has been focused on improving teacher preparation to integrate instructional technologies within their instruction. Scholarly efforts have been, and continue to be, devoted to the design and development of effective learning environments that capitalize on the capacity of instructional technologies to change teaching and learning.

The existing literature base for WBLEs is largely anecdotal, but growing in volume and preponderance (see Bibliography). To the extent that this case study contributes to that literature base, the practice of distance development and instruction can be informed and elaborated.

Some important generalizations from this case study include: (a) students need time to formulate and contribute higher quality responses, (b) the quality of on-line interactions improves over time, (c) group interaction is a motivating factor, and (d) students in WBLEs tend to work harder and produce higher quality products than in a traditional setting.

The content of the WBLE described in the case study was distance education. Thus, the design of the WBLE was grounded in both cognitivist and constructivist principles: cognitivist in that specific content was identified and delivered, readings required, projects prescribed; constructivist in that multiple distance delivery technologies were embedded in the learner experience as vehicles for content delivery.

The reader should also know that the learners in this WBLE were graduate students representing a broad set of academic disciplines (e.g., Chemical Education, Physical Education, Human Rehabilitation, Educational Technology) and a wide range of prior experience with the Internet, the WWW, computer-based technologies, and distance learning. While this profile presents some challenge to the instructor and designer of WBLEs, it represents the typical on-line experiences with which I have been involved.

This chapter is admittedly colored by my convictions and value systems related to effective technology use, the potential for technology to positively influence and enhance learning, the importance of instructional design process in creating any learning environment, and the capability of WBLEs to meet the diverse needs of individual learners. When well designed, properly managed, and delivered by professional instructors, WBLEs offer a robust alternative to the traditional face-to-face instructional environment.

LESSONS LEARNED

The lessons learned from this novice experience are many. Some are documented in the WBLE literature, while the generalizability of others may be dependent on contextual variables. To bring order to the presentation, these "lessons" will be organized according to the basic principles of the generic instructional design model known as ADDIE (Analysis, Design, Development, Implementation, and Evaluation).

Analysis

In preparing this course for WWW delivery, a variety of analyses were conducted including learner, content, access, and infrastructure. The existing literature related to the typical characteristics of distance learners was valid. While unique in that these were all graduate students, they did fit the profile of adult distance learners (Hanson, Maushak,

Schlosser, Anderson, Sorensen, & Simonson, 1997). These students sought a credible, content-focused course that they could complete with heavy professional and personal commitments. Lack of time to fully engage in campus-based coursework was repeatedly the reason cited by students for their willingness to risk engagement in a nontraditional course. An error of my learner analysis was the assumption that since these students chose to register for an on-line course that was an upper-division graduate course in distance education, they had some minimal level of computer skill and some minimum level of Internet experience. Actually, the desire of students to access a flexibly scheduled course coupled with an apparent over-estimate of their individual ability to be successful in a technology-based "classroom" resulted in nearly half of the students being marginally skilled with computers and actual novices with Internet technologies. Success was achieved largely due to very high levels of motivation and determination on the part of both the learners and the instructor.

The content analysis focused on identifying and incorporating activities within the course that required significant active learner engagement. I was committed to delivering the same course content as for the campus-based course, but the instructional strategies and types of learner interaction would be varied dramatically. As I reflect on the culmination of this class, I did meet my commitment but at a significant cost to the learners and myself in scaffolding their technological skill development and troubleshooting access issues at the same time. This was simply too much content for learners unaccustomed to the environment and a novice on-line instructor.

The analysis of access for distance environments crosses a fairly complex set of issues. One must consider not only the choice of an appropriate delivery system(s), but also student and instructor access to that system(s). These considerations are compounded for WBLEs because of the variety of communication and utilization options available today (e.g., listservs, e-mail, computer conferencing, synchronous and asynchronous discussion) and the access capability of the student to infrastructure, hardware, and software (e.g., ISP bandwidth, amount of RAM, browser configuration) required in the WBLE. I overestimated the students' ability to solve their own technical problems, their ability to clearly define or articulate access problems, the typical in-home access to adequate bandwidth, and my own ability to provide access support to learners in the WBLE. Online communications, browsers, operating system configuration, and ISP capacity are not yet highly compatible or transparent to the user.

Design

Since the content of this course was distance education theories and principles, and the primary delivery system was the WWW, it seemed particularly appropriate to embed the content within activities that were both cognitive and constructive. Students were required to: (a) participate in weekly asynchronous on-line discussions that were topically directed and threaded by the instructor; (b) prepare a literature review or position paper on a distance education topic selected from a list that paralleled the weekly readings and on-line lectures; (c) participate in 10 synchronous discussions that began in week three and ended in week 12; (d) respond to the query, "What is distance education?" with a short reflection paper at three different times during the semester; (e) participate in two compressed video sessions with a group of graduate students from another university; and (f) create a full-scale design document for the implementation of a distance learning opportunity for an audience of their choice. The evaluation of student progress was directly correlated with stated course goals and performance rubrics.

The resource support for the content was available within the WBLE. Support strategies included a supplemental reading list, Web links to relevant sites, a brief FAQ section for basic technical questions, a section of the Web site devoted to student sharing and the building of learner community, a course listserv, a clearly defined course schedule, and a syllabus that included extensive descriptions of the student requirements, student samples, and the rubric criteria for evaluation.

Many of the course requirements relied, at least partially, on the student's ability to interact not only with the content but with the other students and the instructor as well. Consequently a number of the learner activities and the resource supports were aimed directly at maintaining high levels of learner-instructor interaction, peer-peer interaction, and feedback mechanisms to provide some boundaries for self-regulation within the constructivist WBLE.

The most important lesson learned from the design of the WBLE was actually a confirmation of the literature that advocates the importance of varied and continuous interaction opportunities in WBLEs. These opportunities allowed the students to maintain their high motivation when frustrated with the technology, overwhelmed by the workload, and geographically removed from their "class." This experience also confirmed the need for students to stay actively engaged with the content for deep, meaningful learning to occur.

Development

The same types of barriers exist for the creation of robust WBLEs that exist for the utilization of other types of technological innovation. Specifically, Leggett and Persichitte (1998) identify five barriers that hindered the customized creation of this WBLE: time, expertise, access, resources, and support (TEARS). The creation and development alone of the WBLE consumed approximately 150 hours. Perhaps we will eventually reach such a point of experience with WBLEs that their creation will be as common as that of traditional didactic instruction, but we are far from that point today. WBLEs are very human resource intensive to develop. My preparation in the discipline of educational technology prepared me for some of the expertise demands of this effort. However, the advances in telecommunications continue to explode with little chance to maintain that level of expertise with all applications of Internet technologies. Access to adequate hardware and software for development purposes is often an issue for on-line development. Resources during and after development are often nonexistent or minimal in their impact. Administrative support (before development and during implementation) can be a serious barrier to WBLE creation and utilization.

Implementation

Successful implementation of a WBLE is highly dependent on accurate and complete analyses as previously described. The students in this WBLE praised the opportunities for sharing and interaction and expressed deep frustration with access issues. Both the students and instructor were surprised by the amount of extra time required within the on-line delivery environment as compared to the traditional classroom delivery.

I cannot stress enough the importance of utilizing an instructional design model far in advance of the actual course start date. Without significant analysis, planning, design, development, and formative testing of the environment, the WBLE is likely to miss the mark with meeting student needs or developing learner knowledge. The asynchronous discussions and the reflection papers allowed me to formatively monitor both the attitude and the cognitive growth of the students. I found it important to temper my requests, expectations, and feedback with the results of these formative evaluations in order to maintain and cultivate a necessary sense of community among these learners.

Evaluation

Every instructional technology has a set of capabilities and limitations. WBLEs are not exempt from either category. Capabilities of WBLEs include:

- Provision of student-centered environments that allow for enhanced cognitive supports,
- A variety of opportunities to incorporate interaction and communication (group and individualized),
- The ability to meet the academic needs of learners who find themselves heavily constrained by professional and personal obligations,
- An increased potential to meet and adapt to individual learner needs in the affective, cognitive, and social domains, and
- The potential to provide almost immediate feedback at the individual learner level.

Limitations of WBLEs include:

- Increased student responsibility for monitoring, directing, and self-evaluating their own learning,
- A serious misperception among many learners and instructors that WBLEs will be "easier" than traditional classroom instruction,
- The potential for misinterpretation given that the content delivery is entirely media-based, and
- The expectation of students that this is an "immediate feedback" technology, so the instructor must set boundaries to their personal access.

In order to capitalize on the capabilities and design around the limitations of the WWW, I offer the following suggestions (Persichitte, 1999). Early on, emphasize the use of the WWW for communications. Use individual e-mail, class listservs, mailing lists, synchronous and asynchronous discussion areas to open as many electronic channels of communication as possible. Students will develop their reliance on these communication tools as use is modeled and encouraged by the instructor.

Scaffold the use of the Web for research purposes. There is a tendency to expect that students in online environments already possess basic skills associated with research and information management...that they simply need to transfer those skills to the WWW. This has not been my experience even though my work has been exclusively with graduate students. The WWW presents a unique information structure for the novice that requires suggestions and support from the instructor to be effectively used by the student. These skills must be developed and practiced over time.

Clearly articulate the class structure. The feelings of isolation are quite real for most first time students in WBLEs. Those emotions are heightened if students do not have a clear understanding of what they are expected to do, when they are expected to do it, where they can find resources to support their efforts, and how their performance will be evaluated. Identify opportunities for students to interact with each other and with the instructor.

Define student activities (participation, activities, assessments, assignments, etc.).

Details that are often shared informally in face-to-face settings need to be documented in WBLEs. Consider the questions that you are asked when teaching in traditional classrooms about class requirements and address those in detail within the WBLE.

Be creative and flexible with instructional strategies. Creativity is imperative if we are to provide online students with the same (or better!) quality of learning experience as provided for traditional on campus students. The ability to capitalize on the capabilities of the Web for instructional purposes relies heavily on our re-thinking the status quo of instructional strategies. To prevent WBLEs from becoming monotonous environments, I encourage you to be flexible with your selection of instructional strategies, as well. For instance, do not rely completely on asynchronous communication - find a way to incorporate some synchronous communication.

Encourage and design for collaborative activities. This suggestion is related to the previous paragraph and to the prior discussion about the importance of developing a sense of learner community among on-line students. The purposeful incorporation of collaborative activities in WBLEs requires creativity, flexibility, and instructor commitment that collaboration and sharing are important for many reasons in on-line environments.

RECOMMENDATIONS

Like all instructional environments, WBLEs are complex in their design. Ask yourself these ten fundamental redesign questions as you begin to create a WBLE:

What are the course objectives?
What are the anticipated learner characteristics?
What content can be learned by discovery and what must/should be scaffolded?
What can be learned via peer interaction and collaboration?
What instructional strategies and media allow me to meet these criteria?
Does technology exist that would eliminate or alter this activity?
What are the anticipated differences in feedback to my on-line learners?
How will I mentor and monitor active student engagement?
What type(s) of assessment are appropriate?
What provisions are in place for summative and formative course evaluation?

CONCLUSION

By reflecting upon and describing this first experience with on-line instruction, I have provided a number of suggestions, concerns, and recommendations related to the creation and implementation of WBLEs. Certainly, the designers and instructors of these environments must be cognizant of particular differences related to the WWW as a delivery system for instruction. On the other hand, a number of the "lessons learned" might be as easily descriptive of *any* instructional environment. The importance of instructional design process and maintaining a focus on the learner apply regardless of the delivery system.

REFERENCES

Bates, A. W. (1995). *Technology, open learning and distance education.* New York: Routledge.

Cuban, L. (1986). *Teachers and machines: The classroom use of technology since 1920.* New York: Teachers College Press.

Cyrs, T. E., & Conway, E. D. (1997). *Teaching at a distance with the merging technologies: An instructional systems approach.* Las Cruces, NM: New Mexico State University.

Franklin, N., Yoakam, M. & Warren, R. (1995). *Distance learning: A guide to systems planning and implementation.* Bloomingdale, IN: Indiana University.

Hannafin, M. J. (1995). Open-ended learning environments: Foundations, assumptions, and implications for automated design. In R. D. Tennyson & A. E. Barron (Eds.), *Automating instructional design: Computer-based development and delivery tools* (pp. 101-130). Berlin: Springer.

Hanson, D., Maushak, N. J., Schlosser, C. A., Anderson, M. L., Sorensen, C, & Simonson, M. (1997). *Distance education: Review of the literature* (2nd ed.). Washington, DC: Association for Educational Communications and Technology.

Jonassen, D. H. (Ed.). (1996). *Handbook of research for educational communications and technology.* New York: Simon & Schuster Macmillan.

Keegan, D. (1996). *Foundations of distance education* (3rd ed.). New York: Routledge.

Khan, B. (Ed.). (1997). *Web-based instruction.* Englewood Cliffs, NJ: Educational Technology.

Leggett, W., & Persichitte, K. A. (1998). Blood, sweat, and TEARS: 50 years of technology implementation obstacles. *Tech Trends, 43*(3), 33-36.

Lockwood, F. (Ed.). (1995). *Open and distance learning today.* New York: Routledge.

McHenry, L., & Bozik, M. (1995). Communicating at a distance: A study of interaction in a distance education classroom. *Communication Education, 44*(4), 363-370.

Mood, T. A. (1995). *Distance education: An annotated bibliography.* Englewood, CO: Libraries Unlimited, Inc.

Moore, M. G., & Kearsley, G. (1996). *Distance education: A systems view.* Belmont, CA: Wadsworth.

National Center for Education Statistics (NCES). (1997). *Distance education in higher education institutions.* Washington, DC: Office of Educational Research and Improvement.

National Telecommunications and Information Administration (NTIA). (1997). *Falling through the Net II: New data on the digital divide.* Available online: http://www.ntia.doc.gov/ntiahome/net2/falling.html

Persichitte, K. A. (1999). Tips for course conversion to the Web. In J. D. Price, J. Willis, D. A. Willis, M. Jost, S. Boger-Mehall, & B. Robin (Eds.), *Society for Information Technology and Teacher Education Proceedings of SITE 99* (p. 237-239). Charlottesville, VA: Association for the Advancement of Computing in Education.

Porter. L. R. (1997). *Creating the virtual classroom: Distance learning with the internet.* New York: J. Wiley & Sons.

Rivard, J. D. (1998). *Educational technology: Reflection, research, practice* (2nd ed.). Needham Heights, MA: Simon and Schuster.

Schlosser, C. A., & Anderson, M. L. (1994). *Distance education: Review of the literature.* Washington, DC: Association for Educational Communications and Technology.

Schrum, L., & Berenfeld, B. (1997). *Teaching and learning in the information age: A guide to educational telecommunications*. Boston: Allyn & Bacon.

Simonson, M. R. (1995). Does anyone really want to learn at a distance? *Tech Trends, 40*(5), 12.

Witherspoon, J. P. (1997). *Distance education: A planner's casebook*. Boulder, CO: Western Interstate Commission for Higher Education.

Chapter XIII

Examining the Range of Student Needs in the Design and Development of a Web-Based Course

Susan M. Powers and Sharon Guan
Indiana State University, USA

Distance learning is by no means a new phenomenon. However, new technologies provide a twist to distance learning that is making it grow and expand at an overwhelming rate. The National Center for Educational Statistics reported that in 1995, a third of U.S. post-secondary schools offered distance education courses with another quarter of these schools planning to do so in the next three years. During the summer of 1999, the UCLA Extension Service will offer more than 100 Web–based courses in continuing higher education to anyone and anywhere (*Business Wire*, 1999). When the rapid proliferation of Web-based courses as a distance learning option is considered, and then couple that proliferation with the fact that the World Wide Web (WWW) has only been "popular" for the past five years, this expansion is indeed overwhelming.

While the numbers alone are enough to amaze and dazzle, what is more interesting, and should be of greater concern, are the instructional design and pedagogical issues that should form the foundation of Web-based courses (Ritchie & Hoffman, 1997). The technical proficiencies necessary to build a course Web site and all of its technological accompaniments are merely psychomotor skills that range from the simple to the highly complex. However, one of the reasons for the rapid proliferation of Web-based courses is the development of courseware packages (Web Course-In-A-Box, WebCT, ILN CourseInfo, etc.) that remedy the needs for instructors to worry about acquiring these technical skills (Hansen & Frick, 1997). Unfortunately, while these courseware packages, and the many Web editors available, may facilitate the development of Web-based courses, these tools don't address the myriad of instructional design and pedagogical issues that must be considered before and during development. Hill (1997) lists some of these key issues, which include pedagogical, technological, organizational, institutional, and ethical questions. Many of these issues must be resolved prior to the development of the first Web page.

In this chapter, we explore some of the research that has been done on Web-based courses, but our intent is to largely delve into the practical realities of designing pedagogically effective and accessible Web-based instruction (WBI). Specifically, we explore the importance of a needs assessment of learner characteristics in the design process to determine and therefore design for the technological abilities and capacities of target students. Additionally, potential solutions and recommendations on how to design a virtual classroom environment that fosters and facilitates active student learning are discussed. Finally, the authors examine the very real issue of course accessibility for all students and how various design elements can enhance the accessibility.

BACKGROUND

As described above, the educational community is turning to the Web in ever increasing numbers to deliver and receive instruction. What is the appeal of the Web for teaching and learning? The Web has experienced phenomenal growth, with currently well over four million Web servers worldwide. That figure doesn't even begin to indicate the number of users, which remains a difficult number to determine (Zakon, 1999). This growth makes WBI an accessible medium for distance education for many users. It is also affordable from the delivery standpoint; colleges and universities already have the Internet infrastructure in place. At most, the institution might choose to license one of the aforementioned courseware packages to facilitate WBI delivery; however, faculty may also opt for the development of their own original Web sites. Either way, the university does not need to invest in new classrooms or technologies, and expenses may ultimately be offset by attracting new students to courses.

Although WBI may be growing because it is convenient for the student and for the institution, it also has some inherent advantages as an effective instructional tool. The world's job market is constantly changing; there are jobs that will exist in the future that do not exist at this moment. In many ways, we are preparing students for what is a moving target. Therefore, what we are really preparing students for is the process of lifelong learning whereby they control their own learning needs (Romiszowski, 1997). The power of WBI is that to varying degrees, students have control over when and where they gain their new knowledge. Research has shown that students can be effective learners over the Web, and learn as much if not more than in traditional courses (Mory, Gambill, & Browning, 1998; *Business Wire*, 1999b). However, are there factors that must go into the design of these courses to ensure that students are developing this self-directed learning style and can gain the skills needed to be successful in the long-term?

To design an effective course, whether it is Web-based, traditional, or presented in other formats, a student-centered needs assessment should form the central core of the instructional design. Witkin (1984) defines a needs assessment as the process of using information to make decisions, set priorities, and allocate resources for course design. Burton and Merrill (1991) suggest that a need is present when "there is a discrepancy or gap between the way things 'ought to be' and the way they 'are'" (p.21). As an instructor, and as an instructional designer, part of a needs assessment is determining if these "gaps" can be resolved through instruction, or if the possible resolution lies outside those bounds (Mager & Pipe, 1970). These views of needs assessment largely deal with determining discrepancies. By highlighting discrepancies in knowledge and information, for example, an instructor can piece together the components that create a course.

For WBI, an effective needs assessment must consider more than discrepancies. It is still important to determine what students know and don't know as that information forms the basis of the course. However, there are a number of other factors that can't be left to chance and must be designed into the course. For example, the instructor or designer must be familiar with the learner characteristics of the students. This issue is also critical to the success of other forms of instruction, like face-to-face courses; yet, most effective instructors can learn about these elements and about their students as the class progresses and make course adjustments as necessary. What are these factors? They are the elements of a course that are specific to the students themselves, such as the ability of the student to become actively involved with the course information, the ability to manage course information, and the ability to process course information.

Once the needs of the course and the learner characteristics are understood, there still remains the issue of designing the course. There are many aspects to the instructional design process. Beyond the needs assessment and the determination of learner characteristics, we will also delve into the instructional strategies that can be used to create interactive learning experiences and course accessibility. The instructional strategy provides the sequences and methods for achieving course objectives. Effective strategies will help the learner to make connections between what s/he already knows and the new information of the course (Kemp, Morrison, & Ross, 1998). Strategies and the design process should focus on the learners and the learning process rather than the content.

FACTORS TO BE CONSIDERED IN THE DESIGN PROCESS

In this section, we address those factors that can and should be considered in the design process. They are factors that can greatly impact the success of students in WBI, and may even affect the ability of students to access the course itself. The factors considered here are the computing capacity and ability of students, the design of an active learning environments, and the equity of student access to the course.

Determining and Designing for Computing Capacity of Students

Instructors who plan to teach a course on the Web automatically add two new responsibilities to their usual teaching task. One is to construct a course with technological "bells and whistles", and the other, to walk the students through the process of accessing and utilizing those technologies. The former is likely to ignite the enthusiasm (and perhaps terror in more than a few people) of course designers to use cutting-edge technology. Student use of the technology can be the splash of cold water of hard reality when slow modem speed, narrow bandwidth and limited storage space are considered.

The multimedia components of WBI consist of five elements: (1) text and graphics; (2) audio or streamed audio; (3) video or streamed video; (4) graphic user interface (GUI); and (5) compression technology (Khan, 1997). Although text and graphics are still the most commonly used elements for the Web, there has been enormous effort to enrich Web pages with audio and video clips, and to make Web graphics more attractive with complex design.

Emerging technologies continue to make the design of these elements even easier for the non-programmer. It is also possible to find companies that offer software- and hardware-based full motion video experience on the Internet. Video streams via new 56.6 kpbs modems may be optimized to deliver the maximum performance. However, the most prevalent connection rate on the Internet will continue to be 28.8 and 14.4 kpbs for some time to come (Azarmsa, 1998). Furthermore, most audio and especially video files are too large to run through small Internet pipes or even over most corporate and educational intra-networks.

While the glitz of technology might be appealing, it is important to once again consider the design of the instruction and the needs of the student. The intentional sense of teaching can lead to the success sense of teaching only through the right choice of media (Soltis, 1978). In other words, if the Web technologies that can create the "bells and whistles" are chosen without consideration of the learner's perspective, successful learning might not be achieved. The students might learn in spite of the technology.

When constructing an on-line course, technology availability and accessibility should be analyzed from the user's perspective, and from the perspective of the instructional need. To gain a sense of the student perspective, a course designer or instructor should prepare some sort of end-user technology checklist that includes:

- Hardware capacity (hard drives, RAM, sound cards, video cards, multimedia input and output devices, such as a microphone, speakers, etc.);
- Internet accessibility (modem speed, connection types);
- Software setup (types and versions of Internet browser, plug-in programs – Quick Time, RealAudio, RealVideo, Shockwave, Adobe Acrobat Reader, etc); and
- Server capacity and capability (bandwidth, FTP, CGI support).

This information can seem dry and uninteresting, even tedious to collect, but it would be far worse to design a course that contained critical, instructional components a remote student was unable to access because of a lack of computer power or necessary modem speed.

The designer of WBI should keep in mind that the driving force behind a distance course is the effective learning of subject matter, not the enforcement of state-of-the-art distance education technologies. Despite knowing the strength and limitation of a student's computing capacity, an advanced Web technology may not be the best way to successfully present information to the student, i.e., just because something can be done does not necessarily mean that it should be done.

Finally, when designing WBI, the computing ability of the student must also be considered. For example, an instructor might be safe in assuming that a student who elects to enroll in WBI is able to send and receive e-mail, and to navigate the Web. Depending on the student population, that might not necessarily be true. It is also highly possible that students may not know how to e-mail an attached file, to properly respond to e-mail discussion group messages, to participate in chatrooms, or download Internet helper applications or class files. To combat these potential discrepancies between proficiency and course demands, the instructor either needs to carefully determine the skills of students at the beginning of the class and be prepared to modify the course design, or be prepared to provide instruction on how to use any tools that are required in the class.

To accomplish all of this, the instructor can do a number of things. To determine student computing power and ability, the instructor can send out a brief survey to the students at the beginning of the class, or earlier if class lists are available. The survey can ask students information regarding computing capacity (hardware issues) as presented earlier. The survey can also be used to ask students how often they have used the Web and e-mail in the past, whether or not they have ever participated in chatrooms or an e-mail discussion group, or sent e-mail attachments (depending upon the expectations of the course).

Finally, the instructor must remember that instructor expectations aren't always clear to students in the beginning of a course, and WBI will cause some additional confusion. For example, the instructor might expect all papers to be turned in as e-mail attachments, to be opened, read and returned as attachments using Microsoft Word. However, the student may have a different word processing package on his or her computer and will be submitting attachments that have been created in Claris Works, for example. Instead of frustrating the student by informing him or her that the file is unreadable, or at least not formatted as intended, it is important for the instructor to establish protocols to distribute to students. The instructor might require that all papers or other attachments be turned in using a specific version of a software title. Yet, that might be considered an excessive requirement of the student. What might be more reasonable is to have the students attach their papers in Rich Text Format (RTF). This format retains the appearance of the student's formatting, and can be retrieved through a variety of software. The instructor must also be aware that many students may not know how to save their documents as RTF files, and a tip sheet might need to be provided.

A set of protocols can also provide guidelines for how electronic conversations are conducted (e.g., addressing messages, signing messages, etc.), any restrictions for electronic discussion groups (e.g., no social discussion allowed), and repercussions for violating the protocols. In many ways, this type of information is not any different than the class rules or policies that might be introduced into a traditional classroom. However, in a traditional class, students have had years to understand and practice that they should raise their hands to be called upon, to hand in papers that are stapled and neat, etc. The time span of WBI has not yet allowed for this general culture of understanding and expectation to develop. Therefore, effective instructional design for WBI must consider the student computing capacity, ability and experience.

Online Active Learning Environments

After years of educational experiments, educators at all levels have begun to realize that an effective education is a learner-centered education. Successful learning occurs only when students are actively involved in the process of inquiry, reflection, conceptualization and application. Mel Silberman (1996) describes an active learning environment as a place where students' needs, expectations, and concerns influence the teacher's instructional plans.

When the research shows that the majority of classes taught by faculty rated highest by students are predominately non-interactive, lecture-based courses (Nunn, 1996), and student discussion may comprise less than 2% of the course, it seems discouraging to expect faculty to make WBI interactive. However, the research does show that WBI that employs a variety of instructional strategies and creates interactive experiences for students (Mory et al., 1998; *Business Wire,* 1999b) leads to students who are successful and are assumedly developing self-directed learning skills (Romiszowski, 1997).

To construct a Web course that fosters student interaction and meets their expectations requires a better understanding of students from the cognitive, psychological and social perspectives. An active on-line learning environment built to meet the needs of the learner does the following:

1) Explores and stimulates learners' motivation;
2) Fosters and encourages participation and interaction among the students; and
3) Contains a great amount of personal and humanistic elements.

Motivation

Lynnette Porter (1997) points out, "the most successful distance learners are self-motivated; you want to learn and you make sure you participate fully in the course" (p. 97). The less self-motivated students then contribute to the high drop out rate of 30-50% in distance education courses (Moore & Kearsley, 1996). Given the relationship of motivation to student success, it is imperative that the underlying cause of student self- motivation is explored when planning WBI (Carlson, Downs, Repman & Clark, 1998).

Motivation is a large and complex subject that has been investigated by many psychologists. Given the existence of multiple kinds and sources of motivation, says Gagné (1985), the task of the instructional designer is to identify the motives of students and to channel them into activities that accomplish educational goals. In other words, the task of motivating students in distance learning requires the designer to: 1) identify the motives of the students; and 2) stimulate their motivation with course-related activities.

Three factors have been reported to help identify students' motivation: intention to complete the course, early submission of work, and completion of other distance education courses (Armstrong, Toebe & Watson, 1985; Billings, 1989; Moore & Kearsley, 1996; Cornell & Martin, 1997). Information regarding these three factors may be obtained by an on-line questionnaire posted on the course site prior to or at the beginning of the course, or e-mailed to students (such a questionnaire could be combined with the information being gathered about students' computing ability and capacity). Some of the elements that can be included in the questionnaire are:

- Demographic information (gender, age, ethnicity, etc.);
- Academic information (pursued degree, major, specialized area, etc.);
- Previous experience with the subject matter;
- Previous experience with distance education (the number of Distance Ed courses taken, types of Distance Ed, i.e. video-based, correspondence, or Web-based);
- Reason(s) for taking the course through the Internet (degree requirement, time and space bound, personal interest, the only delivery mode available, etc.);
- Perceptions of Web-based instruction in comparison with traditional instruction;
- Anxieties and concerns (technological and personal);
- Identification of learning style (visual, auditory, or kinesthetic learner), interpersonal orientation (a loner or a group person), time management and pace control of project and assignment skills (an "on-timer" or procrastinator); and
- Strategies that students think can help them succeed in this class (technical support, study groups, a tutoring program, regular instructor feedback, etc.).

The questionnaire will serve not only as a database for the instructional designer to conduct a learner analysis, but also a reminder for the learners to be more aware of or alert to their potential barriers.

In order to use motivation effectively within instructional design, Gagné (1985) suggests that the learner must be informed of the nature of the achievement expected as an outcome of learning. The purpose is to establish an expectancy of the performance to be achieved as a result of learning and that "the primary effect of providing learners with an expectancy of the learning outcome is to enable them to match their own performances with a class of performance they expect to be 'correct'" (Gagné, 1985, p.309). As discussed with student computing ability and capacity, in WBI the instructor needs to be purposeful about the expectations and communicate clearly with all students. For example, in a face-to-face class situation, if a student raises a hand and asks about instructor expectations, the whole class hears the answers. In WBI, if a student sends an e-mail question to the instructor, and the instructor replies back just to the student, only that one student has had the expectation clarified.

Student Participation and Interaction

Jerome Bruner (1966) recognizes that there is a deep human need to respond to others and to work together jointly toward an objective. Such need of the students is described as the social side of learning, or the psychosocial environment of the classroom (Fraser, 1989; Moos, 1974). Learning is enhanced when it is more like a team effort than a solo race. Good learning, like good work, is collaborative and social, not competitive and isolated. Working with others often increases involvement in learning. Sharing one's ideas and responding to others improves thinking and deepens understanding (Chickering & Gamson, 1987). However, in terms of distance learning, Verduin and Clark (1991) state that the separation of teacher and learner does not allow for a truly shared learning experience. While the separation may not allow for these important interactions, is it possible to intentionally design interactions and purposefully engineer shared learning experiences for the WBI learning environment?

Research on factors influencing students' perceived learning in WBI indicates that the percentage of the grade weight based on discussion and the instructor's specification of requirements of students' contributions in discussion are significantly and positively correlated to students' perceived amount of learning (Jiang, 1998). Although the level of an instructor's participation was not significantly correlated with students' perceived amount of learning, it had a significant correlation with the level of students' participation. These findings indicate that student learning outcomes can be enhanced when an instructor intentionally designs student interactions into WBI. Furthermore, Jiang (1998) found that students learn better through a social, shared construction of meaning. Grading of interactions is just one technique that could be used to foster active learning. Silberman (1996) has introduced a number of ideas on how to create an active learning environment for face-to-face instruction. Minor modifications make these same activities possible in the WBI arena. Some examples are presented here:

- **Trading Places** – to promote self-disclosure or an active exchange of viewpoint
  1. Ask students to post a note on a course bulletin board or listserv on the following (for example):
     - A value they hold;
     - An enjoyable experience they have had recently; or
     - A Web site (or page) that they like the most.
  2. Ask students to negotiate the trading of posted notes with one another over the

listserv or through e-mail. The exchange should be based on a desire to possess a particular value, experience, idea and taste. Make sure that all trades are two-way deals. Post on the course bulletin board or on listserv the result of the exchange and the reason for it.

- **Group Resume** – geared toward the subject matter or computer skills
  1. Divide students into groups of 3 to 5.
  2. Suggest an imaginary job, such as a Web Usability Test Group that will be in charge of using, evaluating and analyzing a certain Web site or resources on the Web.
  3. Ask each group to apply for the job by posting on the course site or course listserv a group resume that will include Education Background, Experience with the Web, Computer Skills, Accomplishment, and Special Talents (make sure the data represents the group as one unit).
  4. Respond to the applicants with a nice sense of humor, such as "Your resume has been put into our company's data bank for future opportunities."
- **Web search** – Scavenger Hunts on the Internet
  1. Distribute the class roster at the beginning of the course.
  2. Ask each student to conduct a search on the Internet for the information related to his/her classmates, such as personal Web pages, links, people with similar names, etc. (For a big class, students can be assigned with names of two or three classmates.)
  3. Post the information on the Listserv. (Call it a "Got Ya" message.)
- **Paired Activity** –getting acquainted or study with a friend
  1. Pair up students according to one of the following criteria:
     - Students who express a desire to work together;
     - Students from the same department/major; or
     - Students who have taken classes together.
  2. Encourage them to exchange learning experiences on a regular basis. The instructor might ask to be cc'ed on any e-mail correspondence they share.
  3. Assign projects to the teams.

In many instances, active learning is the product of creative teaching, which comes from either careful planning or impromptu wisdom. For success in WBI, the former is more critical.

Personal and Humanistic Elements

The greatest advantage of a dynamic instructor over all other instructional media and methods is human interaction and reciprocal caring expressed through relationship listening (Bohlken, 1998). Such a statement from a different angle implies the potential disadvantage of distance education. Porter (1997) points out that distance learning turns teaching and training into publication and presentation. WBI runs the risk of easily becoming impersonal and mechanical. In the virtual classroom where eye contact, body language, facial expressions, and other types of non-verbal communication are missing, how to break through the boundary of "distance" and develop a close personal relationship with students becomes a big challenge in the design of courses.

Research indicates that "perceived caring" on the part of the students in regard to the instructor enhances the students' attitudes toward the class and their perception of what they learn (Bohlken, 1998). Frequent student-faculty contact in and out of class is an important factor in student motivation and involvement. Knowing a few faculty members well enhances students' intellectual commitment and encourages them to think about their own values and plans (Chickering & Gamson, 1998).

While there might not be an ideal resolution for the lack of "physical presence" of an instructor, some of the following methods can be used to enhance the humanistic aspects of the Web-based course:

- *Create a friendly instructor page.* A Web page of a mug shot and some academic information is not enough for the students to get a complete image of the instructor. A Chinese proverb says, " A heart can only be traded by another." To win the trust of the students, the instructors should expose more information about themselves, e.g., hobbies, family, and favorite sites or stories.
- *Call every student on the phone at the beginning and during the semester.* Sometimes written words in e-mail cannot carry the tone that the voice can. A phone conversation or greeting makes a big difference especially to those who are used to "reading" information on the computer all the time.
- *Display a sense of humor.* A joke a day may be too big a burden, but some jokes once in a while on the listserv or through e-mail may help break the boundary between the instructor and students.
- *Be available and approachable.* Being physically apart from the group, distance learners are more likely to feel insecure since one of the key ways to attain that sense of safety and security is to gather connections to other people and to feel included in a group (Silberman, 1996). Instructors must make the line of connection available all the time. Remind students regularly that they may send e-mail or phone at any time with questions or concerns. Then, be quick to respond to these virtual connections when they do come from students.

Course Accessibility

One of the advantages of WBI over traditional instruction is that is provides for anytime, anywhere learning. In other words, the learner is not prevented by physical time or space from participating in a class; and as seen in previous sections, a carefully designed, interactive course can provide a learning environment where students can flourish. However, all the design efforts and needs assessments conducted by the instructor or designer are for naught if the course is inaccessible to the student. We have already looked at some student issues that might impact accessibility, such as desktop computing power or technical ability. These issues are often visible or at least easy to detect if a proper needs assessment is completed. What must also be of concern to the instructor and course designer are those more hidden factors that might affect accessibility. These factors include learning and physical disabilities.

Learning Disabilities

The numbers are difficult to determine, but consider that in 1986, 14% of the disabled students who registered with college disability offices reported being learning disabled (HEATH, 1997), and that nationally, 15-20% of the population has some form of learning disability (National Center for Learning Disabilities, 1999). The future impact is also amplified when it is considered that during a ten-year period between the mid-1980s and mid

1990s the number of children in public schools identified with learning disabilities more than doubled.

The Rehabilitation Act of 1973 and the Americans With Disabilities Act of 1990 (Reamer, 1997) serve to protect the civil rights of persons with disabilities. They also require that higher education must provide reasonable, timely and effective accommodations for disabled persons at the institution. The expectation for accommodation does not include the expectation that programmatic requirements are altered or established academic standards are diminished. Once a student is registered with the appropriate university office, the student is expected to notify instructors and propose a number of accommodative strategies. For instance, the student (and if necessary the support office) may ask for permission to tape lectures, have extended periods of time for exams, or use a computer for the writing of essay exams (Reamer, 1997). Faculty have become familiar with these accommodations as they occur during typical face-to-face instruction. However, how do these accommodations work in the on-line classroom?

There is not a direct instructional correlation between the face-to-face environment and the on-line teaching environment. Gilbert (1997) does observe that there are basic characteristics shared such as the focus on the transfer of knowledge, application of the understanding, and evaluation. However, the instructional strategies chosen will not be the same as those used in the traditional classroom (Powers, 1997). Therefore, the strategies that a learning-disabled student might know and be familiar with will not necessarily translate neatly into the Web-based environment. The challenge becomes one of determining what type of accommodations would be necessary and practical, given the variety of electronic communication and amount of reading and writing of text WBI requires.

The typical expectation for accommodation is that the student presents options and the instructor grants permission. However, given the unique and new nature of Web-based course delivery, students may not be aware of what useful accommodation options might work and what might be possible. Additionally, since many of the accommodations suggested below require advanced planning (as does most of Web-based course delivery), an instructor is well-served to consider these options during the design of Web-based instruction and prior to being approached by a learning-disabled student.

Reading Guides. Often in Web-based instruction, the instructor takes the role of a learning facilitator leading students through readings that enhance and elaborate upon the topic. In other words, a greater dependence upon written materials may exist in the Web-based classroom environment. To facilitate this heavy reliance on reading for the learning-disabled student, an instructor might elect to develop reading guides which direct the student to the most critical components of a reading passage. For example, imagine that a class has been assigned to read and review a Web site. A comprehensive Web site includes a multitude of links that lead the reader to many directly and indirectly related topics. A reading guide leads the student to the relevant links to follow, as well as highlights the most important parts, much as voice inflection does in a traditional class.

It might appear that providing a written reading guide simply compounds the problem for the student. However, if done in a simple outline format, the amount of reading necessary is cursory. The organization of a reading guide can also help the student organize the information in ways similar to traditional learning strategies. Another option, and possibly more viable, is to provide the student with an audio reading guide. Much like the tape-recorded guide through a museum, an audio guide highlights the key points of readings on which the student should concentrate. Audio can be placed on the Web site or on a CD for the use of the student.

Voice E-mail. E-mail quickly becomes a critical component of on-line instruction. Whether used to submit assignments, to ask questions of an instructor to receive guidance and feedback, or to participate in electronic discussion lists, successful electronic communication will translate into a successful class (Powers & Dutt-Doner, 1998). The student who has difficulty reading and writing electronic transmissions is therefore at an immediate disadvantage. Limited success can be achieved by having another person read the e-mail messages to the student or transcribing his or her words into a message. Success can be limited because the sheer bulk of email during an on-line course can tax even the most willing helper.

Another alternative comes in the form of voice e-mail. Voice e-mail works on the same principle as text e-mail; however, the sender's message is recorded with audio and sent to the e-mail address and then played with a voice e-mail client. The software is compatible with a number of different e-mail programs such as e-mail access through popular Web browsers and some of the more popular POP email programs. There is a cost associated with the software needed to create and send voice email, but the client software needed to play the message is free.

Telephone. The newer technology of voice e-mail provides one set of options for communication between instructor and student and the familiar telephone offers other possibilities. For those times when a learning-disabled student needs verbal instructions from the instructor, or needs to transmit information to the instructor verbally, the phone is still be an immensely useful mechanism. The great advantage of this option is that the phone is convenient and available. There are no hardware or software requirements for using the phone, and no training is required to begin use! However, some of the disadvantages of the phone are more evident when voice email is considered.

When a synchronous phone conversation is taking place, it is difficult to keep a record of the conversation (unless the parties have agreed that the conversation can be taped). When the conversation is not synchronous and messages are being left on answering machines and voice mail (either of which are necessary to make this option workable), those messages are not easily stored. Voice mail generally has limitations on the size of storage and does not allow the user to save a large number of messages. Answering machines with tapes have a greater capacity for storage but also lend themselves to easy erasure of messages. Also, the messages can't be saved in a selected order, only in the order in which they were left on the machine. Finally, most answering machines and voice mail limit the length of a message. Voice email does not have that limitation (although the longer the message, the larger the file size).

CD-ROM. Another option is the development of a companion CD-ROM for the course. A CD-ROM is suggested instead of a floppy disk because of the likely size of an appropriate companion disk. The companion CD-ROM can provide an off-line opportunity for the student to access information that would enhance course understanding. It can include materials such as:

1. *Audio recordings of lectures*. If the course includes Web-based lectures or readings created by the instructor to explain the course material and content, the text of those documents could be digitally recorded on the computer and saved to individual files identified by date or topic. The student could then select the appropriate file and listen to, rather than read, the material.

2. *Graphical representations of content.* An instructor may have content that lends itself to explanation to some students through concept mapping or other graphical representation. The CD-ROM can contain graphics files for those items. Many of these graphics might be free form, hand-drawn representations by the instructor that are scanned into digital format.
3. *PowerPoint Presentations.* This option once again utilizes text, but a well-constructed PowerPoint presentation will provide highlights of the material in a visually pleasing manner and may help guide the student through the required lectures and readings.
4. *Helper Applications.* This option makes available any software (keeping in mind copyright restrictions) that allows students to access other information placed on the CD ROM, e.g., an audio player for digitized audio or a graphics viewer for graphics files.
5. *Reading Guides.* This option was presented earlier, but it is important to consider that the CD-ROM could store these guides in a variety of formats—text, audio, or video —for retrieval.
6. *Index.* Like the index of a reference book, a CD ROM index, perhaps provided as both text and audio even as hypertext, assists an individual in finding the needed resources on the CD-ROM.

This list is not meant to convey every option of what could be placed on a CD-ROM, but rather to provide a starting point. Other students as well might appreciate the variety that such materials lend to a text-laden Web-based course.

***Web-Based Multimedia*.** The options discussed under the CD ROM heading can just as well be offered through the format of the Web site. The student who needs the additional resources can download presentations, graphics, concept maps, audio files, etc. However, the use of these features in WBI that require certain levels of computing capacity and student ability should be considered only if the student needs assessment indicate that those tools are accessible to all students.

Physical Disabilities

There are millions of Americans who are deaf, hard-of-hearing, blind or visually impaired, or with other physical limitations who are also computer users. Many of these individuals also need to be provided with the option of WBI. We do not explore the hardware and software devices that can be used by these individuals to enable interactions with the computer, but rather explore how features in the *Web Content Accessibility Guidelines* (W3C, 1999) point to instructional design issues for WBI.

- *Text.* Text is the most heavily used aspect of WBI. Fortunately, text is able to be rendered (through text readers, Braille readers, etc.) that makes it accessible to almost all users.
- *Multiple Channels.* By providing your information through multiple channels (i.e., what is offered in audio or video is also offered in a text format), accessibility is enhanced. This option also provides an option for those students who don't have the computing capacity to view Web-based multimedia. Text equivalents also need to be offered for graphics for the visually impaired (the text must convey the same function or purpose as the image). Reversing this principle, providing a non-text equivalent of text can enhance accessibility for those with reading difficulties (as described in the section on Learning Disabilities).

- *Color*. Ensure that information can be conveyed equally well when users are unable to discern color differences. This factor applies to graphics, hypertext links, and emphasis in text.
- *Tables*. It is becoming a common practice to use tables on Web pages to make a visually pleasing layout design. However, layout tables present problems for screen readers (software that reads aloud the content of the screen). Use tables only to present data and content.
- *Movement*. Items on a Web page that move, blink, or scroll can disrupt the information processing of people with visual difficulties, learning disabilities, or medical conditions like epilepsy. Screen readers cannot read moving text. Persons with physical disabilities might not be able to move quickly enough to interact with moving objects. For these reasons alone, it is best to avoid features like animated graphics, blinking text, scrolling text, etc.
- *Orientation and Navigation*. Clear and consistent navigation tools and content organization helps to ensure that students with disabilities are able to find information within the course Web site. This factor actually benefits all users, but poor navigation and orientation can particularly hinder those students with visual or learning disabilities.

The items presented here do no reflect all of the guidelines available to make a Web site accessible. However, they do represent those features that an instructor or designer should carefully consider as the course is being developed.

FUTURE TRENDS

In an interview with Alan Chute, at the Center for Excellence in Distance Learning, the opinion was offered that current Web-based instruction is little more than downloaded face-to-face courses, or at best computer-based training (Christiansen & Cowley-Durst, 1998). The power of the Web and its related interactivity has barely begun to be explored. WBI can be truly interactive and use the many resources that are available through the Web. The challenge also comes in finding a balance between interaction and personalization, as well as synchronous and asynchronous learning.

Costs are dropping for the technologies and the speed of Internet access is continually being enhanced. There may always be a discrepancy between the technologies that are available, the minimum computer configuration required to access those technologies, and the technology available to students, but student capacity is sure to increase with time, as are student capabilities.

New technologies that are being developed for the Web are likely to make the issues of instructional design more complex for WBI as more features demand more planning to ensure accessibility and interactivity. However, there might also be innovations that work to make the design process easier for instructors or university processes to aid with accessibility issues.

In terms of the design process, Web-based Electronic Performance Support Systems (EPSS) offer some dramatic possibilities for education. An EPSS is an integrated system that provides on-demand resources, as well as tools and support systems, to help the user (Kirkley & Duffy, 1997; Romiszowski, 1997). An EPSS could be used to help faculty create WBI. Such a tool would contain more than the existing courseware packages that provide essentially a course template. This system could instead prompt instructors to include strategies that encourage student interaction and automatically create Web features that ensure course accessibility.

Beyond being a WBI creation tool, EPSS could also function as the WBI itself. The many features that could assist an instructor in the creation of a well-designed course, could also function to present the well-designed course to the student. A Web-based EPSS can combine the content of the course with the tools that enable interaction and access.

The development or purchase of such systems by a college or university demonstrate a commitment to more than WBI, but a commitment to the development of WBI that is truly accessible and promotes effective learning. As WBI continues to grow and expand, and the competition for distance students increases, institutions will need to make additional commitments to ensure that their Web-based courses are accessible and use instructional strategies to encourage interaction. Colleges and universities need to consider what their ethical and legal obligations are in regard to WBI accessibility for all students. If the university is willing to accept the responsibility for accessibility, it then needs to provide the resources that make courses accessible to all students, regardless of type of disability. Finally, if the university chooses to develop Web-based courses and programs that will require the use of high-end Web technologies that require higher skills from students and greater capacity from computers and Internet connections, they also need to develop either program requirements that make those expectations clear to students or find ways to assist students to meet those expectations.

CONCLUSION

Even those who will agree that to design effective WBI, the factors presented above must be considered and incorporated into the instructional design process, might still wonder and question whether WBI should even be utilized. These individuals might question whether or not students can truly learn effectively in an on-line environment. One recent study might quell some of these concerns. A study of 200 undergraduates enrolled in a macroeconomics class found that the group of students who took the class online scored, on average, 15% higher than those who took the class in a traditional format, regardless of gender, ethnicity, academic background, computer skills, or academic aptitude (*Business Wire,* 1999b). One of the researchers who completed the study noted, however, that online courses only work if they are designed well and are more than just digitized textbooks.

The implications for course design are vast. All of these many issues need to be given serious consideration before the class is designed. Although some of the learner characteristics gathered through needs assessment may not be available until the very beginning of the semester, a careful design process can provide preliminary observations on many of these factors. Regardless, in order to provide students with a course that takes full advantage of anytime, anywhere learning, the course design and instructional strategies must be planned in advance of course delivery. It is important to remember that one of the purposes and benefits of Web-based instruction is to make education accessible to a greater variety of students and populations. Therefore, when designing a course that will be delivered over the Internet, keep in mind the significance of planning and designing in advance, and the consideration of the needs of all students.

REFERENCES

Armstrong, M., Toebe, D., & Watson, M. (1985). Strengthening the instructional role in self-directed learning activities. *Journal of Continuing Education in Nursing*, *16*(3), 75-84.

Azarmsa, R. (1998). Digital video: In the classroom and on the net. *Syllabus*, *11*(5), 18-20.

Billings, D. M. (1989). A conceptual model of correspondence course completion. In M. G. Moore & F.C. Clark (Eds.), *Reading in Distance Learning and Instruction*. University Park, Pennsylvania: ACSDE.

Bohlken, B. (1998). *Reciprocal listening with and from the heart in the electronic classroom.* (ERIC Document Reproduction Service. No. ED 416 554)

Bruner, J. (1966). *Toward a Theory of Instruction.* Cambridge, MA: Harvard University Press.

Burton, J.K. & Merrill, P.E. (1991). Needs assessment: Goals, needs and priorities. In L.J. Briggs, K.L. Gustafson, & M.H. Tillman, *Instructional Design Principles and Applications*. Englewood Cliffs, NJ: Educational Technology Publications.

Business Wire (1999, May 25). UCLA Extension offers more than 100 online courses this summer. *NewsEdge* [Online] Available at: http://www.newspage.com

Business Wire (1999, May 25). Online learning triumphs over the traditional classroom. *NewsEdge* [Online] Available at: http://www.newspage.com

Carlson, R. D.; Downs, E.; Repman, J.; & Clark, K. F. (1998, March). So you want to develop Web-based instruction—points to ponder. In *Proceedings of the 9th conference of the Society for Information Technology & Teacher Education International Conference*. Washington, DC. (ERIC Document Reproduction Service. No. ED 421 097)

Chickering, A. & Gamson, Z. (1998, March). Seven principles for good practice in undergraduate education. *AAHE Bulletin*, *39*(7), 3-7.

Christiansen, H.D. & Cowley-Durst, B. (1998, November/December). Thoughts on distance learning: An interview with Alan Chute. *Performance Improvement*, [Online] Available at: http://www.lucent.com/cedl/thoughts.html.

Cornell, R. & Martin, B.L. (1997). The role of motivation in Web-based instruction. In Badrul H. Khan (Ed.) *Web-based Instruction*. Englewood Cliffs, New Jersey: Educational Technology Publications, Inc.

Fraser, B.J. (1989). Twenty years of classroom climate work: Progress and report. *Journal of Curriculum Studies*, *21*(4), 307-327.

Gagné, R.M. (1985). *The Conditions of Learning and Theory of Instruction (4th ed.).* New York: CBS College Publishing.

Gilbert, K. (1997). Teaching on the Internet: The world wide Web as a course delivery system. In N. Millichap (Ed.), *Beginnings: Initial Experiences in Teaching via Distance Education*. Indiana Partnership for Statewide Education (IPSE). [Online] Available at: http://www.ihets.org/distance_ed/fdpapers/1997/gilbert.html

Hansen, L. & Frick, T.W. (1997). Evaluation guidelines for Web-based course authoring systems. In Badrul H. Khan (Ed.) *Web-based Instruction*. Englewood Cliffs, New Jersey: Educational Technology Publications, Inc.

HEATH Resource Center (1987). Learning disabled adults in postsecondary education. In *LD On-Line* [On-line]. Available at: http://www.ldonline.org/ld_indepth/postsecondary/reamer_trans.html.

Hill, J. (1997). Distance learning environments via the World Wide Web. In Badrul H. Khan

(Ed.) *Web-based Instruction.* Englewood Cliffs, New Jersey: Educational Technology Publications, Inc.

Jiang, M. (1998). Course design, instruction, and students' online behaviors: A study of instructional variables and students' perceptions of online learning. Paper presented at the Annual Meeting of the American Educational Research Association (AERA), San Diego, CA, April 1998. (ERIC Document Reproduction Service. No. ED 421 970)

Kemp, J.E., Morrison, G.R. & Ross, S.M. (1994). *Designing Effective Instruction.* New York: Merrill/Prentice Hall.

Khan, B. H. (1997). Web-based instruction (WBI): What is it and why is it? In Badrul H. Khan (Ed.), *Web-based Instruction.* Englewood Cliffs, New Jersey: Educational Technology Publications, Inc.

Kirkley, J.R. & Duffy, T.M. (1997). Designing a Web-based electronic performance support system (EPSS): A case study of Literacy Online. In Badrul H. Khan (Ed.) *Web-based Instruction.* Englewood Cliffs, New Jersey: Educational Technology Publications, Inc.

Mager, R. & Pipe, R. (1970). *Analyzing Performance Programs.* Belmont, California: Lake Publishing Company .

Moos, R.H. (1974). *The Social Climate Scales: An Overview.* Palo Alto, California: Consulting Psychologists Press.

Moore, M.G.; & Kearsley, G. (1996). *Distance Education: A Systems View.* Belmont, CA: Wadsworth.

Mory, E. H.; Gambill, L. E.; & Browning, J. B. (1998, March). Instruction on the Web: The Online student's perspective. In *Proceedings of the 9th International Conference of Society for Information Technology & Teacher Education International Conference,* Washington, DC. (ERIC Document Reproduction Service. No. ED 421 090)

National Center for Learning Disabilities (1999). *Information About Learning Disabilities.* [Online] Available at: http://www.ncld.org/ld/info_ld.html

Nunn, C.E. (1996). Discussion in the college classroom: Triangulating observation and survey results. *Journal of Higher Education, 67,* 23-26.

Porter, L.A. (1997). *Creating the Virtual Classroom: Distance Learning with the Internet.* New York: Wiley Computer Publishing.

Powers, S.M. (1997). Designing an interactive course for the Internet. *Contemporary Education, 68*(3), 194-196.

Powers, S.M. & Dutt-Doner, K.M. (1998). Replacing the tin can: creating an effective electronic communication environment. In S. McNeil, J.D. Price, S. Boger-Mehall, B. Robin, & J. Willis (Eds.), *Technology and Teacher Education Annual* [CD ROM].

Reamer, A. (1997). Transition to college. In *LD On-line.* [On-line]. Available: http://www.ldonline.org/ld_indepth/postsecondary/reamer_trans.html

Ritchie, D.C. & Hoffman, B. (1997). Incorporating instructional design principles with the World Wide Web. In Badrul H. Khan (Ed.). *Web-based Instruction.* Englewood Cliffs, New Jersey: Educational Technology Publications, Inc.

Romiszowski, A.J. (1997). Web-based distance learning and teaching: Revolutionary invention or reaction to necessity? In Badrul H. Khan (Ed.) *Web-based Instruction.* Englewood Cliffs, New Jersey: Educational Technology Publications, Inc.

Silberman, M. (1996). *Active Learning: 101 Strategies to Teach Any Subject.* Boston: Allyn & Bacon.

Soltis, J. F. (1978). *An Introduction to the Analysis of Educational Concepts (2nd ed.)*. Boston: Addison-Wesley Publishing Co.

Verduin, J. R., & Clark, T. A. (1991). *Distance Education*. San Francisco: Jossey-Bass, Inc., Publishers

W3C (1999). *Web Content Accessibility Guidelines 1.0* [Online] Available at: http://www.w3.org/TR/WAI-WEBCONTENT-19990505/

Witkin, B.R. (1984). *Assessing Needs in Educational and Social Programs*. San Francisco: Jossey-Bass, Inc., Publishers..

Zakon, R. (1999). *Hobbes' Internet Timeline v. 4.1*. [Online] Available at: http://info.isoc.org/guest/zakon/Internet/History/HIT.html

Chapter XIV

Layers of Navigation for Hypermedia Environments: Designing Instructional Web Sites

Patricia L. Rogers
Bemidji State University, USA

As an instructional medium, computer-based hypermedia environments (e.g., Web sites or CD-ROM materials) enable distinct and enriched activities that facilitate learning. With the pressure on educators to produce Web-based courseware and other distance educational materials, more and more instructional Web sites have been developed. However, simple access to the World Wide Web (WWW) in any course does not guarantee that learning takes place: "No computer technology in and of itself can be made to affect thinking" (Salomon, Perkins, & Globerson, 1991, p. 3).

Too often, Web sites are developed for instructional uses without the aid of sound instructional design principles. Content is presented as static, verbal information pages linked to other information pages that may or may not include obvious or intuitive navigational cues for making the cognitive connections necessary for knowledge construction. That is, critical information is delivered in a potentially rich learning environment but the format of the presentation confuses or "loses" the novice learner. Such environments are most often the result of an educator's first few attempts at Web site development.

Even with the use of Web site builders and intranet templates, designing instruction for instructional hypermedia requires thoughtful attention to certain aspects of learning. Over-simplification of the complexities of an ill-structured or even a well-defined domain encourages novices to reduce the "solutions" of domain-specific problems to simplified or cookbook answers, which is known as reductive bias (Spiro, Feltovich, & Coulson, 1992). Thus what is learned from some Web sites is often not what the designer or educator intended. A deliberate instructional design strategy for educational hypermedia environments is needed.

This chapter focuses chiefly on the development of deliberate navigation cues and describes strategies for three blended levels or "layers" of navigation that support knowledge construction. Characteristics of hypermedia learning environments (learner and site specific elements) and cognitive flexibility theory are discussed in relation to navigation strategies. Recommendations for application of the navigation strategies to hypermedia environments conclude the chapter.

Specifically, the objectives of this chapter are:

- to identify and define learner and site elements present in hypermedia environments,
- to introduce cognitive flexibility theory in relation to higher order learning in hypermedia environments, and
- to examine strategies for navigating in hypermedia environments (based on learner and site elements) that facilitate higher order learning.

HYPERMEDIA AND LEARNING

Successful educational hypermedia environments are more than the information presented. That is, in successful educational Web sites, there appears to be a synergistic relationship between the information at the site, the authors of the site, and the users of the site. Several articles have identified elements of this synergy (Barrett, 1992; Carlson, 1991; Corry, Frick, & Hansen, 1997; Hill & Hannafin, 1997; Jonassen, 1991; Jonassen & Wang, 1993; Locatis, Charuhas, & Banvard, 1990; Schroeder, 1994; Spiro et al., 1992; Spiro, Feltovich, Jacobson, & Coulson, 1991), but few have presented them as a unified whole. Table 1 is an attempt at illustrating the learner and site characteristics designers consider when developing successful educational Web sites.

Learner Elements

Computer skills. The ability to use the computer and by implication a WWW browser, is described by Hill and Hannafin (1997) as "system knowledge" (p. 39). Word processing, e-mail, and basic WWW familiarity are competencies most graduating high school students have upon entering post-secondary institutions. In fact, the prevalence of computer skills among K-12 students is increasing. Even as far back as 1993, "...more than two-thirds of all students in grades 1–12 used a computer either at home or at school, with a majority, 66 percent, using a computer at school" (National Center for Education Statistics, 1995). Currently, that number is predicted to be much higher, though current national data is not yet available.

Content knowledge. Content knowledge is the understanding of certain domain-specific building blocks of information. As learners add to their building blocks (i.e., learn new things), new knowledge is linked to prior knowledge. Such prior knowledge is critical

Table 1: Elements of Hypermedia Learning Environments

Learner Elements	Site Elements
Computer Skills	Content
Content Knowledge	Presentation
Self-efficacy	Navigation
Learner Control	Links and Nodes
Task Type	Task Type

to the acquisition of new subject or content knowledge. The building of content knowledge and linking prior knowledge to new things is quite simply the real business of education and what it means to be educated. There are many ways to describe "knowing" (Belenky, Clinchy, Goldberger, & Tarule, 1986; Bereiter, 1991; 1994; Brent, 1991; Brown, Collins, & Duguid, 1989; Gardner, 1993; Kimpston, Williams, & Stockton, 1992) but few would dispute the basic necessary connection between new and prior understanding.

Self-efficacy. This element "...refers to a personal judgment of one's capability to execute actions required to perform" (Hill & Hannafin, 1997, p. 39). In other words, the confidence of the learner in his or her ability to use the computer and link new information to previously learned information has a great impact on how one uses the site and on how much the learner will persevere in acquiring new information. The degree of confidence a learner has in using computer-based media is directly related to how much control the learner requires or expects in a learning environment.

This degree of learner influence on what is learned, typically referred to as *learner control,* is another element that has been discussed at length in designing effective instruction (Hooper, Temiyakarn, & Williams, 1993; Malone & Lepper, 1987; Morrison, Ross, & Baldwin, 1991; Ross & Morrison, 1992) and is of particular relevance in hypermedia environments. Learner control is the degree of managing the depth, breadth, speed, and sequence of learning new knowledge. Hypermedia environments are designed on a continuum from total program control (design dependent) to total learner control (to the extent that the learner may explore anywhere in or outside of the designed environment). However, because of the complexity of many content areas, total learner control may not be an effective design feature. Cognitive overload can occur as learners branch further and further from the Web site in search of critical content knowledge (Spiro et al., 1992).

Task type. Highly related to learner control is *task type.* The type of task in which a learner engages when entering an educational hypermedia environment appears to determine his or her path through the site (Barab, Bowdish, & Lawless, 1997). From a learner's perspective, task type (and its successful completion) results in an interpretation of the new knowledge, some demonstration of learning, and a deeper understanding of domain knowledge. Task type is closely tied to depth of prior knowledge and confidence (self-efficacy) to complete the task.

Site Elements

Previous researchers (Conklin, 1987; Jacobson & Spiro, 1995; McLellan, 1993; Recker, 1994; Schroeder, 1994) have identified site elements using a variety of terms. The site elements: content, presentation, navigation, and links and nodes; refer to the information itself, how it is presented to the learner, how the learner moves within the site, and how information is linked to other information respectively. Task Type appears as a site element based on certain "built-in" features of the content.

Content. The information and its supporting activities provided at the site are the major component of any educational Web site. Content, intimately connected to links and nodes and to task type (below), can be thought of as the segment of domain knowledge presented to the learner. The scope and sequence (and control of sequence) of the content is determined by the characteristics of the intended learners. One does not design a math Web site for second grade that includes complex physics computations (unless of course the second graders are unusually sophisticated).

Presentation. Presentation of the content is the interface of the learner with the materials. Presentation includes the graphic interface (colors, layout, design), location and order of links and content items, speed of access, use and choice of multimedia (text, graphics, sounds, movies), and degree of dependence on learner control.

Navigation. How one moves through hypermedia is a site element often relegated to secondary status in Web site development. Navigation cues within an educational Web site include hot-linked words, buttons, textual directions, site-controlled sequences, colors, sounds, and the overall flow of content concepts. Navigating or "finding one's way" through the content is necessary to learning in any instructional setting and, as discussed in this chapter, is absolutely critical to learning in hypermedia environments.

Links and nodes. Perhaps the most familiar aspect of hypermedia are the links and nodes. Links and nodes are the generic descriptions of navigation cues and sites or other destinations containing domain content. Navigation cues that lead to other information (links) connect content within a Web site and among Web sites (nodes) to form the hypermedia environment for any specific domain content. Links are the text or graphic symbol (cue) and the noun, phrase, or image associated with the linked information. Nodes are the destinations for the linked information.

Task type. Task type appears in the site elements list (see Table 1) and in the learner elements list. While task type as a learner element is the interpretation of content, attitude, and understanding held by the learner, task type as a site element is interpretation of content, attitude, and understanding held by the designer. Task type as a site element is the organization of the content determined by the designer. What is the scope of the content? How is the content linked to other information to help the learner through a task?

Though learner and site elements may be considered separately, good hypermedia design appears to be *most successful when it is purposefully designed to cross learner elements with site elements.* Hypermedia materials that are based on the concerns of instructional design (learners, goals of instruction, teaching strategies, appropriate instructional media, and so on) should by default address all of the elements in some degree. However, most educational Web sites are not deliberately designed with learner and site elements in mind and can be weak in critical areas. Major weaknesses may be in over-simplifying complex information or over-loading learners with too much complex information without including some means of organization.

Cognitive Flexibility

Novices in ill-structured domains have several difficult obstacles to overcome before they are welcomed into the world of the expert. Medical students encounter patients whose symptoms do not conform to textbook examples, budding physicists struggle to leap from ordered word problems to speculating on the nature of planetary motion, and student teachers find that teaching methods are seldom performed "by the book" in real classrooms.

Ill-structured domains (and more expert levels of any domain) are those which may be characterized as having two distinct and interconnected properties: "concept- and case-*complexity*," and "across-case *irregularity*" (Spiro et al., 1992, p. 25). Briefly stated, concept and case complexity requires that learners hold several and often conflicting concepts in mind when confronting a case within the domain. In art, cases may be particular problems in aesthetics, history, criticism, or creating a work of art. For example, seeking to understand an artwork from another culture, such as a 19th century Lakota parfleche case, may require one to hold in mind such diverse concepts as climatic conditions, the relationship of geometric shapes, and pre-industrial art-making techniques (Erickson, 1996). One can easily argue that higher order learning in all domains reaches such complex levels of thinking.

The irregularity of similar cases, that is, the necessity of applying different concepts and actions to a case that might resemble a previously encountered case, is often encountered in lessons designed for higher order thinking in any content area. Staying with art for a moment, an example of case irregularity might be an aristocratic portrait from Colonial New Spain; a representation of the Mexican Revolutionary hero, Zapata; a mural by Diego Rivera; and a feminist self-portrait as the Virgin of Guadalupe (Erickson & Cárdenas, 1997). These art works are examples of an application of very different concepts and actions to the "common" problem case of painting a portrait.

Well-designed instructional hypermedia environments should offer learners rich and challenging instructional contexts that foster learning, as described in the complex and irregular cases above. Yet novice learners in such domains as art or medicine are largely struggling to understand the complexities of the domain itself. Add to this the necessity of learning with and from an educational technology that affords a non-linear mode of accessing information, and the result can be disorientation and cognitive overload (Conklin, 1987; Jacobson & Spiro, 1995; Spiro et al., 1992). Designing strong navigation strategies for hypermedia is identified as the most critical factor in minimizing much of the confusion and disorientation without sacrificing the presentation of the complexities of the content.

However, "the most questionable assumption...is that merely providing structural cues in the user interface [navigation] will result in greater structural knowledge acquisition" (Jonassen & Wang, 1993, p. 6). Buttons that move learners forward and back, labels with the word "next" and so on are inadequate. Rather, it seems that, in order for higher order learning to occur, the navigation cues must be somehow inextricably linked to learner elements and site elements with respect to task type such that learners at various competency levels might intuitively move within the site. Such learning requires deliberate design strategies.

Layers of Navigation

Considering the brief discussion (above) on cognitive flexibility and learner elements (see Table 1) and the complexities of all domains at higher levels, it would seem that educational hypermedia environments should be somehow customized for individual learners. Such customization is not always possible or feasible, considering the diversity of learner characteristics in most distance education settings. How then should site elements in educational hypermedia materials be organized to address the needs of learners? How might navigation strategies guide learners through a site without over-simplifying the content, limiting learner control, or over loading the learner with too much information?

These questions were considered during the prototyping phase of two educational Web sites: Our Place in the World (OPITW) and Chicana Chicano Space (CCS) (Erickson, 1996; Erickson & Cárdenas, 1997). The two Web sites described are designed to guide and support the novice art educator in developing curriculum for art education while providing some sense of case complexity and irregularity. The above examples of case complexity (seeking to understand artwork from another culture) and case irregularity (portrait painting) are illustrations drawn from the two Web sites. These Web sites were developed specifically for an ill-structured domain (art) and provide a good illustration (pun intended!) of the need for deliberately designing layers of navigation.

The overall task for these Web sites is to help the novice teacher become familiar and knowledgeable in the business of teaching. The site designers found that the natural flow of the content design in these materials could become too linear if translated directly from the print-based materials to a hypermedia environment. When the materials are presented in a classroom to beginning teachers, a large amount of dialog and experimentation with themes and questions becomes the focal point of the class. The intent was to create a site that could provide rich interaction with the content and at the same time guide the novice teacher through the materials.

To accomplish this goal, deliberate attention was given to learner and site elements. Three layers of navigation—near-linear, guided, and self-directed exploration—were then developed to address the needs of novice teachers without sacrificing the complexities of the content. Not surprisingly, the navigation layers roughly parallel the three levels of use described in the Jasper Series (Cognition and Technology Group at Vanderbilt, 1992), one of the first sets of instructional laser disks intended to foster higher order thinking.

Through a series of scenarios, K-12 learners are presented with learning tasks that are "anchored" to "real-world" problems; an approach described as anchored instruction. The Jasper Series allowed three levels of use, with each level progressively less dependent on direct instruction. The *Basics First* level of use provides a means of teaching the components of solving Jasper problems, such as decimals, measurements, time, etc. before viewing the problem scenarios. *Structured Problem Solving*, the second level in the Jasper Series, provides a means of introducing complex problems with simple problems to help students avoid error and to break down complex problems into simple components. The third level, *Guided Generation*, provides a flexible context in which the problem is approached through cooperative groups, some guidance by the teacher as a resource, and the development of inquiry skills based on the concept of scaffolding (Vygotsky, 1978).

The three layers of navigation are specifically intended for learners as users, allow greater learner control than Web sites with only one or two layers of navigational strategies, and are less prescriptive than materials such as the Jasper Series. Novice teachers and those who are more experienced may move through the sites using three distinct navigation paths. Each layer is described below with brief examples from the OPITW and CCS Web sites; however, the navigation strategies are intended for application to any educational Web site.

Three Layers Defined

Near-linear navigation. Near-linear navigation may be defined as the path through the Web site most apparent from the homepage. The task assignment that matches a near-linear approach would be fairly simple with learners moving through the site in sequence and working out the problems. For example, text cues in the OPITW and CCS Web sites imply a path from Lesson One to Lesson Two and so on through each site. Supplements and extensions to these lessons would typically be accessed *after* all of the core lessons have been completed, which is very similar to a more traditional instructional approach. This strategy layer is "near-linear" in the sense that users typically follow the path from one step to the next in sequence, but there is always an option for branching to other links, sections of the site, or different sites.

Guided navigation. The guided navigation strategy layer allows the user to access a set of outlines, questions, or thematic paths provided online to structure navigation through the site. In a guided navigation strategy layer, a set of simple icons is often included to graphically represent themes, sets of inquiry questions, or other guided paths. Materials may be accessed selectively for specific applications guided by the needs and parameters of the assigned task.

Another guided navigation strategy may include an on-line discussion, either synchronously or asynchronously accessed. In this way, the guided navigation layer may be designed into the site as icons, themes, and inquiry questions; and/or may be added by an instructor as an on-line seminar or discussion.

Tasks associated with this layer of navigation are most likely to be of a higher order and require learners to think beyond what is presented. That is, learners may be asked to develop a theme, pursue a series of inquiry questions across the site, or follow a specific sequence of delivering content with the option of adding additional content from other sources.

Self-directed exploration. Most Web sites appear to be open for a self-directed tour. However, if the designer has not attended to the site elements of content, navigation, or links and nodes, the learner is easily lost within the site or may consciously choose to leave the site. In other words, the learner may have sufficient content knowledge and confidence, but may become frustrated with the site's lack of navigation cues and obvious links to critical nodes.

OPITW and CCS are organized in such a way that ideas, key artworks, detailed information, inquiry questions, and icons, as well as specific themes are likely to inspire more in-depth exploration of a topic throughout the WWW. For example, "Protest and Persuasion" on the CCS site concludes with a lesson in which students are asked to use the theme to guide their own cruising of the WWW. OPITW and CCS offer a framework for lesson planning and curriculum development, yet at the same time foster further in-depth exploration of the domain.

Recommendations

Based on experiences with the two example Web sites described above and on sound instructional design practices, the following set of considerations are offered as a framework for deliberate navigation design for hypermedia:

1. *Consider the elements of hypermedia environments and deliberately design for "cross over" between learner and site elements.* By striving to merge site and user characteristics as listed in Table 1, designs for educational hypermedia environments become more useful, relevant, and accessible for a variety of learners, novice to expert. Sites that focus only on one set of elements (learner or site-specific elements) may be appropriate for presenting verbal information, but are not useful for learning in ill-structured domains or for higher order learning.

2. *Use a guided navigation strategy to engage students in the content and to control cognitive overload.* The sites discussed in this article make no attempt to cover the entire world of art. Rather, they guide learners through a series of strategies for moving through the domain by asking questions and by attending to suggested themes. Web sites designed for any content area should ensure that the domain is well represented, yet cognitive overload is reduced.

3. *Reduce reductive bias by presenting a variety of cases with open-ended solutions.*

Increase complexity of the cases by presenting alternative extensions to the cases. Thematic inquiry-based learning provides a means of presenting cases with increasing complexity. Examples of case complexity and case irregularity must be present to ensure higher order thinking. The layers of navigation strategies allow novices and more advanced learners to experience complexity and case irregularity without overwhelming or misleading. By encouraging elaborations and curriculum extensions, case complexity and irregularity can be addressed as typical of an ill-structured domain and higher order learning. Carefully selected links and nodes aid learners in inquiry activities.

4. *Use a "layers of navigation" approach to support a variety of strategies for moving through the site and to facilitate learning.* Guided navigation is perhaps the most efficient method of supporting learners through educational Web sites. However, different levels of support are needed to address novices, intermediate learners, and those more expert in a domain. Novices following near-linear navigation cues are exposed to certain aspects of the guided navigation cues as they become familiar with the content and with learning in a hypermedia environment. More advanced learners may revert to using near-linear strategies for ease of use or to help clarify connections among concepts. Self-directed navigation may be dependent on task type and inquiry path, which could be facilitated by guided navigation features.

FUTURE TRENDS AND CONCLUSION

This chapter discusses some possible deliberate navigational design features for hypermedia environments. Based on learner elements of hypermedia environments (computer skills, content knowledge, self-efficacy, learner control, and task type) and on site elements (content, presentation, navigation, links and nodes, and task type), a case is made for the necessity of layers of navigation. A brief list of recommendations is presented above.

Throughout this chapter, Web sites are referred to as "hypermedia environments." I use this phrase in anticipation of the future of learning on the Web, distance learning, and the changing face of education. The lines between Web site and library, real-time classroom and virtual reality, CD-ROM technology and video streaming are becoming indistinct. What was once a fairly simple task of coding text into HTML has taken on the trappings of a movie production. Web sites as mere destinations are becoming events. I am not sure that we will use the same language to describe them three years from now.

For the present, further experimentation in designing layers of navigation strategies for educational hypermedia is needed. The flexibility of instructional hypermedia designs provides great potential to address higher order thinking. By attending to the elements of instructional hypermedia environments (learner and site specific), designers can meet the needs of learning. If the designer pays attention to the interaction of site and user elements as an interconnected whole rather than to any particular individual elements, and is capable of designing navigation strategies, the design has a greater chance of presenting the complexities of the domain while reducing disorientation. Developing and refining navigation strategies for instructional hypermedia, such as the three layers of navigation described above, will aid novices and experts in understanding the complexities of complex content while avoiding reductive bias.

REFERENCES

Barab, S. A., Bowdish, B. E., & Lawless, K. A. (1997). Hypermedia navigation: Profiles of hypermedia users. *Educational Technology Research and Development*, 45(3), 23-41.

Barrett, E. (Ed.). (1992). *Sociomedia: Multimedia, hypermedia, and the social construction of knowledge.* Cambridge: The MIT Press.

Belenky, M. F., Clinchy, B. M., Goldberger, N. R., & Tarule, J. M. (1986). *Women's ways of knowing.* New York: BasicBooks.

Bereiter, C. (1991). Implications of connectionism for thinking about rules. *Educational Researcher*, 20(3), 10-16.

Bereiter, C. (1994). Constructivism, socioculturalism, and Popper's world 3. *Educational Researcher*, 23(7), 21-23.

Brent, D. (1991). Oral knowledge, typographic knowledge, electronic knowledge: Speculations on the history of ownership. *EJournal*, 1(3), 2-16 (EJournal@ALBNYVMS).

Brown, J. S., Collins, A., & Duguid, P. (1989). Situated cognition and the culture of learning. *Educational Researcher,* 18(1), 32-42.

Carlson, H. L. (1991). Learning style and program design in interactive multimedia. *Educational Technology Research and Development*, 39(3), 41-48.

Cognition and Technology Group at Vanderbilt. (1992). The Jasper experiment: An exploration of issues in learning and instruction. *Educational Technology Research and Development*, 40(1), 65-80.

Conklin, J. (1987). Hypertext: An introduction and survey. *Computer*, 20(9), 17-41.

Corry, M. D., Frick, T. W., & Hansen, L. (1997). User-centered design and usability testing of a Web site: An illustrative case study. *Educational Technology Research and Development*, 45(4), 65-76.

Erickson, M. (1996). Our place in the world [Online]: Getty Education Institute for the Arts Available: http://www.artsednet.getty.edu/ArtsEdNet/Resources/Erickson/Place.

Erickson, M., & Cárdenas, G. K. (1997). Chicano/Chicana art space [On-line]: Getty Education Institute for the Arts Available: http://mati.eas.asu.edu:8421/ChicanArte/html_pages/Protest-home.html.

Gardner, H. (1993). *Multiple intelligences.* New York: Basic Books.

Hill, J. R., & Hannafin, M. J. (1997). Cognitive strategies and learning from the World Wide Web. *Educational Technology Research and Development*, 45(4), 37-64.

Hooper, S., Temiyakarn, C., & Williams, M. D. (1993). The effects of cooperative learning and learner control on high- and average-ability students. *Educational Technology Research and Development*, 41(2), 5-18.

Jacobson, M. J., & Spiro, R. J. (1995). Hypertext learning environments, cognitive flexibility, and the transfer of complex knowledge: An empirical investigation. *Journal of Educational Computing Research*, 12(4), 301-333.

Jonassen, D. H. (1991). Hypertext as instructional design. *Educational Technology Research and Development*, 39(1), 83-92.

Jonassen, D. H., & Wang, S. (1993). Acquiring structural knowledge from sematically structured hypertext. *Journal of Computer-Based Instruction*, 20(1), 1-8.

Kimpston, R. D., Williams, H. Y., & Stockton, W. S. (1992). Ways of knowing and the curriculum. *The Educational Forum*, 56(2), 153-172.

Locatis, C., Charuhas, J., & Banvard, R. (1990). Hypervideo. *Educational Technology Research and Development*, 38(2), 41-49.

Malone, T. W., & Lepper, M. R. (1987). Making learning fun: A taxonomy of instrinsic motivations for learning. In R. E. Snow & M. J. Farr (Eds.), *Aptitude learning and instruction: Cognitive and affective process analysis* (pp. 223-253). Hillsdale, NJ: Lawrence Erlbaum Associates.

McLellan, H. (1993). Hypertextual tales: Story models for hypertext design. *Journal of Multimedia and Hypermedia*, 2(3), 239-260.

Morrison, G. R., Ross, S. M., & Baldwin, W. (1991). Learner control of context and instructional support in learning elementary school mathematics. *Educational Technology Research and Development,* 40(1), 5-13.

National Center for Education Statistics. (1995). *Student use of computers [On-line]*. Available WWW: http://nces.ed.gov/pubsold/CoE95/05txt.html [1995, December 1995].

Recker, M. M. (1994). A methodology for analyzing students' interactions with educational hypertext. *Proceedings of ED-MEDIA 94—World Conference on Educational Multimedia and Hypermedia*, 474-479.

Ross, S. M., & Morrison, G. R. (1992). In search of a happy medium in instructional technology research: Issues concerning external validity, media replications, and learner control. *Education Technology Research and Developmen*t, 37(1), 19-33.

Salomon, G., Perkins, D. N., & Globerson, T. (1991). Partners in cognition: Extending human intelligence with intelligent technologies. *Educational Researcher*, 20(3), 2-9.

Schroeder, E. E. (1994). Navigating through hypertext: Navigational technique, individual differences, and learning. *Proceedings of Selected Research and Development Presentations of the Association for Educational Communications and Technology,* 789-824.

Spiro, R., Feltovich, M. J., & Coulson, R. L. (1992). Cognitive flexibility, constructivism, and hypertext: Random access instruction for advanced knowledge acquisition in ill-structured domains. In T. M. Duffy & D. H. Jonassen (Eds.), *Constructivism and the Technology of Instruction: A Conversation* (pp. 57-75). Hillsdale, NJ: Lawrence Erlbaum.

Spiro, R. J., Feltovich, P. J., Jacobson, M. J., & Coulson, R. L. (1991). Knowledge representation, content specification, and the development of skill in situation-specific knowledge assembly: Some constructivist issues as they relate to cognitive flexibility theory and hypertext. *Educational Technology*. (22-25)

Vygotsky, L. S. (1978). *Mind in society.* Cambridge,MA: Harvard University Press.

Author Note

The author wishes to acknowledge the contributions of Dr. Mary Erickson (School of Art, Arizona State University) to earlier versions of this chapter.

Chapter XV

Strengthening Learning on the Web: Programmed Instruction and Constructivism

Karen Smith-Gratto
North Carolina A&T State University, USA

In the brave new world of cyberlearning, we need to look back as well as forward to create the best learning environments for students. All fields of study require the learning of facts and definitions that have been mediated within that field of study. In addition, individuals must learn to manipulate both information and procedures within any given field to achieve expert status within that field. It can be argued that learning facts is different from learning how to solve a problem within the same field. The mental processes needed to learn facts and those needed to solve problems involve different ways of learning. If we believe that there are different types of learning, then it is logical to assume that different learning theories will contribute more to one type of learning than another.

Programmed instruction as developed by B. F. Skinner (1968) was based upon operant conditioning principles. The material to be learned by students is presented in small increments, students are given a chance to answer questions related to the information, given feedback (and reinforcement) and the process continues until the end of the programmed instruction. Earlier computer software tutorials most often followed modified forms of programmed instruction (Poppen & Poppen, 1988), and while Web-based instruction can follow this model, there are basic differences that will result in less designer control than was possible with stand-alone software. Students using Web-based instruction that follows the programmed instruction paradigm will have more opportunity to leave the planned instruction and go elsewhere on the Web. However, the basic principles can be used and combined with constructivism to address learning in different ways.

Constructivism is defined in a variety of ways. Biehler and Snowman (1997) define constructivism as a view of learning in which the learning is meaningful and involves learners in the active creating of their own knowledge structures. This perspective is most often based on Piaget's (1954) view of learning as accommodation or assimilation of new information based upon the learners' previous experiences and the schema that resulted from those experiences. However, another definition of constructivism includes a view that learning is constructed through social interaction (Von Glaserfeld, 1989). If one considers both definitions of constructivism, the Web can be considered primarily a constructivist environment because learners move through material on the Web and construct individual understandings of the material they encounter. Indeed, students can also engage in conversations with others during the information-gathering and problem-solving processes and this becomes social mediation.

While the Web allows open-ended exploration, most educational objectives must be met in a timely manner. So while students can gain a great deal from the exploration, there is also a need to keep students focused and headed toward required outcomes. It is suggested here that students can be best served by combining programmed instruction with constructivist activities to achieve a more efficient and effective learning experience. Activities that are not behavioral in nature can be incorporated into programmed instruction programs on the Web.

This chapter will explore how the two perspectives can be combined to create Web-based instruction that draws on the strengths of both theoretical perspectives. It is the view here that factual information is often the foundation on which more complex activities are built. Programmed instruction can contribute to the foundation-building aspect of learning, while constructivism can contribute to the advanced manipulation and problem-solving aspects of learning.

PROGRAMMED INSTRUCTION

Why look at programmed instruction in relation to instruction presented via the World Wide Web? When considering programmed instruction one considers the control by the instructional designer as almost absolute. Before the World Wide Web, early educational software often followed the behavioral paradigm. Even the Web has certain characteristics that can allow a modified application of programmed instruction. The nature of instructional delivery on the Web has certainly become more open than the closed programmed instruction software available in the past. However, programmed instruction has proven itself useful for some forms of learning and could be worth modifying to enhance some aspects of learning via the Web. It is worth considering how programmed instruction was implemented for computer instruction in the past and how that might be combined with other theories to enhance instruction delivered via the Web.

In the early days of computers in education, the design of educational software was usually based on a behaviorist paradigm (Jonassen, 1990; Case & Bereiter, 1984; Hannafin & Reiber, 1989). According to Hannifin and Reiber (1989) when learning theory was employed, programmed instruction as developed by Skinner was most often the design model of choice. While Poppen & Poppen (1988) agree with the idea that programmed instruction was the model employed, they state that it was often inadequately implemented.

Programmed instruction as developed by Skinner (1968) involves providing a learner with a stimulus. The student then responds to the stimulus and is provided with a consequence in the form of feedback. The steps taken during the learning process must be small enough that the learner can respond correctly so that the behavior can be shaped. Skinner applied these techniques to "teaching machines." In part because of the example of teaching machines and in part because of the screen-by-screen presentation inherent in computer-based instruction, programmed instruction presented an easily adapted technique or design model for instructional development on the computer.

Various people have written about the appropriate design of educational software based upon behavioral principles (Case & Bereiter, 1984; Tennyson, 1981; Hazen, 1985). When comparing their ideas with those of Skinner (1968), a set of design principles emerges. These principles are: 1) gathering the necessary information for the content of the software; 2) stating the objectives for the students; 3) organizing the information to be learned into small segments; 4) assessing the student responses on a continual basis to insure mastery of one part before students move on; 5) reinforcing the desired responses; and 6) pacing controlled by the student.

These steps seem to be dismantled by the open-ended nature of the Web. For example, if a tutorial Web site is developed and we base it on the above programmed instruction principles, there is nothing to stop the student from typing in a different address or going to a previously bookmarked site and "escaping" the tutorial. Cruthirds and Hanna (1996) suggest that while the learner can "surf" away from a programmed instruction tutorial, the effort to develop multimedia and take advantage of the unique characteristics of the Web may well be worth that effort. They suggest that research needs to be done in order to build upon what has been previously learned about programmed instruction and adapt its use for multimedia and use on the World Wide Web.

Some Web sites that state they are designed around programmed instruction principles are readily available to any Web user. While these sites purport to implement the principles of programmed instruction, some do so inadequately. For the purpose of examples, three sites will be briefly discussed.

One site, *Connected: An Internet Encyclopedia,* is online at http://cie.motor.ru/Course/index.html and is advertised as a "Programmed Instruction Course". While the site provides a lot of information it does not truly follow the accepted principles of programmed instruction. The information is presented in large chunks with little opportunity for frequent student to media interaction. Link after link takes one to more and more textual information without provision for more than "page turning". While there is interaction in the program, you must go through many links and read large amounts of text before reaching any activities which truly require interaction.

Another site, *Programmed Instruction Using Web Pages* (Kjell, 1997), is a somewhat better example, but still violates some of the programmed instruction principles. This site can be found at http://www./cs.ccsu.ststaeu.edu/~kjell/lecture/talk1.html. The information is presented in small chunks that are followed by a question. Both the length and question are appropriate when following programmed instruction techniques. However, there were two weaknesses noted with the questions. In some cases the answer is not found within the reading (as with the first question on the site). The other weakness is in the type of interaction and feedback used. The questions do not require the user to respond by typing in a response. Therefore, in this type of interaction students could just click on the next link and move on to the next frame. The feedback consists of text that gives a possible answer to the question and allows students to compare their response to the desired response. This is the accepted technique with paper or book programmed instruction. However, the technology employed allows the user to type in a response and for that response to be checked. In fact, fill-in-the-blank questions can be programmed to respond to a variety of answers and even include checking answers for misspellings. Such programming would require the student to respond (or leave the Web site). If the site required answers from users, then branching could be used to reteach when needed.

The best site found was *The Sheep Brain Dissection* at http://academic.uofs.edu/department/psych/sheep/, created by Robert A. Wheeler, Anne E. Baldwin, Richard S. Reid, Jennifer J. Quinn, and J. Timothy Cannon of the University of Scranton. The program is a linear tutorial that guides the user through the parts of a sheep's brain. The information is presented in small chunks that allow for student success, and reinforcement is provided. Each section of the tutorial must be mastered before the next section can be entered. The program contains high interactivity through the use of quizzes. If a quiz is answered incorrectly, students are sent back in the program to review the information. Students must master one concept before going on to the next. While the program does not use branching to reteach the concepts, it appropriately follows the principles of programmed instruction.

According to research, programmed instruction works as well as other kinds of instruction, takes less time for students to learn when using it than traditional forms of instruction, and learners liked it as well as other kinds of instruction (Hanna, 1971). It has been suggested that behavioral theory principles are appropriate for instruction that deals with basic skills and basic knowledge (Heinich et al., 1996). However, while programmed instruction has proven to be efficient and effective in the past, it may not be appropriate for all areas of learning.

CONSTRUCTIVISM

Constructivist theory explains learning as an active process in which the learner builds knowledge and understanding from individual experiences. Individuals learn by using accommodation or assimilation to adjust their schema when confronted with new experiences (Piaget, 1954). As a learner encounters new experiences, the learner usually places the new experience within a mental framework. This can be done by either fitting the new experience into an existing schema (assimilation) or by restructuring the mental framework (accommodation). Schemas are abstract mental constructs that connect concepts and form a sort of web of concepts that contribute to the individual's interpretation of experiences. When a concept such as farm is activated, other concepts such as animals, fields, and so forth will be activated. While each individual has unique schemas, there is some overlap between the schemas of individuals that allows for common understandings of concepts.

When a new experience does not fit into an individual's existing schema, the individual experiences disequilibrium. The individual must then readjust and restructure or create new schema to accommodate the new experience. Each individual has a unique understanding of the environment. According to Brooks (1990) when individuals have a flawed understanding of a concept, they should be provided with experiences that lead to disequilibrium. The disequilibrium will cause individuals to clarify their understanding to achieve a sense of mental balance.

Opportunities for the creation of disequilibrium in a student abound on the World Wide Web. Depending on the area of instruction, sites can be found that contain information that won't easily fit into the learner's existing understanding of the world. If the instructor chooses the sites in advance, the student's experience can be guided toward an intellectual balance. When students explore the Web in search of information, they need to know how to evaluate and verify the information found on those sites before taking the information as correct.

If students do not have the ability to evaluate sites, the Web offers opportunities for gross misinterpretations by the naive learner. For example, a site that gives very interesting information about tree cows is *Bovinus Arbitrary: The Common Tree Cow* found at http://austin.brandonu.ca/~ennsnr/Cows/treecow.html. The site is well prepared in that it describes the tree cow in both what appear to be scientific terms and common terms. While most of us know that there is no such thing as a tree cow, a young student learning about cows could access this site. Imagine the disequilibrium this can cause. Indeed, when the site was discovered in one of my university classes, one of the students viewing the site said, "I didn't know there were cows that lived in trees." To my surprise the student believed the information was true. Of course this led to a discussion about the reliability of Web sites and the need to evaluate and verify the information presented on Web sites. Just imagine how that student's schema would have been restructured if the student had accessed that site and there had been no intervention!

Another aspect of constructivism is the use of realistic problem-solving to enable meaningful learning (Duffy & Jonassen, 1991; Bednar et al., 1992; Brown, Collins & Duguid, 1989). In order to develop complex schemas, students need to be involved in solving problems that require students to explore a variety of viewpoints. When solving problems, individuals must develop an assortment of techniques. An instructor can facilitate student development of these techniques and guide students to appropriate sources for solving the problem at hand.

According to Bruner (1961) learners understand better if they take part in hands-on activities. Through the manipulation of concrete objects students "discover" the conditions within the environment. While the search for information on the Web is not strictly a "hands-on" activity, it is a "minds on" endeavor. If students approach the Web armed with good basic tools for evaluating the information on sites, they can glean a variety of information that can be applied to solving the problem at hand. For example, if students are working on a project to determine weather patterns there are a variety of reputable sources to be found on the Web. *The National Weather Service* found at http://www.nws.noaa.gov/; *Global Hydrology and Climate Center* found at http://wwwghcc.msfc.nasa.gov; and the *Earth Watch* site found at http://www.earthwatch.com/FCST_CTR/fcst_ctr.html can be accessed by students collecting data to analyze. This would allow students to work in an authentic manner using Web-based resources.

Social interaction is another aspect that is often emphasized in constructivist theory. Individuals negotiate meaning through interactions with others (Vygotsky, 1981). Vygotsky believed that social activities were the beginning of complex mental processes. Through social interaction individuals learn about other points of view and build more complex understandings of the world. A common understanding of meaning is arrived at by individuals through the exchange of information and by clarifying abstractions through symbolic exchanges (which can consist of verbal or textual exchanges). While each individual will maintain a unique understanding, some aspects of the concepts explored through the interchange will overlap (Von Glaserfeld, 1981). While students have individually constructed meanings for language, language can be used to help students make sense of the world (Yager, 1991).

The Web enables social interaction through the use of chat rooms, e-mail, and discussion lists. Unlike discussions within the traditional classroom setting, on-line discussions can include individuals from around the world. This offers students a unique opportunity for expanding their understanding of the world. In addition, students have direct access to experts in a variety of fields.

Chat room discussions offer real-time exchanges among individuals. This type of discussion can be confusing at times. For example, one student can ask a question and several can respond. While those students are typing, another question is asked. This means that two questions may appear on the computer screen before the first set of the answers. However, once one adjusts to the environment, this becomes less of a problem. The ideal chat room situation would involve a small group. The small group could consist of students only or an expert and a student or students. These real-time exchanges could help students clarify their understanding of a topic.

The use of e-mail and discussion lists offers the opportunity for students to carefully consider and frame their thoughts on a topic. Because of the lag time between exchanges, students can think about the topic and even do research on the topic before responding. This enables the student to refine and readjust their understanding of the topic. Both e-mail and discussion lists have strengths and weaknesses.

Ideally e-mail would be used between two individuals, rather than for large groups because the exchanges for large groups would be time intensive. With e-mail the overall coherency of a group discussion could become lost as e-mail messages could cross and mix-up, just as often happens in the chat room situation. However, e-mail can allow two or three individuals to not only discuss a topic, but create products that can be sent back and forth as they are revised.

In the traditional classroom some students are reluctant to ask the instructor questions. For whatever reason, students who have not asked questions in class are now using e-mail to send questions to me. The perceived privacy of the medium seems to encourage students to ask questions that they believe other students might consider "dumb". This allows students to use social interaction to clarify their thoughts without fear of being embarrassed in front of their peers.

Discussion lists are ideal for open discussions in which the object is to help students mediate the meaning of the material being discussed. When left totally alone as a group, students may mediate a meaning entirely inappropriate for the content. However, when shared meaning within the context of the content is desired, the instructor needs to take an active role. This does not mean that the instructor should correct misunderstandings by directly correcting the students' current understanding of the topic. If the desire is to follow a constructivist path, the instructor needs to carefully devise questions that will lead students toward the desired mediated meaning. In a way, each entry into a discussion list is like a stone. When the stones come together and bump against each other each stone changes shape. The students' written entries, which represent their understanding, are like the stones. As students read other entries, new perspectives are added and the students' previous understanding is changed; just as the stones changed shape, so to does the students' schema.

In most instructional contexts instructors must meet required goals and objectives. This is true whether you teach in a university setting, in business, or in a K-12 environment. Whatever the case some of the objectives will require students to learn facts, skills, and basic concepts. If we approach this type of learning using only constructivist methods, three concerns arise.

The first is that students may not meet the required objectives because facts, skills and basic concepts may not have been learned. This can happen if students are required to make meaning from unfamiliar content. After all, under constructivist theory students must be able to gain meaning based on past experiences. If students' experience does not overlap with the new information, it will be like trying to get meaning from a foreign language with which one is unfamiliar.

The second concern is that students will not have a foundation on which to build. We might look at this as a carpenter building a house. In order to build the house, the carpenter needs basic tools, such as hammers, saws, levels, and so forth. The carpenter cannot build the house even with a blueprint, if he does not have the basic tools. Learners can be viewed in much the same way. For example, if students are learning about learning theory and the students have no concept of what a theory is, the students can never reach a higher level of understanding learning theories. The concept of theory is essential to understanding that all learning theory is a matter of perspective, which is often supported by philosophy, logic, and research. While students can learn the definition of theory through programmed instruction techniques, their understanding can be refined through student/teacher interactions and having students address problems related to theory building and/or application.

This brings us to the last concern, which is one of time. As anyone who has ever been given the task of guiding student learning can attest, "time is limited". One thing that constructivist activities require is time and lots more time. According to Hanna's (1971) review of the literature programmed instruction enabled students to meet objectives in less time than traditional methods. It is commonly accepted that constructivist activities take more time then traditional methods. This being the case, we need to move toward a sense of balance between what each theory has to contribute.

Principles for designing a constructivist learning environment could include the following: 1) create opportunities for students to experience disequilibrium; 2) provide students with activities which help them restructure their understanding; 3) provide authentic problem-solving activities; and 4) provide activities which require social interaction.

As can be seen so far constructivism and programmed instruction have different perspectives and benefits to offer in the design of on-line instruction. By taking advantage of the strengths of each it may be possible to create stronger learning environments online.

THE CASE FOR COMBINING PROGRAMMED INSTRUCTION AND CONSTRUCTIVISM

Many will believe that combining programmed instruction and constructivism for Web-based instruction is illogical. However, the two learning theories can be considered as contributing to different types of learning. Programmed instruction has been shown to be successful when used for helping students learn a set of terms, very structured content, or a sequence of steps when developing a skill. Constructivism, on the other hand, is considered effective when addressing individual understanding of information and higher cognitive processes, such as are needed for successful problem solving.

While under constructivism the parts of the individual's cognitive structure are distinctive, the syntax or structure of the actual information is not (Merrill, 1991). Therefore, a knowledge base can be independent from individual understanding. Knowledge can be represented in a knowledge base that contributes to a somewhat shared reality (Merrill, 1991). The aspect of constructivism that contributes to the construction of shared reality is that of social interaction. The communication of ideas helps to create an overlap among individuals with regard to meaning. In order to begin construction of the basic knowledge within a well-structured domain, the information needs to be explicitly taught (Winn, 1991). In support of this view, Jonassen (1991) states that constructivist learning may be most appropriate for advanced learning. He adds that basic or introductory knowledge may be best approached by other means. It can also be argued that there is a difference between training to acquire skills and helping students to build understanding (Von Glaserfeld, 1989).

If one considers this point of view, it becomes logical to use programmed instruction to provide a foundation on which constructivism can build. Programmed instruction could be used to introduce basic terms a student would need in order to sift through information to solve a particular type of problem. Within reading materials for a specialized field of study, technical vocabulary is needed. Therefore, part of the instruction could take form of programmed instruction to help students learn the technical vocabulary. Even within a programmed instruction format, some activities could be constructivist in nature. For example, students' prior knowledge could be activated first, then through programmed instruction techniques, the prior knowledge could be connected to the specialized vocabulary. While the primary design of the lesson would use programmed instruction, the activation of students' prior knowledge would help students to make connections to the new material, which would help students restructure their schema. This is a small way in which the two theories can be combined.

The combination of programmed instruction and constructivism also demands different responses from designers/instructors and students. Programmed instruction puts the management of the learning enterprise in the hands of someone other than the learner, either the teacher or an instructional designer. Constructivism requires students to take more responsibility for managing their own instruction (Perkins, 1991). The position of constructivists in this instance has more to contribute to the development of students as independent learners than does programmed instruction. In designing on-line instruction, the basic structure of the lesson could be one of creating a constructivist environment. For example, students could be given a simulation to do. Students would need to known how the simulation operates and, if sources on the Web were to be used during the simulation, how to use those sources. A menu could be provided that would give students a choice of short programmed instruction modules to help them learn the skills necessary. Students could choose to complete the modules depending on their individual needs. When designing this type of lesson, keep in mind that students may need to be provided with guidance about how to solve problems within the simulation itself. This can be accomplished via e-mail with the instructor and other students.

GUIDELINES FOR PLANNING A COMBINATION LESSON

When considering how to combine programmed instruction and constructivism for an on-line lesson, the following questions can help guide designing the learning environment:

1) What goals and objectives are best addressed by programmed instruction?
2) What goals and objectives are best addressed by constructivism?

3) If the majority of goals and objectives are constructivist:
   a) What is the most appropriate primary activity (problem solving, simulation, or discussion). In some cases, a series of constructivist activities may be more appropriate than using one primary activity. This is determined by the objectives of the lesson.
   b) What additional support would be beneficial? (For example, if the primary activity is problem solving, are there sources that you can recommend to students that would help guide them?)
   c) What type of on-line social interaction component would work best? (If students are working in pairs, e-mail might be the choice. However, if you want students to compare and discuss progress or problems they encounter, a discussion list might be more appropriate.)
   d) What areas within the lesson are most likely to require instructor guidance? (While not all areas can be planned for in advance, some can be prepared for in advance.)
4) If the majority of goals and objectives are geared toward programmed instruction:
   a) What is the information needed for the content?
   b) How will the statement of objectives for the students be expressed? (There may be some differences in the way they are expressed when constructivist-type goals are included within the lesson.)
   c) What small segments will make up the lesson?
   d) What feedback do students receive for each item that students answer? (This will

Figure 1. Example of a Web-based Constructed Response Screen for Programmed Instruction.

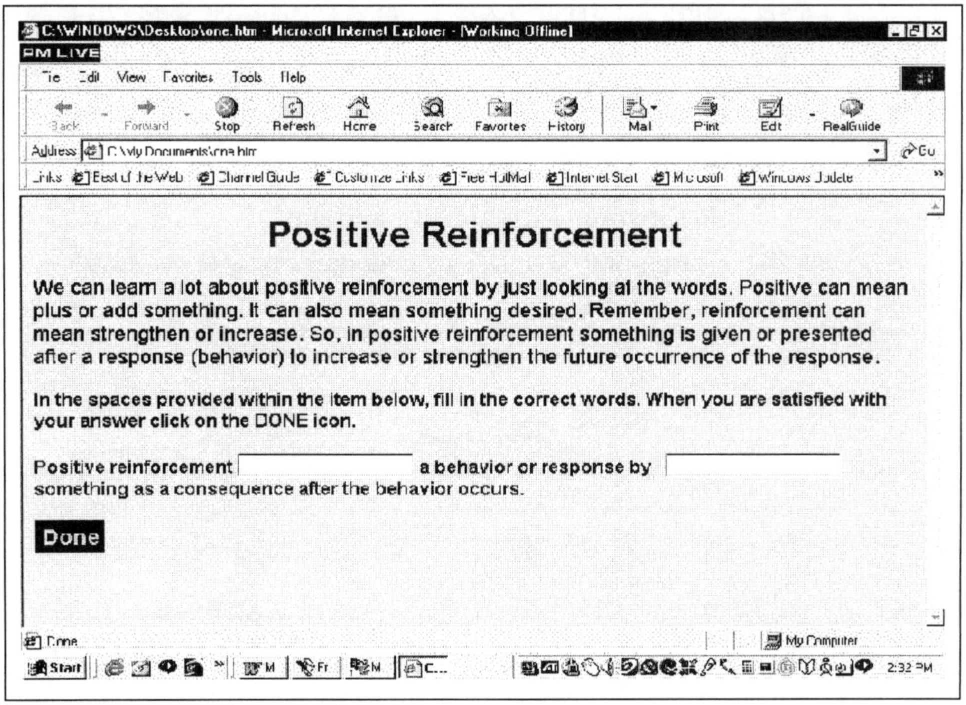

help decide what branching, if any, will be used and how that will affect the overall structure.)

e) What form of reinforcement is most appropriate for this group of students?

5) Are there aspects of the other theory that would contribute to some aspects of the lesson? If the answer is "yes," review numbers 3 and 4 then add suitable elements from those to the lesson.

EXAMPLE OF PLANNING TO DEVELOP A COMBINED LESSON

First goals and objectives need to be considered. The general goal for this lesson is "Students will learn about reinforcement and punishment." This requires articulation of objectives because the goal is extremely broad. The goal and the following objectives are for a Web-based lesson that is currently under development. As each objective is stated, it is labeled as behavioral or constructivist.

At the end of this lesson you will be able to:

1. Define positive reinforcement, negative reinforcement, type I punishment, and type II punishment.—This is determined as behavioral because the objective requires definitions.
2. Compare and contrast positive reinforcement and negative reinforcement.—This

Figure 2. Example of the instructions for constructing a frame as part of a web- based Constructivist based learning activity.

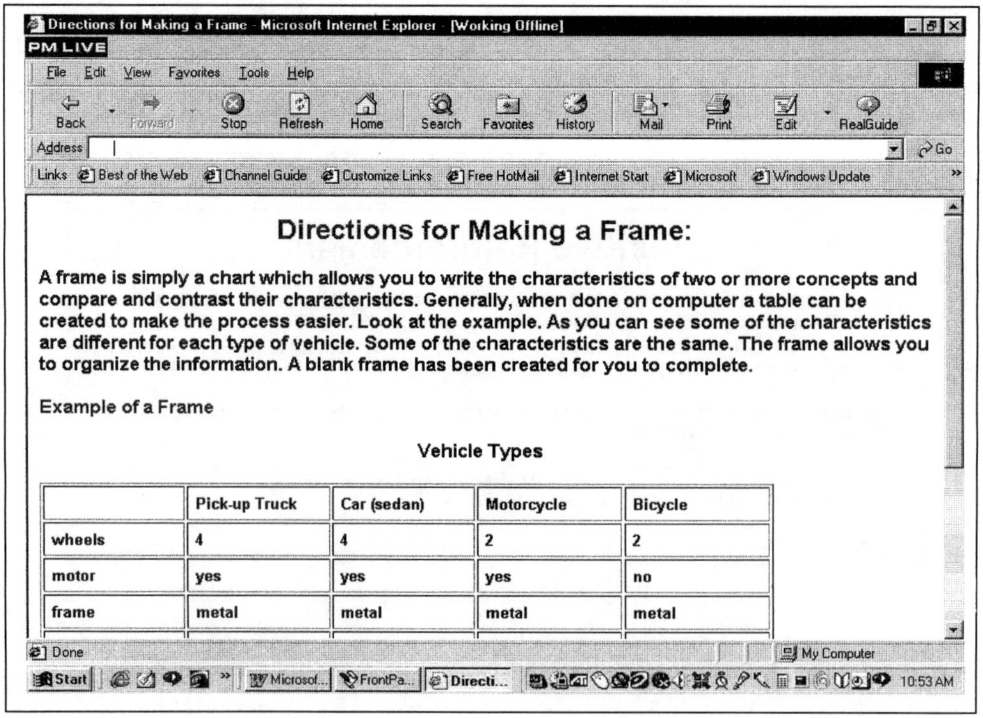
Directions for Making a Frame - Microsoft Internet Explorer - [Working Offline]
PM LIVE
File Edit View Favorites Tools Help
Back Forward Stop Refresh Home Search Favorites History Mail Print Edit RealGuide
Address
Go
Links Best of the Web Channel Guide Customize Links Free HotMail Internet Start Microsoft Windows Update
Directions for Making a Frame:
A frame is simply a chart which allows you to write the characteristics of two or more concepts and compare and contrast their characteristics. Generally, when done on computer a table can be created to make the process easier. Look at the example. As you can see some of the characteristics are different for each type of vehicle. Some of the characteristics are the same. The frame allows you to organize the information. A blank frame has been created for you to complete.
Example of a Frame
Vehicle Types
Pick-up Truck | Car (sedan) | Motorcycle | Bicycle
wheels | 4 | 4 | 2 | 2
motor | yes | yes | yes | no
frame | metal | metal | metal | metal
Done
My Computer
Start
Microsof...
FrontPa...
Directi...
10:53 AM

objective can be either constructivist or behavioral depending on how it is approached. If the designer/instructor chooses to present the information, the student could learn the information through programmed instruction techniques; however, if the designer/instructor decides to have students work through the material to determine the similarities and differences then the activity associated with this objective makes the objective constructivist. In this case, the choice was to use the constructivist model.

3. Compare and contrast type I and type II punishment.—Refer to 2.
4. Develop models for positive reinforcement, negative reinforcement, type I punishment, and type II punishment.—This is considered constructivist because each student will have to overtly "construct" a model for each of the items in the objective. Each model will demonstrate how the student is making meaning about what is being learned.
5. Determine whether a scenario is an example of positive reinforcement, negative reinforcement, type I punishment or type II punishment and defend your position. – The choice for this is similar to the second objective. The designer/instructor could use programmed instruction techniques to present rules for determining the type of scenario or approach the objective through constructivist methods and require students to develop their own rules. In the instruction being developed the designer/instructor has chosen to use constructivist methods.
6. Given problem situations students will determine the type of reinforcement or

Figure 3. Example of the setup for a web-based Constructivist activity in which students construct a model.

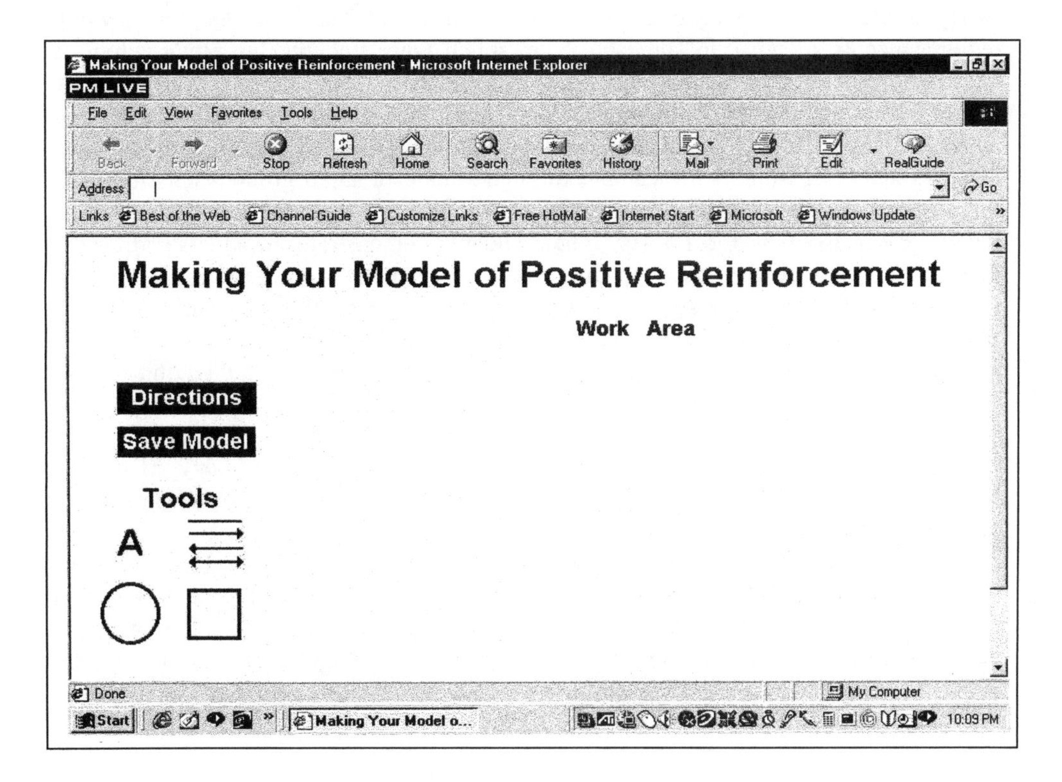

punishment that should be used and explain why.—This is a problem-solving activity and as a result is clearly constructivist in nature.

The majority of the objectives for this lesson are constructivist in nature. While it can be argued that some of the objectives contain elements of both theory bases, the primary focus of the lesson is determined by how the designer and instructor perceive each objective.

The next step is to consider whether to use a primary constructivist activity or a series of constructivist activities. When studying the objectives, it becomes evident that different constructivist techniques will be most appropriate. Since that is the case, each objective can be addressed at this point. This means that as each objective is examined, the appropriate placement in the on-line lesson should be determined.

The first objective is one that addresses definitions and has been identified as behavioral. This is a "fact" level building block type of objective. Students sometimes need basic terms and definitions in order to work with more advanced learning. Since this is foundational information, it will be the first part of the lesson. The designer/instructor decides to create constructed response screens in which information will be presented to the students and the students are required to type in answers (refer to Figure 1, which is a constructed response screen). The answers will be evaluated and students branched to the appropriate Web page. Once students have mastered the definitions, they will be routed to other portions of the lesson.

Since the objectives in this lesson have been placed in the sequence that the designer/instructor believes will allow for the gradual building of knowledge and skills, the students are routed to activities that address objectives 2 and 3. Students would be asked to create, compare or contrast frames (see instructions for frame construction in sample instructional Web page in Figure 2). The learners would be expected to organize the characteristics of the two types of reinforcement and the two types of punishment. The frame assignment would require students to "construct" the table from scratch. Once students finish their individual tables, the tables can be shared with a partner through document sharing via the on-line program or as an attachment to e-mail. Students can then discuss the differences in their tables and "mediate" their understanding of the material. Since students are "constructing" meaning and discussing their meanings through e-mail (or small-group discussion lists), this is clearly a constructivist endeavor. Once students have mediated their frames, the instructor can examine the frames. When students demonstrate an understanding that diverges from the accepted understanding within the field, the instructor can ask questions to guide the students toward that common understanding. This is simply providing scaffolding for students to reshape and refine their understanding.

The development of models as required by the fourth objective would require the use of on-line tools such as lines, boxes, circles, text, and so on (refer to Figure the 3). The student would then construct a model that provides a combination of graphics and text to demonstrate their interpretation of positive and negative reinforcement, and type I and type II punishment. This extends the definition and compare/contrast portions of the lesson, and deepens the students' level of understanding.

Once students have completed these activities, they can be presented with scenarios to examine and respond either individually or in cooperative groups. As students work to identify what kind of reinforcement or punishment the scenario describes, they would be developing their own set of rules. These rules can be tested and refined as the students examine different scenarios. In the planned design, students will work cooperatively to develop rules and analyze the scenarios.

After students finish the rule development and type analysis, they will work cooperatively through additional scenarios. These scenarios will provide careful descriptions of situations in which a particular behavior is targeted for change and information about what the individual in the scenario would perceive as reinforcement and punishment. Students will be expected to determine the most appropriate consequence for changing the behavior and explain why that would be the best choice. As the final learning activity, students would complete at least two scenarios individually. The example described here is only one possible way that programmed instruction and constructivist theory can be combined to meet the listed objectives.

CONCLUSION

Since more and more institutions are providing on-line instruction, it is important to consider how we may best design that instruction. Different learning theories can contribute to student learning in different ways. While constructivism and programmed instruction are at opposite ends of a theoretical spectrum, they each have aspects that can contribute to stronger on-line learning environments.

Each theory approaches learning from a different perspective, and can help us address different learning requirements. The careful consideration and classification of the goals and objectives as behavioral or constructivist allows the designer/instructor to break the designing task into separate theory bases. After the identification occurs the specific theory-based activities can be developed and combined. Since each theory has its strengths and weaknesses, combining the two can provide students with a richer and more effective learning environment.

REFERENCES

Bednar, A. K., Cunningham, D., Duffy, T. M., & Perry, J. D. (1992). Theory into practice: How do we link?. In Duffy, T. M, & Jonassen, D. H. (Eds.). *Constructivism and the technology of instruction.* Hillsdale, NJ: Lawrence Erlbaum.

Biehler, R. F. and Snowman, J. (1997). *Psychology applied to teaching.* (8th ed.). Boston: Houghton Mifflin Company.

Brooks, J. G. (1990). Teachers and students: Constructivists forging new connections. *Educational Leadership, 47*(5), 68-71.

Brown, J. S., Collins, A. & Duguid, P. (1989). Situated cognition and the culture of learning. *Educational Researcher, 18*, 32-42.

Bruner, J.S. (1961). The act of discovery. *Harvard Educational Review, 31*, 21-32.

Case, R., & Bereiter, C. (1984). From behaviorism to cognitive behaviorism to cognitive development: Steps in the evolution of instructional design *Instructional Science, 13*, 141-158.

Cruthirds, J., & Hanna, M. S. (1996, March). *Programmed Instruction and Interactive Multimedia: A Third Consideration.* Paper presented at the Annual Meeting of the Southern States Communication Association in Memphis, TN. [Online.} Available: http://cctr.umkc.edu/user/jaitken/vol11/programmedvol11.html

Duffy, T. M., & Jonassen, D. H. (1991). Constructivism: New implications for technology?. *Educational Technology, 31*(5), 7-12.

Hanna, M.S. (1971). *A Comparative Investigation of Three Modes of Instruction in Organization of Ideas.* Unpublished doctoral dissertation. University of Missouri, Columbia.

Hannafin, M. J., & Reiber, L. P. (1989). Psychological foundations of instructional design for emerging computer-based instructional technologies: Part I. *Educational Technology Research and Development, 37*(2), 91-101.

Hazen, M. (1985). Instructional software design principles. *Educational Technology, 25*(11), 18-23.

Heinich, R., Molenda, M., Russell, J.D., & Smaldino, S.E. (1996). *Instructional Media and Technologies for Learning.* 5th ed. Englewood Cliffs, NJ: Prentice-Hall, Inc.

Jonassen, D. H. (1990). Thinking technology: Toward a constructivist view of instructional design. *Educational Technology, 30*(9), 32-34.

Kjell, B. J. (1997). *Programmed Instruction Using Web Pages.* Lecture presented at 11th CSU Annual Academic Computing Conference, April 12, 1997. (Adapted for use on the World Wide Web). [Online]. Available: http://www./cs.ccsu.ctstaeu.edu/~kjell/lecture/talk1.html.

Piaget, J. (1954). *The Construction of Reality in the Child.* New York: Basic Books.

Perkins, D. N. (1991). What constructivism demands of the learner. *Educational Technology, 31*(9), 19-21.

Poppen, L., & Poppen, R. (1988). The use of behavioral principles in educational software. *Educational Technology, 28*(2), 37-41.

Skinner, B.F. (1968). *The Technology of Teaching.* New York: Appleton-Century-Crofts.

Tennyson, R. D. (1981). Interactive effect of cognitive learning theory with computer attributes in the design of computer-assisted instruction. *Journal of Educational Technology Systems, 10*(2), 175-186.

Von Glaserfeld, E. (1989) Cognitition, construction of knowledge, and teaching. *Synthese, 80*, 121-140.

Vygotsky, L.S. (1981). The genesis of higher mental functions. In J. V. Wertsch (Ed.), *The concepts of activity in Soviet psychology.* Armonk, NY: Sharpe.

Yager, R. E. (1991). The constructivist learning model. *Journal of Science Teaching, 58*(6), 52-57.

Chapter XVI

Designing Technology-Enhanced Learning Environments

J. Michael Spector and Pål I. Davidsen
University of Bergen, Norway

ABSTRACT

There are now many educational research and technology projects reporting a variety of outcomes and lessons learned with regard to how to effectively integrate technology into learning and instruction. What can we learn from these projects and experiences? Is there a clear and coherent instructional design framework for technology-enhanced learning environments? What are the most promising approaches to instructional design? Are there particular tools that can assist? What kinds of evaluations will insure that the process of designing such environments will become progressively more effective? These are the questions explored in this chapter. The discussion includes a short review of the possibilities afforded by new technologies, with special emphasis on collaborative tele-learning and Web-based simulations. After illustrating the rich and diverse kinds of interactions now possible in Web-based settings, we shall argue that instructional design is more critical than ever before. It is not the case that technology has simplified instructional planning. Quite the contrary; new technologies have made the design of effective learning environments even more challenging than before. While our concept of learning remains relatively intact, the settings in which instruction can and does occur and the kinds of resources which can be brought to support learning in those various settings has changed dramatically. As a consequence, the subject of this chapter is relatively unexplored territory, and the findings and conclusions suggested herein should be regarded as tentative and preliminary.

INTRODUCTION

There are now many educational research and technology projects reporting a variety of outcomes and lessons learned with regard to how to effectively integrate technology into learning and instruction. What can we learn from these projects and experiences? Is there a clear and coherent instructional design framework for technology-enhanced learning environments? What are the most promising approaches to instructional design? Are there particular tools that can assist? What kinds of evaluations will insure that the process of designing such environments will become progressively more effective?

These are the questions we shall explore in this chapter. The discussion will include a short review of the possibilities afforded by new technologies, with special emphasis on collaborative tele-learning and Web-based simulations. After illustrating the rich and diverse kinds of interactions now possible in Web-based settings, we shall argue that instructional design is more critical than ever before. It is not the case that technology has simplified instructional planning. While our concept of learning remains relatively intact, the settings in which instruction can and does occur and the kinds of resources which can be brought to support learning in those various settings has changed dramatically. Not only is instructional planning for technology-enhanced learning environments more crucial than ever before, it is also much more challenging.

Based on a review of projects and learning environments with demonstrated and credible learning outcomes, we shall elaborate a tentative framework for the design of effective technology-enhanced learning environments. This framework contains some familiar elements found in previous design guidelines, including most especially those found in the cognitive apprenticeship literature (see, for example, Collins, 1991). Other elements are drawn from activity theory (Leontiev, 1975; Nardi, 1996), cognitive complexity theory (Spiro et al., 1992), coordination theory (Malone & Crowston, 1993), distributed cognition (Salomon, 1993), and sociocultural learning theory (Vygotsky, 1975). How this framework can be effectively applied to the design of learning for a complex domain will then be illustrated (Spector & Davidsen, 1997). Special attention will be given to the analysis of learning in and about complex domains (Dörner, 1996).

One of the findings with regard to Web-based environments is that they have potential to promote distance collaborations, but they rarely succeed in approaching the effectiveness of small-group, face-to-face collaborations. Another finding is that technology-enhanced learning environments, even those which are professionally produced and appear quite robust, can fail to achieve any recognizable learning benefits. What some offer as an explanation for such uneven results with such promising technology is lack of vision or lack of a coherent design perspective. Others argue that no single paradigm or perspective is adequate for the design of technology-enhanced learning environments (see, for example, Sfaard, 1998).

We shall argue that what has changed and continues to change is not our concept of learning, but the settings in which instruction can and does occur and the kinds of resources which can be brought to support learning in those various settings. It is just these changes and possibilities which have made instructional design much more complicated than before. It is precisely that complexity which the proposed design framework attempts to address.

A FALSE DICHOTOMY

It should be noted that there are some researchers who will argue that our fundamental perspective on education and our conception of learning should change on account of the possibilities offered by new technologies. We view this as a radical stance which is not well founded and which is likely to result in further fragmentation of the research community.

Such an argument first produces a grossly simplified view of traditional, classroom-based instruction, indicating that such instruction implies that education is merely knowledge transfer and that learners are passive and receptive. Many of those who are critical of the traditional classroom setting adopt an activity theory perspective (Nardi, 1996). In such a perspective, learning should be viewed as involving an activity system, which includes a variety of persons (students, tutors, teachers, parents, etc.), a variety of roles (advising, coaching, exploring, experimenting, etc.), a collection of various artifacts (documents, computer-based tutorials, on-line chat groups, interactive simulations, etc.), various intentions, and so on. In short, according to activity theorists, a proper analysis of a learning situation should take into account all associated aspects and not focus on a specific learning task.

Ironically, when critiquing traditional learning environments, this view is all too often abandoned. If one examines what actually occurs in such classroom settings, one often finds private meetings with teachers, discussions of various side-aspects of a topic, chats in the café, and so on. Many classroom settings are quite rich in terms of the quantity, the diversity, and the quality of interactions and activities which occur and are well supported.

Moreover, our view, which is well supported with historical evidence, is that technology has yet to make significant improvements in the quality of education by any reasonable measure. The reason for these failures to make pervasive and lasting improvements in education through innovative use of technology is not a failure of technology nor is it a failure to find the right learning perspective or theory. It is primarily a failure caused by the widespread belief that one single and typically simple approach to using technology to support learning will succeed. This kind of failure is based on a confusion between science and polemics, and it has resulted in many meaningless debates concerning whether media has an impact on learning or whether constructivism can create a society of self-motivated learners.

The reality that we perceive is that technology can offer new kinds of interactions and activities for both learners and teachers; new instructional settings can be created; new opportunities for learning can be designed. However, these are all quite difficult and costly to achieve. If one thinks about the kinds of interactions typically found on the Internet, for example, one will see that these include browsing, searching, occasionally making a query, still less often engaging in an ongoing discussion on a focused topic, hardly ever conducting an experiment, and so on. Let us be realistic. Learners often desire structure and guidance. Learners do not magically become scientific explorers or investigative inquirers. Technology is fascinating. However, technology does not automatically support exploration, investigation, sustained interaction, and such activities often associated with education. In the remainder of this chapter, we shall explore an area in which technology can provide new opportunities which we believe are well suited to support learning about complex subjects. We shall describe the landscape of that territory, including how it might be modeled using system dynamics. We shall then indicate one design approach which we believe works well. It is not simple, it does not generalize to all technology-intensive settings, and it does not presuppose that we need to change everything in order to make progress.

SYSTEM DYNAMICS

The system dynamics community is firmly committed to and believes in the value of using system dynamics in order to improve understanding of complex, dynamic systems. Much has been written about the uses of systems dynamics to support learning in and about complex systems (see, for example, Sterman, 1994). Unfortunately, there is insufficient evidence to establish that or how system dynamics has contributed in significant ways to improved understanding. Moreover, what has been shown to be effective with system dynamics students and practitioners has not been established to be generally effective outside the system dynamics community. What is lacking is an instructional design methodology to support the design of system dynamics-based learning environments.

In order to make progress in this regard, we believe that the appropriate place to begin is with the design of learning support (i.e., instruction) for simpler dynamic systems. The focus of this chapter, therefore, is on an instructional design methodology to facilitate learning in and about relatively simple dynamic systems. The paper is primarily conceptual in nature, drawing on lessons learned from the system dynamics literature as well as from the cognitive psychology and instructional science literature. We have applied the principles illustrated here in a number of learning environments and will also present selected findings from those efforts.

In order to develop an appropriate instructional design methodology for system dynamics-based learning, it is necessary to identify a number of relevant assumptions and then to elaborate a perspective on learning appropriate for supporting understanding in and about dynamic systems. We share with most system dynamicists the general belief that system dynamics has much to contribute to understanding complexity. Specifically, we shall assume that a learning environment that integrates system dynamics models and simulations can facilitate learning. We are especially interested in supporting those who are not system dynamicists in coming to understand dynamic systems. As a consequence, our first two assumptions are as follows:

1. System dynamics can be used to facilitate understanding dynamic systems.
2. One need not become a system dynamicist or a skilled system dynamics modeler in order to understand a particular complex system.

The learning perspective which informs our thinking is based on principles derived from cognitive psychology, learning theory, and instructional design. The learning perspective we find most appropriate is based on notions derived from situated and problem-based learning (Barrows, 1985; Lave, 1988; Lave and Wenger, 1990), especially as informed by cognitive flexibility theory (Spiro et al., 1987; 1988). Instructional design methods and principles consistent with this learning perspective can be derived from elaboration theory (Reigeluth & Stein. 1983) and cognitive apprenticeship (Collins et al., 1989).

In the course of elaborating these principles for the design of interactive learning environments (ILEs), we shall indicate why such principles are relevant and how they can inform a design rationale. We shall pay special attention to the concepts of a unit of instruction (which has an identifiable learning goal) and a learning module (a collection of related units of instruction). We shall call our instructional design approach model-facilitated learning (MFL). Our fundamental argument is that MFL is an appropriate methodology to support the design of system dynamics-based learning environments for complex domains. We shall illustrate MFL for a simple dynamic system, because we believe that will make the methodology most clear and is in fact consistent with one of our primary design perspectives: graduated complexity (Spector and Davidsen, 1998).

A third assumption we share with many persons designing system dynamics-based learning environments is that a deep understanding of dynamic systems is based on an understanding of the relationships between structure and behavior. To put it differently, understanding how a complex system behaves involves being able to provide causal and structural explanations for observed system behavior, and, further, being able to anticipate and explain changes in those underlying causes and structures that may occur as the system evolves over time. This kind of understanding is not acquired easily nor is it likely to be acquired from observations of either real or simulated behavior (Dörner, 1996). Additional support is required. This paper elaborates one way to conceptualize and design such support.

Broadly stated, we adhere to a principle we have called graduated complexity (Spector and Davidsen, 1998), according to which learners are confronted with increasingly complex aspects of a problem. This principle is necessary due to the need to begin with simple, cognitive representations of complex realities. In the development of ILEs, implementation of this principle leads to graduated transparency and support for learner-directed evaluation. Yet another assumption, consistent with the principle of graduated complexity, is that learning is most effective when interactions are cognitively engaging. The design of cognitively engaging interactions and activities around system dynamics in order to support learning is, therefore, the primary focus of this chapter. First, however, we wish to briefly review the relevant learning and instructional design theories.

Theoretical Framework

As already indicated, we derive our model facilitated learning (MFL) perspective from learning and instructional theories. That these theories are reasonably well established and articulated but have not been embraced by the system dynamics learning community is somewhat disturbing. Situated learning (Lave, 1988) is a general theory of knowledge acquisition which is based on the notion that learning (stable, persisting changes in knowledge, skills and behavior) occurs in the context of activities that typically involve a problem or task, other persons, and an environment or culture. This perspective is based on observations indicating that learners gradually move from newcomer or novice status (operating on the periphery of a community of practitioners) to advanced or expert status (operating at the center of the community of practitioners). As learners become more advanced in a domain, they typically become more engaged with the central and challenging problems that occupy a particular group of practitioners.

Situated learning has been most directly and successfully applied in the domain of medical training. The medical community has embraced the notion of problem-based learning, which is a particular application of situated learning theory (Barrows, 1985). In the last 20 years, the medical community has gradually recognized that physicians gain diagnostic skills and understanding as a consequence of treating patients, not as a consequence of traditional medical training. In order to promote the acquisition of diagnostic skills and understanding, many medical training curricula now integrate clinical problems and experience into the education of physicians. Typically, small groups of learners encounter actual clinical problems and they work individually and together to develop a diagnosis and recommended treatment plan. The learning typically proceeds in five stages: problem presentation, problem analysis, problem synthesis, problem abstraction, and problem reflection (Barrows, 1985). These stages are derived from clinical practice and integrate collaborative interactions that naturally occur among specialists in such settings.

These stages are consistent with our notion of graduated complexity and fit nicely into the general instructional design guidelines provided by cognitive apprenticeship and elaboration theory. The particular stages that are emphasized in terms of our units of instruction described later in this chapter are analysis, synthesis and abstraction.

Learning in complex and ill-structured domains places significant cognitive demands on learners, as appropriately recognized by the medical community. Ill-structured domains include those which do not remain constant over time, those which involve variables and constraints which are not well-defined, and those which are influenced in not easily predictable ways by a number of internal and external factors. According to cognitive flexibility theory (Spiro et al., 1987; 1988), understanding in such domains requires the following: the ability to construct multiple representations (mental models) of a problem, the ability to relate apparently disconnected parts of a system, and the ability to integrate information on a holistic level (to view problem and system features as interconnected rather than as compartmentalized). As a consequence, learning to support the acquisition of such understanding should be designed so as to promote multiple representations, to promote appreciation of the underlying complexity of the system, and to promote the ability to interrelate various components of the system. Moreover, learning should be supported with a variety of problems and cases. Cognitive flexibility theory shares with situated and problem-based learning the view that learning is context dependent, with the associated need to provide multiple representations and varied examples so as to promote generalization and abstraction processes. Additionally, cognitive flexibility places particular emphasis on the importance of learner-constructed representations. In MFL, this would mean that learners are provided the opportunity and challenge to become model builders and experiment with those models. We agree that this is an appropriate activity for advanced learners, but model building and construction is not always required in order to understand dynamic systems. Moreover, we believe that the units of instruction to be illustrated are appropriate precursors to model-building activities.

According to elaboration theory (Reigeluth and Stein, 1983), an instructional design theory, consistent with many cognitive learning principles, is that units of instruction should be designed in accordance with clear and consistent elaboration sequences (e.g., simple to complex, depth first, breadth first, etc.). The basic presupposition is that sequencing of units of instruction is a fundamental instructional design and/or learning task that should not be taken lightly. The first item in an elaboration sequence should be an epitomizing example. An epitomizing example need not and should not demonstrate all of the complexity of the final targeted learning outcome, but it should be rich enough to provide learners with an appreciation for the scope and complexity of the problems associated with a particular learning module (collection of units of instruction). The goal behind a well-articulated elaboration sequence is to help the learner develop stable cognitive structures that can accommodate increasingly rich and complex subject matter. The particular elaboration sequence which we believe generally appropriate for complex domains is one that progresses from the relatively simple to the more complex, and we have already referred to that as graduated complexity. It should be noted that some educational researchers draw on these same theories and argue that learners should not be provided simplified versions of real systems, and that some other elaboration sequence should be supported, or even that learners should be left to develop their own elaboration sequences. Some go so far as to say that it is wrong to think of learning objectives or goals. We find insufficient evidence to adopt such views. In other words, we do believe that there is a need to support and facilitate learning, that learners have and want to have goals, and that it is possible to design support to help learners achieve those goals (i.e., to design instruction).

According to cognitive apprenticeship (Collins et al., 1989), one elaboration sequence which should be supported follows the path of the learner from novice to more experienced practitioner. Specifically, those new to a challenging domain often desire and require more initial support and guidance than more experienced persons. Consequently, there should be a variety of support structures to scaffold learning processes and assist new learners in developing appropriate representations of problem domains. As we shall illustrate, causal loop diagrams and stock and flow diagrams can provide relevant scaffolding. Indeed, one affordance of technology in general is the ability to support multiple representations of a problem or situation. As learners become more sophisticated, the burden is shifted to the learner to provide explanations for observed problematic behavior. Consistent with cognitive flexibility theory, learners may even construct and test their own system dynamics models as part of the learning process. In this chapter, however, we do not illustrate such units of instruction, although as already stated, we do believe that they can facilitate learning, especially for more advanced learners. We briefly address this issue in the next section and then turn to an elaboration of our units of instruction for a system dynamics-based ILE.

To summarize our overall learning and instructional perspective, we adopt the basic notion from situated and problem-based learning that concepts are best learned in a context of use—a problem setting in which it is then necessary for the learner to apply and use the relevant concepts. Such learning should improve retention by providing a clear and relevant context, and it promotes transfer of learning to work-task situations by providing relevant aspects of a learning situation which can be realistically compared with real-world settings.

Piaget (1929) argued that children pass through four identifiable stages of mental development: sensorimotor, pre-operational, concrete operational, and formal operational. There is a clear progression in these stages from physical action towards abstract reasoning. We believe it reasonable to extend the last two stages to adult learners. For a particular topic, learners may begin with concrete operations, physically manipulating objects in order to solve specific problems. As these operations are mastered, they can then progress to more abstract representations and solve increasingly complex problems. This is consistent with the notion of graduated complexity already presented. One such elaboration sequence for a set of MFL learning modules for an entire curriculum might be as follows:

1. Start with concrete operations. Introduce a specific problem in the context of manipulating physical things. In system dynamics, a board game (e.g., the Beer Game) is typically used for such purposes. This physical manipulation of orders and shipments and inventories provides a setting in which the concepts of delays and feedback mechanisms are then introduced. This fits well with the classical notion of problem-based learning — introduce concepts in a problem setting, especially one involving concrete objects which can be manipulated. In this context, the problem to be solved is how to place and fill orders in order to avoid excess, inadequate or badly oscillating inventory.
2. The next stage towards formal operational understanding is to introduce the first level of abstraction, still within the context of solving specific kinds of problems. This can be accomplished by asking students to engage in some kind of hypothetical reasoning.

The problem to be solved then becomes something like this: What would happen if X does this, and Y does that, and Z remains constant, all within the context of the Beer Game, for example. This shifts the problem-solving context into something more appropriately supported with a dynamic or interactive simulation so that alternative scenarios and hypotheses can be tried out. This kind of learning is more abstract and can be characterized as inquiry-based learning to indicate that it is a different form of problem-based learning than that associated with the first and more concrete stage. A management flight simulator such as SimCity, Beefeater or People Express supports this stage of learning as has been demonstrated by a number of researchers (see, for example, Sterman, 1994). At this stage, it is important to begin to form a holistic view of a system, and causal loop diagrams can help facilitate this process. Technology (e.g., interactive simulations) now has a clear role to play and offers new opportunities for learning activities not easily constructed in classroom settings.

3. A higher level of understanding occurs when a learner is able to explain why things happen the way they do in a complex system. The focus of this kind of learning is not only to be able to predict what would happen under different circumstances but to be able to explain exactly why they will happen that way. In stage two, one formulates what one believes to be a reasonable hypothesis in response to an inquiry about a complex system and then checks to see if the hypothesis fits observed behavior (either in a simulation or in a real setting). In this more formal operational stage, learners are asked still more challenging questions about causes for and reasons underlying observed and hypothesized behavior. This might be called policy-based learning to distinguish it from the second stage. At this stage it is important to introduce some representation of a system's structure so as to make clear exactly what kinds of feedbacks and delays exist within the system. It is also important to support discussions, learner-learner collaborations, and learner-tutor interactions. Again, technology can support such collaboratively constructed explanations, especially in settings where those with ideas and comments are not all physically co-located. Email, chat rooms, and collaborative workspaces are all important technology supports. In addition, recording results of various simulation-based experiments and sharing those in such collaborative settings is an important new affordance made possible by information and communications technologies.

It is at the third stage that transparency becomes important for system dynamics-based ILEs, and it is at this stage that we provide elaborated units of instruction consistent with the MFL perspective. By transparency we refer to the notion that learners need to be able to see through an interface to a high level representation (e.g., a causal loop diagram) through to deeper structures and causal mechanisms (e.g., stock and flow diagrams). Just as there has been a progression from simple and concrete to more complex and abstract when going from stage 1 to stage 3, within stage 3 we can image a similar progression from simpler representations to more complex representations, consistent with our principle of graduated complexity. The emphasis in the remainder of this paper is on the first level of elaboration within stage 3 of a system dynamics-based learning environment.

Learning by Modeling Versus Learning with Models

There is a general consensus among system dynamicists that learning that results from modeling a reality is more effective than learning that results from the use of a model that is made to represent reality (synthetic reality). There are a number of interesting questions to be addressed when making such a comparison, and it is not our intention to argue one way or the other on that issue. Probably, there is insufficient empirical data to support a definitive argument either way. Probably, both approaches have an appropriate role to play in learning. One main point is, however, that modeling in the face of reality is quite a different exercise than experimenting with an existing model as if it represented such a reality. Our main concerns are with the learning contexts in which synthetic realities might support and facilitate learning.

One way to compare these two learning approaches (by modeling versus using models) is to challenge the learner to understand the synthetic reality in just the same way the modeler is challenged to understand reality. In that case, a synthetic environment should help us emulate the situation that a learner might later face as a modeler (consistent with the learning perspective already presented). In principle, one can come a long way towards providing such a realistic context for modeling. In that case, the synthetic reality is represented in the form of a model that is valid in the sense that the assumptions included serve as the basis for learning just as well as the facts of reality would have. This ensures that the learning gained from such a model is relevant and applicable to the reality it represents. In short, we accept the notion from situated learning that the learning context should be realistic and authentic. Furthermore, we accept the notion from the system dynamics community that identifying and understanding causal structures are critical for learning about dynamic systems.

In many ways, existing ILEs do not provide an appropriately rich environment to facilitate this kind of learning. Too often, ILEs do not provide a view of or access to an underlying causal model. Thus, learners cannot benefit from an explicit model-centered approach to learning. We do believe that people, when confronted with an ILE, either consciously or subconsciously, seek to capture or reconstruct that synthetic reality in some kind of mental representation, a representation that is internal, hidden (even from the learner), individual and intermittent. In the design of ILEs, little has been done to elicit an explicit representation of such mental models, although according to cognitive flexibility theory (Spiro et al., 1987; 1988) developing multiple mental representations is critical to understanding complex systems. In existing ILEs few tools and techniques have been made available to the learner for that purpose. In principle, however, there is nothing preventing us from furnishing the learner with such modeling tools and techniques. Moreover, model-based ILEs provide the learner with a synthetic reality that, in ways that are well known, offer a number of advantages to experimenting with and learning from reality (e.g., cost and time efficiencies). Moreover, providing learners with explicit models should facilitate their ability to construct their own models and internal representations. This premise is fundamental to our model facilitated learning perspective. Again, we can see that technology can provide an important learning affordance, in this instance it is in the form of modeling tools.

As indicated, we are not arguing that emulating a formal modeling process is the only way by which we can learn about a complex, dynamic domain. There are other strategies for learning that could, conceivably, be successful. We do assume, however, that they all involve some kind of representation or modeling activity, at the very least the construction of a mental model. For that purpose, according to MFL, learning should be situated in a real or synthetic, complex, dynamic environment.

In the following discussion, we will focus on learning based on a synthetic reality (i.e., model facilitated learning). This implies that we can assume that the designer of a model-based ILE fully understands (see below) that synthetic reality, and, based on that insight, can provide ILE support according to the principles of MFL to facilitate learning at different stages in a learner's development. In reality-based learning, the instructional designer is forced to rely on other methods.

Designing an Interactive Learning Environment for Complex Domains

The point of departure for a system dynamics based activity is a problem, a conflict that exists between what is desired and what exists. The embodiment of such a conflict may range from a pure curiosity to be satisfied to the state trajectory of a system that does not follow an expected or a predetermined path. The real reference attributes with which the conflict is associated are represented by the reference variables in a system dynamics model. The model is intended to represent the problem at hand. It is an expression of our understanding of that problem. To be more specific, the model embedded in a learning environment is intended to represent the system underlying that problem, and should generate the problem (reference) behavior. The reference variables are expected to reproduce the reference behavior, exhibited by the reference attributes, under the influence of the underlying model. If it does so for the right reasons (Barlas, 1996), the model can be said to embody a theory for why the problem exists. In system dynamics, such a problem identification is considered a prerequisite for problem solving. You need to understand some aspects of a problem before embarking on a solution activity.

Understanding is a key concept here as in other sciences. What we need to understand is the relationship between structure and behavior—how the behavior characteristics arise from the structure and how the structure that essentially dominates the behavior varies in response to the behavior exhibited over time. The ultimate target for learning in system dynamics is such an understanding acquired for the purpose of decision making and management. Such management might take the form of strategy development, policy design or, simply, decision making and implementation. Consequently, learning includes the application of systems understanding to the identification of a strategy, a policy or a decision that modifies the reference behavior of the system towards a goal or desired behavior. We are not arguing that there is a single correct goal or a single correct decision to achieve a goal or a single correct representation of a problem state. We do argue, however, that representing goals, behaviors and decisions are essential to problem-solving activities in complex settings.

By "complexity" system, dynamicists usually mean structural complexity. This implies that complexity is associated with the characteristics of the relationships that constitute the system structure. Implicit is the fact that people find it difficult to analyze dynamic systems that are characterized by a complex structure and cannot easily infer behavior from knowledge about the system structure. For the same reason, people find it difficult to synthesize dynamic systems for a particular purpose. When challenged to define the concept "complexity," system dynamicists typically list feedback, delay, non-linearity and, possibly, uncertainty and vagueness. We believe that this characterization leaves out a significant feature of dynamic systems that contributes to complexity, namely, the integration process. Consequently, our interactive learning environments are designed with particular emphasis on the integration processes that take place within a complex system (e.g., the accumulation process for a backlog of unfilled orders, or the depletion of an important resource over time, or the accumulation of detrimental aspects of fatigue caused by overwork).

We also believe that a process that leads up to an understanding of complex, dynamic systems must rely on an alternation between analysis and synthesis. This implies iteratively synthesizing models of component structures and subsequently analyzing them in terms of their behavior. We assume that it is not possible to understand a model as a whole unless we understand key components. The implication is that we generally need to understand key model components before we synthesize them. An integrated packet of structure and associated behavior can be considered a unit of analysis or a unit of synthesis, depending on which mode of investigation we are in, related to the specific problem at hand. Once again, technology affords the opportunity to support the analysis mode and also the synthesis mode in this learning process.

A model results from a synthesis and, associated with that, there is, ideally, an improved understanding of the relationship between the model and the characteristic set of behavior patterns that can be generated using the model. A complete systems understanding may not necessarily result from such a modeling exercise. If we abstract from the specifics of a model and its behavior, we obtain a generic model and associated generic behavior, a general unit of investigation that potentially can be transferred and reapplied in a variety of contexts, especially if we are careful to avoid attaching too much confidence with regard to what those generic models imply with regard to specific situations.

A learning environment should help the learner uncover problems with regard to complex systems. To facilitate this process, we adopt the notion of a unit of instruction (UoI). Learners are generally expected to acquire an understanding of the relationship between structure and behavior presented in a particular UoI. To assess a learner's understanding, the learner is challenged to develop a policy relevant to the system covered by a single unit of instruction.

So, what do these units of learning look like in a complex, dynamic environment and how do we identify them? How do we utilize them for learning purposes? In association with ILEs, we suggest six basic principles to guide the development of a model facilitated learning environment. Such principles cannot predetermine the outcome of a learner's investigation. There are typically several opportunities pursuing alternative learning paths, and, presumably, it is not always obvious which branch to follow. In fact, at each stage of the investigation of a problem, a learner can engage in a number of activities, but only one can be selected at a particular point in time. We expect the principles offered here to provide guidelines that improve the likelihood of a successful investigation of a model on the part of a learner. In each unit of instruction, there is a problem to be resolved. The six basic principles for designing model facilitated learning for complex domains are as follows:

1. Challenge the learner to identify and characterize the reference mode or standard behavior of the system.

As a learner explores a system, that system will be represented in a model. The system attributes will be represented by variables, and their properties by values. The reference mode of behavior is assumed to identify a problem. By implication, there is a preference associated with each of these system attributes called *target attributes* that defines the reference mode of behavior. In a model, they are represented by *target variables*. Target

Figure 1. Reference and target behavior.

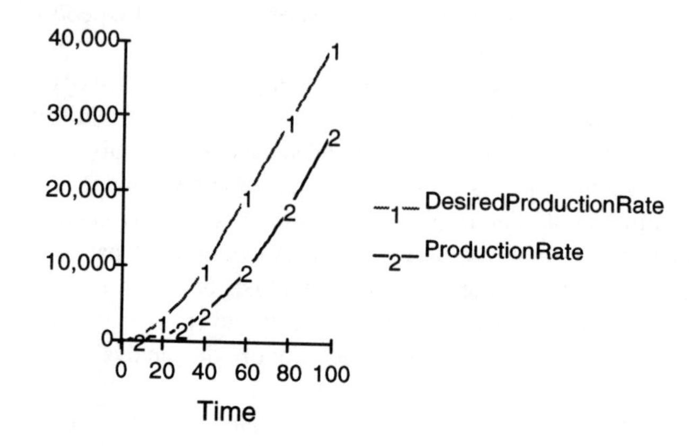

attributes are interrelated by the structure of an underlying system. To uncover the problem, the learner needs to identify that system, called the *target system.* A model of the system, a *target model*, is a record of learner findings. The model structure is assumed to inter-relate the target variables the same way the system structure inter-relates the target attributes. In the subsequent discussion, we will simplify our terminology and refer to variables, whether we discuss the system attributes or the model variables.

2. Challenge the learner to identify the preference variables, each associated with a target variable and uncover the underlying preference structure.

Since a problem is assumed to exist, there is a preference or desire associated with some target variable. Consequently, the learner is asked to define a *preference variable* associated with each target variable. In system dynamics, the preference variables are often identified by the prefix *desired*, such as *DesiredProductionRate.* A preference variable can be a constant. Typically, however, its value varies relative to other variables in the system. A structure that relates a preference variable to other variables is called a preference structure.

A *preference structure* is a preferred relationship between a (sub)set of preference variables and, possibly, other variables (i.e., between the values they take). In our example, it may be desirable for the production rate to follow our expectations regarding an exogenously generated order rate, *OrderRate.* If we disregard expectation biases, the implication is that the *DesiredProductionRate* should be equal to the *OrderRate.*

As we shall see, preference variables can be related to other preference variables and to parameters and variables in the target system so as to adjust to that system as well. Note that the fact that the order rate is considered exogenous does not imply that it will remain so forever. In fact, the gradual uncovering of a system, implies that we establish temporary and changing boundaries to support investigations. Consequently, variables that are initially defined as parameters (constants) or exogenous variables (external to the system), may later be incorporated in the model to serve as endogenous variables.

The educational purpose of identifying the preference variables is to explicitly establish a *goal behavior* that can be compared to the reference behavior as early as possible in the learning process. The discrepancy between the two provides a concrete and realistic setting for a problem.

3. Challenge the learner to identify the structure (or causes) underlying each target variable in the associated preference structure.

In the form of a precedence analysis, the learner is expected to trace the causes underlying the behavior of the target variable. This may uncover variables that are themselves preference variables or that influence such variables.

In our example, the target variable, *ProductionRate*, is influenced by the size of the *Workforce*, and the *Productivity* of that workforce, one multiplied by the other. As illustrated in Figure 2, neither workforce nor productivity is currently mirrored by preference variables.

The learner is now challenged to infer a secondary preference from the key preference. This way, a learner can create a mirror system of preferences to the target system. The educational value of that is that it allows the learner to identify the systemic implication of the original key preference in the form of secondary preferences and to compare the desired state of affairs in the target system to the actual state of affairs. Thus, it is possible to identify the origin of discrepancies between the preferred and the actual values of the original preference variables. This refers to the diagnostic approach of problem-based learning.

The implication of preferring a certain production rate, given a certain productivity, is to prefer a certain workforce, *DesiredWorkforce*. Alternatively, the implication of preferring a certain production rate, given a certain workforce, is to prefer a certain productivity, *DesiredProductivity*. The first one of these alternatives is illustrated in Figure 3.

The learner's choice leads us to a situation where a preference variable is not only related to exogenous factors characterizing the environment, but also may be related to parameters or variables in the target model. By anchoring a preference variable, such as *DesiredWorkforce*, to a parameter, such as *Productivity*, the preferred state of affair comes to rely on the static characteristics of the target system. Since the preference system must be expected to influence the target system, there is a mutual interdependence between the two.

One of the important reasons for introducing the preferred magnitudes explicitly as preference variables in the model of a learning environment is to be able to investigate the consistency of the model, representing the target system and the associated system of preferences. If all the variables in the model take their preferred values, the equations that

Figure 2. Desired and actual production rate.

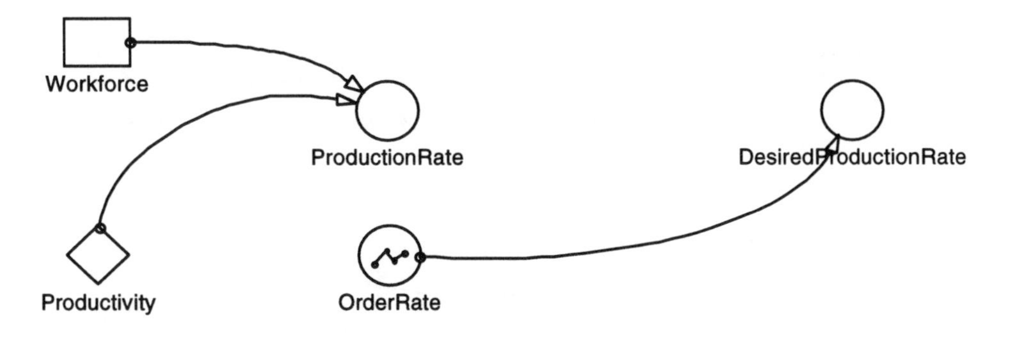

describe the structure of the system should all be satisfied simultaneously. When the workforce matches the desired workforce, for example, the production rate should match the desired production rate. If not, the preferences associated with the model cannot be satisfied simultaneously due to the constraints of the target system structure. From an educational point of view, it is important for the learner to eventually discover whether the model is consistent or not, because this determines whether or not the expectations regarding the preferences can be satisfied, that is, whether or not there is a solution to a problem. A significant and deep affordance of system dynamics-based learning environments is that they allow learners to explore the consistency of alternative representations of a system.

4. Challenge the learner to reflect on dynamic characteristics, to infer associated preferences, and to develop a desired management policy.

From a key variable, we trace back along the causal links until we identify a stock (i.e., an accumulation/depletion entity). Stocks provide clues to the dynamics of a system. A stock is a state variable and its level constitutes an element in the state of the system. The stocks are accumulators. They change their state over time as a consequence of various influences. The stock equation is the only kind of equation in system dynamics models that span a time period. Stocks thus constitute the memory of the system.

So far, the model developed is static. All relationships are instantaneous. Having identified the first stock in the target system, *Workforce*, the learner moves on to investigate the structure that governs its dynamics. The learner needs to identify the associated flows and the rates that govern these flows. Since the learner's problem indicated a need to increase the workforce, the learner might start with an inflow of persons governed by the *HiringRate*.

The accumulation process is the core of the dynamic system and, at the same time, the most difficult process to understand. Consequently, at this stage the investigation includes a thorough analysis of the behavior of the stock. Therefore, it is reasonable to provide the learner with a simple unit of instruction and an associated ILE that affords an investigation of how the workforce responds to a variety of hiring and layoff patterns (see Figure 4). The goal of such a unit of instruction is for the learner to develop a dynamic intuition based on familiarity with integration processes. Since the designer of the learning environment is familiar with the behavior pattern potentially exhibited by the model upon completion, such

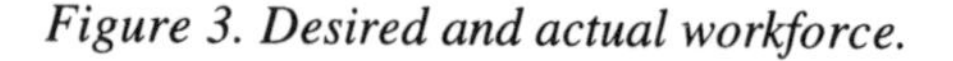
Figure 3. Desired and actual workforce.

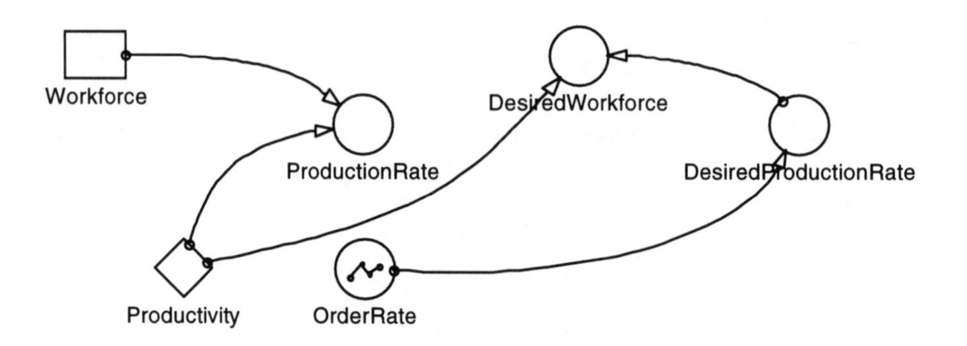

patterns of behavior can be used to assess the learner's dynamic intuition and support subsequent investigation. The *Workforce*, for example, responds with a phase shift to a cyclical hiring and layoff pattern, considered common in our case. Therefore, such a pattern should be available among the behavior patterns that potentially may characterize the *HiringRate*. In Figure 4 we illustrate a very simple control on those rates for that very purpose. As seen in the last button, the learner is also allowed to experiment freely with both rates.

In this first unit of instruction, the learner is challenged to meet the demand for workforce in view of the current order rate. A control can also be assigned to the order rate so as to select between the current problem behavior and a variety of synthetic conditions, such as steps, oscillations, and so on. Moreover, a variety of delays can be introduced in the hiring and layoff process so as to challenge the learner. The purpose of this is to enable the learner to develop a robust hiring policy for a variety of order rate patterns so as to consolidate understanding of the relevant integration processes.

The learner is thereafter challenged with a second unit of instruction, where an attrition mechanism is in place causing the workforce to leave after an average duration of employment (*ADE*). Moreover, we introduce the current hiring policy that is based on the desired workforce. As illustrated in Figure 5, this policy determines the preferred hiring rate, *DesiredHiringRate*. The equation governing the policy is of course:

DesiredHiringRate =
MAX(0, LayoffRate + (DesiredWorkforce – Workforce) / TimeToHireAndTrain)

DesiredHiringRate is a preference variable that relates the preferred to the actual workforce in the target system, taking into account the average time it takes to hire and train a new member of the workforce, *TimeToHireAndTrain*, and compensating for the attrition. Consequently, it is a policy that adjusts to the current state of affairs in the target system.

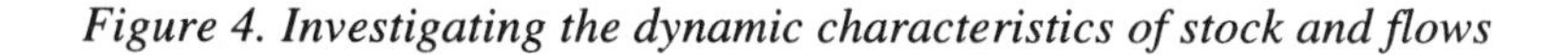

Figure 4. Investigating the dynamic characteristics of stock and flows

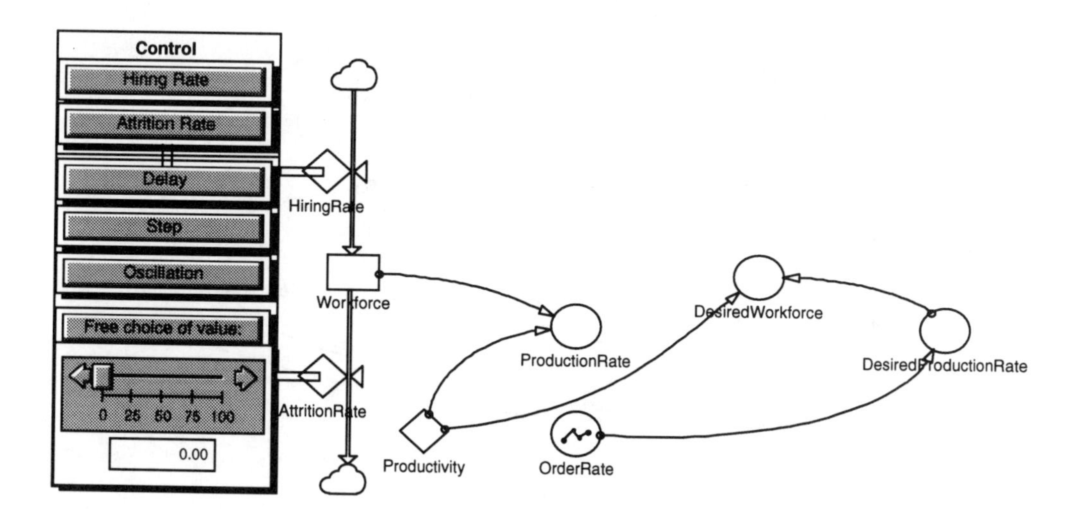

The policy constitutes a negative (or balancing) feedback loop (from the perspective of the underlying system – not from an instructional perspective). Based on the understanding of the integration process gained from the first unit of instruction, the learner is expected to understand the logic behind this policy and is provided the opportunity to change the *TimeToHireAndTrain* within a pair of reasonable boundaries. Thus, the learner begins to take a more active part in calibrating policies and adjusting model parameters.

5. Challenge the learner to encapsulate the unit of instruction and incorporate it into a meaningful body of active knowledge.

Having understood the relationship between the structure and behavior in this second UoI, the learner is assumed to recognize the response of this system to typical input patterns of behavior. By encapsulation, we mean the successful integration into a repertoire of deployable knowledge and skills. In the analysis of the model behavior, it is no longer necessary for the learner to investigate this structure in great detail. The learner now understands the first order response of this system to a change in the order rate, to a change in productivity, and to a change in the time to hire and train the workforce. A key affordance of this technology is that it not only facilitates the process of understanding such systems, it also provides the means to assess such understanding.

6. Challenge the learner to diversify and generalize.

Figure 5. Investigating a negative feedback loop governing the hiring rate.

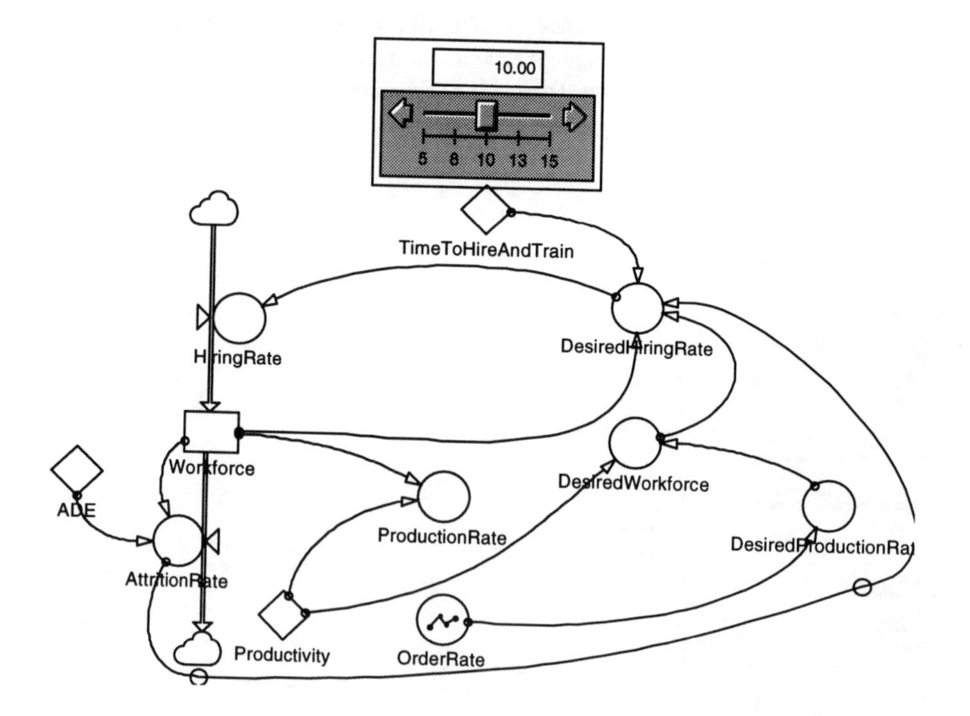

The next unit of instruction challenges the learner with the following problem: The workforce is not homogeneous and can be split into an experienced and an inexperienced workforce, characterized by very different productivities. The learner is challenged to make an abstraction from the model developed and to question to what extent the structure governing the two different workforce segments resembles the structure already developed for the workforce as a whole. The learner may consider the workforce to be a generic workforce, with attrition applying to both experienced and inexperienced workforces, for example. Figure 6 is an illustration of one possible resulting model.

The learner may recognize that attrition is equivalent to the recruitment from one segment of the workforce to the next so that the two components of the model in Figure 6 might be integrated as illustrated in Figure 7.

The learner is challenged to investigate whether the remaining structure generalizes and, in that case, how each component integrates into a model of the workforce as a whole. The learner may recognize that the assimilation of the inexperienced workforce into the experienced one is similar to attrition in general. The average duration of employment transfers to the average duration of assimilation, or how long it takes for inexperienced workers to reach the productivity of an experienced worker.

This implies that the recruitment of the experienced workforce is no longer governed by the desired rate of recruitment of the experienced workforce. Therefore, the learner typically stops at this stage. The learner may conclude that recruitment of workers in general can only take place through the recruitment of inexperienced workers.

The learner is then directed to the preferences that apply to the system. The original preference attribute, *DesiredWorkforce*, must be diversified into secondary *DesiredInexperiencedWorkforce* and *DesiredExperiencedWorkforce*, respectively. This is no trivial matter, and, is in a sense dependent upon the definition of desired workforce. The learner is led to apply the productivity of one of the kinds of workforce, say that of the experienced workforce. Thus *DesiredWorkforce* is measured in experienced equivalents, that is to say in terms of the number of experienced workers that is required.

As in the case of the *DesiredProduction* leading to a *DesiredWorkforce* and/or a *DesiredProductivity*, we now face the following situation: the learner could arbitrarily prefer a certain amount of experienced workers and let the remaining workload be carried by the inexperience workforce. In this case, however, restrictions apply. In an interactive learning environment associated with a third unit of instruction, the learner is challenged to identify other conditions in the target model that limit the degrees of freedom that a

Figure 6. Stock and flow indicating diversification and generalization in learning.

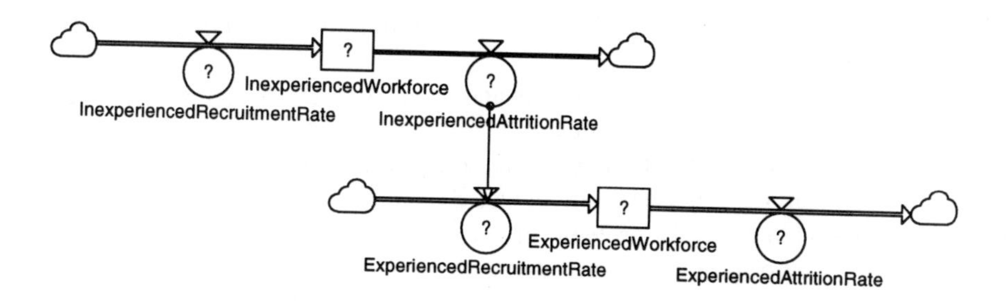

Figure 7. Stock and flow diagram indicating an integrative learning process.

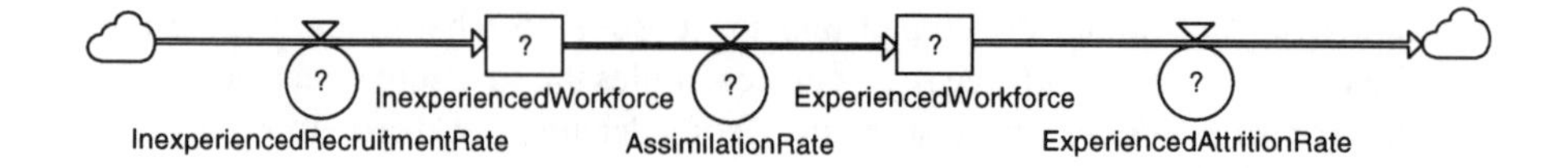

workforce manager would be facing in this context.

By operating in that learning environment, the learner comes to the realization that, in equilibrium, the ratio between the experienced and the inexperienced workforce remains the same. The learning environment also allows the learner to identify the parameters that determine this ratio. Thus, based on the assumption that the system is in equilibrium, the learner is able to find a closed form expression for the ratio existing between the two. As such, the learning environment helps the learner not only to identify the equilibrium condition, but also to understand the significance of that condition. Moreover, this discovery can be utilized to identify the need for recruitment in view of a certain preferred production, *DesiredProduction*.

CONCLUSIONS

In this chapter, we have presented some of the considerations we typically face while designing interactive learning environments for simple dynamic domains. We expect the same considerations to apply to the design of environments for complex domains. These considerations are rooted in learning theory and lead to the definition and application of units of instruction. We are still far from a formal definition of such units, and realize that more formal definitions of units of instruction for system dynamic-based learning environments may not exist. Yet we do believe that focusing on units of instructions does provide a clear framework for designing (structuring and sequencing) system dynamics-based learning activities. Learning goals remain important both for learners as well as for instructors and designers. Moreover, understanding dynamic domains can both be facilitated and assessed using the technology and methodology described here. It is critical in understanding dynamic systems to represent the relationship between structure and behavior, and this technology supports multiple representations (causal loop as well as stock and flow diagrams). It also facilitates learner interaction with and exploration of those representations. Finally, it provides the means to assess how well learners can apply the knowledge gained to various altered scenarios. In short, this type of interactive, on-line, simulation-enabled environment enables and facilitates the integration of understanding concerning dynamic domains.

We believe that with regard to learning in and about complex domains, it is important to begin with simpler systems and to build gradually toward the more complex. We do not regard this as a violation of the notion of situated learning. Rather, we regard it as vital to promoting the appropriate use of enabling knowledge at key points of difficulty. Furthermore, we believe that in general a problem-based learning approach is preferable, but we identify different types of problems associated with different kinds of units of instruction. Some problems are primarily focused on the manipulation of concrete or concretely representable objects, and we arbitrarily call this stage the problem-based stage. Some problems are primarily associated with the manipulation of more abstract representations and what-if analysis using models and simulations. We call this inquiry-based learning. Some problems are associated with very abstract manipulations of models and reasoning about rules to guide decision making and formulate policies that generalize across a wide variety of system behaviors. We call this policy-based learning. We call all three together model-facilitated learning, and we regard model-facilitated as a general form of situated and problem-based learning appropriate for understanding complex systems.

Finally, the use of on-line technologies provides unique opportunities for learners to interact with other learners who may be located elsewhere. We have argued that collaborative learning is highly effective with regard to complex systems. Most of our discussion focused on details pertaining to how this technology affords multiple representations, how those representations can be structured and sequenced so as to facilitate an active and activity-centered learning process, and how the same system dynamics technology allows genuine assessment of learner understanding since the models are both interactive and executable. None of this is easily accomplished. However, if we are to make good uses of technology to improve learning outcomes, then we must take seriously the specific kinds of activities in which learners might engage in order to improve understanding of complex systems. It will not happen without careful planning and continued serious investigation of which learning technologies work, when, and why.

REFERENCES

Barlas, Y. (1996). Formal aspects of model validity and validation in system dynamics. *System Dynamics Review*, 12(3), 183-210.

Barrows, H. S. (1985). *How to Design a Problem-based Curriculum for the Preclinical Years*, Springer-Verlag, New York.

Collins, A. (1991). Cognitive apprenticeship and instructional technology. In L. Idol & B. F. Jones (Eds.), *Educational values and cognitive instruction: Implications for reform.* Mahwah, NJ: Erlbaum.

Collins, A., Brown, J. S., & Newman, S. E. (1989). Cognitive apprenticeship: Teaching the crafts of reading, writing, and mathematics. In Resnick, L. B. (ed.), *Knowing, learning, and instruction: Essays in honor of Robert Glaser,* Erlbaum, Mahwah, New Jersey, 53-494.

Davidsen, P. I. (1994). The systems dynamics approach to computer-based management learning environments: Implications and their implementations in Powersim. In J. D. W. Morecroft, & Sterman, J. D. (eds.*), Modeling for learning organizations*, Productivity Press, Portland,301-316.

Davidsen, P. I. (1996). Educational features of the system dynamics approach to modelling and simulation. *Journal of Structured Learning,* 12(4), 269-290.

Davidsen, P.I. (1993). System dynamics as a platform for educational software production. In Barta, B. Z., Eccleston, J. & Hambusch, R. (eds.), *Computer mediated education of information technology professionals and advanced end-users*, North Holland, Amsterdam, 27-40.

Dijkstra, S., Seel, N., Schott, F., & Tennyson, R. D. (Eds.) (1997). *Instructional design: International perspectives.* Mahwah, NJ: Erlbaum.

Dörner, D. (1996) (Translated by Rita and Robert Kimber). *The logic of failure: Why things go wrong and what we can do to make them right.* New York: Holt.

Driscoll, M. (1998). *Web-based training: Using technology to design learning experiences.* San Francisco: Jossey-Bass.

Forrester, J. W. (1985). "The" model versus a modeling "process". *System Dynamics Review 1(1)*, 133-134.

Forrester, J. W. (1992). Policies, decision, and information sources for modeling. *European Journal of Operational Research 59(1), 42-63.*

Lave, J. & Wenger, E. (1990). *Situated learning: Legitimate peripheral participation*, Cambridge University Press, Cambridge, UK.

Lave, J. (1988). *Cognition in practice: Mind, mathematics and culture in everyday life*, Cambridge University Press, Cambridge, UK.

Leontiev, A.N. (1975). *Activity, Consciousness, Personality*. Moscow.

Malone, T. & Crowston, K. (1993). The interdisciplinary study of coordination. *Computing Surveys*, 26(1), 87-119.

McCormick, C. & Jones, D. (1998). *Building a Web-based educational system.* New York: Wiley.

Nardi, B. (Ed.) (1996). *Context and consciousness: Activity theory and human-computer interaction.* Cambridge, MA: MIT Press.

Piaget, J. (1929). *The Child's Conception of the World*, Harcourt, Brace Jovanovich, New York.

Reigeluth, C. M. & Stein, F. (1983). The elaboration theory of instruction. In Reigeluth, C. M. (ed.), *Instructional-design theories and models: An overview of their current status*, Erlbaum, Mahwah, New Jersey.

Salomon, G. (1993) (Ed.). *Distributed cognitions: Psychological and educational considerations.* New York: Cambridge University Press.

Sfard, A. (1998). On two metaphors for learning and the dangers of choosing just one. *Educational Research, 27*(2), 4-12.

Silbermam, M. (1998). *Active training: A hanbdbook of techniques, designs, case examples, and tips.* San Francisco: Jossey-Bass.

Spector, J. M. & Davidsen, P. I. (1997). Creating engaging courseware using system dynamics. *Computers in Human Behavior, 13*(2), 127-155.

Spector, J. M. & Davidsen, P. I. (1998). Constructing learning environments using system dynamics. *Journal of Courseware Engineering 1*, 5-12.

Spector, J. M. (1994). Integrating instructional science, learning theory, and technology. In R. D. Tennyson (Ed.), *Automating instructional design, development, and delivery.* Berlin: Springer-Verlag, 243-259.

Spector, J. M. (1995). Integrating and humanizing the process of automating instructional design. In R. D. Tennyson & A. E. Barron (Eds.), *Automating instructional design: computer-based development and delivery tools,* Berlin: Springer-Verlag, 523-546.

Spiro, R. J., Vispoel, W., Schmitz, J., Samarapungavan, A., & Boerger, A. (1987). Knowledge acquisition for application: Cognitive flexibility and transfer in complex content domains. In Britton, B. C. (ed.), *Executive control processes*, Erlbaum, Hillsdale, New Jersey, 177-200.

Spiro, R.J., Coulson, R.L., Feltovich, P.J., & Anderson, D. (1988). Cognitive flexibility theory: Advanced knowledge acquisition in ill-structured domains. In Patel, V. (ed.),

Proceedings of the 10th Annual Conference of the Cognitive Science Society, Erlbaum, Mahwah, New Jersey.

Spiro, R.J., Feltovich, P.J., Jacobson, M.J., & Coulson, R.L. (1992). Cognitive flexibility, constructivism and hypertext: Random access instruction for advanced knowledge acquisition in ill-structured domains. In T. Duffy & D. Jonassen (Eds.), *Constructivism and the technology of instruction*. Hillsdale, NJ: Erlbaum.

Sterman, J. D. (1994). Learning in and about complex systems. *System Dynamics Review 10(2-3),* 291-330.

Vygotsky, L. S. (1978*). Mind in society: The development of higher psychological processes*. (M.Cole, V. John-Steiner, S. Scribner & E. Souberman, Editors and Translators). Cambridge, MA: Harvard University Press.

About the Authors

BOOK EDITOR

Beverly Abbey earned her doctorate of philosophy from the University of North Texas in Information Science, specializing in Computer Education and Cognitive Systems. The idea for this book was conceived while she was an assistant professor in Educational Technology at Texas A&M University-Commerce teaching graduate courses in instructional design, instructional technology theories and multimedia authoring. She has a consultancy business specializing in instructional design and training serving the Dallas-Fort Worth area. Abbey is currently working on research in ethics, cognitive problem solving, instructional technology evaluation and multimedia instructional design. Currently, she is Director of Instructional Technology at Austin College in Sherman, Texas.

CHAPTER AUTHORS

Theo J. Bastiaens is assistant professor at the Educational Technology Expertise Centre of the Open University of the Netherlands. He has been working in the field of Training and Development since 1990. His extensive interest is in Human Resource Development and Organizational Change. For more then seven years now his research has been in the field of Electronic Performance Support Systems and Performance Improvement. The Educational Technology Expertise Centre of the Open University has distinguished itself as a leading international centre of expertise in the field of dinstance education, guided independent study and flexible, student centred education.

Zane Berge, Ph.D. and **Mauri Collins** are widely published in the field of computer-mediated communication used for teaching and learning. Most notably are seven books: *Computer-Mediated Communication and the Online Classroom* (Volumes 1-3) (1995) and a four volume series, *Wired Together: Computer Mediated Communication in the K12 Classroom* (1998). Dr. Berge is director of the Training Systems graduate program at UMBC. Ms. Collins is an instructional designer at Old Dominion University. They conduct research internationally in distance education.

Louis H. Berry is Associate Professor and Coordinator of the Program in Instructional Design and Technology at the University of Pittsburgh. He received his Ph. D. in Instructional Media from Penn State University. He has researched and published in the area of instructional message design, particularly with regard to the effects of color and complexity in visual learning. This interest currently extends into the design of on-line museums. Dr. Berry has been active in the Association for Educational Communications and Technology and is a past president of the Research and Theory Division of that organization.

Curt Bonk is an associate professor in the Department of Counseling and Educational Psychology as well as adjunct in the Instructional Systems Technology Department at Indiana University. Currently, he is a core member of the Center for Research on Learning and Technology located in the IU School of Education. Curt is interested in enhancing college and K-12 pedagogy with technological supports, scaffolded instruction, alternative instructional strategies, and nontraditional learning tools. He recently edited: "Electronic Collaborators: Learner-Centered Technologies for Literacy, Apprenticeship, and Discourse" published by Erlbaum and was technology contributor for the 9th edition of Houghton Mifflin's educational psychology textbook, Psychology Applied to Teaching by Jack Snowman and Robert Biehler. Further information can be found at: http://php.indiana.edu/~cjbonk or by contacting him at: cjbonk@indiana.edu.

John Burton has been at Virginia Tech since completing his Ph.D. in Educational Psychology at Nebraska in 1977. Currently a Professor of Educational Psychology and Instructional Technology, Dr. Burton has published extensively in the areas of memory, problem solving, and hypermedia.

Jack Cummings is Professor and Chair of the Department of Counseling and Educational Psychology at Indiana University-Bloomington. He has directed interactive video projects funded by AT&T and the U.S. Department of Education. Since the mid-1980's Jack has attempted to infuse technology into the school psychology program at IU. In the spring of 1997, he taught the first undergraduate class to be offered by the IU School of Education. Since that first Web course, he has been experimenting with the Web as a tool to break down the artificial barriers that exist among students, researchers, and practitioners.

Rhoda Cummings is a professor of counseling and educational psychology in the College of Education, University of Nevada, Reno. She received her Ed.D. at Texas Tech University. Her areas of expertise are human growth and development, cognitive development, and learning disabilities. She has written a number of books and articles about learning disabilities, cognition and technology, and adolescent development.

Jared Danielson has a PhD in Instructional Technology from Virginia Tech. He is intrigued by the relationship between instructional design and interface design, a relationship which he has examined first hand. Dr. Danielson is currently the Director of Educational Technology at the University of Virginia's College at Wise, Virginia.

Karen Dougherty is an Instructional Design Consultant at McCormick & Co. Her areas of interest include distance education, CBT, and web-based training. Ms. Dougherty earned a masters in ISD from UMBC and is currently with McCormick & Co, Inc in human performance improvement.

Robert Fischler acquired a Master's degree in Educational Psychology at Indiana University (IU) in 1997 and is now a doctoral candidate at IU in the same field of study. He is interested in on-line education and effective Internet tools for learning, teaching, and academic research. To this effect, Robert founded a company in 1999 entitled Academos to develop and market such tools. He may be reached at rob@academos.com.

Mercedes Fisher is an Assistant Professor with a specialization in Educational Technology, within the Department of Educational Policy and Leadership Studies, in the School of Education at Marquette University. She teaches both traditional and web-based educational technology courses. Her expertise lies in educational technology, project-based learning, instructional telecommunications models and experiential learning pedagogy. Dr. Fisher has published research articles in numerous international journals regarding teaching with technology. For three of the past four years, Dr. Fisher has been selected as a Marquette University Distinguished Scholar. In 1997, Dr. Fisher was selected as an International Group Study Exchange Team Member to study the development of online teaching and learning resources in Denmark and Germany. Prior to Marquette, Dr. Fisher was an Assistant Professor at the University of Southern Colorado (USC) and received the Outstanding Faculty Award in 1995. She served as the Director of USC's Beck-Ortner Technology Center, and conducted research emphasizing instructional design and technology applied to classroom learning for her book entitled, "Technology: Creating High Impact Learning Environments." Dr. Fisher holds a Ph.D. in Curriculum and Instruction from the University of Denver and an M.A. in Secondary Education and B.A. in Psychology and Sociology from Austin College. She can be reached via e-mail: Mercedes.Fisher@Marquette.edu.

Sharon Guan is an instructional designer with Continuing Education and Instructional Services at Indiana State University and an adjunct instructor at St. Mary of the Woods College. She received her bachelor degree in the field of International Journalism from Beijing Broadcasting Institute before coming to the United States to pursue her master degree in Educational Media. As a doctoral candidate at Indiana State University, she is currently working on her dissertation, which focuses on the studying of the relationship between graduate students' interpersonal needs and their preference of the interaction methods in the distance learning environment. <extguan@ruby.indstate.edu>

Noriko Hara is a Ph.D. candidate in the Department of Instructional Systems Technology at Indiana University. Her research agenda includes the investigation of organizational learning, communities-of-practice, and online learning within social informatics. Additionally, she designs and develops information architecture for educational web sites. Her recent publications address the use of information technologies to support learning environments. Noriko is currently writing her dissertation on professional communities-of-practice. Further information can be found at: http://php.indiana.edu/~nhara.

Jan Herrington is a Research Fellow in the School of Communications and Multimedia at Edith Cowan University in Western Australia. She has spent the last 21 years of her professional life supporting and promoting the effective use of educational technologies across all sectors of education. Since 1992, as a Senior Instructional Designer, she has worked principally in the area of multimedia, and in associated web-based projects. Recent research and development interests have focused on moving the design of learning environments to reflect constructivist approaches.

Marshall G. Jones is an assistant professor of Instructional Design and Technology at the University of Memphis. He teaches classes in the design and development of web-based instruction, and works with schools and businesses on the use of the web in education and training. He can be reached at mjones2@memphis.edu or http://www.people.memphis.edu/~mjones2/.

Sun Myung Lee is a doctoral student in Instructional Systems Technology at Indiana University-Bloomington. She has been a Web developer for the Smartweb, an educational psychology web-based course designed at IU. Her research interests are related to technology environment design and consulting aligned with professional development for both teacher education and corporate training. Sun has been involved in designing and implementing classroom and online workshops for K-12 teachers in Indiana as well as developing online knowledge network ("online community of practice") in a corporate setting.

Dorothy Leflore is the Chairperson of the Department of Curriculum and Instruction at North Carolina A&T State University. She received her doctorate from the University of Oregon, Eugene, Oregon. Her major research interest has been computers as a means of managing instruction. More recently, her interest has focused on using learning theories as the bases for designing Web-based instruction.

Barbara Lockee ia an assistant professor in the Instructional Technology program at Virginia Tech. She teaches courses in distance education and co-directs an off-campus IT master's program for professional educators. Her research interests include faculty development for distance education, as well as the socio-psychological implications of distance learning.

Deborah L. Lowther received her Ph.D. in Educational Technology from Arizona State University. She is currently an assistant professor of Instructional Design and Technology at the University of Memphis. Her research is centered on factors influencing the integration of technology into various learning environments, teacher education, and school restructuring. She may be contacted at dlowther@memphis.edu.

Cleborne D. Maddux taught for 10 years in the public schools of Oregon and Arizona before earning his Ph.D. from the University of Arizona in 1978. Since that time he has been an assistant, associate, and a full professor at four different institutions, most recently at the University of Nevada, Reno, where he is a professor in the Department of Counseling and Educational Psychology. He currently teaches classes in statistics and in information technology in education. He is the author of 14 books and more than a hundred scholarly articles, many in the area of information technology in education.

Rob L. Martens is assistant professor at the Educational Technology Expertise Centre of the Open University of the Netherlands. For about 10 years, his main research and development activities have been in the field of ICT and adult education. Research topics are, among others, embedded support devices, electronic intake and student support. The Educational Technology Expertise Centre of the Open University has distinguished itself as a leading international centre of expertise in the field of dinstance education, guided independent study and flexible, student-centred education.

Susan M. Miller earned a doctor of philosophy degree in Educational Psychology from Purdue University. She is currently an assistant professor in the Department of Psychology and Special Education at Texas A&M University in Commerce, Texas. Dr. Miller's primary research interests include: issues in the design and delivery of web-based instruction; assessment of cultural attitudes and behaviors; and early childhood literacy issues.

Kenneth L. Miller earned a doctor of philosophy degree in Counselor Education from Purdue University. His is currently of Grayson Place Consulting located in Commerce, Texas. Dr. Miller's research addresses the following topics: theoretical issues in the design of web-based instruction; measurement of cultural attitudes and behaviors; HIV/AIDS education; and gender-equity issues in counseling.

Ron Oliver teaches in the School of Communications and Multimedia at Edith Cowan University in Western Australia. He has been teaching with, and researching innovative uses of, instructional technologies for the past 20 years in secondary schools and universities. His research interests include the design of effective learning strategies for Web-based learning, the development of generic and key skills, developing sustainable and scalable Web-based learning resources and scaffolding student learning using on-line technologies.

Kay A. Persichitte is an Associate Professor and the Department Chair of Educational Technology at the University of Northern Colorado. She teaches courses in foundations of the field, distance education, and instructional design and development. Kay has a long history in both public education and higher education. Her research emphases are teacher preparation and technology utilization, change and diffusion of innovation, and distance education systems.

Robert T. Plants recently received his doctorate in Instructional Design and Technology from the University of Memphis. He is currently a research associate who is involved with several projects sponsored by the Center for Research on Educational Policy at the University of Memphis. He is email address is: [bplants@bellsouth.net]

Susan Powers is an Assistant Professor in the Department of Curriculum, Instruction and Media Technology at the School of Education, Indiana State University. She received her doctorate from the University of Virginia in Instructional Technology, and holds an M.S. in Education and B.S. in Business from Indiana University. She has developed and currently delivers three graduate courses solely through web-based instruction and consults with a number of organizations on the design and delivery of WBI and instructional technology. Her research interests include the integration of technology in teacher education programs, and the design, delivery and learning environments of distance education. <powers@indstate.edu>

Patricia L. Rogers, Ph.D. is an Associate Professor at Bemidji State University in northern Minnesota. Dr. Rogers is currently on leave from the university to serve as the Interim System Director for Instructional Technology for the Minnesota State Colleges and Universities (MnSCU) system office. Dr. Rogers regularly publishes articles on barriers to technology adoption, instructional design, and distance learning. She is a Getty Fellow (1996) and was recently awarded a Fulbright scholarship to Iceland for Fall 2000-2001.

Karen Smith-Gratto is the Coordinator of the Masters of Instructional Technology at North Carolina Agricultural and Technical State University in Greensboro. She received her doctorate from the University of New Orleans in 1992. Since that time she has held positions at Quincy University in Illinois and Cameron University in Oklahoma. Her research and writing focuses on improving the design of computer-based instruction and the integration of computer activities into curricula.

J. Michael Spector is Chair of the Instructional Design, Development & Evaluation Department at Syracuse University as well as Professor of Information Science at the University of Bergen, Norway. From 1991 through 1997, he was the Senior Scientist for the United States Air Force Research (Armstrong) Laboratory Technical Training Research Division's Instructional Systems Research Branch. He is a distinguished graduate of the United States Air Force Academy (1967); he earned a Ph.D. in Philosophy from the University of Texas at Austin in 1978. Before joining Armstrong Laboratory in 1991, Dr. Spector was an Associate Professor of Computer Science at Jacksonville State University, specializing in Software Engineering and Artificial Intelligence. His recent research is in the areas of intelligent performance support for instructional design and in system dynamics based learning environments. He has published numerous refereed journal articles and book chapters in the area of instructional design research and edited a volume on the concepts and issues involved in automating instructional design processes. He is active in professional associations and serves on the editorial boards of several international journals. He was awarded a Fulbright research fellowship (1995/1996) to work at the University of Bergen creating and testing an interactive simulation of the project dynamics for large-scale courseware development efforts. Dr. Spector helped found and is the President of the International Consortium for Courseware Engineering. He also serves on the International Board of Standards for Training, Performance and Instruction. He is an adjunct member of Göteborg University's faculty of Pedagogical Science and Agder College's faculty of Computer Engineering, and he is a Lecturer and member of the graduate faculty in the Department of Educational Psychology at the University of Minnesota. Dr. Spector's core area of competencies include the following: Automated Instructional Design Systems; Courseware Engineering; Evaluation of Instructional Design and Development Systems; Instructional Systems Design and Development; Intelligent Performance Support Systems; Multimedia and Web-Based Design and Development; Open and Distance Learning and Implications for Universities; System Dynamics Applications in Education and Training.

Index

J

K

L

M

N

O

P

Q

R